Psychology and History

As disciplines, psychology and history share a primary concern with the human condition. Yet historically, the relationship between the two fields has been uneasy, marked by a long-standing climate of mutual suspicion. This book engages with the history of this relationship and the possibilities for its future intellectual and empirical development. Bringing together internationally renowned psychologists and historians, it explores the ways in which the two disciplines could benefit from a closer dialogue. Thirteen chapters span a broad range of topics, including social memory, prejudice, stereotyping, affect and emotion, cognition, personality, gender and the self. Contributors draw on examples from different cultural contexts – from eighteenth-century Britain, to apartheid South Africa, to conflict-torn Yugoslavia – to offer fresh impetus to interdisciplinary scholarship. Generating new ideas, research questions and problems, this book encourages researchers to engage in genuine dialogue and place their own explorations in new intellectual contexts.

CRISTIAN TILEAGĂ is Senior Lecturer in Social Psychology and a member of the Discourse and Rhetoric Group at Loughborough University.

JOVAN BYFORD is Senior Lecturer in Psychology at The Open University.

Psychology and History

Interdisciplinary Explorations

Edited by

Cristian Tileagă

and

Jovan Byford

CAMBRIDGE
UNIVERSITY PRESS

University Printing House, Cambridge CB2 8BS, United Kingdom

Cambridge University Press is part of the University of Cambridge.

It furthers the University's mission by disseminating knowledge in the pursuit of education, learning and research at the highest international levels of excellence.

www.cambridge.org
Information on this title: www.cambridge.org/9781316502846

First published 2014
First paperback edition 2015

A catalogue record for this publication is available from the British Library

Library of Congress Cataloguing in Publication data
Psychology and history : interdisciplinary explorations / edited by Cristian Tileagă, Loughborough University and Jovan Byford, The Open University.
pages cm
Includes bibliographical references and index.
ISBN 978-1-107-03431-0 (hardback)
1. Psychohistory. 2. Psychology. 3. History. 4. Psychoanalysis and history. I. Tileagă, Cristian, 1975– II. Byford, Jovan.
D16.16.P88 2014
901.9–dc23
2013033848

ISBN 978-1-107-03431-0 Hardback
ISBN 978-1-316-50284-6 Paperback

Contents

Figures

Contributors

MICHAEL BILLIG is Professor of Social Sciences at Loughborough University, UK. Originally he trained as an experimental social psychologist under the supervision of Henri Tajfel. He has been interested in developing a more qualitative form of social psychology, which looks at language and ideology. He has written books on a number of topics including rhetoric, Freudian theory, nationalism, fascism and the history of rock 'n' roll. His book *The Hidden History of Critical Psychology* (2008) looks at the similarities between some neglected eighteenth-century theories of mind and modern critical psychological ideas.

MARK E. BLUM is Professor of History in the Department of History at the University of Louisville, Kentucky, USA. He was a Fellow at Carl Rogers Center for Studies of the Person in La Jolla, California from 1970–1. His publications include: *The Austro-Marxists, 1890–1918: a Psychobiographical Study* (1985) and *Continuity, Quantum, Continuum, and Dialectic: the Foundational Logics of Western Historical Thinking* (2006). More recently he wrote three chapters on national historical logics and generational change in historical logics in the volume *Political Economy, Linguistics and Culture*, edited by Jürgen Georg Backhaus (2008).

ROB BODDICE is Assistant Professor (Wissenschaftlicher Mitarbeiter) at the Friedrich-Meinecke-Institut, Freie Universität, Berlin, Germany. He is the author of *A History of Attitudes and Behaviours Toward Animals in Eighteenth- and Nineteenth-century Britain: Anthropocentrism and the Emergence of Animals* (2009) and editor of a collection entitled *Anthropocentrism: Humans, Animals, Environments* (2011). He is currently working on a history of sympathy in the context of early Darwinism.

JEREMY T. BURMAN is the Norman S. Endler Research Fellow in the Department of Psychology and Pierre Elliott Trudeau Fellow at York University in Toronto, Canada. His research blends developmental psychology, history and the public understanding of science. (He is currently working on a book about how the works of Jean Piaget were imported into American Psychology, and their arguments reconstructed in translation, following his "rediscovery" in the 1960s.) He also aims to advance historical research using scientific methods, but without sacrificing historicism, context, thick description, or the devotion to primary sources.

JOVAN BYFORD is Senior Lecturer in psychology at The Open University, UK. His research interests include conspiracy theories, Holocaust survivor testimonies and anti-Semitism. He is the author of four books: *Conspiracy Theories: a Critical Introduction* (2011), *Denial and Repression of Antisemitism: Post-Communist Remembrance of the Serbian Bishop Nikolaj Velimirović* (2008), *Conspiracy Theory: Serbia vs. the New World Order* (2006, in Serbian) and *Staro sajmište: a Site Remembered, Forgotten, Contested* (2011, in Serbian).

CATHIE CARMICHAEL is Professor of History at the University of East Anglia, UK. She is an editor of the *Journal of Genocide Research*, on the International Advisory Board of *Europe-Asia Studies* and on the executive committee of the British Association of Slavonic and East European Studies. Her publications include *Slovenia and the Slovenes* (with James Gow, 2000), *Language and Nationalism in Europe* (with Stephen Barbour, 2000), *Ethnic Cleansing in the Balkans* (2002), *Genocide before the Holocaust* (2009) and *A Concise History of Bosnia* (in press).

ALAN COLLINS is Senior Lecturer in Psychology at Lancaster University, UK. His main research interest is the history of psychology, especially the history of psychological concepts and the history of psychology in Britain. He is currently working on the history of memory and on the emergence and consolidation of neuropsychology in Britain. He is the former Chair of the British Psychological Society's History and Philosophy section.

SUSAN CONDOR is Professor of Social Psychology at Loughborough University, UK. Her research interests concern everyday understandings of the social world and the dialogic construction of social reality. Funded research projects involve the construction of national identities in the mass media, young people's orientations to EU membership and changing understandings of nationality, citizenship and civil society in the aftermath of UK constitutional change.

GEOFFREY CUBITT is Reader in the Department of History at the University of York, UK. His research interests embrace issues of history and memory, and the political and social uses of the past, as well as nineteenth-century French history. He is the author of *The Jesuit Myth: Conspiracy Theory and Politics in Nineteenth-Century France* (1993) and *History and Memory* (2007) and editor of *Imagining Nations* (1998), *Heroic Reputations and Exemplary Lives* (with Allen Warren, 2000), and *Representing Enslavement and Abolition in Museums: Ambiguous Engagements* (with Laurajane Smith, Ross Wilson and Kalliopi Fouseki, 2011).

CAROLYN J. DEAN is Professor of History at Yale University, USA. She is the author of several books, including *The Frail Social Body: Pornography, Homosexuality and Other Fantasies in Interwar France* (University of California Press, 2000) and most recently *The Fragility of Empathy after the Holocaust* (2004) and *Aversion and Erasure: the Fate of the Victim after the Holocaust* (2010).

KEVIN DURRHEIM is a Professor of Psychology at the University of KwaZulu-Natal, South Africa, where he teaches social psychology and research methods. He obtained his Ph.D. in political psychology from the University of Cape Town in 1995. He writes on topics related to racism, segregation and social change. He has co-authored two books, *Race Trouble* (with Xoliswa Mstose, Lyndsay Brown, 2011) and *Racial Encounter* (with John Dixon, 2005); and is co-editor (with Martin Terre Blanche) of *Research in Practice* (1999, 2006) and (with Colin Tredoux) *Numbers, Hypotheses and Conclusions* (2002).

PAUL H. ELOVITZ is the Associate Professor of History, Psychohistory and Interdisciplinary Studies at the Ramapo College of New Jersey, USA. He is a historian, lay psychoanalyst and a founding member of the International Psychohistorical Association (IPA) and the International Society for Political Psychology (ISPP). He serves on the editorial board of the *Journal of Psychohistory* and in 1994 became the founding editor of *Clio's Psyche*, a quarterly psychohistory journal. He is the author of more than 290 publications, mostly on applied psychohistory, biography, methodology, political psychology, psychobiography and teaching.

KENNETH J. GERGEN is Senior Research Professor of Psychology at Swarthmore College, and affiliate professor at Tilburg University, The Netherlands. He has published extensively on social constructionism and psychological theory, including *An Invitation to Social Construction* (2009), *Realities and Relationships: Soundings in Social Construction* (1997), and *Relational Being* (2011).

MARK KNIGHTS is Professor of History at the University of Warwick, UK. He is the author of (amongst other works) *Representation and Misrepresentation in Later Stuart Britain: Partisanship and Political Culture* (2005) and *The Devil in Disguise* (2011), both of which consider partisan publics and the construction of stereotypes in the seventeenth and eighteenth centuries.

IVANA MARKOVÁ is Emeritus Professor at the University of Stirling, UK. She has been a visiting Professor at the Universities of Oslo, Dundee, Berne, Paris, Linköping, Mexico and London. She has published in the field of epistemology of social psychology, language and communication, and has carried out research in political and health psychology. She is a fellow of the British Academy, of the Royal Society of Edinburgh and of the British Psychological Society.

JOAN W. SCOTT is Harold F. Linder Professor in the School of Social Science at the Institute for Advanced Study in Princeton, USA. She is widely known as the author of *Gender and the Politics of History* (1988 and 1999). Her most recent books are *The Politics of the Veil* (2007) and the *Fantasy of Feminist History* (2012).

CRISTIAN TILEAGĂ is Senior Lecturer in social psychology at Loughborough University, UK. His research interests concern the critical social psychology of racism, political discourse analysis, ideological justifications of polity and history. His current research explores how official (controversial) political imaginary and histories of the (Romanian) communist past are constructed in talk and text. He is the author of *Discourse Analysis and Reconciliation with the Recent Past* (in Romanian, 2012) and *Political Psychology: Critical Perspectives* (2013).

GEORGE TURNER is a research student at Lancaster University, UK, where he is writing a history of the term 'self-esteem' from the first half of the sixteenth century to the second half of the twentieth century. He holds a doctorate in education from the University of East Anglia.

Foreword

KENNETH J. GERGEN

One might suppose that in this time when the idea of *consilience* – the unity of scientific knowledge – sweeps across the disciplines, that an integration of psychological and historical studies would be untroubled. After all, they both employ the most sophisticated methods available to generate knowledge of human activity. And yet, if one were to select a key demonstration of the impediments to a unified science of human activity, the alienated relationship between history and psychology would be exemplary. The roots are deep, traceable at least to the late nineteenth-century debates between those favouring a model of the human sciences as *Naturwissenschaft* as opposed to *Geisteswissenschaft*, essentially the difference between claims to an observational versus hermeneutic grounds for knowledge. Closely related to this is the distance between psychologists' penchant for general laws or principles on the one hand, and historians' focal concern with the unique and particular. Indeed the central goal of the psychologist – for prediction and control – stands in contrast to the predominant concern among historians for contextual understanding.

Standing over these multiple estrangements is the implicit fear that each orientation, when extended to its fullest, can eliminate the other. If we fully accept the goals of the psychologist, then historical research is nothing more than a search for instances bearing on general laws, a second-rate enterprise at best, in its lack of experimental methods and predictive capacities. Yet, if we accept the orientation of the historian, the psychologists' claims to trans-historical knowledge are destroyed. We find that whatever psychologists claim to be true about human nature is nothing more than their application of historically and culturally fashioned concepts to the ever-shifting conventions of the times. This was the import of my 1973 paper, 'Social Psychology as History', and a major reason for its vociferous negation among my peers.[1]

[1] K. J. Gergen, 'Social psychology as history', *Journal of Personality and Social Psychology*, 26 (1973), 309–20.

It is against this background that the present volume is a welcome addition. To be sure, strong echoes remain of these longstanding differences. Yet, as the editors so keenly realize, there are significant cracks in the walls of the disciplines. Curious scholars wander across the territories, and, as they do, creative hybrids emerge. One discerns, for example, that virtually all historical accounts contain at least an implicit psychology, unarticulated assumptions about why people act as they do. And one sees that even within the cause-and-effect paradigm of psychology – and its realization in the experimental method – there is a rudimentary narrative at play. Extend the cause–effect sequence into the past and you are soon doing history. The blurring of genres is nowhere as evident as in the recent interest in social memory. Here the laminations of connection are rich indeed. At the outset, this work functions meta-theoretically. That is, it concerns itself with how our understanding of history is socially constituted. At the same time, these accounts are teaming with broadly applicable generalizations about the nature of this process. And as well, the particular cases used to support these ideas are typically the result of research into a specific period of history.

Thus, in the present volume we are treated to a rich array of boundary-crossing adventures. We come to see how psychoanalysis can introduce alternative conceptions of time into historical analysis, the limits and potentials of 'neurohistory,' the historical location of conceptions of self, the wrestling of historians with issues of emotion, the potentials of cognitive psychology for historical understanding, and the blending of disciplines in social representation research. And we are also introduced to ways in which history and psychology can draw from each other in their shared concerns with race prejudice, ideology, national character and self-esteem. Of special note, one sees in these chapters how a given psychological concept (e.g. motivation, emotion, memory, prejudice) can function productively in both psychology and historical inquiry, but in different ways.

I join with the editors of this work in the hope that these chapters will serve as the beginning of a new and more vital relationship between psychologists and historians. Each tradition requires the other in order to reflect wisely on the limits and potentials of its otherwise taken-for-granted assumptions. More importantly, disciplinary boundaries are invariably an impediment to creative scholarship. However, in my view the possibility for future dialogue will be vastly enhanced by casting away the realist/empiricist assumptions still pervading both the disciplines of psychology and history. As long as psychologists and historians continue to believe that their descriptions and explanations are capturing the contours of the world as it is, the alienating tensions will remain. If it is an objective fact that the world of human activity is made of unique composites of action and circumstance, there is no place for general laws or principles. If world leaders are, in fact, free to make decisions, and moral deliberation may change the course of one's action, then the discourse of psychological mechanics is mystifying. Yet, if it is objectively true that the world is composed of continuous repetitions of cause–effect patterns, there is little place for history as we know it. If psychoanalysis, social evolution, sociobiology, or neuro-behaviourism are true, then traditional historical study will perish.

In my view, it is far more promising to adopt a constructionist alternative to the realist/empiricist tradition. If we give up the idea that discourse serves as a potentially accurate map or picture of an independent world, and begin to understand the way in which our forms of representation shape the outcomes of our inquiry, we move into a new space of evaluating our endeavours. To be sure, historians would have to give up 'the noble dream' of an objective history.[2] And psychologists would have to abandon their view of infinite progress in prediction. However, we could begin to ask more generative questions of both pragmatic and moral/ideological import. We would not ask whether any given account – either historical or experimental – is transcendentally true, but what contribution such accounts make to the human condition. Historical accounts are often valuable in stimulating critical and/or appreciative reflection on our traditions, contributing to moral and ideological deliberation, and providing a sense of how we came to be as we are. Psychological accounts can provide an array of lenses through which we can appraise our actions, and thus consider multiple policies and practices of broad utility. At certain times and places, our capacities for prediction may even be improved. All this may occur without claims to obdurate objectivity. Most importantly for the present volume, without the impediments of such claims, we are liberated to create novel amalgams of unlimited variety – merging, borrowing, translating, reducing, and so forth. Removing the quest for transcendent truth, we may cross boundaries and combine resources to generate the kinds of inquiry that contribute to futures of value to humankind. It is neither to the past nor the eternal present that our inquiries in history and psychology properly contribute, but to our future lives together. Such endeavours may bring us all into productive and impassioned deliberation.

[2] P. Novick, *That Noble Dream: the "Objectivity Question" and the American Historical Profession* (Cambridge University Press, 1988).

Acknowledgements

Our thanks are due, first of all, to the contributors for the enthusiasm with which they responded to our invitation and for their continuing support and encouragement. We are especially grateful to Ken Gergen for the illuminating and thought-provoking foreword, which sets the scene for the book.

The contributions by Joan W. Scott, Jeremy T. Burman, Carolyn J. Dean and Ivana Marková have previously appeared elsewhere, either in their entirety or in part. The editors are grateful to the following journals or publishers for the permission to include in this volume work previously published under their auspices. Wesleyan University and Wiley-Blackwell Publishing for Joan W. Scott, 'The incommensurability of psychoanalysis and history' *History and Theory* **51**, 1 (February 2012), 63–83 (reproduced in full in Chapter 2); The American Psychological Association for Jeremy T. Burman, 'History from within? Contextualizing the new neurohistory and seeking its methods', *History of Psychology* **15** (2012), 84–99 (published in modified form in Chapter 3); Springer for Ivana Marková, 'Method and explanation in history and in social representations', *Integrative Psychological and Behavioral Science* **46**, 4 (2012), 457–74 (amended version published in Chapter 5) and Blackwell Publishers for Carolyn J. Dean, 'Redefining historical identities: sexuality, gender, and the self', in L. Kramer and S. Maza (eds.), *A Companion to Western Historical Thought* (Oxford: Blackwell Publishers, 2002), pp. 357–71 (amended version published in Chapter 6).

We would also like to thank Paul Churchland for the permission to reproduce the figure in Chapter 3, and the British Museum for the permission to publish the illustrations that feature in Chapter 12.

We are grateful to the editors at Cambridge University Press and especially Hetty Marx, Carrie Parkinson and Fleur Jones for supporting our project, to Alison Walker for her meticulous copy-editing, and Rob Wilkinson for the efficient management of the production process.

Finally, we would like to thank the family of Vladan Čokić from Mladenovac in Serbia for the exquisite, home-made slivovitz that we enjoyed while poring over the merits of interdisciplinarity.

Introduction: psychology and history – themes, debates, overlaps and borrowings

Cristian Tileagă and Jovan Byford

The main concern of this book is with the possibilities for an interdisciplinary dialogue between psychology and history. At first sight it might seem obvious that psychology and history, as scholarly disciplines, have a lot in common. For one thing the two traditions of enquiry share, and are continuously brought into contact by, their concern with the human condition: with individual and collective beliefs, mentalities, human behaviour and motivation, memory, personality, emotions and feelings. And yet the dialogue between the two disciplines has been, for the most part, sporadic and fraught with both theoretical and epistemological tensions.

Traditionally, both historians and psychologists have been aware of the need for a conversation with each other. Many historians have appealed for greater engagement with psychological literature. As the French historian Jean Chesneaux wrote, 'social psychology and psychoanalysis add substantially to the historian's intellectual equipment and enable him [*sic*] to cope more effectively with problems of collective consciousness and mass mentality'.[1] Historians of genocide and social conflict have similarly appealed for greater engagement with psychological literature, especially when researching topics such as memory, obedience, conformity or intergroup conflict.[2] Meanwhile, the pioneers of the fields of psychohistory and psychobiography (which gradually developed throughout the twentieth century, mainly in the United States) sought to apply the tools of psychoanalysis and depth psychology to the study of historical figures, past events and collective behaviours.[3] Equally, to many prominent psychologists, the engagement with history (and other humanities and social sciences) promised a way of undermining the rigid positivism that reigns

1 J. Chesneaux, *Pasts and Futures or What Is History For?* (London: Thames & Hudson, 1978), p. 130.

2 See C. R. Browning, 'Foreword', in J. Waler, *Becoming Evil: How Ordinary People Commit Genocide and Mass Killing* (Oxford University Press, 2002), pp. vii–viii.

3 See, for instance, W. M. Runyan (ed.), *Psychology and Historical Interpretation* (Oxford University Press, 1988).

within traditional academic psychology. Michael Billig, Kenneth Gergen and Serge Moscovici have all argued that psychology ought to be more attentive to the historical contingency of psychological phenomena and pay closer attention to the issue of how historical conditions, ideologies and cultural traditions produce and sustain particular forms of individual and collective thought and action.[4]

In spite of the increasing awareness that 'history is far too important a matter to be left to the historians' – and the same can be said to apply to psychology and psychologists – the conversation between the two disciplines has been anything but fluent.[5] As Kenneth Gergen once observed, 'psychologists and historians have not always been congenial companions'.[6] Mainstream academic psychology treats history with 'little more than tolerant civility'. Psychologists may 'scan accounts of earlier times', but only in the quest for 'interesting hypotheses and anecdotes', or for confirmation that the results of systematic and controlled empirical research have a wider currency and the much coveted 'ecological validity'. But, history and psychology are seldom seen as being truly complementary. For many psychologists history is an incomplete enquiry, because of the evasive 'messiness' of history and social life.[7] As Michael Billig explains:

> Historians lack complete records of the past. They cannot run experiments to test hypotheses. A historian might claim that Protestantism was vital to the development of capitalism in the early modern period. Supporting evidence might be assembled. A plausible story might be told. But the thesis can never be 'proved' to the rigorous standards demanded by an experimental scientist, such as a chemist or physicist. No controlled experiment could be conducted on past events. One cannot re-run the processes of European history, this time controlling for factors such as Henry VIII's divorce, the doctrines of Martin Luther and the failure of the Catholic Church to stop the selling of pardons, in order to assess what precise weightings these 'variables' would have on the rise of capitalism.[8]

The attitude of 'tolerant civility' found among psychologists is reciprocated by historians who have been sceptical of historical enquiry based on psychological theories and empirical findings. In his 1957 presidential address delivered at the American Historical Association's annual

4 K. Gergen, 'Social psychology as history'. *Journal of Personality and Social Psychology*, 26 (1973), 309–20; S. Moscovici, 'The phenomenon of social representations', in R. M. Farr and S. Moscovici (eds.) *Social Representations* (Cambridge University Press, 1984), pp. 3–70; M. Billig, *Arguing and Thinking: a Rhetorical Approach to Social Psychology*, 2nd edn (Cambridge University Press, 1996).

5 Chesneaux, *Pasts and Futures*, p. 9.

6 K. Gergen, *Social Constructionism in Context* (London: Sage, 2001), p. 82.

7 M. Billig, *The Hidden Roots of Critical Psychology* (London: Sage, 2008).

8 Billig, *Hidden Roots*, p. 10.

dinner, the Harvard historian William D. Langer stated that 'classical or academic psychology ... so far as I can detect, has little bearing on historical problems'.[9] Curiously, Langer was more favourably inclined towards the potential of psychoanalysis and 'depth psychology'. Other historians, however, have been less forthcoming. In Britain, the renowned historian of the twentieth century A. J. P. Taylor once wondered how anyone could take Freud seriously, a sentiment shared by other historians who see psychological reductionism as inherently ahistorical.[10] One critic of psychohistory, Lawrence Stone, went as far as to accuse this approach of developing 'along dogmatically ahistorical lines', in that it emphasized causal factors 'independent of the influence of historically based cultural conditioning' and ignored 'the critical importance of changing context – religious, moral, cultural, economic, social, and political'.[11] Even within the genre of biography, where the link between psychoanalytically informed psychology and history might seem most apparent, the cooperation between the two disciplines has been at best 'uneasy'. Psychobiography has always been largely confined to the peripheries of mainstream academia.[12]

One important cause of the tensions that exist between psychology and history lies in their dissimilar approaches to evidence and 'data'. As Christopher Browning, one of today's foremost Holocaust historians acknowledges, different historians reading the same historiographic sources 'would not produce or agree upon an identical set of "facts" – beyond an elementary minimum – out of which a narrative of events ... could be created'. In other words, the same material – official documents, eyewitness reports, memoirs, and so on – can produce multiple interpretations and explanations. There is no 'objective' or 'scientific' means of adjudicating between competing interpretations, except through scholarly debate and argumentation.[13] This is not something that can be easily reconciled with academic psychology's empiricist credentials, obsession with method and, more often than

9 W. D. Langer, 'The next assignment', *The American Historical Review*, 63 (1958), 284.

10 C. Ginzburg, 'Freud, the Wolf-Man, and the Werewolves', in C. Ginzburg, *Clues, Myths, and the Historical Method* (Baltimore, OH: Johns Hopkins University Press, 1992); S. Nicholas, 'Psychoanalysis and Psychohistory', in P. Lambert and P. Schofield (eds.), *Making History: an Introduction to the History and Practice of a Discipline* (London: Routledge, 2004); A. C. Elms, *Uncovering Lives: the Uneasy Alliance of Biography and Psychology* (Oxford University Press, 1994).

11 L. Stone, *The Past and the Present Revisited* (London: Routledge & Kegan Paul, 1987), pp. 26 and 40.

12 See Elms, *Uncovering Lives.*

13 For the defence of scholarship as method see M. Billig, 'Methodology and scholarship in understanding ideological explanation', in C. Antaki (ed.), *Analysing Everyday Explanation: a Casebook of Methods* (London: Sage, 1988), pp. 199–227.

not, quantification. Furthermore, as Lawrence Stone points out, psychologists exhibit a tendency to adopt 'an almost consciously antiliterary style' sacrificing narrative coherence and clarity, so important in historical writing, in favour of a language that is 'obscure, turgid, repetitive, flatulent, studded either with meaningless jargon and neologisms, or with oversophisticated algebraic formulae and impenetrable statistical tables'.[14]

Also, academic psychology often has a problem with historiographic sources. Because psychology focuses mainly on human behaviour in the present (from which it draws often unwarranted universalist, 'ahistorical' conclusions), psychologists can claim to have a direct and unmediated access to their object of study. Put differently, in the context of experimental research in particular, psychologists are involved in the design and creation of the data they analyse. Historians, on the other hand, do not have that luxury: they deal with 'data' that, because its *locus* is in the past, is always imperfect, incomplete, contingent on interpretation and mediated through sources.[15]

The present collection of chapters hopes to help psychology and history move from their current state of sporadic engagement, towards genuine and authentic interdisciplinary dialogue. The thirteen chapters, authored by internationally renowned psychologists and historians, span a broad range of topics of mutual interest to the two disciplines, such as social memory, prejudice, stereotyping, affect and emotion, cognition, personality, gender and the self. The contributions explore these topics, drawing on examples from different historical periods and cultural contexts – from eighteenth-century Britain, through apartheid South Africa to the conflict-torn former Yugoslavia – and cover diverse issues, such as political decision making, the Darwinian theory of emotion and sexuality. Also, the chapters consider the various issues that arise from conducting research across the boundaries between the humanities and the social or psychological sciences. These include the nature and limitations of psychological and historical enquiries, the different epistemologies within and across the two disciplines, the tensions between the universal and the particular, the relationship between the individual and the social. The main aim of this collection of chapters is to rekindle the dialogue between psychology and history and encourage students and researchers working in the two disciplines to engage in this dialogue more directly and self-reflectively.

[14] Stone, *The Past and the Present Revisited*, p. 8; see also M. Billig, *Learn to Write Badly: How to Succeed in the Social Sciences* (Cambridge University Press, 2013).

[15] L. Jordanova, *History in Practice* (New York: Bloomsbury, 2006), p.170.

Conceptions and meanings of interdisciplinarity

Before we present the outline of the book it is perhaps worth dwelling on the elusive notion of 'interdisciplinarity'. As Ludmilla Jordanova points out, there is a 'certain ambiguity surrounding what is meant by "interdisciplinary" – is it about exchanges between fields that remain distinct or a rather more intimate blending of domains with already blurred edges?'[16]

One notable form of interdisciplinary engagement between psychology and history involves what might be referred to as *merger* or *appropriation*. The sub-disciplines of 'psychohistory' and 'psychobiography' are relevant examples. Historians who embraced psychoanalysis turned it into a critical instrument for uncovering hidden motives, desires, life trajectories, and so on, of both individuals and collectives.[17]

Another common form of engagement is *transfer* or *borrowing*. This is where specific insights, ideas, or vocabulary from one discipline are used to shed light on a specific problem regarding human motivation, behaviour, and so on. The historian engaged in borrowing often takes on the role of the 'seeker' who looks for a particular idea, 'poking about' in the quest for 'some formula, some hypothesis, some model, some method which has immediate relevance to one's own work, and which seems to help one to understand one's data better and to arrange and interpret them in a more meaningful way'.[18] An example of this approach might include Christopher Browning's work on the conduct of the members of the German Reserve Police Battalion 100 in Poland in 1942, which drew on the findings of Stanley Milgram's classic social psychological study of obedience.[19] On the other hand, when psychologists engage in borrowing, they look to history for accounts of real life events, which they then examine through the prism of psychological research and theory. One example is the study by Steve Reicher and colleagues, which looked at the rescue of Bulgaria's Jews during the Holocaust as an example of bystander intervention and the mobilization of pro-social behaviour.[20]

The determining feature of borrowing is that it is selective and focuses on solving a particular problem or issue: how does one account for the

[16] Jordanova, *History in Practice*, p. 80.

[17] P. Loewenberg, *Decoding the Past: the Psychohistorical Approach* (New Brunswick, NJ: Transaction, 1996).

[18] Stone, *The Past and the Present Revisited*, p. 20.

[19] C. R. Browning, *Ordinary Men: Reserve Police Battalion 101 and the Final Solution in Poland* (New York: HarperCollins, 1992).

[20] S. Reicher, C. Cassidy, I. Wolpert, N. Hopkins and M. Levine, 'Saving Bulgaria's Jews: An analysis of social identity and the mobilisation of social solidarity', *European Journal of Social Psychology*, 36 (2006), 49–72.

survival of Bulgaria's Jews? What explains the behaviour of members of a police battalion? Importantly, when historians or psychologists turn to each other, they do so for *suggestions* rather than prescriptions. What is to be borrowed and how much is usually determined by the perceived usefulness, applicability and relevance. As Jordanova argues, 'if conducted correctly, with due acknowledgement' borrowing can be seen, by both sides, as 'a productive transaction'.[21]

Occasionally, transfer or borrowing can lead to the creation of new vocabulary and novel ways of thinking about psychological or historical phenomena. One example of this process of *translation* is the new 'history of emotions' whose vocabulary and academic thesaurus is a transformation and reinterpretation of concepts from disciplines such as psychology, neuroscience and evolutionary science. Translation usually involves topics and concerns that are taken for granted by some researchers, but are seen as 'lost' and then 'found' by others. These 'recuperation' projects involve some degree of (more or less complex) transformation or translation.[22] In the case of the 'history of emotions' the cross-disciplinary process of translation at the same time enriches historical practice, and revitalizes the psychological exploration of emotions, by placing them 'within an economy that depends on, and answers to, cultural expectations and social needs'.[23]

Translation is usually intimately linked to a process of *historicization* of the object of study. For historians, this usually involves recasting individual-level types of phenomena (fear, emotion, etc.) and situating them within a cultural-historical framework.[24] For example, Bourke's cultural history of fear asks, 'how can we understand the way people in the past experienced emotions such as fear' given that, from a historical vantage point, 'subjective feelings are invisible'? [25] One cannot just expect to contemplate historical 'traces' and understand how individuals 'really felt'. 'Knowing' this requires squaring historical scholarship with insights from psychology and cognate domains.[26]

21 Jordanova, *History in Practice*, p. 63.

22 U. Frevert, *Emotions in History: Lost and Found* (Budapest: Centra European University Press, 2011).

23 Frevert, *Emotions in History*, p. 212.

24 J. Bourke, *Fear: a Cultural History* (London: Virago, 2006); W. A. Reddy, *The Navigation of Feeling: a Framework for the History of Emotions* (Cambridge University Press, 2001).

25 Bourke, *Fear: a Cultural History*, p. 6.

26 Importantly, historicization is not in itself a guarantee against reductionism. Quite the contrary, the impetus to account for a certain socio-psychological phenomenon culturally and historically (in a full and comprehensive fashion) can lead someone to disregard particular or deviant cases.

In any project of translation lurks the danger of *reduction* and oversimplification. In broadest terms, reduction can be defined as 'recasting the type and level of phenomena from one that is complex to another that is less so: by implication, one too basic to be satisfying'.[27] A classic example of reduction in history is psychohistory. The majority of critiques levelled at the psychohistorical project have dealt in some way or another with its reductionism, its tendency to reduce complex historical phenomena, or individual biographies, to an (unsatisfactory) basic level, grounded in psychodynamic interpretations. However, as Paul Elovitz argues in his contribution to this volume, psychohistory should be seen as more varied and less reductionist than its critics would allow. Another example that can be given is the new approach of 'neurohistory', with its emphasis on the brain as the material and historical basis of experience.[28] According to Jeremy Burman (this volume), neurohistory suggests a narrative about past events that takes into account the biological underpinnings of experience, which, in any given context, are seen to *cause* the feeling of 'what it was like'. One of the crucial suggestions of neurohistory is that historians need to take into account the 'deep' (evolutionary, physiological) structures, traditionally investigated by neurologists, neuropsychologists and cognitive psychologists. It is assumed that one can delve deeper into the history of the humankind by exploring the neural structures that make possible feelings, emotions, culture, social organization, and so on. Historians' turn to the brain is akin to psychologists' turn towards evolution and neurosciences: some psychologists increasingly see evolutionary, physiological and cortical correlates of behaviour as the sole answer to the various puzzles posed by human action, values and motivations. These are not considered particular to individuals, but rather as universal aspects that can offer the ultimate story of human existence and experience.

One of the problems with this approach is that the diversity of human actions is reduced to the brain, which is seen as determining the forms that cultural life and cultural experience take. What Kenneth Gergen has called the 'expanding romance with cortical explanations of human action' ignores the diversity of experiences, plurality of values and beliefs, issues of cross-cultural variation, and so on.[29] More importantly, what makes this approach reductionist is that it glosses over the idea that 'the brain does not determine the contours of cultural life; cultural

[27] Jordanova, *History in Practice*, p. 68.

[28] D. L. Smail, *On Deep History and the Brain* (Berkeley: University of California Press, 2008).

[29] K. Gergen, 'The Acculturated Brain', *Theory & Psychology*, 20 (2010), 19.

life determines what we take to be the nature and importance of brain functioning'.[30]

Appropriation, borrowing, translation and reduction, as forms of interdisciplinary engagement, are neither mutually exclusive nor jointly exhaustive. In fact, when looking at specific studies, it is not always possible to determine where borrowing turns into translation or where translation might acquire the properties of a merger. Instead, what can be discerned are elective affinities between the two disciplines, which imply the notion of a discretionary, flexible choice. This choice is guided by diverse factors including, but not limited to, the prevailing academic conventions in the two disciplines, hierarchies of specialization and expertise, the implicit or explicit models of the mind and human behaviour, assumptions about possible areas of overlap and dialogue, and so on. Most importantly, as the contributions to this volume testify, the key driver of interdisciplinary dialogue has been the need to solve puzzles and answer questions related to the human condition. Sometimes these puzzles are defined by the conventions of the discipline and previously acquired knowledge, sometimes by real world concerns, and sometimes by the interaction between the two. Also, whether the dialogue between psychology and history involves a one-way or two-way flow is less important than the fact that researchers from two seemingly different traditions of enquiry can and, in fact, do find common ground, and use insights from the other discipline creatively, as a guide to their endeavour. The dialogue between two fields of knowledge and the continuing exchange, transaction, and so on should strive to broaden the scope of both of them and make more meaningful the examination of the variety of assumptions and preconceptions about the human condition. This dialogue should not be mainly about *how* psychology and history ought to relate to each, but about actual ways in which psychologists and historians infuse their enquiries with each other's insights.

The recognition of this plurality of ways of doing interdisciplinarity is central to the present volume. Forthcoming chapters do not offer an 'instructional manual' on how to do interdisciplinarity; nor do they lay out a fully developed, singular interdisciplinary approach. Instead, as the title suggests, what follows is a collection of diverse and engaging interdisciplinary *explorations*, which track the intersection between psychology and history and consider different ways in which each discipline can enhance the understanding of the other. It is hoped that these explorations will raise awareness among researchers from both disciplines about the need to question their unspoken, often taken-for-granted assumptions, to

[30] *Ibid.*, p. 19.

scrutinize their concepts and methods more carefully, to make innovations to existing research strategies, to generate new research questions, and to offer, where relevant, theoretical and contextual *appui* to other disciplines.

Outline of the book

The book is divided into three parts. Part I deals with central aspects of the theoretical dialogue between psychologists and historians. The emphasis is on the distinctive theoretical relevance of interdisciplinary engagement for understanding human behaviour. The opening chapter, by Geoffrey Cubitt, uses the example of social memory – a field of interest for both history and psychology – to examine the manner in which the boundaries between the two disciplines may be kept open or critically interrogated. Joan Scott discusses the possibility/impossibility of a productive dialogue between history and psychology, with particular reference to psychoanalysis. Scott argues that although history and psychoanalysis work with very different conceptions of time and causality, it is important for historians to recognize the latter's potential when examining the historical relevance of unconscious motivation and fantasy. Scott charts part of the history of the 'compatibility' between the two disciplines and the contexts that fostered or hindered their interaction. Jeremy Burman critically appraises some of the recent engagement between history and neuroscience. Burman explores the promises and limitations of 'neurohistory' as an emerging approach that seeks to do 'history from within' and interrogates some of its psychological assumptions. The fourth chapter in this section, by Paul Elovitz, uses the example of psychohistory and psychobiography to consider the successes and failures of some of the previous attempts to bring psychology and history closer together. Elovitz identifies crucial tensions that strained the relationship between historians and psychologists in the past, and suggests remedies for a productive and mutually beneficial interdisciplinary engagement. The concluding chapter of Part I, by Ivana Marková, looks specifically at micro-history and single case studies, and contrasts method and explanation in history and social psychology.

Parts II and III include examples of research in which psychologists and historians have borrowed from, developed, or explored each other's ideas. Part II focuses on *cognition, affect* and *the self*. Carolyn Dean writes about selfhood and sexuality in historical writing. Dean follows the historical trace of conceptions of selfhood and gender identity in historical scholarship, and generally considers the historical and cultural contingency of psychological notions. Rob Boddice critically appraises the 'affective turn' in history by considering how emotions are treated in historical writing. Using the history of evolutionary psychology as a case study, he engages with the question about how to 'do' the history of emotions. Mark Blum looks at 'cognitive orientation' as a factor in the decision-making processes of politicians, and argues that cognition offers a useful tool for the historian trying to understand the psychological underpinnings of political decision making and action. The chapter by George Turner, Susan Condor and Alan Collins explores the history of the concept of self-esteem, and shows that, contrary to popular belief, there existed a psychology of self-esteem in the writings of phrenologists, well before William James used the term in *Principles of Psychology* in 1890.

Part III offers further examples of the dialogue between psychology and history, which consider issues around *prejudice*, *ideology*, *stereotypes* and *national character*. By charting the two 'histories' of the concept of prejudice in social psychology, Kevin Durrheim argues that one cannot understand the social psychology of racism in apartheid South Africa outside of its historical context. Through the analysis of a largely forgotten early social psychological exploration of anti-Semitism, Michael Billig writes about the need for a more historically conscious social psychology, while Mark Knights focuses on the understanding of stereotypes as both psychological and historical constructions, and comments on history's and social psychology's shared interest in the public sphere, the arts of persuasion and the formation of attitudes. The final chapter, by Cathie Carmichael, examines the ways in which psychological and psychoanalytic language and interpretation of national character were mobilized for propaganda purposes in the former Yugoslavia in the late 1980s and 1990s.

The contributions by historians included in this volume show how taking psychology seriously can help construct a more comprehensive stance towards historical phenomena, events, chronologies, and so on, and disentangle the intricate web of human motivation, individual and social memory, values, attitudes, beliefs, social identifications, social representations, stereotypes, and so forth. Equally, the contributions by psychologists demonstrate how taking history and historical context seriously can help avoid the tendency towards unwarranted generalization, and develop a more reflective stance towards the historical contingency of psychological vocabulary and phenomena, such as values, attitudes and collective mentalities. Crucially, the volume does not privilege any specific school of thought within either psychology or history. On the contrary, it covers a whole range of theoretical, epistemological and methodological approaches, and considers myriad issues that arise from conducting research across the boundaries between the humanities and the social or psychological sciences.

We have asked our contributors not simply to try to bring into contact or relate two seemingly separate domains of knowledge and practice, but also to position themselves epistemologically and theoretically in order to generate and explore distinctive kinds of research questions, quandaries and problems. We hope that these explorations can foster the creation of a platform for emancipative and socially relevant forms of self-awareness and critical reflection across both disciplines. We also hope that they raise crucial issues regarding the cultural function of historical and psychological description and explanation, and the status of the knowledge that is generated by interdisciplinary endeavours. We will return turn to these issues in the Conclusion.

In this volume, one will find an engagement with the notion of interdisciplinarity, but without an overt consensus about *how* it can be achieved. The contributions seek to open new channels of communication drawing on different positions and voices within the two disciplines. The reactions to interdisciplinarity are different. Some of the contributors experiment with more direct ways; others approach the issue more tentatively. There is no common recipe, or a unified message, as the chapters collected in this volume reflect the inherent complexity and diversity of interdisciplinary scholarship.

Part I

Theoretical dialogues

1 History, psychology and social memory

Geoffrey Cubitt

In 1973, the psychologist Kenneth Gergen entitled an article 'Social psychology as history'.[1] Twenty-four years later, James Pennebaker and Becky Banasik responded with a subtitle describing 'history as social psychology'.[2] The symmetry of the juxtaposition reduces on closer inspection. Gergen's provocative claim was not that social psychologists should busy themselves with the study of past societies and historical processes, but that they should recognize the historically specific – meaning culturally bounded and socially located – character of what they studied. Rather than seeing themselves as discoverers of general truths about human cognitive processes, they should see the significance of their work as lying in what it revealed about mental functioning in a particular society: they were supplying the material for future histories. Pennebaker and Banasik pointed out that, while challenging psychologists to rethink the credentials of their discipline, Gergen had implicitly accepted the status of history as an impartial and objective form of knowledge. Writing at a time when faith in historical objectivity had receded, they asserted the need to grasp the ways in which historical knowledge itself was continually shaped by social psychological processes. Together, these two articles remind us that thinking about the disciplinary identities of history and psychology and thinking about the relationships of historical knowledge, memory and society are closely entangled.

Over recent decades, memory in general and its social dimensions in particular have become objects of compelling interest across the humanities and social sciences. History and psychology have both participated in this efflorescence of social memory studies, but their paths towards it have not been symmetrical. Psychology, a discipline with a

[1] K. J. Gergen, 'Social psychology as history', *Journal of Personality and Social Psychology*, 26 (1973), 309–20.

[2] J. W. Pennebaker and B. L. Banasik, 'On the creation and maintenance of collective memories: history as social psychology', in J. W. Pennebaker, D. Paez and B. Rimé (eds.), *Collective Memory of Political Events: Social Psychological Perspectives* (Mahwah, NJ: Lawrence Erlbaum, 1997), pp. 3–19.

long tradition of studying memory, but traditionally used to viewing it from an individualizing perspective, has begun to engage seriously with its more social dimensions. History, a discipline traditionally interested in social (including cultural, institutional and political) objects of study, has taken to using memory as a category of analysis in their description: we have witnessed an 'emergence of memory in historical discourse'.[3] In this chapter, I consider some of the currents of thought within the two disciplines that have brought social memory issues into prominence, and seek to use this as a way of exploring relationships between the two disciplines more generally.

'Social memory' (like 'collective memory', 'cultural memory' and just plain 'memory') is a term in danger sometimes of being 'depreciated by surplus use'.[4] I use it here not to designate a particular type of memory, or to privilege a particular theory, but as an umbrella term to cover a range of approaches to memory whose similarities, differences and interrelationships I want to explore. These approaches have in common the fact of engaging seriously with social dimensions of memory; I distinguish them from other approaches whose common characteristic is that of treating memory as a phenomenon of individual mind, to which social influences are marginal or irrelevant. At one end of an imagined spectrum of approaches, taking a social view of memory may mean simply recognizing that much of the content of individual remembering refers to things that are social in character – social occasions, relationships, conversational exchanges, shared endeavours, and so on. At the other end, it might mean positing a 'group mind' endowed with a remembering capacity somehow distinct from that of group members.[5] In between are ranged a variety of ways of thinking of memory as socially inflected or conditioned, interactive, culturally mediated, shared or socially distributed. Middling positions along this spectrum may be thought of as being reached either by 'socializing' the concept of the remembering individual or by 'writing the individual back into collective memory'.[6]

[3] K. L. Klein, 'On the emergence of memory in historical discourse', *Representations*, 69 (2000), 127–50.

[4] A. Confino, 'Collective memory and cultural history: problems of method', *American Historical Review*, 102, 5 (1997), 1386.

[5] For discussion of 'group mind' thinking, see R. A. Wilson, *Boundaries of the Mind: the Individual in the Fragile Sciences* (Cambridge University Press, 2004), chapters 11–12, and R. A. Wilson 'Collective memory, group minds, and the extended mind thesis', *Cognitive Processing*, 6, 4 (2005), 227–36.

[6] S. A. Crane, 'Writing the individual back into collective memory', *American Historical Review*, 102, 5 (1997) 1372–85; also W. Hirst and D. Manier, 'Towards a psychology of collective memory', *Memory*, 16, 3 (2008), 183–200.

The polar opposition between the individual and the collective should not, however, be too readily taken for granted. Current thinking on memory increasingly seeks ways of transcending this opposition. '[W]hat is individual and what is collective, and what is personal and what is societal are not separable – they are interdependent', writes David Middleton.[7] Amanda Barnier and John Sutton see psychology as central to efforts to 'understand the relationships between an individual remembering alone, an individual remembering in a group and the group itself remembering', while Astrid Erll affirms that 'cultural memory studies is decidedly concerned with social, medial, and cognitive processes, and their ceaseless interplay'.[8] A whole series of recent general studies, edited collections, readers and journals (e.g. *Memory*, *Memory Studies* and *History and Memory*) has set out to prepare or map the field for more integrated forms of study.[9] Now is a good moment to consider some of the movements that have contributed to this position.

Schematically, we might map the enterprise of memory studies as having three dimensions: *personal*, investigating memory in relation to the individual; *social*, investigating its relationship to society and culture; and *historical*, investigating its relationship to historical processes. (Work in any of these dimensions may encompass an interest both in memory content and in remembering as a process.) We might expect a concentration on the personal dimension in disciplines like psychology and psychoanalysis, on the social in disciplines like sociology, and on the historical in disciplines like history. But the potential for cross-overs between the three dimensions is such that any attempt to use this schematic division as a way of describing an actual division of labour between disciplines rapidly becomes confusing. Literary scholars, philosophers and oral historians as well as psychologists and psychoanalysts are interested in individual memory; memory in past societies is studied by sociologists and literary analysts as well as historians. The 'social psychology of memory'

[7] D. Middleton, 'Succession and change in the socio-cultural uses of memory: building-in the past in communicative action', *Culture and Psychology*, 8, 1 (2002), 83.

[8] A. Barnier and J. Sutton, 'From individual to collective memory: theoretical and empirical perspectives', *Memory*, 16, 3 (2008), 177; A. Erll, 'Cultural memory studies: an introduction', in A. Erll and A. Nünning (eds.) *A Companion to Cultural Memory Studies* (Berlin and New York: De Gruyter, 2010), pp. 1–15.

[9] For recent general overviews see B. A. Misztal, *Theories of Social Remembering* (Maidenhead: Open University Press, 2003); D. Middleton and S. Brown, *The Social Psychology of Experience: Studies in Remembering and Forgetting* (London: Sage, 2005); G. Cubitt, *History and Memory* (Manchester University Press, 2007); A. Assmann, *Cultural Memory and Western Civilization* (Cambridge University Press, 2011); A. Erll, *Memory in Culture* (Basingstoke: Palgrave Macmillan, 2011), and the important edited collections of P. Boyer and J. V. Wertsch (eds.), *Memory in Mind and Culture* (Cambridge University Press, 2009) and Erll and Nünning (eds.), *A Companion to Cultural Memory Studies.*

is practised, with sometimes different understandings of what it covers, in departments both of psychology and of sociology. The study of memory is not marshalled within neat disciplinary containers.

The specific relationship between history and psychology in relation to memory is also elusive. The frontier between these two disciplines has not, in this area, been an especially busy zone of interdisciplinary traffic. Both disciplines have developed their thinking on memory more through encounters with other disciplines – philosophy, sociology, anthropology, psychoanalysis, literary studies, neuroscience – than through direct exchanges with each other. The history of their relationship is one of cultural differences, indirect connections, parallel engagements with third-party influences, leading to piecemeal and somewhat accidental movements in each other's direction, rather than of open clashes, ardent embraces or direct ransacking of each other's conceptual store-cupboards. The rest of this chapter seeks to make some sense of this elusive picture. It deals inevitably in generalizations, to which exceptions could be found, but which I think capture certain broad-brush differences between the disciplines and between approaches to memory within them. The discussion is in four parts: the first offers certain framing comparisons between the two disciplinary cultures; the second and third describe some of the ways in which historians and psychologists have approached the field of social memory; the fourth seeks on the basis of these descriptions to sketch an area in which the joint energies of the two disciplines can profitably be mobilized in future.

History and psychology: difference and common ground

One important difference between history and psychology relates to the way in which reflections on memory rebound on questions of disciplinary identity. For psychologists, memory, described by some as 'the scaffolding upon which all mental life is constructed', has been a key object of study, intimately connected to many others.[10] No one, however, has seriously claimed that psychology itself is a form of memory, or that it is to society what memory is to the individual, or that it is defined conceptually in opposition to memory, or that its pretensions are to be critiqued by contrasting them with memory's greater authenticity – all claims whose equivalents have repeatedly been made in reference to history. The reason for this difference is that history, like memory but unlike psychology,

[10] G. D. Fischbach, and J. T. Coyle, 'Preface', in D. L. Schacter (ed.), *Memory Distortion: How Minds, Brains and Societies Reconstruct the Past* (Cambridge, MA: Harvard University Press, 1995), p. ix.

deals in past-related knowledge. Two ideas are involved here. The first is that history is itself significantly memory-dependent: it processes information that has passed through memory *en route* to it. A critical awareness of memory's strengths and weaknesses is therefore an important part of historical method. The second is that, if we define memory in the broadest social sense, to encompass the multifaceted presence and articulation of past-related knowledge within human societies, history as a disciplined composition and presentation of such knowledge is itself a significant contributor to social memory processes. Claims about the nature of its contribution, and about the function and credibility of history in relation to other past-regarding discourses or bodies of knowledge are therefore central to history's status in the eyes both of its practitioners and of its critics. This is what debates over the history–memory relationship have usually been about.[11] History has either been discursively aligned with memory, which it has been seen as refining, codifying or extending, or has been legitimated in opposition to it, as a systematically critical discipline designed to transcend and correct memory's notorious subjectivity and partiality.[12] Or else, reversing the polarities, memory's vibrant authenticity has been posited as a corrective to the archival obsessions and elitist proclivities of conventional historical writing.[13] As a means to conceptualizing social memory in general, the recurrent scholarly obsession with the history–memory antithesis may well appear a 'dead end'.[14] Its persistence, however, bears witness to a long history of struggles to define, defend and legitimize a disciplinary identity. It is no accident that the 'turn to memory' in historical studies has coincided with the impact of postmodernist critiques that have destabilized traditional faith in history's claims to deliver objective, methodologically grounded past-related knowledge. As historians have become more aware of the extent to which their own representations of the past are historically 'positioned' and culturally constructed, so the once sternly defended boundaries between history and memory have become porous, and memory itself has been re-evaluated.[15]

[11] Cubitt, *History and Memory*, pp. 26–62; A. Megill, 'History, memory, identity', *History of the Human Sciences*, 11, 3 (1998), 37–62.

[12] For alignment, see, for example, P. H. Hutton, *History as an Art of Memory* (Hanover: University of Vermont Press, 1993). For opposition, see Michael Bentley, *Modern Historiography: an Introduction* (London: Routledge, 1999), for whom history is 'precisely non-memory' (p. 155).

[13] R. Samuel, *Theatres of Memory*, vol. I: *Past and Present in Contemporary Culture* (London and New York: Verso, 1994), pp. 3–6.

[14] Erll, 'Cultural memory studies', p. 7.

[15] P. Burke, 'History as social memory', in T. Butler (ed.), *Memory: History, Culture and the Mind* (Oxford: Blackwell, 1989), pp. 97–114; Cubitt, *History and Memory*, pp. 59–61; K. Hodgkin and S. Radstone (eds.), *Contested Pasts: the Politics of Memory* (London:

Another aspect of this is that history is also implicated in kinds of ethical and political debate over memory that have an important place in the real world – and in the concerns of philosophers and political scientists – but that seldom impinge on the work of psychologists. Whether we, as individuals and as society, have a 'duty to remember' certain people or episodes or experiences; how we enact that duty; how we combat the forms of motivated or accidental forgetting that are produced by hegemonic discourses; how individuals and societies should manage the tension-ridden business of remembering (or forgetting) the past in the aftermath of atrocity or division, navigating between competing memory-postures of remembrance, acknowledgement, forgiveness, amnesty, silence, reparation, retribution and reconciliation – these are questions that show how, in the life of societies, issues of memory are interwoven with emotionally and ideologically charged issues of power and justice and identity.[16] Psychologists, preoccupied with memory as a cognitive function, have usually by-passed these issues. History, by contrast, is implicated in these debates, since the work of historians is itself an influence on the way in which the past is viewed, and hence, at least potentially, a vital vehicle either for building a hegemonic orthodoxy or, in a radical vein, for salvaging those memories and experiences that dominant representations of the past exclude or deny. Thinking about the ethics and politics of memory thus draws historians necessarily into thinking about the responsibilities, limitations and political functions of their own discipline.[17]

While this difference is rooted in history's functional proximity to memory, it also connects to long-established differences in working method. Since Ebbinghaus, the psychological study of memory has been predominantly conducted through controlled experiment.[18] The aim has been to observe recollective activity in its purest form, isolating the remembering subjects from the complex play of social and cultural and historical and

Routledge, 2003), p. 2; K. L. Klein, 'On the emergence of memory in historical discourse', *Representations*, 69 (2000), 127–50.

16 The literatures on such issues are now enormous: for a few starting points see T. Todorov, 'The uses and abuses of memory', in H. Marchitello (ed.), *What Happens to History: the Renewal of Ethics in Contemporary Thought* (New York: Routledge, 2001), pp. 11–22; R. J. Golsan, 'History and the "duty to memory" in postwar France: the pitfalls of an ethics of remembrance' in Marchitello, *What Happens to History*, pp. 23–40; J. W. Booth, *Communities of Memory: On Witness, Identity, and Justice* (Ithaca, NY: Cornell University Press, 2006); J. K. Olick, *The Politics of Regret: On Collective Memory and Historical Responsibility* (New York: Routledge, 2007); J. Blustein, *The Moral Demands of Memory* (New York: Cambridge University Press, 2008).

17 H. Rousso, *The Haunting Past: History, Memory, and Justice in Contemporary France* (Philadelphia: University of Pennsylvania Press, 1998); A. De Baets, *Responsible History* (New York and Oxford: Berghahn, 2009); E. Wyschogrod, *An Ethics of Remembering: History, Hetorology, and the Nameless Others* (Chicago, IL: University of Chicago Press, 1998).

18 H. Ebbinghaus, *Memory: a Contribution to Experimental Psychology* (New York: Columbia University, 1913).

momentary influences that may complicate the business of remembering 'in the wild', and subjecting them to tests that allow the specific influence of particular variables on recollective performance to be measured. The assumption has been that this will allow the assembly of robust and critically answerable sets of empirical data, leading to the formation of conclusions about the basic cognitive operations that underpin human recollection. In recent decades, the gap between the laboratory and the real world has reduced, but a significant contrast to the working methods of historians remains. Historians do not in any obvious sense experiment, partly because those they study are otherwise engaged – usually dead and buried – but also because experimentation, even if possible, would not supply the kind of knowledge they are interested in, which is not knowledge of general principles but knowledge of the specifics of what has gone on in past societies at particular moments. Since these moments are in the past, the historian is in an important sense no more firmly located in the real world that he or she studies than is the laboratory-based psychologist: he or she is forced to work backwards, inductively and reconstructively, from the traces – general texts and material remains – that past happenings have left behind. In critically evaluating these traces, and in considering previous accounts of the past that is being studied, historians inevitably encounter memory not in the abstract, but in a socially embedded, culturally mediated and politically resonant form.

Despite these differences, psychologists and historians working on memory have generally, in recent decades, had one important thing in common: adherence to a reconstructivist conception of remembering. That memory is to be understood not as a mental survival or quasi-photographic representation of past reality, but as a reconstructive process, in which our impressions of that reality are continually reconfigured and reinterpreted in ways that are influenced by our present attitudes and positioning, is a conception nowadays almost universally accepted across the humanities and social sciences. Psychologists usually trace this conception to Frederic Bartlett's account of remembering as a process involving the application of interpretative templates or schemas, whereas historians and social scientists more commonly go back to the sociologist Maurice Halbwachs' theorization of it as a process fundamentally structured by group-specific mental frameworks (*cadres sociaux*), the intersection of which determines what the individual remembers or forgets.[19] Whatever the emphasis, the understanding that what is to be studied is a continuous process of meaning production, always fluid, selective,

[19] F. Bartlett, *Remembering: a Study in Experimental and Social Psychology* (Cambridge University Press, 1995); M. Halbwachs, *Les Cadres sociaux de la mémoire* (Paris: Albin Michel, 1994); M. Halbwachs, *La Mémoire collective* (Paris: Albin Michel, 1997).

interpretative and organizational, supplies an important measure of common ground on which different approaches can be brought into contact.[20]

Approaches to social memory in history

Jeffrey Olick has influentially distinguished between individualistic and collectivist understandings of social memory. He sees these as rooted in two different conceptions of culture, the first of which sees it as 'a subjective category of meanings contained in people's minds', while the second sees it as lying in 'patterns of publicly available symbols objectified in society'.[21] It is fair, as a generalization, to say that most work on social memory in psychology has started from the first of these conceptions, and most in history from the second. In both cases, this reflects the pre-existing general orientation of the discipline.

History has traditionally concerned itself primarily with collective experiences – the affairs of societies and states and cultures and classes and social or political movements. It has been interested in individuals either as prominent figures who are deemed to have influenced the shape and fortunes of collectivities or as representative figures whose lives and thoughts are felt to shed light on broader collective experiences. In adopting memory as a category of analysis, historians have not abandoned these perspectives. Their work on memory has run in two main directions, the first of which (embodied in work on the politics of memory, 'difficult' pasts, *lieux de mémoire* and mnemonic practices) has focused essentially on group-level phenomena and common culture, while the second (chiefly in oral history) has engaged with individual memory as a way of gaining insight into social experiences and cultural mentalities.

Work on memory politics has hinged on issues of identity and power. Groups, it is affirmed, require a shared identity if they are to be coherent and purposeful communities. Memory is central to this identity: it supplies a vision of a group's origins and former history that can motivate togetherness in the present and give a sense of common purpose for the future. Cultivation of a shared or collective memory strengthens the group collectively and gives its members a place in society, but conversely denying or marginalizing a group's memory undermines its position and disempowers its members. Control over collective memory – the ability to impose and maintain a particular vision of the collective past and

20 D. L. Schacter (ed.), *Memory Distortion: How Minds, Brains and Societies Reconstruct the Past* (Cambridge, MA: Harvard University Press, 1995).

21 J. K. Olick, 'Collective memory: the two cultures', *Sociological Theory*, 17 (1999), 336.

to prevent other possible visions from finding satisfactory expression – is therefore an important lever of power within societies. When identity is challenged or contested or debated, memory becomes an important arena of contention.[22]

It is this conflictual aspect that has usually drawn the attention of historians. Some have studied the politics of memory in an international plane, analysing for example the ways in which transnationally disseminated narratives of the Second World War or the Holocaust or the Cold War have influenced politics within, between and across countries.[23] Most studies of the politics of memory, however, have adopted a national frame of reference. The emphasis of most has been on public culture, especially on formally commemorative or official elements like memorials, museums and anniversaries, but often also including a wider range of media (political speeches, literature, film, etc.); in some cases, use is made of other sources, for example oral history or folklore, as a means of accessing non-elite perspectives.[24]

Work of this kind generally seeks to probe the tension between surface appearances of unity and consensus and underlying tensions, exclusions and resistances. The conceptual frameworks employed have often posited some form of opposition between an *official* or *dominant* memory, taken to be unitary, hegemonic, elite-generated, enshrined in high-profile forms of public culture, and often state-supported, and a *popular* or *vernacular* memory, usually viewed as plural, localized and rooted in the grass-roots memories, experiences and traditions of ordinary – and often disadvantaged – groups or communities. In some cases, the diffuse forms of vernacular memory are seen as capable of being marshalled – possibly with the assistance of radically minded historians – into a 'countermemory' capable of resisting or subverting the official one.[25] In others, the model allows for the idea of transaction or negotiation. In John Bodnar's

22 J. R. Gillis, 'Memory and identity: the history of a relationship', in J. R. Gillis (ed.), *Commemorations: the Politics of National Identity* (Princeton, NJ: Princeton University Press, 1994); Megill, 'History, memory, identity'.

23 Examples of the former include T. G. Ashplant, G. Dawson and M. Roper, 'The politics of war memory and commemoration: contexts, structures and dynamics', in T. G. Ashplant, G. Dawson and M. Roper (eds.), *Commemorating War: the Politics of Memory* (New Brunswick, NJ and London: Transaction, 2000), pp. 3–85; D. Levy and N. Sznaider, *The Holocaust and Memory in the Global Age* (Philadelphia, PA: Temple University Press, 2006); A. Assmann and S. Conrad (eds.), *Memory in a Global Age: Discourses, Practices and Trajectories* (Basingstoke: Palgrave Macmillan, 2010).

24 For example Gillis (ed.), *Commemorations*. On monuments see K. Savage, *Standing Soldiers, Kneeling Slaves: Race, War, and Monument in Nineteenth-Century America* (Princeton, NJ: Princeton University Press, 1999).

25 G. Lipsitz, *Time Passages: Collective Memory and American Popular Culture* (Minneapolis: University of Minnesota Press, 1990); Y. Zerubavel, *Recovered Roots: Collective Memory and the Making of Israeli National Tradition* (Chicago, IL: Chicago University Press,

study of civic commemorative cultures in the twentieth-century United States, for example, public memory reflects the inequalities of American society, but is, nonetheless, the terrain on which different ethnic or local communities, each with its own vernacular memories, stake claims to legitimacy and to inclusion within the larger national society.[26] Recent work by Beiner, using folklore sources to explore popular memory of the events of 1798 in Ireland, reveals a complex 'dialogue' of official and popular: official commemorations generated a 'porous metanarrative', which 'accommodated certain micronarratives but marginalized others'.[27]

Although the official versus vernacular model remains an influential way of structuring accounts of memory politics, its essential emphases on domination and subordination have been challenged or qualified by others. Alon Confino has suggested that emphasis on conflict in social memory needs to be balanced by analysis of the 'common denominators of variousness' that allow entities like nations to hold together as memory communities despite the tensions within them.[28] Jay Winter, in influential work on First World War remembrance, has proposed a 'social agency' approach that in many ways reverses the traditional emphasis on elite hegemony. Approaching the culture of remembrance 'from the angle of small-scale, locally rooted social action', Winter shows how the interaction of multiple social agencies – families, municipalities, veterans' organizations, and so on – shaped its development: far from being the embodiment of a hegemonic elite design, the national commemorative framework that emerged was 'a thin cover over a host of associative forms arduously constructed over years by thousands of people, mostly obscure'.[29] Challenging from a different angle, the literary scholar Michael Rothberg has taken issue with two notions underpinning conventional approaches: first, 'that the boundaries of memory parallel the boundaries of group identity' (so that each group is constituted by its own discrete memory formation); and second, that memory is 'a zero-

1995). On the role of radical historians, see Popular Memory Group, 'Popular memory: theory, politics, method', in R. Johnson, G. McLellan and B. Schwarz (eds.), *Making Histories: Studies in History-Writing and Politics* (Minneapolis: University of Minnesota Press, 1982), pp. 205–52.

26 J. Bodnar, *Remaking America: Public Memory, Commemoration and Patriotism in the Twentieth Century* (Princeton, NJ: Princeton University Press, 1991).

27 G. Beiner, *Remembering the Year of the French: Irish Folk History and Social Memory* (Madison: University of Wisconsin Press, 2007), pp. 306 and 309.

28 A. Confino, *The Nation as a Local Metaphor: Württemberg, Imperial Germany and National Memory, 1871–1918* (Chapel Hill, NC: University of North Carolina Press, 1997).

29 J. Winter, 'Forms of kinship and remembrance in the aftermath of the Great War', in J. Winter and E. Sivan (eds.), *War and Remembrance in the Twentieth Century* (Cambridge University Press, 1999), pp. 59–60; for critical discussion, see Ashplant *et al.* 'The politics of war memory', pp. 39–43.

sum game' – an inherently competitive affair in which the success of one memory is always at the expense of others. Against these assumptions, Rothberg views the public sphere as 'a malleable discursive space' in which both groups and memories are fluidly constructed through 'dialogical interactions'. Memories, in this view, are 'multidirectional' – not owned by particular groups, but available for varied, evolving and unpredictable uses and appropriations.[30] Such a view may not rid us of the need to be alert to issues of domination and exclusion in studying social memory: essentialist, zero-sum notions of memory and identity, however misplaced, remain an important influence on social behaviour. An emphasis on multidirectionality does, however, supply an important reminder of the transactive complexity of memory formation, especially in modern media-dominated societies: collective memories are not a stable form of cultural property, but are crafted in realms of discourse whose frames of reference are continually shifting and whose elements are continually recombining in new patterns of meaning.

An important category of historical social memory studies analyses the impact of 'difficult' or 'traumatic' experiences like civil war or genocide – especially the Holocaust – on memory in the affected countries. Studies of this kind have usually focused less on competition between official and vernacular memory than on the idea of a need for society to 'come to terms' with the past in question, which seems in most interpretations to involve a combination of historical understanding, ethical acknowledgement and political reparation. Discussion hinges on issues of guilt and denial, acceptance and atonement, and the connection of these to remembering and forgetting, both public and private. A common type of analysis delineates stages in a process of public remembering, sometimes linked to generational shifts, and marked by changing orientations towards the past in question. Henry Rousso's pioneering account of the memory of the Second World War in post-war France set an example in using a quasi-psychiatric vocabulary of neurosis to describe what he called the 'Vichy syndrome' – a fixation of French society with the wartime experience that he saw as passing through different phases of recrimination, repression, crisis, obsessive remembering, and so on.[31] More recently, however, such approaches have been criticized both for their over-ready transferring of concepts from the psychology of individuals to the description of collective dispositions, and for a tendency to over-homogenize societal responses. Probing beneath

[30] M. Rothberg, *Multidirectional Memory: Remembering the Holocaust in the Age of Decolonization* (Stanford, CA: Stanford University Press, 2009), p. 5.

[31] H. Rousso, *The Vichy Syndrome: History and Memory in France since 1944* (Cambridge, MA: Harvard University Press, 1991).

the surface of official commemorative practice often reveals a more complex persistence of contradictory currents, sustained in private and sporadically articulated.[32] Wulf Kansteiner has suggested that the habit of interpreting the social processing of difficult histories as a trauma-driven collective process of repression and working-through obscures the extent to which it is the politics of present interests and inequalities of cultural leverage between interested groups that determines which ways of viewing a 'difficult' or compromising past become publicly dominant.[33] The emphasis in recent studies has shifted, at least partially, from memory's relationship to trauma to a more complex reading of memory's relationship to power – to the ways in which memory constrains policy-making, and to the strategies of remembering and forgetting that are deployed in specific political contexts.[34] Work along these lines is supported by differentiations of the various forms of purposeful 'forgetting' or 'silencing', some of them conciliatory rather than repressive, that may be evident in post-conflictual settings, and by fresh understandings of the ways in which the category of 'trauma' itself is discursively constructed in a context of social and political action.[35] Rather than being located in a special realm of post-traumatic collective neurosis, the problems of coming to terms with a difficult past are intrinsically interwoven with political practicalities and unfolding social dynamics.

Alongside the broad structural and developmental analyses of social memory just alluded to, historians have often dealt in a more narrowly focused and 'archaeological' form of study, probing the evolving commemorative histories or mnemonic 'afterlives' of specific events or symbolic foci. Widespread use of Pierre Nora's term *lieux de mémoire* (memory sites), defined broadly to include 'any significant entity, whether material or non-material in nature, which by dint of human will or the work of time has become a symbolic element of the material heritage of any

[32] For example R. G. Moeller, *War Stories: the Search for a Usable Past in the Federal Republic of Germany* (Berkeley and Los Angeles: University of California Press, 2001).

[33] W. Kansteiner, 'Finding meaning in memory: a methodological critique of collective memory studies', *History and Theory*, 41 (2002), 187–8.

[34] J.-W. Müller (ed.), *Memory and Power in Post-War Europe: Studies in the Presence of the Past* (Cambridge University Press, 2002); S. Kroen, *Politics and Theater: the Politics of Legitimacy in Restoration France, 1815–1830* (Berkeley, CA: University of California Press, 2000), chapter 1; P. Aguilar, *Memory and Amnesia: the Role of the Spanish Civil War in the Transition to Democracy* (New York and Oxford: Berghahn, 2002); S. Nuttall and C. Coetzee (eds.), *Negotiating the Past: the Making of Memory in South Africa* (Oxford University Press, 1998).

[35] L. Passerini, 'Memories between silence and oblivion', in K. Hodgkin and S. Radstone (eds.), *Contested Pasts: the Politics of Memory* (London: Routledge, 2003), pp. 238–54; P. Connerton, 'Seven types of forgetting', *Memory Studies*, 1, 1 (2008), 59–71; J. C. Alexander, *Trauma: a Social Theory* (Cambridge: Polity, 2012).

community', has helped to legitimize an approach to social memory that takes the in-depth investigation of such specific 'sites' – places, texts, legends, iconic images, personal reputations, symbolic ideas, canonical experiences – as its essential mode of entry.[36] At their best, for example in the historical sociologist Barry Schwartz's analysis of the changing historical orientations embodied in the pictorial imagery commissioned over time for the US Capitol building in Washington, 'site'-specific studies offer insights not just into the shifting representations of particular pieces of the past, but into the ways in which visions of the past are institutionalized and embodied in public culture.[37] Taking the *lieu de mémoire* as a kind of primary unit of study can, however, produce a somewhat fragmented body of analysis, not assisted by the fact that the *lieu de mémoire* remains an 'inchoate and undertheorized' conception.[38] How one decides what constitutes, within any given society, a *lieu de mémoire* worthy of investigation is surprisingly rarely discussed. Without necessarily abandoning the study of sites and representations, recent scholarship has focused attention increasingly on how these are 'embedded in social practice' – on the structured and often routinized deployment of the past in concrete social settings (state, family, workplace, marketplace), and to the social relationships that such practices sustain or generate.[39] Understandings of what constitutes 'memory-work' within society are diversified: Chris Healy, for example, tracks particular ways of remembering Australian history 'through a variety of institutional and habitual practices, from property law to naming country, public rituals and language'.[40] One effect of reconnecting the study of memory to the analysis of social practice is to break down the somewhat block-like reifications of memory that sometimes characterize more traditional accounts: social memory appears 'not as something complete but as a shifting, heterogeneous, partial and repetitive assemblage of acts, utterances and artefacts',

[36] P. Nora (ed.), *Realms of Memory*, vol. I: *Conflicts and Divisions* (New York: Columbia University Press, 1996), p. xvii. Studies of this kind, not all inspired directly by Nora, are too numerous to cite.

[37] B. Schwartz, 'The social context of commemoration: a study in collective memory', *Social Forces*, 61 (1982), 374–402.

[38] Erll, 'Cultural memory studies', p. 10.

[39] A. Confino and P. Fritzsche, 'Introduction: noises of the past', in A. Confino and P. Fritzsche (eds.), *The Work of Memory: New Directions in the Study of German Society and Culture* (Urbana and Chicago: University of Illinois Press, 2002), pp. 4–5; J. K. Olick and J. Robbins, 'Social memory studies: from "collective memory" to the historical sociology of mnemonic practices', *Annual Review of Sociology*, 24 (1998), 105–40; H.-J. Grabbe and S. Schindler (eds.), *The Merits of Memory: Concepts, Contexts, Debates* (Heidelberg: Winter, 2008).

[40] C. Healy, *Forgetting Aborigines* (Sydney: University of New South Wales Press, 2008), p. 9.

always adapted to particular situations, and liable to evolution as new needs and conditions emerge.[41]

Focusing on memory as an activity rather than as a body of symbolic representations also opens space for the individual rememberer as participant in social memory processes. Using individual memories as a means of exploring the social has, within history, been the particular province of oral historians. Unlike other historians (but like psychologists) oral historians engage directly with individual living subjects, and employ a research method – the oral history interview – that actively generates the data on which they base their conclusions. But while psychological experimentation traditionally seeks to separate the remembering subject from outside influences, the aim of oral historians is to make the interview speak of realities that lie beyond it. While the methodological ethics of the psychological experiment are dominated by the requirements of scientific method, which include a carefully regulated manipulative relationship between researcher and experimental subject, those of oral history have come to focus on allowing the informant to speak in his or her own distinctive voice of his or her own experience, and on wariness of the potential for appropriation or manipulation which is inherent in the interview setting.

In its early years as a distinctive field of study, oral history was an extension of social history that sought, first, to restore a neglected experiential dimension of history, and second, to recover the hidden histories of the marginalized and disadvantaged that conventional histories excluded. Oral testimony was assumed to encapsulate memory, which in turn was assumed to offer the historian retrospective access to past realities. Over time, however, and partly through interactions with disciplines like literary studies and psychoanalysis, oral historians' research agendas have been significantly refashioned. Increasing awareness of memory's reconstructive character, of its complex relationship to narrativity, and of the complicating effects of the social dynamics of the oral history interview itself, have produced a clearer sense of the methodological difficulty of using oral sources as straightforward evidence of past experiences. With this awareness, however, has come the hope of turning the 'so-called unreliability of memory' into 'a resource, rather than a problem, for historical interpretation'.[42] Remembering itself, as a sense-making activity and as a socially embedded experience, has become a central

[41] *Ibid.*

[42] A. Thomson, 'Fifty years on: an international perspective on oral history', *Journal of American History*, 85 (1998), 585.

focus of oral historians' concerns. Some have analysed specific memory 'distortions' as clues to the psychological and symbolic and narrative logics that frame an understanding of the past for individuals and local communities.[43] Others have focused on the gendered dynamics of memory, or on the narrative templates and stereotypical self-representations that make autobiographical narrations culturally recognizable, or have begun to explore the common elements and interactions that constitute generational memories.[44] Work along these lines intersects in one direction with the movement towards the analysis of memory practices in history more generally, and in another with approaches to social memory that psychologists have developed.

Approaches to social memory in psychology

In contrast to historians, psychologists have moved towards social memory against the backdrop of strongly individualizing traditions. The unit for most psychological study has been the individual mind, and the prevailing assumption among psychologists has usually been that individual minds are to be understood in terms of their internal functioning, rather than their external connections. Social influences are considered as external variables enhancing or inhibiting recollective performance, rather than as integral ingredients of memory processes. Occasional figures in the earlier history of psychology can be looked to for a more socializing perspective: Pierre Janet's account of memory as an adaptive capacity developed in response to evolving communicative needs, and Lev Vygotsky's view of it as an activity mediated through the use of cultural tools, are examples.[45] But the divided reception of the theories of the most prominent of these figures, Frederic Bartlett, is significant: while his account of the schema-dependent reconstructive character of remembering was adopted as foundational in the discipline's turn towards a cognitivist orientation in the 1960s and 1970s, his suggestion that the schemas involved were typically shaped by group-specific social

[43] For example A. Portelli, 'The death of Luigi Trastulli', in A. Portelli, *The Death of Luigi Trastulli and Other Stories: Form and Meaning in Oral History* (Albany, NY: State University of New York Press, 1991), pp. 1–26.

[44] For example L. Passerini, *Fascism in Popular Memory: the Cultural Experience of the Turin Working Class* (Cambridge University Press, 1987), pp. 17–63; P. Summerfield, *Reconstructing Women's Lives: Discourse and Subjectivity in Oral Histories of the Second World War* (Manchester: Manchester University Press, 1998); L. Passerini, *Autobiography of a Generation: Italy, 1968* (Hanover: Wesleyan University Press, 1997).

[45] P. Janet, *L'Evolution de la Mémoire et de la Notion du Temps* (Paris: Chahine, 1928); L. S. Vygotsky, *Mind in Society: the Development of Higher Psychological Processes* (Cambridge, MA: Harvard University Press, 1978), chapter 3, written in 1930.

and cultural influences was largely overlooked.[46] Much of the recent history of the discipline has been dominated by studies of 'social cognition', but these have focused on the individual mind as a self-contained information-processing system: it is the contents of mental representations, rather than their processes of formation that are deemed to be social.[47]

Much of the ground for movements in a more social direction was prepared by the strong appeal to psychologists to engage with real-world psychological issues and to develop more 'ecologically valid' research methodologies launched by figures like Ulric Neisser and Jerome Bruner in the 1980s.[48] Allowing psychology to breathe outside the laboratory did not necessarily mean abandoning an essentially individualizing perspective, but it gave a significant impetus to a whole range of new research interests – in childhood development, narrative, conversation, discourse, culture, material objects, social identity formation, memory for real-world events, generational experiences, ritual, emotion, and so on – that could hardly fail in the long run to breach some of the boundaries between psychology and other disciplines and to raise questions about memory's connectedness to cultural frameworks and social processes. The radical perspectives on cognition in general developed by 'social constructionists', arguing that what is basic in mental processes is 'not the inner subjectivity of the individual, but the practical social processes going on "between" people', also prompted new thinking on memory in particular.[49]

Approaches to social memory in psychology have generally started not from the collectivity but from the idea of the individual as a socially and culturally embedded agent.[50] Cognition, including memory, is viewed here

[46] M. S. Weldon, 'Remembering as a social process', *Psychology of Learning and Motivation*, 40 (2000), 73–4.

[47] For critical discussion of the 'overwhelming individualistic orientation' in social cognition studies, see M. Augoustinos, I. Walker and N. Donaghue, *Social Cognition: an Integrated Introduction*, 2nd edn (London: Sage, 2006), pp. 7–8; see also E. E. Sampson, 'Cognitive psychology as ideology', *American Psychologist*, 36, 7 (1981), 730–43.

[48] U. Neisser (ed.), *Memory Observed: Remembering in Natural Contexts* (San Francisco, CA: W. H. Freeman); E. Winograd and U. Neisser (eds.), *Remembering Reconsidered: Ecological and Traditional Approaches to the Study of Memory* (Cambridge University Press, 1988); J. Bruner, *Acts of Meaning* (Cambridge, MA: Harvard University Press, 1990).

[49] J. Shotter, 'Social accountability and the social construction of "you"', in J. Shotter and K. J. Gergen (eds.), *Texts of Identity* (London: Sage, 1989), p. 136; also K. J. Gergen, 'The social constructionist movement in modern psychology', *American Psychologist*, 40 (1985), 266–75.

[50] For example J. Brockmeier, 'After the archive: remapping memory', *Culture and Psychology*, 16 (2010), 9; J. V. Wertsch and H. L Roediger, 'Collective memory: conceptual foundations and theoretical approaches', *Memory*, 16, 3 (2008), 318–26. For useful surveys of different psychological approaches to social memory, see Weldon, 'Remembering as a social process' and Middleton and Brown, *The Social Psychology of Experience*.

as 'the property of individuals, but only insofar as these individuals are situated in certain physical environments and social milieux'.[51] Remembering is understood not as a simple processing of information about past experiences, but as 'a meaningful action we perform in the sociocultural contexts that we take part in creating, and within which we live'.[52] From this starting point, research has run in a number of different but interconnecting directions, of which two will be explored here. The first focuses on autobiographical remembering, and the second on what may be called the extended, mediated or transactive aspects of memory processes.

Within the first approach, two main emphases can be traced: on the social character of the contents of autobiographical remembering, and on the social character of the processes by which humans develop as agents who engage in it. Autobiographical remembering – the remembering by individuals of their own life experience – may appear, from one angle, to be the most personal form of memory, but since our lives are lived in society, it is permeated at every level with social experience. Maurice Halbwachs (in whose ideas some psychologists have recently shown a new interest) argued long ago that autobiographical remembering is socially framed: we locate our own experiences in memory by relating them to shared or group experiences, so that changes in our memories of the past are 'explicable by the changes that are produced in our relationships to the various collective milieux' through which we have passed.[53] Against this, psychological analyses of autobiographical memory tended in the past to assume that the structures of autobiographical remembering were inwardly generated. Recently, however, a more social orientation of research has emerged. Recent theorizations, even when not directly analysing social influences, see autobiographical memory not as a simple memory of events, but as mobilizing several more general kinds of information, relating to 'lifetime periods', 'repeated or extended events' and the 'lifetime goals' governing particular phases of the individual's existence.[54] All of this brings the study of autobiographical memory much closer to the study of the ways in which human lives are continuously

[51] Wilson, 'Collective memory', p. 229.

[52] D. Manier, 'Is memory in the brain? Remembering as social behavior', *Mind, Culture, and Activity*, 11, 4 (2004), 256.

[53] Halbwachs, *La Mémoire collective*, pp. 95–6. See, for example, Middleton and Brown, *The Social Psychology of Experience*, chapter 3; E. Reese and R. Fivush, 'The development of collective remembering', *Memory*, 16 (2008), 201–12.

[54] M. A. Conway, 'The inventory of experience: memory and identity', in J. W. Pennebaker, D. Paez and B. Rimé (eds.), *Collective Memory of Political Events: Social Psychological Perspectives* (Mahwah, NJ: Lawrence Erlbaum, 1997), pp. 21–45; H. Williams and M. A. Conway, 'Networks of autobiographical memories', in Boyer and Wertsch (eds.), *Memory in Mind and Culture*, pp. 33–60.

structured by social relationships, institutional routines, cultural expectations, career patterns, and so on. Psychological researchers have begun to make these connections explicit, suggesting for example that autobiographical remembering is influenced by 'cultural life scripts' embodying 'culturally shared expectations about the order and timing of life events in a prototypical life course'.[55] Psychological studies of the self are also relevant here. Where once selfhood was viewed as embodying some kind of internal intuition of individuality, concepts of the self are now positioned 'at the interface between individual and collective memories'.[56] The self itself is seen as constructed with culturally supplied materials, and in ways influenced by social relationships and communicative needs.[57]

Reinforcing these directions in the study of autobiographical memory is a now well-established literature in developmental psychology dealing with the ways in which the skills and habits of autobiographical narration are acquired and developed in childhood and adolescence.[58] This is seen as a form of situational learning: the child serves a kind of apprenticeship through conversation with more experienced autobiographical narrators. In the early stages, his or her efforts at recollection are largely scaffolded by adult interlocutors (in the psychological literature usually parents): the narrative habits that are internalized, and which in turn are presumed to shape the way the child will remember, reflect parental strategy but are also indicative of broader cultural norms, in ways that comparative studies of children from different cultural backgrounds may reveal. American children, for example, have been observed to display a facility in forms of recollection embodying individualistic conceptions of agency and identity, while Chinese children's memories are more likely to foreground social roles and collective identities.[59] The same processes that fashion

[55] D. Berntsen and A. Bohn, 'Cultural life scripts and individual life stories', in Boyer and Wertsch (eds.), *Memory in Mind and Culture*, pp. 62–3.

[56] D. L Schacter, A. H. Gutchess and E. A. Kensinger, 'Specificity of memory: implications for individual and collective remembering', in Boyer and Wertsch (eds.), *Memory in Mind and Culture*, p. 84.

[57] Bruner, *Acts of Meaning*, chapter 4; Q. Wang and J. Brockmeier, 'Autobiographical remembering as cultural practice: understanding the interplay between memory, self and culture', *Culture and Psychology*, 8 (2002), 45–64.

[58] For a useful summary, see K. Nelson and R. Fivush, 'Socialization of memory', in E. Tulving and F. I. M. Craik (eds.), *The Oxford Handbook of Memory* (Oxford University Press, 2000), pp. 283–95.

[59] Wang and Brockmeier 'Autobiographical remembering'; more generally M. D. Leichtman and Q. Wang, 'A socio-historical perspective on autobiographical memory development', in D. B. Pillemer and S. H. White (eds.), *Developmental Psychology and Social Change: Research, History and Policy* (New York: Cambridge University Press), pp. 34–58; A. H. Gutchess, and M. Siegel 'Memory specificity across cultures', in A. Assmann and L. Shortt (eds.), *Memory and Political Change* (Basingstoke: Palgrave Macmillan, 2012), pp. 201–15.

a person as a self-consciously individual remembering subject also train him or her in the ways of remembering that are culturally prevalent: 'Individualization and socialization are thus by no means opposites, but instead concurrent.'[60]

Pursuing such lines of thought has brought developmental psychologists into a closer relationship to the understandings of social or collective memory that have circulated in the social sciences. Elaine Reese and Robyn Fivush have recently drawn attention to the ways in which the diversified circles of social interaction that human beings encounter across childhood and adolescence provide frameworks for integrating their own autobiographical recollections with larger narrations: the stories individuals tell of themselves expand to incorporate information relating to the individual but not personally remembered, and beyond that to include other stories about the collectivities to which they belong, information relating to past generations, and larger cultural and historical contexts.[61] All these become part of what the sociologist Eviatar Zerubavel has called 'sociobiographical memory' ('the existential fusion of one's own biography with the history of groups or communities to which one belongs').[62]

Socially focused work on memory development involves thinking about the individual's interactive relationship to culture and to other individuals. In the second approach, these issues are engaged from a different angle. One starting-point here is the idea that, as individual mnemonic agents, we habitually use elements in the world around us as instruments or resources in our processes of remembering.[63] These elements may include people, places and objects as well as cultural devices (including non-tangible ones like rhyme schemes and narrative conventions) and technologies, and the idea encompasses a variety of possible forms of instrumentality; such elements may help us to store and retrieve information, or to encode meaning, or may act as reminders or as symbolic foci for practices of remembrance. The key idea is that our use of instruments or resources from the world around us should be seen not as a kind of incidental 'add-on' to the core process of remembering, but as an integral part of that process: the use of such instruments and resources shapes the whole way in which we remember. Remembering, in other words, is to be seen as a form of 'mediated action', always involving tools

[60] H. Welzer, 'Communicative memory', in Erll and Nünning (eds.), *A Companion to Cultural Memory Studies*, p. 291.

[61] Reese and Fivush, 'The development of collective remembering', pp. 201–12.

[62] E. Zerubavel, *Social Mindscapes: an Invitation to Cognitive Psychology* (Cambridge, MA: Harvard University Press, 1997), pp. 91–2.

[63] Middleton and Brown, *The Social Psychology of Experience*, chapter 8.

of one kind or another, and as an activity that is 'fundamentally distributed between active agents, on the one hand, and the cultural tools … that they employ, on the other'.[64] Whether or not such thinking should prompt the adoption of an 'extended mind thesis', in which the mind is no longer seen as 'physically bounded by the body', but as 'extend[ing] into the environment of the organism' is a largely philosophic question.[65] More important is to recognize the ways in which psychological research on 'mediated' or 'distributed' remembering connects with the interests of historians, media and literary theorists, anthropologists, archaeologists and others in a wide range of areas: the role of monuments and rituals in structuring practices of remembrance, the role of narrative structures and stereotypes in oral testimony, the mnemonics of oral tradition, the effects of literacy on the cultural (including legal and administrative) uses of memory, the mediation of memory through literary texts or visual imagery or material culture, and the impact of particular communicative technologies (print, television, the Internet) both on individual remembering and on the circulation of representations of the past within society, are cases in point.

The importance of external instruments for remembering lies not simply in the 'extension' of the individual, but in the sharing of resources. 'What makes collective remembering collective is the fact that these narrative tools are shared across the members of the group', write James Wertsch and Henry Roediger.[66] The fact that different individuals employ the same narrative devices in framing their memories creates a community of use and allows communication of memories around the members of the group. Thinking about cultural mediation thus connects to thinking about social interaction. Psychological work on 'conversational remembering', however, extends beyond the idea that individuals help each other to remember. By studying the dynamics and collectively improvised structures of conversations about the past, such work explores the ways in which members of a conversational group interactively negotiate a shared account of the past that is being remembered – 'a continuously reworked collective memory'.[67] This takes the form not necessarily of a

[64] J. V. Wertsch, *Voices of Collective Remembering* (New York: Cambridge University Press, 2002), p. 172; also J. V. Wertsch, 'Social memory and narrative templates', *Social Research*, 75 (2008), 133–56; J. V. Wertsch, 'Collective memory', in Boyer and Wertsch (eds.), *Memory in Mind and Culture*, pp. 117–37.

[65] R. A. Wilson, 'Collective memory, group minds, and the extended mind thesis', *Cognitive Processing*, 6, 4 (2005), 230; R. Menary (ed.), *The Extended Mind* (Cambridge, MA: MIT Press, 2010).

[66] Wertsch and Roediger, 'Collective memory', p. 324.

[67] D. Middleton and D. Edwards, 'Conversational remembering: a social psychological approach', in D. Middleton and D. Edwards (eds.), *Collective Remembering* (London:

formally agreed narrative, but of more or less convergent understandings of what is important, coupled to mutual assumption of the parameters (e.g. conceptions of continuity and change) that give structure to discussions of shared experience, and that shape the ways in which individual and collective experiences are related to each other.[68] Psychological studies of this kind contribute to an understanding both of group dynamics and of the ways in which the past as an object of discourse is socially constructed.

Another connecting strand of research, under headings like 'transactive memory' or 'socially distributed remembering', pursues the idea of collaboration in a different direction, via ideas of networking and a mnemonic division of labour. Rather than jettisoning the information-processing model familiar in individualizing studies of cognition, work of this kind extends that metaphor to interpersonal relations: the focus here is less on the joint negotiation of meaning than on collective strategies for handling, retaining and combining information. Daniel Wegner defines a 'transactive memory system' as 'a set of individual memory systems in combination with the communication that takes place between individuals'.[69] Such systems vary from dyads (e.g. married couples) to much larger collaborative teams. Transactive systems exist when groups establish divisions of labour, in which different participants are entrusted with the task of remembering different kinds of data, and of feeding that data back in at appropriate moments to group operations or deliberations; such divisions may be improvised in the course of a conversation, or in established groups may be developed over a longer period and embodied institutionally. Transactive systems require not just division of mnemonic labour, but 'mechanisms of co-ordination and communication', which allow the members collectively to bring 'differentiated knowledge' from around the system together as 'shared new emergent knowledge'.[70] Work on transactive systems has often focused on questions of mnemonic and operational efficiency that are of secondary interest to scholars chiefly interested in how collective memories of the past are generated. Attention to mnemonic divisions of labour and integrative practices nevertheless

Sage, 1990), p. 26; also Middleton and Brown, *The Social Psychology of Experience*, chapter 5.

[68] D. Middleton, 'Succession and change in the socio-cultural uses of memory: building-in the past in communicative action', *Culture and Psychology*, 8, 1 (2002), 79–95.

[69] D. M. Wegner, 'Transactive memory: a contemporary analysis of the group mind', in B. Mullen and G. R. Goethals (eds.), *Theories of Group Behavior* (New York: Springer-Verlag, 1987), p. 186.

[70] J. Sutton, C. Harris, P. Keil and A. Barnier, 'The psychology of memory, extended cognition, and socially distributed remembering', *Phenomenology and the Cognitive Sciences*, 9, 4 (2010), 547.

offers a way of thinking further about how the social organization of remembering connects to other facets of social structure, for example to gender divisions in the family or status hierarchies within institutions.

Conclusion

The task that faces historians and psychologists jointly is that of understanding the social and psychological processes through which individuals become embroiled in, are influenced by, and contribute to the making of a society's historical memory. These are complex processes. The ways in which individuals remember and make sense of their own experiences dovetail with – that is to say, simultaneously draw on and feed into – the ways in which collective understandings are formed, consolidated, publicized, circulated, perpetuated, challenged and transformed. They involve on the one hand multiple interactions between shifting groupings of ordinary people thrashing out working understandings of the past within limited – though nowadays sometimes geographically extensive and electronically sustained – circles of interaction, and on the other the construction and maintenance of durable and institutionally supported bodies of knowledge, and of cultural products capable of publicly encapsulating the elements of shared understandings. They are processes of transmission and convergence and consolidation (as William Hirst and David Manier have indicated), but also of contestation and exclusion: they are characterized both by tension and by its submergence.[71] They are also an integral part of the larger historical process, for the ways in which societies, and groups and individuals within those societies, make sense of the past and of the past's relationship to the unfolding present are not an external commentary on history but part of what drives it and shapes it. It is important also to realize that, despite the frequent tendency of studies of social memory to concentrate on the dramatic and traumatic, these processes are continuous, driven as much by 'low intensity' routine and repetition as by towering cultural achievements or coercive interventions.[72]

Large-scale conceptual frameworks for talking about the overall shaping of collective memory are available. The most influential, derived from the work of Jan Assmann, distinguishes two levels: the short-term, non-institutionalized, inherently evanescent *communicative memory* that works itself out in everyday exchanges, and the more durable (but still gradually evolving) long-term *cultural memory*, institutionally organized,

[71] Hirst and Manier 'Towards a psychology', p. 192.
[72] Kansteiner, 'Finding meaning in memory', pp. 189–90.

'exteriorized, objectified, and stored away in symbols that ... are stable and situation-transcendent', that gives a society or community its durable sense of identity.[73] It is on the transitions between these levels that work is needed – on how thoughts and data on the past move from the fluidities of conversation and rumour into the stabler realm of culture, and how the durable reference points of culture shape and structure conversational remembering. The interests of psychologists in cultural mediation, conversational remembering, situated memory development and mnemonic divisions of labour come into contact here with the interests of historians in issues of power and identity, institutional structures, historical narrativity, and the long-term structuring of continuity and change.

I shall end by proposing one area of investigation in which historical and psychological approaches may profitably be brought together: the study of how historical events are mentally and culturally constructed. Traditionally, events are part of the historian's stock in trade: off-the-cuff definitions of history often assume that it is the study of past events and their consequences. But events are not to be taken for granted: they are not automatically evident units of experience, but 'mental constructions – products of the organizational mental labour by which we impose order and meaning on what would otherwise be the ceaseless, seamless and bewildering flow of our impressions and perceptions'.[74] Psychologists are well aware of this, and have studied the ways in which individual memory composes events by binding together assorted data, locates them chronologically, links them thematically or narratively, models them with event schemata, and sometimes disaggregates them or blurs the distinctions between them. But analogous processes operate in the production of historical knowledge. What determines which clusters of experiences and impressions get retained in social memory as distinct events, whether momentary (the Battle of Waterloo or the assassination of President Kennedy) or extended (the Napoleonic Wars or the Great Depression), and which get marshalled instead as period information (what things were like in the later Middle Ages) or other forms of experiential knowledge (the condition of women, the harsh realities of working-class life)? What determines which of these events go on being remembered, which are simply forgotten, and which dissolve over time into vaguer generalities? How do particular events get placed in larger historical narratives? How do societies handle or resolve tensions between narrative arrangements,

[73] J. Assmann, 'Communicative and cultural memory', in Erll and Nünning (eds.), *A Companion to Cultural Memory Studies*, pp. 110–11; also J. Assmann, 'Collective memory and cultural identity', *New German Critique*, 65 (1995), 125–33.

[74] Cubitt, *History and Memory*, p. 83.

such as arise when we debate, for example, whether the dropping of the atom bomb should be remembered as ending a destructive global war, or as an escalatory moment in the nuclear arms race, or as a key symbolic moment in the general history of human atrocity?[75] Answering such questions requires a mobilization of political, sociological, institutional, cultural and historiographical knowledge that obviously goes beyond the usual remit of psychological study. But studies of the social memory of public events that focus only on public statements and cultural reifications give a flat and misleading picture. Deepening it requires studies that explore reception – including use – as well as production – that look, for example, at how visitors to a memorial experience it, move around it, use it and interpret it.[76] James Young's advocacy of the notion of 'collected memory' (as distinct from 'collective memory'), to encompass 'the many discrete memories that are gathered into common memorial space and assigned common meaning' offers one way forward here.[77] James Wertsch's analysis of the different levels of 'mastery' and 'appropriation' that can characterize an individual's use of the narrative templates of an officially promoted view of history offers another.[78] Also needed are more analyses of the ways in which multiple individual memories, articulated initially in private or small-scale social settings, themselves contribute to the formation of a society's historical knowledge. Under what kinds of circumstance and through what mechanisms do separate individual stories, or recurrent elements in those stories, develop 'narrative coalescence' or fuse into the collectively recognizable 'figures of remembrance' that can carry weight in the shaping of a broader (for example national) memory culture?[79] Efforts to answer this kind of question may draw support from studies of vernacular or localized historical practices (family history, local history, etc.), from oral history, from literary studies of life-writing genres (captivity narratives, conversion narratives, etc.), and from ethnographic observation, but must also be enriched by the work of psychologists on conversational remembering, cultural mediation and transactive systems.

[75] E. T. Linenthal and T. Engelhardt (eds.), *History Wars: the Enola Gay and Other Battles for the American Past* (New York: Henry Holt, 1996).

[76] K. A. Hass, *Carried to the Wall: American Memory and the Vietnam Veterans Memorial* (Berkeley and Los Angeles: University of California Press, 1998).

[77] J. E. Young, *The Texture of Memory: Holocaust Memorials and Memory* (New Haven, CT and London: Yale University Press, 1993), p. xi.

[78] Wertsch, *Voices of Collective Remembering*, pp. 119–223.

[79] B. Attwood, '"Learning about the truth": the stolen generations narrative', in B. Attwood and F. Magowan (eds.), *Telling Stories: Indigenous History and Memory in Australia and New Zealand* (Sydney: Allen & Unwin, 2001), pp. 183–212; K. R. Jarausch and M. Geyer, *Shattered Past: Reconstructing German Histories* (Princeton, NJ: Princeton University Press, 2003).

The processes by which a set of occurrences gets bound together and labelled as 'the Great Depression' or 'the Second World War' has effects on two levels. In the realm of public discourse, such events get written into larger narratives of collective history, which may themselves be reconfigured by this inclusion. Narrative relations are established between this event and others: it becomes a marker of progress or decline or recovery, or a moment of crisis or foundation or fulfilment. On another level, the act of labelling and incorporation has an effect on individual and group remembering: what might otherwise be dispersed or indeterminate memories get cast as memories of a larger and more significant collective experience. They are brought within the scope of emerging narratives of collective struggle and endurance, suffering or victory, opportunity or disappointment, and of the various myths and stereotypes and lower-level narrative templates that are generated as these narratives are constructed. Elements in individual memory that are readily assimilated to these narrative structures get reinforced, sometimes with empowering consequences; discrepant elements become discordant, and may be forgotten or suppressed, or possibly defiantly reasserted. Historians have offered illuminating case studies of the complex and often ambiguous relationships that can develop between publicly accredited mythical accounts of collective experience and the efforts of individuals to make acceptable and sustainable sense of their own experiences and memories.[80] Psychologically informed studies of how culture is used in individual remembering, and of how relationships between the personal and the collective are negotiated in different kinds of social setting, can help to sharpen research on these issues.

Exploring the interdependencies and tensions between individual memory formation, social interaction, cultural mediation and the generation of collective histories forms part of a larger task of understanding the historical process. As such, it is a challenging, long-term project, which requires the mobilization of research energies generated in many different corners of the academic forest, and which prompts individual researchers to become accustomed to facing in several directions at once. It is a project to which both historians and psychologists, working separately but also together, have much to contribute.

[80] For example A. Thomson, *Anzac Memories: Living with the Legend* (Oxford University Press, 1994); C. Merridale, 'War, death and remembrance in Soviet Russia', in J. Winter and E. Sivan, *War and Remembrance in the Twentieth Century* (Cambridge University Press, 1999), pp. 61–83.

2 The incommensurability of psychoanalysis and history

Joan W. Scott

'Clio ... to thee, O Muse, has been vouchsafed the power to know the hearts of the gods and the ways by which things come to be.'[1] So wrote the Roman Valerius Flaccus in the first century CE.[2] In the language of Lacanian psychoanalysis, we might say that this invocation takes the Muse of History to be an (imagined) authoritative subject; she who is supposed to know. Historians become, in this reading, Clio's analysands, pinning our hopes for enlightenment on the knowledge we presume she can impart to us. In this way, we either/both attribute to the knowledge she reveals a standing independent of us, or/and turn to her for interpretation of the facts we have at hand. In another reading, though, Clio and the historian become one: she imbues us with her authority; we identify with her power. We become the analysts in relation to our subjects, those for and about whom we produce knowledge; to the extent that our own subjectivity matters, it functions in the service of imparting meaning to their lives. It is important to note here that, in psychoanalytic theory, whoever is in the analyst's position is only imagined to have authoritative knowledge. The lack of distinction between real and imagined knowledge is at the heart of the transference, the setting in which unconscious desires are allowed to emerge.

[1] This chapter is a revised version of the third *History and Theory* lecture, presented on 4 April 2011, at Columbia University in New York. The *History and Theory* lecture is given annually, and is jointly sponsored by *History and Theory* and the consortium for Intellectual and Cultural History centred at Columbia University (www.columbia.edu/cu/cich/ [accessed 8 March 2013]). The lecture was published in the February 2012 issue of the journal *History and Theory*. I am extremely grateful to Brady Brower, Brian Connolly, Ben Kafka, Judith Surkis, and Elizabeth Weed, whose critical suggestions pushed me beyond my own limits and made this a much better chapter than it otherwise might have been. I also wish to thank Peter Loewenberg for many helpful suggestions, and Sam Moyn and Ethan Kleinberg, who invited me to give the *History and Theory* lecture.

[2] Valerius Flaccus, *Argonautica* 3: 15, trans. J. H. Mozley. Loeb Classical Library, vol. CCLXXXVI (Cambridge: MA: Harvard University Press). www.theoi.com/Text/ValeriusFlaccus3.html [accessed 8 March 2013].

The relationship between fact and interpretation has long preoccupied the discipline of history. The issue turns on the location of authority: who knows and how do we know? It is crucial for the coherent narratives we construct that they refer to reality: events and behaviours whose occurrence we can document, even as we know they are differently interpreted at different points in time. A whole body of disciplinary rules guides the collection of evidence, its organization and presentation, and this, in turn, is meant to confer authority. But discipline achieves only a measure of the authority it seeks precisely because interpretations are always subject to revision. Revisionist controversies periodically disrupt the established order of things, calling into question facts, interpretations, the use of evidence and the motives of historians. The repetition of such controversies about the meanings of the past in the present creates doubt: is it the facts or the interpretations that are produced by the historian? And do the facts ground the interpretation, or is it the other way around?

Periodically, solutions are offered in the form of outside help; various theories of causality come into and out of favour (the latest is neuro- or cognitive psychology – brain science as the ultimate explanation for human behaviour). They occasion heated debate and then fade, some becoming part of the eclectic grab bag of explanation, some incorporated into disciplinary common sense (or the historian's 'intuition') in ways that make their provenance virtually unrecognizable; still others marking out territory for a subgroup that sets apart its members within the mainstream. Psychohistory is an example of this last possibility and the focus of this chapter.

Although the influence of Freud can be found in history-writing throughout the twentieth century, the emergence of something like a movement came only in the 1970s, at least in the United States. Then, inspired by Erik Erikson's ego-psychological approach to Martin Luther and by a body of advocacy and example developed in the 1950s and 1960s, historians founded journals and training institutes, and published compendia of essays to elaborate and demonstrate the importance of psychoanalysis to historical thinking.[3] Uncovering the hidden motives

[3] E. Erikson, *Young Man Luther: a Study in Psychoanalysis and History* (New York: Norton, 1962). Articles and books will be mentioned later in this chapter. Among the journals founded were the *History of Childhood Quarterly* (1973) and the *Journal of Interdisciplinary History* (1969). In 1971, UCLA established research training fellowships, in conjunction with the Southern California Psychoanalytic Institute, for scholars with Ph.D.s in academic fields who wanted psychoanalytic training. Those involved – Peter Loewenberg was a key figure – managed to win repeal of a California law in 1977 that had prohibited the practice of psychoanalysis by anyone other than a certified psychologist. This training programme still exists today. For a full account, see P. Loewenberg, 'Psychoanalytic research training: a California success story', *American Psychoanalyst*, 27 (1973), 11–12.

for individuals' actions would offer new insight into issues that had long perplexed the field; 'the dead do not ask to be cured', Frank Manuel commented, 'only to be understood'.[4]

Manuel, not a psychohistorian himself, talked about psychoanalysis as 'a historical instrumentality'. William Langer suggested, in 1957, that psychoanalysis should become part of the 'equipment' of young historians.[5] A generation later, Peter Loewenberg, who played a key role in establishing the institutions as well as the scholarship of the subfield, wrote of the way in which analysis sensitized the historian to his own unconscious investments as well as to those that inhered in material from the past.[6] What all of these examples share is the idea that history can usefully appropriate psychoanalytic authority for its own ends.

That is surely one way to think about interdisciplinarity – as the importation of useful concepts into an existing field, expanding its scope, augmenting the stock of its explanatory arsenal. But there is another way, as well, one that looks to the encounter as disruptive and ultimately unreconcilable. Elizabeth Wilson (speaking of neuroscience and psychoanalysis) refers to the productive qualities of 'incommensurability'.

> If a theory of the unconscious is unruly, at its core and necessarily so, this will make efforts to synthesize psychoanalysis with other kinds of epistemological projects difficult; for it will demand from any prospective partner a high degree of tolerance for disjunction, overdetermination and displacement, and a waning interest in consilience as an epistemological goal. These difficulties strike me as uniquely productive: when methodologically disparate, perhaps antagonistic, domains are brought into a relation of mutuality, this is often when interdisciplinarity is most acute, most unstable and most promising. This kind of interdisciplinarity procreates not through conventional plots of compatibility but through the logic of incommensurability.[7]

[4] F. Manuel, 'The use and abuse of psychology in history', *Daedalus* (Winter 1971), 209.

[5] W. L. Langer, 'The next assignment', *American Historical Review*, 63 (January 1958), 283.

[6] P. Loewenberg, *Decoding the Past: the Psychohistorical Approach* (New York: Knopf, 1983). See esp. pp. 3–8.

[7] E. Wilson, 'Another neurological scene', *History of the Present*, 1 (2011), 156. Writing in 1977, literary scholar Shoshana Felman argued that the traditional method of applying psychoanalysis to literary study was a mistake. She offered instead the notion of 'implication', something similar to the idea of incommensurability proposed by Wilson. '[T]he interpreter's role would here be not to apply to the text an acquired science, a preconceived knowledge, but to act as a go-between, to *generate implications* between literature and psychoanalysis – to explore, bring to light and articulate the various (indirect) ways in which the two domains do indeed *implicate each other*, each one finding itself enlightened, informed, but also affected, displaced, by the other', S. Felman, 'Literature and psychoanalysis: the question of reading: otherwise', *Yale French Studies*, 55, 56 (1977), 8–9. Wilson cites others, among them Eve Sedgwick, who have made similar suggestions.

I want to argue that, by endorsing the 'plot of compatibility', psychohistory, as developed in the United States, tended to reaffirm the discipline of history's concept of itself. A more critical approach, one exemplified in the work of the French historian and Lacanian analyst Michel de Certeau, used psychoanalysis to pose a challenge to history's conventional self-representation.

When I say a challenge to history's concept of itself, I do not mean the things that historians who scorn psychoanalysis rail against: that abstract 'psychological theory' is being substituted for solid 'documentary proof'; that reliable evidence cannot be produced to document unconscious motivation; that 'Freudian biological determinism' is a poor explanatory substitute for rational calculations based on economic interest; that a focus on passion feeds the anti-intellectualism of the general population; that psychoanalysis was developed to treat individual neurotics and so cannot offer insight into collective action; that Freudian theory is a product of Western modernity and so cannot be used to think about other cultures and other times; and that the reason of historical actors deserves respect.[8] A particularly outraged reaction on that last point came in the pages of *History and Theory* from Gerald Izenberg in 1975:

> Intellectual historians often deal with complex and sophisticated systems of ideas which are carefully thought through and intellectually well defended. What right does the historian have to dismiss or denigrate the importance of the intellectual processes by which historical thinkers have arrived at their beliefs and refer instead to unconscious impulses, phantasies, defenses, or conflicts in order to explain them?[9]

Figuring the unconscious as a threat to reason (its denigration or outright erasure) is characteristic of historians' resistance to psychoanalytic thinking and has played an undeniably powerful role in curbing its influence. Yet these objections seem to me predictable, almost banal, a displacement of more disturbing worries. The critical challenge of psychoanalysis lies elsewhere, in the way it can be understood to conceive of history itself.

[8] Examples of these views are: E. Saveth, 'Historians and the Freudian approach to history', *New York Times Book Review*, 1 January 1956; R. L. Schoenwald, 'The historian and the challenge of Freud', *Western Humanities Review*, 10 (1956), 99–108; P. Pomper, 'Problems of a naturalistic psychohistory', *History and Theory*, 12 (1973), 367–388; M. Curti, 'Intellectuals and other people', *American Historical Review*, 60 (January 1955), 260–281; W. Reddy, 'Against constructionism: the historical ethnography of emotions', *Current Anthropology*, 38 (June 1997), 327–51.

[9] G. Izenberg, 'Psychohistory and Intellectual History', *History and Theory*, 14 (1975), 140.

From one perspective, history and psychoanalysis have some things in common, but these similarities mask their different epistemological approaches. Like psychoanalysis, the discipline of history acknowledges that facts are in some sense produced through interpretation, but each understands this production to take place differently. Historians refer to a rational interpretive process that attributes different meanings to established facts, depending on the context or framework within which a scholar works. In contrast, Freud used the term *Nachträglichkeit* ('deferred action') to indicate the way in which events acquired significance through revision: 'rearrangement in accordance with fresh circumstances ... a re-transcription'.[10] As he wrestled with the timing of the primal scene in the Wolf Man case, Freud insisted on 'the part played by phantasies in symptom-formation and also the "retrospective phantasying" of later impressions into childhood and their sexualization after the event'.[11] Although he concluded that the obsessional neurosis of his patient must have originated when he witnessed his parents' coitus, there was no way finally to establish that fact. Freud acknowledged the difficulty of attributing the dream of a four-year-old boy, recalled by a grown man undergoing analysis some twenty years later, to a trauma experienced by a one-and-a-half-year-old child. But finally he dismissed the effort at precision as beside the point: 'It is also a matter of indifference in this connection whether we choose to regard it as a primal *scene* or a primal *phantasy*.'[12] Events are not the starting point of the analysis, but are deduced from their effects. As Certeau puts it, 'Analysis establishes history by virtue of a relation among successive manifestations.'[13] Historians, in contrast, replace one set of interpretations (of facts or events) with another.[14]

If historians assume that the linear narratives they create capture the past's relationship to the present (and, in some cases, the present's to

[10] Cited in J. Laplanche and J.-B. Pontalis, *The Language of Psychoanalysis*, trans. D. Nicholson-Smith (New York: Norton, 1973), p. 112.

[11] S. Freud, 'The history of an infantile neurosis', in *The Complete Psychological Works of Sigmund Freud* (The Standard Edition), trans. and ed. J. Strachey, 24 vols. (New York: W. W. Norton, 1976), vol. XVII, p. 103.

[12] *Ibid.*, p. 120.

[13] M. de Certeau, *The Writing of History*, trans. Tom Conley (New York: Columbia University Press, 1988), p. 303. It is noteworthy that Certeau was largely neglected by American psychohistorians as well as by those historians who turned to post-structuralism in the 1980s and 1990s in the writings of Foucault, Derrida, and even Lacan (a primary influence on Certeau).

[14] This is how Philip Rieff put it: 'If for Marx the past is pregnant with the future, with the proletariat as the midwife of history, for Freud the future is pregnant with the past, with the psychoanalyst as the abortionist of history', P. Rieff, 'The Meaning of history and religion in Freud's thought', *Journal of Religion*, 31 (April 1951), 114–31, reprinted in B. Mazlish (ed.), *Psychoanalysis and History* (New York: Grosset and Dunlap, 1971), pp. 23–44. Citation is on p. 28.

the past), psychoanalysts take the transference to operate in more than one temporal register. There is the time of the analysis and the times remembered in analysis, and these do not add up to a single chronology. Brady Brower puts it this way: 'Within the practical time of the analysis, the analysand's speech designated a second temporality, one that made it possible for the analyst's speech to be attributed a role with little or no correspondence to his actual personal characteristics or his formal capacities as an analyst.'[15] Unlike the historian who makes an object (an other) of the denizens of the past, the analyst refuses objectification, seeking instead to bring the analysand to recognition of the unconscious agency – the condition and limits – of his or her own subjectivity. It is not, as some have noted, that for Freud, the past always haunts the present, but that the objective times of past and present are confused, often indistinguishable. The point is that time is a complex creation, a constructed dimension of subjectivity, and not a chronological given. Freudian theory is sceptical of the evolutionary chronology that shapes professional historians' presentations, attending instead to the role repression or nostalgia play in the construction of memory, and to the interruptions and discontinuities that characterize the necessarily uneven and often chaotic interactions of past and present in the psyche.

Above all, though, it is the unconscious that knows neither time nor contradiction that distinguishes the psychoanalytic version of history from that of the disciplined historian. Not because it denies the operations of reason, but because it influences them in unpredictable ways, defying reliable or systematic explanation. Indeed, reason itself is read as the outcome, at least in part, of its engagement with what Wilson refers to as the 'unruly' unconscious. Reason and unconscious are thus not diametrically opposed in Freudian theory, as Izenberg's complaint insists, but are taken to be interacting, inseparable facets of thought.

On the question of time and causality, and subject and object, there is thus an incompatibility between psychoanalysis and history. Certeau captures the disparity: 'Now I must ask: what disturbing uncanniness does Freudian writing trace within the historian's territory, where it enters dancing? Reciprocally, in what fashion will my question, born of an archival and scriptural labor that cultivates this territory, and seduced by the fiction of psychoanalytical history, be enlightened/distorted through Freud's analysis?'[16] For Certeau the seductive dance of Freudian analysis necessarily distorts even as it sheds new light on the

[15] M. Brady Brower, 'Science, seduction, and the lure of reality in Third Republic France', *History of the Present*, 1, (2011), 172.
[16] Certeau, *The Writing of History*, p. 309.

territory of the historian. He designates writing as 'fiction' in the sense both of fabrication and deception. The Freudian 'dance' is counterposed to the historians' 'labor'; 'dance' refers to the multiple and mobile forms taken by imaginative representation, whereas 'labor' stresses the imposition of order on the materiality of archives and their transcription. Historical writing, he says, is the unconscious or unacknowledged way of working through the historian's relationship to death, at once erasing it by resurrecting the past and avowing it through its very erasure. For Certeau the crucial term is 'uncanniness' – psychoanalysis brings back something once familiar, but now estranged through the operations of distance and repression. The 'uncanny' refers to that which historians know but must deny: 'historiography tends to prove that the site of its production can encompass the past: it is an odd procedure that posits death, a breakage everywhere reiterated in discourse, and that yet denies loss by appropriating to the present the privilege of recapitulating the past as a form of knowledge. A labor of death and a labor against death.'[17]

It is the clash, not the compatibility, of the two different concepts of history that proves productive for Certeau. '[T]he interdisciplinarity we look toward would attempt to apprehend epistemological constellations as they reciprocally provide themselves with a new delimitation of their objects and a new status for their procedures.'[18] Any other approach simply reproduces, with new terminology, history's conventional self-representations.

I suggest that – at least in the United States – psychohistory has, for the most part, selected aspects of psychoanalytic theory that are least challenging to history's epistemology and so have constructed 'conventional plots of compatibility'. In contrast, Certeau and some others illustrate the critical possibilities that are inherent in a relationship of incommensurability.

Instrumentalization

The designation of the subfield as 'psychohistory' suggests, if not a marriage, then a certain mutuality. Psychohistorians made the case for compatibility by instrumentalizing psychoanalysis, conceived of as equipment or tools for approaching the past. These tools were diagnostic labels and developmental narratives that comported comfortably with established historical chronologies.

[17] *Ibid.*, p. 5. [18] *Ibid.*, p. 291.

Diagnostic categories proved useful for introducing new arguments about causality. There was, for example, Preserved Smith's 1913 article on Martin Luther, which anticipated by nearly half a century Erik Erikson's monumental study of the Protestant reformer. Smith published 'Luther's Early Development in the Light of Psycho-Analysis' in the *American Journal of Psychology*. Citing Freud, Otto Rank, Ernest Jones, and William James, among others, Smith probed Luther's life for intimate expression and found him to be 'a thoroughly typical example of the neurotic, quasi-hysterical sequence of an infantile sex-complex; so much so, indeed, that Sigismund [*sic*] Freud and his school could hardly have found a better example to illustrate the sounder part of their theory than him'.[19] Smith turned to psychoanalysis, he said, for greater understanding of Luther's spirituality. 'Far more than we realize or like to admit', he wrote, 'our highest impulses of love, religion, and morality are rooted in physical, even in pathological conditions. If the branches of the tree reach toward heaven, its roots strike deep into the dark bowels of the earth.'[20]

Smith wrote as a secular thinker, deeply committed to science. Having studied for his Ph.D. (1907) in history with James Harvey Robinson at Columbia, Smith believed in 'science and the idea that knowledge of history was a way to improve human prospects for the future'. In his essay on Luther the science of Freudian analysis becomes a tool of secularity in its struggle against religion, reducing religious belief to sexual fantasies shaped in early childhood.[21]

Diagnostic labels were used, too, to probe the effects of historical events on psychic experience. William Langer's presidential address to the American Historical Association in 1957 is an example of this approach. Langer was a European diplomatic historian, so his field made his words doubly surprising. Entitled 'The Next Assignment', the speech called for historians to deepen their historical understanding 'through exploitation of the concepts and findings of modern psychology'.[22] Langer went on to suggest that 'some of our own younger men' ought to undergo

19 P. Smith, 'Luther's early development in the light of psycho-analysis', *American Journal of Psychology*, 24 (1913), 362.

20 *Ibid.*, p. 361.

21 Smith's work probably served another end as well: the vindication of his father, biblical scholar Henry Preserved Smith (1847–1927). Henry was tried for heresy by the Presbytery of Cincinnati in 1892 for teaching that there were errors in the books of Chronicles. The son's attack on religion as rooted in 'the dark bowels of the earth' was in effect a denial of the independent force of religious spirituality, the reduction of it to psychic pathology – perhaps a way of avenging his father's suffering. For a recent rereading of Luther, see L. Roper, 'Martin Luther's body: the "Stout doctor" and his biographers', *American Historical Review*, 115 (April 2010), 351–84.

22 Langer, 'The next assignment', p. 283.

psychoanalytic training as a way of broadening their scholarly 'equipment'.[23] He pointed to Freud's work on Leonardo da Vinci as an example of how biography could be illuminated by psychoanalytic concepts, and he took the Black Death of 1348–9 as an illustration of the way in which psychoanalysis might be used to think about collective (cultural or social) states of mind. The historical experience of mass death could be illuminated, he said, by Freudian concepts of trauma and survivor guilt, which, in individual cases, pointed back to 'the curbing and repression of sexual and aggressive drives in childhood and the emergence of death wishes directed against the parents'. There was reason to believe that when disaster and death threatened an entire community, these same forces could engender 'a mass emotional disturbance, based on a feeling of helpless exposure, disorientation, and common guilt'.[24]

Seeking to explain what many of Langer's dismayed colleagues took to be a mad moment in the life of a distinguished historian (his Harvard colleagues wondered whether he had lost his mind; Princeton historians thought him 'a strange man lacking in common sense'), Peter Loewenberg offered a diagnosis of his own.[25] Loewenberg, whose practice of psychohistory came into its own in the 1970s and for whom Langer was a prescient forefather, offered an explanation of the AHA president's apparently perplexing turn in a 1980 essay. In it, Loewenberg acknowledged the more obvious explanations for Langer's interest in psychoanalysis: his role in wartime intelligence at the Office of Strategic Services and then in the CIA, where researchers were developing psychological profiles of Soviet politicians and others to advance Cold War objectives. Langer also had a younger brother who was a psychiatrist and who had provided the OSS with expert diagnoses of Hitler's character. Given these experiences, it made sense to think about equipping historians with methods that could help serve the nation's policy objectives.

But Loewenberg took these reasons to be 'superficial'.[26] He provided instead a compelling reading (based on both Langer brothers' memoirs) of the unconscious motives at work in William Langer's speech. These included the early loss of his father associated with 'a vague childhood recollection of hearing about the assassination of President McKinley in 1901' and memory traces of the 'intense grief, anxiety and panic of his [fatherless] childhood home'.[27] Such unconscious influences,

[23] *Ibid.*, p. 303. [24] *Ibid.*, p. 299.

[25] The Harvard story was told to me by a then-grad student there; the Princeton story is cited in P. Loewenberg, 'The psychobiographical background to psychohistory: the Langer family and the dynamics of shame and success', in Loewenberg, *Decoding the Past: the Psychohistorical Approach* (New York: Knopf, 1983), p. 81.

[26] *Ibid.*, p. 83. [27] *Ibid.*, pp. 82–3.

Loewenberg suggested, led the historian of modern Europe to choose catastrophic death in the Middle Ages as his example. As for the turn to psychoanalysis itself, Loewenberg revealed that Langer had developed a 'crippling' neurotic symptom, a phobia about speaking in public, which analysis with Hanns Sachs helped him manage but not cure. Loewenberg understood Langer's 'stage-fright' in terms of a dynamic in which shame is erected as a defence against 'exhibitionist impulses' driven by ambition and competitiveness.[28] He took Langer's appreciation for psychoanalysis to be a recognition of the role of the unconscious in human behaviour – and more: 'Would that we may have the freshness of mind and the personal insight to apply creatively our neuroses and personal misfortune to new perspectives and innovations in research method as he did.'[29] The diagnostic tool is doubly applied here as Langer's own preoccupation with death becomes the occasion for his insight into the medieval emotional response to a massive epidemic. Psychoanalysis is both cause and effect; as the title of the article asserts, psychobiography is the 'background' to psychohistory.

Langer's address to the AHA elicited enormous disapproval among orthodox disciplinarians, but it did not come out of the blue. In the 1950s, as he wrote, psychoanalysis was very much in the air.[30] Though much of the theoretical discussion was located outside of the discipline, in sociology and anthropology particularly, historians were not immune to the possibilities of Freudian analysis. The argument that attention to the psyche could illuminate human behaviour became increasingly attractive in the 1940s as scholars tried to explain the rise of Nazism in Germany and the appeal of communism, and then extended their investigations to other historical instances. As was the case with Langer's analysis of the effects of the Black Death, these accounts tended to focus on cases considered excessive or pathological, examples of extraordinary aggression, overreaction, or seemingly irrational politics. Thus Richard Hofstadter explained the American conquest of Cuba and the Philippines in terms

[28] *Ibid.*, p. 87. [29] *Ibid.*, p. 94.

[30] A very small sampling of the preoccupation with psychology and psychoanalysis in relation to history in the 1940s and 1950s includes: G. Watson, 'Clio and Psyche: Some interrelations of psychology and history'; and F. Alexander, 'Psychology and the interpretation of historical events', both in C. Ware (ed.), *The Cultural Approach to History* (New York: Columbia University Press, 1940); S. Ratner, 'The historian's approach to psychology', *Journal of the History of Ideas*, 2 (January 1941), 95–109; C. Kluckhohn, 'Politics, history, and psychology', *World Politics*, 8 (1955), 102–19; C. Schorske, 'A new look at the Nazi movement', *World Politics*, 9 (1956), 88–97; H. Lasswell, 'Impact of psychoanalytic thinking on the Social Sciences', in L. D. White (ed.), *The State of the Social Sciences* (Chicago: University of Chicago Press, 1956), pp. 84–115; H. Meyerhoff, 'On psychoanalysis as history', *Psychoanalytic Review*, 49 (1962), 3–20.

of a national psychic crisis. And, turning to political groups he called 'pseudo-conservative' (using Adorno's term), he wrote of their 'paranoid style'. As he put it, 'of course, the term "paranoid style" is pejorative, and it is meant to be; the paranoid style has a greater affinity for bad causes than good. But nothing entirely prevents a sound program or a sound issue from being advocated in the paranoid style.'[31] Despite this qualification, the power of the argument rested on the light the diagnostic label could shed on 'bad causes'. In a similar vein, seeking to explain the appeal of Hitler to Nazi youth, Loewenberg suggested that the attraction of young Germans to the demagogue could at least in part be explained by the extreme deprivation they had suffered after the First World War: food shortages had a dramatic impact on maternal lactation; fathers were killed or maimed in the war; military defeat undermined belief in national values. This led to identification with a distant, idealized father-figure who promised not only economic but also moral and psychological salvation.[32]

Of course, not all psychoanalytic readings of history sought to diagnose pathology; some wanted to shed light on the idiosyncratic, or on the private lives and hidden motives of public figures (Luther, Gandhi, Woodrow Wilson, Thomas Jefferson, Benjamin Franklin, Kaiser Wilhelm, Henry VIII, Freud himself). Other work extended insights about individuals to groups, locating the psychic bases for social cohesion in Oedipal struggles, rituals of mourning, displacements of aggression, and the like. These studies are surely important, for they provide new and often neglected causal factors to consider, but they do little to disrupt the temporal logic of disciplined history, to question the present's relationship to the past, or historians' attraction for their subject(s). Indeed, with diagnostic categories, historians act not as subjects '*supposed* to know', but as those who *do* know, whose authority is vested in their ability to deploy psychoanalytic terminology.

Diagnostic categories usually referred to developmental narratives, chronological stages from infancy to adulthood. For example, when Loewenberg interpreted the effects of childhood deprivation on German youth, he followed Freud's account of 'the phase-specific psychosexual development of the child … the traumas of the oral phase, of separation-individuation from the mother, the struggles with aggression and control that constitute the anal phase, the Oedipal conflict, the latency years

[31] R. Hofstadter, *The Paranoid Style in American Politics and Other Essays* (Cambridge, MA: Harvard University Press, 1964), p. 5. See also his *Anti-Intellectualism in American Life* (New York: Knopf, 1966).

[32] P. Loewenberg, 'The psychohistorical origins of the Nazi youth cohort', in Loewenberg, *Decoding the Past*, pp. 240–83.

of grade-school political socialization, to the crisis of adolescence that precedes adulthood'.[33] John Demos, locating Puritan personality traits in the child-rearing practices of these early Americans, invoked Erikson's adaptation of this Freudian model according to which there were 'eight stages of man'. Having studied the treatment of infants and young children in these terms, Demos concluded: 'It is tempting, indeed, to regard puritan religious belief as a kind of screen on which all of their innermost concerns – autonomy, shame, doubt, anger – were projected with a very special clarity.'[34] The seeming compatibility between psychoanalysis and history rested, in part at least, on the familiarity of chronology. Despite the differences in the narratives, there was coherence, and a logic of succession from past to present: 'a long and continuing sequence of growth and change'.[35] The adult was foreshadowed by the child, as the present was the outcome of the past.

The move from individual to collective psychology always involved analogy: individuals shared a developmental narrative that resulted in common traits within a specific cultural/historical context. It was already evident in Freud's writing (*Group Psychology* and *Totem and Taboo*). In *Moses and Monotheism* Freud wrote of tradition – the culturally or socially transmitted legacy of a people – as 'equivalent to repressed material in the mental life of the individual'.[36] This analogical reasoning was extended by anthropologists, psychologists and others associated with the 'culture and personality' school in the 1950s and 1960s (among them Abram Kardiner, Margaret Mead, Clyde Kluckhohn, Erik Erikson and Theodor Adorno), who directly influenced historians like Demos. Here the attempt was to think about personality in its social and cultural contexts and to collectivize individual trajectories as theorized by Freud. Taking into account the diversity of individuals in any society, Kardiner, for example, proposed a 'modal personality', defined as 'that constellation of personality characteristics which would appear to be congenial with the total range of institutions comprised within a given culture'.[37] The emphasis was on institutions (the family, the school, religion, law – topics familiar to historians and increasingly so as social history assumed predominance in the 1970s and 1980s) that shaped behavioural characteristics – what

[33] *Ibid.*, pp. 267–8.

[34] J. Demos, 'Developmental perspectives on the history of childhood', in G. M. Kren and L. H. Rappoport (eds.), *Varieties of Psychohistory* (New York: Springer, 1976), p. 188. Here, as in the case of Preserved Smith, there is a secular impulse informing the turn to psychoanalysis, taking religion not as a credible system of belief, but locating it in a deeper, irrational psychic cause.

[35] *Ibid.*

[36] Freud, *Moses and Monotheism*, in The Standard Edition, vol. XXIII, p. xxx.

[37] Cited in Demos, 'Developmental perspectives', p. 182.

would later become 'cultural construction', with attention moved from psychodynamics to regulatory norms. The assumption was that individuals identified with the social representations offered them; so, for example, women and men were said to internalize the prevailing gender system, realizing in their lives the idealized images of their cultures. Changes in the culture led to changes in personality. The process of internalization depended, if only implicitly, on the narrative of individual psychological development. This focus on 'modal personality' as a reflection of cultural institutions had a deeply normative aspect to it; difference was either ignored or diagnosed (according to Freudian categories) as deviation or pathology.[38] The appeal to historians had to do with the cultural side of things; attention to the psychological consequences of institutional change did little to disrupt the frame within which they already operated. As Frank Manuel put it, the future use of psychology for history lay in its ability to address the question of 'what change signified on an unconscious psychic level'.[39]

Manuel wrote in 1971 in a special issue of *Daedalus* devoted to a survey of historical studies. His piece, gesturing to Nietzsche, was called 'The Use and Abuse of Psychology in History'. Like Preserved Smith's invocation of the deep, 'dark bowels of the earth', it emphasized the need to glance 'below the navel', to get at the sexual side of human motivation:

> Few historians have yet coped with the intricacies of presenting to their readers the varying patterns of libidinal satisfaction in different epochs ... The history of fashion, clothes, sexual and marital custom, punishments, style, and a hundred other questions which have traditionally belonged to *la petite histoire* and the antiquarians need to be explored for their symbolic content. Freud's second most important legacy to a historian may well be the dissolution of a hierarchy of values among historical materials. If all things can become vehicles of expression for feelings and thoughts, then the state document, grand philosophical affirmation, and scientific law may lose some of their prestige to other more intimate records of human experience. The day of Dilthey's elitist psychological history is over. Conversely, classical psychoanalysis, with a dubious future as a therapy, might be reborn as a historical instrumentality.[40]

There are several interesting aspects about this comment: the first is the imperial gesture – the subordination of psychoanalysis as a 'historical

[38] Given the normative disposition of so much of psychohistory, it is ironic that those who attacked it found that it threatened notions of the normative or normal. Hence Izenberg insisted that attention to the rational was the object of historical investigation because rationality was defined by its acceptance of cultural norms. It was only irrational actions (by those few who refused such norms), he said, that called for inquiry into 'unconscious motives and intentions'. Izenberg, 'Psychohistory and intellectual history', pp. 146–7.

[39] Manuel, 'Use and abuse', p. 196.

[40] *Ibid.*, pp.192, 209.

instrumentality'. The second, even more telling, is that, in the 1970s and 1980s, social historians stripped the erotic dimension from the topics Manuel set out – the family, childhood, emotions, sexual custom and punishment – and invested them instead with concepts of power, politics and social reproduction.[41]

The reasons for this are many, and there is no space here to discuss them all. The key points have to do first with social history's focus on power, whereas psychohistory had a more normative approach, and second, with psychohistory's turn away from sex and sexuality, another of the factors that assured its compatibility with conventional history. Even as Manuel wrote about the need to look 'below the navel', attention was already focused on the upper regions. The influence of ego-psychology is particularly important here and can be traced in a series of studies issued by the Social Science Research Council in 1946 and again in 1954. The 1954 bulletin was called 'The Social Sciences in Historical Study', and its various sections (on political science, economics, sociology, anthropology and psychology) were based on memoranda submitted by members of those disciplines (Clyde Kluckhohn and Alfred Kroeber for anthropology; Gardner Murphy and M. Brewster Smith for social psychology).

The section on social psychology provided a rundown of various approaches to the field (behaviourism, Gestalt, psychoanalysis), emphasizing the importance of Freud's discoveries for a 'theory of motivation' and the non-rational components of human behaviour. It stressed the influences of culture ('the impact of society') on individuals, and the importance of group experience (shared symbol systems, beliefs and expectations of others' actions) in the formation of personality. It also provided a kind of theory of social change, though it was one that would make it hard to account for revolutionary upheaval or major epistemic shifts: 'each person assimilates culture in his own idiosyncratic version – so he contributes to change even as he sustains continuity'.[42] The emphasis on the formative role of culture diminished the side of Freud that was so

41 Lynn Hunt in 'Psychoanalysis, the self, and historical interpretation', *Common Knowledge* 6 (1997), 10–19, noted the connection: 'The effacement of the psychological ... seems paradoxically connected to the rise of social history.' I would argue that there was nothing paradoxical about it. In the article, Hunt suggests that the incompatibility between psychoanalysis and history has to do with an opposition between the universalist and scientific emphasis of psychoanalysis and the historians' preference for contextual social explanation. She calls for a 'historicization of the self', as if that were not the project of psychoanalysis, when it seems to me to be at the heart of its theoretical and practical work.

42 Social Science Research Council, *The Social Sciences in Historical Study* (New York: SSRC, 1954), 64.

appealing to Preserved Smith – the sexual fantasies of children and their unconscious influence on adult behaviour – even as it stressed the need to study family influences and methods of child rearing.[43]

> Neo-Freudians like Karen Horney and Erich Fromm have rejected the biological assumptions of libido theory (the dominant importance of the sexual drive and its assumed transformations) and have attempted to assimilate into psychoanalysis the theories of sociology and cultural anthropology regarding the cultural and social determination of many factors Freud believed to be biologically ordained ... recent developments in 'ego-psychology' have shifted the emphasis from the realm of irrational urge and wish (the id) to that of the constructive operations of personality in mediating between wish and outer reality (the ego).[44]

There were, in this period and in the decades that followed, any number of experiments by historians using various kinds of psychoanalytic approaches. There were also notable attempts – by philosopher Herbert Marcuse, classicist Norman O. Brown, political scientist Michael Rogin, and others outside the discipline – to bring psychoanalysis, especially theories of the unconscious, to bear on history.[45] But among psychohistorians the approach associated with ego-psychology seems to have predominated.

Assuming that sexuality was 'biologically ordained' placed it on the side of the immutable and irrational (outside history's domain), whereas rational human action was on the side of the social and the cultural (the province of history). A good example is H. Stuart Hughes' 1961 lecture on history and psychoanalysis presented to a psychiatric training group at Beth Israel Hospital in Boston (thus an accounting to psychiatrists of historians' ambivalence about and attraction to their work). It is instructive for what it emphasizes and leaves out. Hughes rejected the utility of a 'one-to-one relationship between the causality of a childhood event and later behavior', preferring instead to focus on adolescence and early manhood.[46] This was Erikson's approach, he said, and was 'far more congenial to the historian's mind than the earlier (and almost exclusive) stress on the first six or seven years of life. Almost by definition, history prefers to deal with epochs of full consciousness, whether in the evolution of

[43] *Ibid.*, pp. 65. [44] *Ibid.*, pp. 62–3.

[45] H. Marcuse, *Eros and Civilization: a Philosophical Inquiry into Freud* (Boston: Beacon Press, 1955); N. O. Brown, *Life against Death: the Psychoanalytical Meaning of History* (Middletown, CT: Wesleyan University Press, 1955); Brown, *Love's Body* (Berkeley: University of California Press, 1966); M. Rogin, *The Intellectuals and McCarthy: the Radical Specter* (Cambridge, MA: MIT Press, 1967); and Rogin, *Fathers and Children: Andrew Jackson and the Subjugation of the American Indian* (New York: Knopf, 1975).

[46] H. Stuart Hughes, 'History and psychoanalysis: the explanation of motive' (1961), reprinted in Hughes, *History as Art and As Science: Twin Vistas on the Past* (New York: Harper & Row, 1964), p. 58.

peoples or in the career of an individual'.[47] The link between individuals and groups, Hughes observed, lay in shared 'emotional affinities'.[48] What is striking about the piece is, first, its rejection of one of the fundamental premises of Freud's theory, that early childhood experiences are not objectively distinct from what comes later, but are constantly revisited and revised in dreams, fantasies and memories; the past is not only returned to, but reimagined in subsequent contexts so that 'later behaviour' cannot be understood without its complex relation to a regularly reimagined past. No linear narrative can capture these workings of the mind. Second is its omission of any discussion of the unconscious and its links with sex and sexuality. Eliminating early childhood meant effectively ruling out infantile sexuality and, with it, the conundrum of sexual difference that young children face. The elimination of sexual difference – that original psychic incommensurability – effectively foreclosed acknowledgement of incommensurability *tout court*, including that of history and psychoanalysis. Hughes referred, oddly, to an individual's 'spiritual biography', which somehow meant conscious self-creation, and he repeated several times that 'individual consciousness' was the 'bedrock' of both psychoanalytic and historical knowledge.

The de-emphasis on sex and sexuality (the preference for the ego over the id) and the emphasis on social and cultural factors reproduced the binaries that traditional historians used to refuse psychoanalysis: sex vs reason; heart vs head; body vs mind; the lower parts vs the upper regions; passion vs interest; unconscious vs conscious. (It is interesting to note that these were the same binaries embraced by the ego-psychologists, hence assuring compatibility between the disciplines.) The turn away from sexuality also blurred the lines between social history and psychohistory, assuring compatibility, on the one hand, and a certain loss of prominence for psychohistory, on the other – and this at the very moment when the history of sexuality became an increasingly important area of inquiry, whether in the translation of Foucault's first volume of *The History of Sexuality* (1978), in Albert Hirschman's *The Passions and the Interests* (1977), or in the manifestos that emerged from women's and gay liberation movements.[49]

[47] *Ibid.*, p. 59. [48] *Ibid.*, p. 64.

[49] M. Foucault, *The History of Sexuality*, vol. I: *An Introduction*, trans. R. Hurley (New York: Random House, 1978); A. O. Hirschman, *The Passions and the Interests: Political Arguments for Capitalism before its Triumph* (Princeton, NJ: Princeton University Press, 1977). I now read Hirschman's book as a jab at orthodox political economists who argued that rational self-interest was the motive for economic behaviour. Hirschman shows how this discourse emerged from an earlier one on the passions. Some eighteenth-century theorists argued that capitalism would make avarice the ruling passion, subsuming all the others. Self-interested behaviour is then understood not as rational, but as the effect of greed, now the dominant passion!

The 1970s and 1980s were a period of tumultuous disciplinary and national politics marked by calls for the inclusion in the annals of history of the histories of neglected groups: workers, peasants, women, African-Americans, homosexuals, and others. The advocates for these histories did not turn to psychohistory, even though it was a lively and expanding area at the time. One reason was that psychohistory was primarily the province of intellectual history, a largely (white) male field.[50] Another was that the quest for inclusion involved proving that those who had been left out of historical accounts were credible historical subjects, and this meant presenting them as rational actors, agents, heroes of their own lives. Although the 'new social history' usually involved the exposure of prevailing biases among conventional historians, its practitioners worried that a resort to psychological interpretation might be perceived as 'hitting below the belt', impugning scholarly motives with dubious Freudian theories. But the main issue was that psychohistory had no ready way to theorize inequality. Indeed, for those seeking critical analysis of prevailing power relations, psychohistory's normative predisposition – accepting Freudian categories not simply as descriptive of the psychic organization of modern bourgeois society (as British feminist Juliet Mitchell argued they were), but as prescriptive – was part of the problem. If the direction of desire was always already known – a function of the Oedipal crisis – then deviations from it could be explained only as pathologies. Thus feminist historians were appalled by Christopher Lasch's *Haven in a Heartless World* (1977), a book that attributed the ills of contemporary society to imperfect 'Oedipalization', and the subsequent loss of patriarchal authority in families.[51] And they found little enlightenment in the many articles that diagnosed historical figures in terms of their narcissistic projections and regressive tendencies, or that attributed what for feminists were oppressive gender relations to psychic norms of masculinity and femininity. For the emerging gay liberation movement the diagnosis of homosexuality as a failure of masculine or feminine identification made psychoanalysis suspect, if not completely unacceptable. And on matters of race, there was general scepticism about white theories of

[50] In Kren and Rappoport (eds.), *Varieties of Psychohistory*, all the authors are male, with the exception of a husband and wife co-authorship. Similarly, in Mazlish, *Psychoanalysis and History*, all the authors are men. More recently, in M. Roth (ed.), *Rediscovering History: Culture, Politics, and the Psyche. Essays in Honor of Carl E. Schorske* (Stanford, CA: Stanford University Press, 1994), all but three of twenty-six authors are men, and the women are notably not feminist in subject matter or approach.

[51] C. Lasch, *Haven in a Heartless World: the Family Besieged* (New York: Basic Books, 1977). For one feminist critique, see S. Faludi, *Backlash: the Undeclared War Against Women* (New York: Crown Books, 1991), p. 281.

any kind. As Audre Lorde warned, 'the master's tools will never dismantle the master's house'.[52]

It was not that interest in sex was lacking; witness the questions posed by feminists in the introduction to a 1983 volume of essays, *Powers of Desire: the Politics of Sexuality*. '[E]very assumption about sex lies in uncharted terrain', the editors wrote. 'Is there a basic energy source, a primary, early experience of pleasure necessarily connected to sex? Should we define heterosexuality as one sexual mode among many, or is it politically important to identify it as a primary institution of women's oppression? Is monogamy a possibility of sexual liberation or will it wither away, like the state?'[53] The mix here of the political and the sexual is telling, as is the assumption that political intervention is possible in matters of sex. What is at stake is both understanding sex and sexuality in the past and present and searching for a way to theorize – and enact – change in the power dynamics of sex and gender relationships.

When feminist historians did turn to psychoanalysis, they did not define themselves as psychohistorians, but they did instrumentalize Freudian theory in a similar way. Taking as a given the male–female relationship to be one of domination and subordination, they showed, for example, how it was maintained by 'libidinization'. Cultural symbols and rituals invested gender relationships with sexual energy; in this way 'cultural construction' achieved its aim at the level of the unconscious.[54] What the essays did not interrogate were the operations of sexual difference, assuming instead fixity in the male–female division, even though it was one they wanted to change. Nor did they pose critical questions about the history they were writing. In this way, feminist history paralleled psychohistory. In both cases the compatibility of psychoanalysis and history was taken for granted; psychoanalysis was seen as an authoritative instrument to be applied in the practice of history.

52 A. Lorde, 'The master's tools will never dismantle the master's house', in her *Sister Outsider* (Berkeley, CA: Crossing Press, 1984), pp. 110–14. There was also, perhaps, a warning in the reaction by mainstream historians to Fawn Brodie's 1974 'intimate history' of Thomas Jefferson. Her suggestion that Jefferson's sexual relationship with Sally Hemings and the children he fathered with her had something to do with his failure to free his slaves, and with his political views more generally, was met with hostility, scorn and indifference. For details and the reviews of the book, see N. G. Bringhurst, *Fawn McKay Brodie: a Biographer's Life* (Norman: University of Oklahoma Press, 1999).

53 A. Snitow, C. Stansell and S. Thompson (eds.), *Powers of Desire: the Politics of Sexuality* (New York: Monthly Review Press, 1983), p. 41.

54 An example is A. Boboroff, 'Russian working women: sexuality in bonding patterns and the politics of daily life', in *ibid.*, pp. 208 and 212.

Incommensurability

The alternative to treating psychoanalysis as simply a tool for historians is to take up Wilson and Certeau's notion of incommensurability. For Certeau the notions of subject, time, desire and unconscious provide a way of thinking differently about history, allowing him to question the unexamined premises of the discipline. So the quest for 'meaning' is read as a quest for the Other, which at once establishes and conceals 'the alterity of this foreigner'.[55] So chronology and periodization are 'less the result obtained from research than its condition', a way of selecting not only what must be understood, but 'what must be forgotten in order to obtain the representation of apparent intelligibility'.[56] So narrative 'makes oppositions compatible ... substitutes conjunction for disjunction, holds contrary statements together, and, more broadly, overcomes the difference between an order and what it leaves aside'.[57] So the event is not an undisputed factual occurrence, but rather 'the hypothetical support for an ordering along a chronological axis; that is, the condition of a classification. Sometimes it is no more than a simple localization of disorder: in that instance, an event names what cannot be understood'.[58] History at once memorializes the dead and, by bringing them to life, covers over their absence. It is the way 'a society furnishes itself with a present time', but so also creates the 'rift of a future', that points not just to change, but inevitably to death.[59] This kind of thinking about history allows the historian a critical reflexivity, but one that is not at all the same as the self-reflection psychohistorians invoke. There it is a matter of examining their own motives, perhaps their personal reasons for taking up or avoiding certain projects, but it does not place them in critical relationship to the assumptions and practices of the discipline as a whole.

For Certeau it is not diagnostic labels borrowed from psychoanalysis that usefully inform history's mission. He writes:

> In both ethnology and history, certain studies demonstrate that the general use of psychoanalytical concepts runs the risk of blossoming into a new rhetoric. These concepts are thus transformed into figures of style. Recourse to the death of the father, to Oedipus or to transference, can be used for anything and

55 Certeau, *The Writing of History*, p. 2.

56 *Ibid.*, p. 4. 57 *Ibid.*, p. 89. 58 *Ibid.*, p. 96.

59 *Ibid.*, p. 101. Of history, Certeau writes: 'As it vacillates between exoticism and criticism through a staging of the other, it oscillates between conservatism and utopianism through its function of signifying a lack. In these extreme forms it becomes, in the first case, either legendary or polemical; in the second, it becomes reactionary or revolutionary. But these excesses could never allow us to forget what is written in its most rigorous practice, that of symbolizing limits and thus of enabling us to go beyond those limits.' *Ibid.*, p. 85.

everything. Since these Freudian 'concepts' are supposed to explain all human endeavor, we have little difficulty driving them into the most obscure regions of history. Unfortunately, they are nothing other than decorative tools if their only goal amounts to a designation or discreet obfuscation of what the historian does not understand. They circumscribe what cannot be explained, but they do not explain it. They avow an unawareness. They are earmarked for areas where an economic or a sociological explanation forcibly leaves something aside. A literature of ellipsis, an art of expounding on scraps and remnants, or the feeling of a question – yes; but a Freudian analysis – no.[60]

An instrumental use of psychoanalysis is effectively impotent – 'decorative tools' do not do any work. For Certeau a Freudian analysis consists in recognizing one's complicated connection to others: that it is we who impose a certain temporality on our relationship with them, that it is our (unconscious) desire that (at least in part) motivates the search for their meaning, that historical facts, like those presented by analysands, are always in some sense 'fabrications' – impositions of order on the confusions of reality, fantasy, memory and desire – and that the place from which we write inevitably informs 'the situation created by a social or analytical relation'.[61] This is a dynamic notion of the transference, one that necessarily disrupts the temporal order of conventional history.[62]

But it goes beyond that, to the nature of the analysis offered as well. Here it is not a standardized developmental narrative that is required, but attention to language and the ambivalence, ambiguity and tension it reveals. Language operates in two ways, as a structure of subjectivation (the inauguration of a subject into the social/symbolic order) and as a vocabulary (the cultural repertoire through which psychic states such as ambivalence are expressed), and it is this double operation that Certeau argues psychoanalysis brings to historians' attention. So he cites Freud's treatment of a seventeenth-century case of demonological neurosis as a way of thinking both psychoanalytically (about ambivalent identifications) and historically (ambivalence is expressed in this period in terms of allegiances to God or the devil). And he undertakes his own histories of early modern religion in these terms as well.

The British historian Lyndal Roper offers brilliant readings of similar phenomena in *Oedipus and the Devil: Witchcraft, Sexuality and Religion in Early Modern Europe* (1994) and *Witch Craze* (2004).[63] Arguing for

60 *Ibid.*, p. 289. 61 *Ibid.*, pp. 296, 69.

62 This is a somewhat different notion of the transference from the one evoked in Dominic LaCapra, 'Is everyone a *Mentalité* case? Transference and the "culture concept"', in LaCapra, *History and Criticism* (Ithaca, NY: Cornell University Press, 1985), pp. 72–3.

63 L. Roper, *Oedipus and the Devil: Witchcraft, Sexuality and Religion in Early Modern Europe* (New York: Routledge, 1994); and *Witch Craze* (New Haven, CT: Yale University Press, 2004).

the importance of the body and sexual difference as a physiological and psychological fact, she employs 'a dynamic model of the unconscious' to examine the 'constant interaction between desire and prohibition'.[64] Like Certeau, she rejects the idea of 'cultural construction', insisting on its ahistoricity. 'What I want to avoid is a developmental account of collective subjectivities which turns individual acts into mere exemplars of a narrative of collective historical progression'.[65] Or, as Certeau puts it a bit differently: 'The labor by which the subject authorizes his own existence is of a kind other than the labor from which he receives permission to exist. The Freudian process attempts to articulate this difference.'[66]

Roper goes on to analyse fantasies of witchcraft in terms of 'women's condensations of shared cultural preoccupations'.[67] Her psychoanalytic approach enables her to listen differently to the testimonies of those accused of witchcraft, even as she attributes a shared repertoire of images and anxieties to them. 'Sexual fantasies to which witches give voice often also display a ... vision of a disorganized body ... [W]hat we encounter ... is a disordered imagination in which anal and oral sex don't reinstate the heterosexual norm of which they are the inverse, but dissolve the categories of the discrete, functioning body altogether.'[68] Criticizing notions of fixed masculinity, she opts instead for an examination of the relationship between 'the rigors of repression' and the 'exuberance of excess'. 'At every turn ... civic authorities found themselves confronted with the anarchic disruption caused by masculine culture – the feckless husband, the drunkard, the threatening collectivities of guild and gang. So far as its public manifestations were concerned, masculinity was far from functional for the patriarchal society of the sixteenth century.'[69]

Psychoanalysis allows Roper to look beyond categorical distinctions and normative representations of masculinity and femininity. Not only does she think in terms of the distinctive process of subject formation – it is precisely not the predictable fulfilment of cultural representation, but an engagement with it, affected by fantasy, the unconscious, slippages

[64] Roper, *Oedipus and the Devil*, p. 8. [65] *Ibid.*, p. 13.

[66] Certeau, *The Writing of History*, p. 303. On this point Joan Copjec, a literary and film theorist working with Lacanian psychoanalysis, wrote in 1989: 'We are constructed, then, not in conformity to social laws, but in response to our inability to conform to or see ourselves as defined by social limits. Though we are defined and limited historically, the absence of the real, which founds these limits, is not *historicizable*. It is only this distinction, which informs the Lacanian definition of cause, that allows us to think the construction of the subject without being thereby obliged to reduce her *to* the images social discourses construct *of* her', J. Copjec, 'Cutting up', in T. Brennan (ed.), *Between Feminism and Psychoanalysis* (New York: Routledge, 1989), pp. 241–2.

[67] Roper, *Oedipus and the Devil*, p. 20.

[68] *Ibid.*, p. 25. [69] *Ibid.*, p. 111.

of language, particular investments of symbols and objects with psychic significance, and the ways in which identification with others affects individual identity – she also adds contradiction and ambivalence to her interpretation of collective behaviour (the relationship of desire to law and its transgression).[70] Indeed, desire, in her account, follows unpredictable directions; its attachment to objects can neither be stabilized nor predetermined. Desire – its perpetual quest and the impossibility of its satisfaction – is a psychic determinant with historical effects. Her approach eschews diagnostic categories and instead engages with the indeterminacies of human behaviour; the point is to operate as an analyst would in a transferential relationship, to 'uncover the psychic logic of the tale before we can guess at its meaning'.[71] The use of the term 'logic' here has nothing to do with the insistence on rationality that critics of psychoanalysis regularly evoke. Nor does it refer solely to the Oedipal struggles of individuals within their private families (a favourite theme of early psychohistory). Rather, 'psychic logic' is (in Brady Brower's terms) 'the relation between the … desire for knowledge and the already constituted field of knowledge. The desire for knowledge is conditional on the transgression of the established field of knowledge, and this transgression is, in turn, always ambivalent toward the constituted laws that it breaks … [I]nnovation is the product of this ambivalence.'[72]

Psychoanalysis does not provide Roper with either a clear causality or a theory of change. It cannot account definitively for the rise and fall of the mass phenomenon she describes as a 'witch craze' in the sixteenth and seventeenth centuries (with a focus on Germany). 'The problem I faced was how to build the details of subjectivity and the sheer power of unconscious forces as they emerged in the confessions [of witches] into a history that would be about a whole society and not just individuals, and that would deal with historical change.'[73] For that she returns to history: to the influences of social and cultural contexts; demographic pressures; anxieties about fertility and reproduction; shared vocabularies of maternity, sex and theology. As a result of urbanization, the growth of a middle class, an end to widespread scarcity, changes in household structure, in childbirth practices and moral codes, the demographic regime that had underpinned belief in witchcraft gradually vanished.

The iron grip of population control relaxed … The moral codes of the Reformation and Counter-Reformation years, which punished fornication and adultery, forbade swearing and regulated dress, had fallen into disuse. They became matters

[70] *Ibid.*, p. 228. [71] *Ibid.*, p. 233.

[72] Brower, personal email correspondence, 17 March 2011.

[73] Roper, *Witch Craze*, p. xi.

of convention and education, not of law and politics ... The baroque imagination, which had made witches fearsome and required their actual death, had finally faded away.[74]

Psychic logic here gives way to the logic of history, individual fantasies are contained within the frames of changed social norms, and a coherent narrative is imposed on what has been a story of the 'unruly' unconscious.

This account of change, although it does not eclipse the book's emphasis on the operations of fantasy and unconscious influences on behaviour, suggests a certain collective conformity of individual imagination and desire to objective conditions. On the one hand, fantasy has been the primary focus and explanation for people's 'acts of appalling ferocity against apparently harmless old women'.[75] 'Witchcraft was a fantasy ... it had deep roots in the unconscious. The fantasies of witchcraft were formed in a particular period of European culture, but they drew their force from their relationship to the primary material of infantile experience, feelings about feeding and eating, about where the body of the child begins and the mother's ends, about emptiness and death.'[76] On the other hand, the end of witchcraft is attributed to conditions that surely influence, but are also external to these concerns. What is the relationship between infantile experience and cultural custom? There is a necessary and uneasy tension around the question of how and under what conditions psyches change and of how (and which) psychic elements taken to be universal matter in the making of history.

The productive incommensurability of psychoanalysis and history emerges in the course of *Witch Craze*. Psychoanalysis provides a way of thinking about fantasy as a universal human psychic operation and so brings the puzzle of witchcraft past into the understanding of present-day readers. Its elements are familiar, and they include aggression, anxiety (about sexual difference, birth and death), the displacements enabled by humour, the difficulty of drawing sharp lines between illusion and reality, and the notion that pleasure can be found in experiences of terror and pain. History provides the repertoire of language and imagery to situated actors; it gives them collective preoccupations even as they are experienced in peculiarly individual terms. It also provides historians with a way of thinking about long-term or large-scale processes of change.

But the conceptions we have of change, rooted as they are in modernist demands of narrative and periodization, can serve to distract us from the insights psychoanalysis provides.[77] The 'unruly' unconscious

[74] *Ibid.*, p. 251. [75] *Ibid.*, p. xi. [76] *Ibid.*, p. 10.

[77] K. Davis, *Periodization and Sovereignty: How Ideas of Feudalism and Secularization Govern the Politics of Time* (Philadelphia: University of Pennsylvania Press, 2008).

gets tamed by the requirements of narrative. Historical time has different rules from the time of the psyche. Thus, Roper concludes *Witch Craze* with a discussion of the reasons for the end of fantasies about witchcraft, and, in so doing, implies that the forces of 'history' tamed the psychic excesses of early modern Europe. The arrival of modernity relegated the questions of sex and reproduction, fear and damnation, to matters of individual psychology; in the course of these developments, fantasies of witchcraft declined and disappeared.[78] The implication, if not the actual conclusion, is that collective obsessions of the kind described in the book – perhaps the very phenomenon of fantasy itself – belong to another age; the fantasies of these early modern 'others' serve to confirm our own fantasies of a new and improved modernity. We are likely to forget Roper's introductory assertions about fantasy as a perpetual feature of the human psyche and instead conclude that it is a historical artefact. Despite her best intentions, Roper's story can be read as effectively consigning fantasy (along with witchcraft) to an era long past.[79]

There is no easy resolution to this lack of fit between the disciplines. Instead it provides the ground for continued conversation and debate about the possibilities, and also the limits, of a collaboration between the different temporalities of psychoanalysis and of history. Recognizing these limits can have the paradoxical effect not of securing boundaries but of loosening them. Certeau referred to history-writing as a form of labour that necessarily addressed the ambiguities and tensions inherent in any confrontation with the past. Writing becomes, for him, a way of 'working through' these matters, but never finally resolving them (death is the only resolution). This 'working through' provokes critical assessment not only of what counts as knowledge within disciplinary parameters, but also of how that knowledge is produced through interdisciplinarity. The point of such interdisciplinarity, writes Brian Connolly, 'should be to live in the incommensurable interstices of disciplines'.[80] That often unsettled, but tremendously exciting, place is where rethinking can occur, a rethinking that 'makes history', in the sense both of its writing and of effecting change.

78 Roper, *Witch Craze*, p. 256.

79 I would have been happier with a conclusion that gestured to the effects of fantasy in later periods of history, the one, for example, that made working women the object of collective fear and solicitude (witness in France Jules Simon's 1861 tract called, fittingly 'L'Ouvrière: Mot impie, sordide'), or the various nineteenth-century obsessions with the masturbatory excesses of young single men, or, for that matter, since Germany is Roper's focus, the recurring fantasies there about the dangers Jews posed for their fellow countrymen.

80 Brian Connolly, personal email correspondence, 15 March 2011.

3 Bringing the brain into history: behind Hunt's and Smail's appeals to neurohistory

Jeremy T. Burman

The value of a tighter connection between psychology, neuroscience and history is to afford an approach that I have elsewhere called 'history from within'.[1] This label was intended to describe the approach sought by Lynn Hunt in her recent essay on the 'experience' of revolution: she asked historians to try to engage with *what it was like* in the past, rather than just engaging with historical texts.[2] In this, she sought to understand how historians 'project' their intuition, and how present understanding is leveraged, in order to enable the historian to step into a world from the past.

Hunt explains her position by way of reference to the notion of a 'paradigm', which she uses in the sense of Thomas Kuhn's highly influential book, *The Structure of Scientific Revolutions*.[3] There, building on his earlier work, Kuhn argued that what-it-is-which-makes-meaning is not limited

[1] J. T. Burman, 'History from within? Contextualizing the new neurohistory and seeking its methods', *History of Psychology*, 15 (2012), 84–99. This chapter is an abridged, reworked, and updated version of that article. I am grateful to the American Psychological Association for permission to use the article as the basis for what appears here. In addition, references to 'what it is like' allude to Thomas Nagel's classic article on mental states and experience: T. Nagel, 'What is it like to be a bat?', *The Philosophical Review*, 83 (1974), 435–450. The consequence of including this, here, is that the larger philosophical purpose of this chapter is to argue that 'organization' is a key missing component in materialist theories of mind. Providing evidence for the differences and similarities in this organization, in terms of grouping, is thus a key 'neurohistorical' contribution. The appeal to Nagel then also implicitly accepts that we may not ourselves be able to have the Other's experience as a kind of felt-subjectivity; we must instead assume *that* it makes sense to that group, then uncover *how* it makes sense. Indeed, that is what makes 'history from within' a kind of *history*. It is also what makes it necessary to address the incommensurability problem, which in turn provides the connection back to Kuhn (whom Hunt cites).

[2] L. Hunt, 'The experience of revolution', *French Historical Studies*, 32 (2009), 671–8.

[3] T. S. Kuhn, *The Structure of Scientific Revolutions* (Chicago, IL: University of Chicago Press, 1962); see also L. L. Downs, 'Lynn Hunt, de la Révolution française à la révolution féministe: entretien avec Laura Lee Downs [Lynn Hunt, From the French Revolution to the Feminist Revolution: Interview with Laura Lee Downs], *Travail, Genre et Sociétés*, 10 (2003), 16. Available online at www.cairn.info/revue-travail-genre-et-societes-2003-2.htm [accessed 8 March 2013].

to the evidence at hand. Rather, the act of interpretation is embedded in a cultural framework composed of examples of previously successful attempts. In other words, for Kuhn, interpretation is a function of projecting evidence through an implicit a-priori 'thought collective' and then reading the implications.[4] This then not only provides the basis for shared belief, such as in a 'scientific knowledge claim', but also for shared feeling (a kind of aesthetics).

This separation between these two kinds of experience – scientific and aesthetic – is important to make because Kuhn did not intend his system to apply to non-scientific knowledge. Still, though, both are experienced by individuals. And, as has come to be generally accepted, an individual's beliefs and feelings are a function of the state of their brain; their separation from it dismissed as 'Descartes' error'.[5]

By making explicit that 'knowing' and 'feeling' are both materially caused by the brain, the intent of the proposal Hunt endorsed – the 'new neurohistory' – reaches beyond that of previous attempts to blend history with psychology. Its goal is to find a way to inject into the interpretation of historical evidence new possibilities for meaning-making; to help historians understand what it felt like to be *there, then*; to encourage historians to ask new questions, while at the same time being constrained in new ways. It is thus intended to augment present contextualist approaches and, in a strong sense, seeks to offer a means of universalizing the resulting stories. For, after all, every historical actor has had a brain, so – argue the proponents of neurohistory – why not use that common factor as a means to make the narratives commensurable?

The problem

Hunt's present desire to focus on historically situated *individual-feeling* is derived from her work on the history of human rights.[6] Her challenge in that earlier book was in justifying a claim that the appearance at the end of the eighteenth century of an interest in universal rights was *causally tied* to the emergence, as a result of reading by the mass public, of *socially-directed* individual-feeling. That new experience then afforded a broadening of what David Hume and Adam Smith at the time called 'sympathy' (or, using a related term that is more consistent with my reading of Hunt's larger argument, of what Theodor Lipps and Edward Titchener

[4] See also T. S. Kuhn, 'Foreword', in L. Fleck (ed.), *Genesis and Development of a Scientific Fact* (Chicago, IL: University of Chicago Press, 1979), pp. vii–xi.

[5] A. R. Damasio, *Descartes' Error: Emotion, Reason, and the Human Brain* (New York: G. P. Putnam, 1994).

[6] L. Hunt, *Inventing Human Rights: a History* (New York: W. W. Norton, 2007).

later called 'empathy').[7] In short, her argument was that reading caused a broader concern for the Other, but felt as deeply as if it were concern for oneself or one's family.

To make Hunt's case simply, since that background is tied intimately to her present call, we will begin with the less controversial of her two claims: a new form of writing was invented in the late eighteenth century that enabled readers to enter into a sympathetic relationship with a fictional protagonist. This new invention, the epistolary novel (storytelling using diary entries and letters), provided the means for the reader to directly experience another's mind by making visible the contents of that Other's consciousness. The new visibility of feelings then encouraged an abstraction: a mental leap of the form, 'my feelings are identical with this Other's feelings, which means that they must feel as I would in the situation described'. And this led to the identification by the reader with that character's emotional and mental states: the reader was made to feel morally commensurable with the Other whose 'mind' they read, enabling them to 'project' themselves into that Other's experiential milieu. The advance made by the epistolary novel was therefore to cause a shift, among readers, from emotional solipsism and the chauvinism of tribal ties to a kind of shared intersubjectivity.

Hunt's suggestion in *Inventing Human Rights* is not that *empathy* was *invented* as a result of the appearance of this new literary form. Rather, her suggestion is that the epistolary novel enabled the universalization of a pre-existing predisposition to feel; that the new literary form parasitized an already-existing human capacity for sympathy and extended it to apply beyond the circle of close relations; that it provided a new way to make individual meaning at the social level. This *expansion*, she argues, is what then enabled the eighteenth-century *extension* of human rights to all Others. To wit: if you are like me, brother, then we should both be free and treated equally – *liberté, égalité, fraternité.*

Her larger claim, however, is unthinkable under the current historiographic paradigm. And she recognizes this: 'there is no easy or obvious way to prove or even measure the effect of new cultural experiences on eighteenth-century people, much less on their conception of rights'.[8] There is, in other words, a lacuna in method: there is no way to show *causation.* As a result, she also has no way to defend from scepticism the implication that this new way of reading 'had physical effects that transplanted into brain changes and came back as new concepts about the organization of social and political life'.[9] And it is this interest that led to her endorsement of an attempt to bring the brain, as material cause, into history.

[7] See G. Jahoda, 'Theodor Lipps and the shift from "sympathy" to "empathy"', *Journal of the History of the Behavioral Sciences*, 41 (2005), 151–63.

[8] Hunt, *Inventing Human Rights*, p. 32. [9] *Ibid.*, p. 33.

The endorsement

What Hunt ultimately calls for is a historiography of *felt meaning*, rather than of *the doer* or *the done-to*. Yet this is not so much an expansion of the call to do 'history from below' as it is for a new kind of history, which is why I offered a new label: 'history from within'. And although this seems like it would produce results reminiscent of Alain Corbin's wonderful examination of the relationship between olfaction and the social imagination, or Steven Shapin's more recent move towards a cultural history of the 'goodness' of wines, Hunt calls instead for a history of the experiencing individual self: 'An historicization of sensation, if you will'.[10] The challenge, then, is to find a set of methodological tools that could bind these changing individual experiences together in a historical narrative. This, she suggests, is where neuroscience might add value: it would provide a pivot around which meaningful experiences could be understood to change in different contexts.

Hunt thus summarizes her purpose in plain language: 'I am insisting that any account of historical change must in the end account for the alteration of individual minds.'[11] As she interprets its value for historians, a neurological approach to history might offer a way to do this: a way to speak about past events that takes into account the biological underpinnings which, in any given context, cause the *feeling* of *what it was like*.[12]

The goal of her incorporation of brains into history is therefore, in a sense, to give historians a new tool to 'read' the *minds* of Others; a way to interpret historical evidence from the perspective of what it would have been like to *feel it*. But this is not a strictly brain-based proposal. Indeed, its success or failure will be driven primarily by how readers understand the underlying appropriation from evolutionary theory, as well as its reliance on some implicit philosophical arguments (namely, a means of overcoming Kuhnian incommensurability).

[10] A. Corbin, *The Foul and the Fragrant: Odor and the French Social Imagination*, trans. M. L. Kochan, R. Porter and C. Prendergast (Cambridge, MA: Harvard University Press, 1986); S. Shapin, 'The tastes of wine: Toward a cultural history', *Rivista di Estetica*, 52 (2012), 49–94 See also S. Shapin, 'The sciences of subjectivity', *Social Studies of Science*, 42 (2012), 170–184. The quotation is my translation of Hunt in Downs, 'Lynn Hunt, from the French Revolution to the feminist revolution', p. 21.

[11] Hunt, *Inventing Human Rights*, p. 34.

[12] The further allusion, after Nagel, is to a typical reference in such discussions: A. Damasio, *The Feeling of What Happens: Body and Emotion in the Making of Consciousness* (New York: Harcourt Brace, 1999). My point here, though, is to problematize what is there offered as an explanation. The neuroscience, alone, is insufficient.

The argument

The 'new neurohistory' proposal was first discussed by Hunt in November 2006 as part of her Natalie Zemon Davis Lectures at the Central European University in Budapest.[13] There, she referred to an argument presented in a then-unpublished manuscript by Daniel Lord Smail.[14] And, indeed, Smail's presentation is so intimately tied up with Hunt's present call for revolution that it is worth reviewing in detail.

Underlying Smail's argument is a view of evidence that is similar to Hunt's. Indeed, for Smail, it is the evidentiary *trace* – not just texts – which makes historical studies empirical (and thus, also, a reflection of unseen causes). Archaeology is like this, he explains: it treats sedimentary layers as if they were an archive. As a result, evidence can be dated, extracted and 'read'. The same standards apply to genetics. Some of the resulting found-objects are inherently meaningful. Others are not.

If, at the top of the hierarchy of evidence, we replace documents with *traces* in general, then we widen the scope of the kinds of stories historians can tell. Doing so requires only that we eliminate *omniscient* intentionality as a historical virtue. Since this is already underway in some quarters, such as through the banishing of Great Man histories, Smail's purpose in this respect can be achieved simply by making his point explicit:

> as most historians recognize, documents are not necessarily used only for what authors intend to put in them. Some of the richest historical information comes from documents that are made to reveal the information they unintentionally possess. There is very little distinction between documents and the sorts of unintentional traces examined by archaeologists and geneticists when the information is handled in this inferential way.[15]

The result, then, is a small shift in how we interpret historical objects: from what an object *says* to *what it implies*. By this shift, trace evidence becomes fuel for the engine of historical inference. But Smail goes further. He also turns to the material cause underlying interpretation: the brain. And he does so in the context of what he sees as the 'biological turn'.[16]

Smail suggests that the implicit biological model underlying most historical scholarship was provided originally by Lamarck. His theory of

[13] This was published as L. Hunt, *Measuring Time, Making History* (Budapest: Central European University Press, 2008).

[14] This later became D. L. Smail, *On Deep History and the Brain* (Berkeley: University of California Press, 2008).

[15] *Ibid.*, p. 59.

[16] See, for instance, M. Fitzhugh and W. Leckie Jr, 'Agency, postmodernism, and the causes of change', *History and Theory* 40 (2001), 59–81; cited in Smail, *On Deep History*, p. 114.

evolution through the inheritance of acquired characteristics proposes, in broad strokes, that natural change occurs as a result of passing down the effects of past effortful actions. (The famous caricature: giraffes have long necks because their ancestors were forced to stretch to reach the leaves on the tallest trees, so the habit and its associated structures got passed down.) Such a position is useful, historiographically, because it allows for individual agency and unintended consequences. At the same time, however, it is also inconsistent with the historian's aim because – as Smail explains – it is driven by a fundamental presentism: 'if there *has* been progress, then that progress can be explained by virtue of the inheritance of acquired assets'.[17] This circularity is a problem: other possible material causes become unthinkable.

In his approach to history, Smail skirts around the implicit Lamarckism.[18] After this, and recognizing that culture is the primary source of human behavioural change, the question then becomes one of determining what it is that culture *is* biologically: *what is it that historians are really talking about when they reconstruct the contexts in which their actors act?* (Or, in terms more consistent with our examination of Hunt's goals, *what conceptual framework ought to inform the intuition used to 'read' historical experiences?*)

In attempting to engage such questions, Smail dismisses the popular misunderstanding of memes-as-idea-viruses.[19] Instead, he endorses Richard Dawkins' later proposal regarding what he called 'the extended phenotype'.[20] In Smail's reading, this then becomes justification for the claim that cultural phenomena can have biological effects: 'Certain species of parasites that hijack the neural pathways of their hosts provide

But see also R. Leys, 'The turn to affect: A critique', *Critical Inquiry* 37 (2011), 434–472; N. Rose and J. M. Abi-Rached, *Neuro: The New Brain Sciences and the Management of the Mind* (Princeton University Press, 2013).

17 Smail, *On Deep History*, p. 83, emphasis in the original.

18 A different approach, leading to similar ends, is provided by J. Burman, 'Updating the Baldwin Effect: the biological levels behind Piaget's New Theory', *New Ideas in Psychology*, 31 (2013), 363–373. There, the biological theory is updated and integrated with Jean Piaget's view of the development of knowledge. Because Piaget and Kuhn overlap in many respects, showed in an earlier essay, the results seem fully compatible with what is discussed here. See J. Burman, 'Piaget no "remedy" for Kuhn, but the two should be read together', comment on Tsou's 'Piaget vs. Kuhn on Scientific Progress', *Theory & Psychology*, 17 (2007), 721–32.

19 See J. Burman, 'The misunderstanding of memes: biography of an unscientific object, 1976–1999', *Perspectives on Science*, 20 (2012), 75–104.

20 This is the idea that the effective reach of genes extends beyond the individual body; that all behaviour – and its material and cultural products, including their effects on different species (in both symbiotic and parasitic relationships) – can be viewed as a consequence of natural historical processes. R. Dawkins, *The Extended Phenotype: the Long Reach of the Gene*, 2nd revised edn (Oxford University Press, 1999).

the classic examples in biology, but the principle extends to other kinds of interactions, such as birdsong.'[21] Yet Smail then connects this to an evolutionary model that, in its historical form, appears decidedly non-Dawkinsian: 'exaptation'.[22]

It is ultimately 'exaptation' that provides the biological foundation for Smail's argument. It also provides the necessary justification for Hunt's turn towards the brain. To understand both sides of the story fully, therefore, we must also understand this.

The term itself was introduced in 1982 by Steven Jay Gould and Elizabeth Vrba to distinguish between sub-types in the category of natural phenomena called 'adaptations'. The reason for its introduction follows from two assumptions: (*a*) the generation of structures is driven, in evolution, by natural selection. But (*b*) present use is driven by functional value irrespective of origins: inherited structures are used for whatever they are good for now, not for whatever reasons led to their inheritance.[23] Gould and Vrba therefore suggested that this coopted present use (*b*) be recognized – when it is unrelated to the causes of its generation (*a*) – as a subject worthy of examination in its own right. So they gave it a name: 'exaptation'.[24]

The value of making the distinction between exaptation and adaptation, when encountering apparently adaptive features, is that it reopens debate. Indeed, the very recognition that something is an exaptation – that natural change occurs with more nuance than what is usually understood from the phrase 'blind variation and selective retention' – enables the asking of new questions. And that is exactly how Smail uses the idea.

Smail proposes that we adopt what I have called 'the *exaptive stance*' in examining the relationship between the human brain and human culture.[25] Briefly, then: the brain did not initially evolve *in order to produce*

21 Smail, *On Deep History*, p. 97.

22 See K. Sterelny, *Dawkins vs. Gould: Survival of the Fittest* (Cambridge: Icon, 2001), for a review of why and how the two positions – and the larger systems in which the extended phenotype and exaptation became thinkable – are understood to be in conflict.

23 Following S. Gould and R. Lewontin, 'The Spandrels of San Marco and the Panglossian Paradigm: a critique of the Adaptationist Programme', *Proceedings of the Royal Society B: Biological Sciences*, 205 (1979), 581–98.

24 S. Gould and E. Vrba, 'Exaptation: a missing term in the science of form', *Paleobiology*, 8 (1982), 4–15; see also S. Gould, 'Exaptation – a crucial tool for an evolutionary psychology', *Journal of Social Issues*, 47 (1991), 43–65.

25 If we accept this stance, even if only as a way to ask new questions, then the human brain can also be reconceived as a kind of exaptive mechanism: it spins off evolutionarily unintended consequences almost constantly (i.e. the brain is 'creative'). And this, in turn, has two interpretations. Following Dawkins, these productions are simply extensions of the human phenotype; uninteresting consequences of the long reach of the gene. From this first perspective, therefore, exaptive spin-offs can be reduced and dismissed: since no structure can emerge except through natural selection, it is unnecessary to be concerned

culture. Following Gould and Vrba, in other words, culture is not – formally – an adaptation. Rather, it is an exaptation that came to be selected-for, and then became 'entrenched'.[26] Human brains and human culture thus co-evolved, shaping each other through a process that is more familiarly called 'the Baldwin Effect'.[27]

The Baldwin Effect, in its simplest form, is the process whereby behavioural changes (such as those caused by a learning brain) in turn cause a change in the selection pressures, which are themselves understood to cause evolution by natural selection. The result is a kind of looping: if individual learning can be shared through teaching, or more simply through imitation, then the imitating–learning–teaching population moves further and further away from its original pressured-position. This has been advanced as the explanation for a huge number of natural changes that would otherwise be difficult to explain.[28] Indeed, that Smail makes the connection between the Baldwin Effect and exaptation is what justifies Hunt's claim that reading could, by its impact on the imitating–learning–teaching brain, lead to the universalizing of human rights: 'The feelings that wash through your body when you read a particularly good novel ... are entirely exaptive.'[29] Less obliquely, however, this is because – as an extension of the human phenotype, following Dawkins – culture serves to modulate and regulate the brains of others; it serves as a source of 'downward completion'.[30]

Smail then provides the connection back to our larger discussion:

> The exaptive capacity of the human brain-body system to be modulated by behaviors of this kind is central to the idea of neurohistory. Behaviors and the institutions that accompany them are crucial components of any human culture, though the institutions clearly vary from one culture to the next. The human capacity to have culture, to this extent, has been built on neurophysiology.[31]

with functions and therefore with the brain's role in history. Events simply unfold, following a pattern determined by natural selection. Following Gould and Vrba, however, it is the brain's (and evolution's) tendency to produce unintended consequences which makes a non-deterministic history possible. And that is very exciting indeed: the observable structures of culture are not *necessary*, except with respect to how they have had functional value and thereby became entrenched (i.e. they are 'pseudo-necessary'). This then aligns our biology with our epistemology.

[26] See also W. Wimsatt, *Re-Engineering Philosophy for Limited Beings: Piecewise Approximations to Reality* (Cambridge, MA: Harvard University Press, 2007).

[27] See T. Deacon, *The Symbolic Species: the Co-evolution of Language and the Brain* (New York: Norton, 1997).

[28] See especially B. Weber, and D. Depew (eds.), *Evolution and Learning: the Baldwin Effect Reconsidered* (Cambridge, MA: Bradford/MIT Press, 2003).

[29] Smail, *On Deep History*, p. 128.

[30] Burman, 'Updating the Baldwin Effect'.

[31] Smail, *On Deep History*, p. 128.

To put it another way: the combination of exaptation and the Baldwin Effect provides the means for high-level effects (cultural norms) to shape low-level causes (brains), top-down, in a way that then also becomes causal of future effects (bottom-up). From this perspective, the new neurohistory proposal therefore offers a new way to think about the sort of circular, looping causality implied by interacting bio-cultural systems.

What does this contribute to history?

Histories based on texts tell stories about the activities of minds in context. But such stories do not tell the complete history of humanity. That history goes deeper, into the earliest sedimentary layers of our existence as feeling creatures. Recognizing this, Smail attempts to transcend the disciplinary division between history and not-history (e.g. archaeology) by transcending Cartesian dualism: by recognizing that *the mind*, the producer of history, is *what the brain is doing*.[32]

From this perspective, micro-histories of minds are necessarily about brains-in-context. Yet Smail is also explicit in making clear that he does not argue for the emergence of an evolutionary psychohistory: 'evolutionary psychologists, working in the manner of Sigmund Freud, have tried to explain behaviours that otherwise seem inexplicable or pathological'.[33] His purpose is not to diagnose biological problems through their manifestation as cultural phenomena.[34] In fact, in advancing a 'new' neurohistory, Smail follows our new conception of causality among biocultural kinds to completely reverse the old reading of the biological–cultural divide:

[32] For those readers trained in contemporary neuroscientific approaches to psychological phenomena, this assumption will seem entirely reasonable. It can also be useful, if we adopt the exaptive stance: it allows us 'to see' previous attempts to construct something like a neurohistory, see J. Peterson, *Maps of Meaning: the Architecture of Belief* (New York: Routledge, 1999). Yet others will find it problematic. Regrettably, there is no space here to delve into this as a metaphysical disagreement. Interested readers are directed instead toward Fernando Vidal's suggestion that 'brainhood' is a modern ideology, as well as Eran Klein's discussion of 'neuroscepticism'. My own position is closer to Ken Gergen's and Christina Toren's; namely, that discussions about brains are also about the embeddedness of brains in history and context. F. Vidal, 'Brainhood, anthropological figure of modernity', *History of the Human Sciences*, 22 (2009), 5–36; E. Klein, 'Is there a need for clinical neuroskepticism?' *Neuroethics*, 4 (2011), 251–9; K. J. Gergen, 'The acculturated brain', *Theory & Psychology*, 20 (2010), 795–816; C. Toren, 'Anthropology and psychology', in R. Fardon, J. Gledhill, O. Harris, R. Marchand, M. Nuttall, C. Shore and M. Strathern (eds.), *Handbook of Social Anthropology* (New York: Sage, 2012).

[33] Smail, *On Deep History*, p. 141.

[34] *Contra* A. Ione and C. Tyler (2003), 'Was Kandinsky a synesthete?', *Journal of the History of the Neurosciences*, 12 (2003), 223–6.

> Culture is made possible by the plasticity of human neurophysiology. With this insight, we can finally dispense with the idea, once favoured by some historians, that biology gave way to culture with the advent of civilization. This has it all backward. Civilization did not bring an end to biology. Civilization *enabled* important aspects of human biology.[35]

In other words, culture affords new opportunities for high-functioning.

Culture makes *value* possible, thereby making different structures possible to select-for naturally, or sexually, and so on. That culture enables biology is an effect of exaptation: culture can make functional different biological structures at different times and in different ways. Thus, for Smail, that which makes it possible to incorporate the brain into history also affords new ways to think about culture and the human condition that has arisen therefrom. Culture itself – not just texts – is therefore the source of constraint in this new historiographic paradigm, expanding the evidentiary possibilities well beyond what one would normally find in the usual regolith examined by disciplinary historians.

To summarize: as selection pressures change (through the imposition of the Baldwin Effect), different biological predispositions are exapted for use. These exaptations not only then change our biology in ways that are consistent with the shifting of the extant selection pressures, but – in so far as they affect the brain – they also provide the lenses through which changing contexts are 'read' and have meaning. The value proposition of neurohistory for historians is therefore in using these insights to engage critically with the implicit folk psychologies we bring to our interpretations of evidence. At this point, however, we are without a means to do this formally: neurohistory, as it is reflected in the writings of Hunt and Smail, is an ideal. If disciplinary historians are to benefit, then there must be a neurohistorical method to be implemented.

Towards method

The promise of neurohistory for Hunt's new paradigm is in its provision of tools for thinking about the *feeling of what happened* and, more generally, in what it affords for storytelling. But if we are to implement this, and thereby use neurohistory to *do* history (rather than just talking about doing it), these tools must be made explicit. So far, however, very little progress has been made in that direction; indeed, that is the value of this volume.

Rather than chasing the vivid imagery presented in the conclusion of Smail's *On Deep History*, which is still sketchy in many of its details, a

[35] Smail, *On Deep History*, p. 155, emphasis in the original.

much closer approximation of an explicitly neurohistorical method can be 'read out' of one of his earlier works: *Imaginary Cartographies*.[36] This book presented a tool for thinking about late-medieval Marseillaise property records, which would seem on its face to be unrelated to the present concern. Yet Smail did in fact make a connection to the brain: he appealed to an argument from evolutionary psychology suggesting that the predisposition towards mapping is a human universal resulting from how the brain works.[37] This earlier book can therefore be tied to the present discussion, and 'read in' to the new neurohistory, as we attempt to follow the implications of his argument as it has developed.

Since there was no map of Marseille in the fourteenth and fifteenth centuries (or at least none we would presently recognize), Smail constructed an 'imaginary cartography' from the language used by different groups to describe similar locations. The divergences between these descriptions then made visible the territories of social conflict: incommensurable language became a guide to cultural clash.[38]

Yet this does not need 'neurohistory' to be thinkable. Instead, it can be read as if it were the result of taking a late-Wittgensteinian approach to history: different groups 'play' different 'language games'.[39] And this, in turn, is consistent with the late-Kuhnian approach: the playing of different games implies the existence of different conceptual 'worlds'.[40] It was therefore not necessary, *a priori*, to adopt a neuroscientific perspective in order for such a line of questioning to have been pursued. But, since Smail and Hunt wish to move beyond textually driven language games towards something more grounded in experience, aspiring towards a neurohistorical perspective can help us to see these older approaches from a new angle (i.e. adopting the exaptive stance to examine our shared inheritance can help us to ask new questions).

In taking this position, we can reread Smail's argument in *Imaginary Cartographies* through his new proposals. In doing so, his basic insight can be reconceived using the terms excavated above: the invention of

36 D. L. Smail, *Imaginary Cartographies: Possession and Identity in Late Medieval Marseille* (Ithaca, NY: Cornell University Press, 2000).

37 Smail, *Imaginary Cartographies*, p. 6.

38 See J. Burman, 'Convergent plurality or basic incommensurability? (Toward the formalizing of Goertzen's Solution to the 'crisis' in psychology)', *History and Philosophy of Psychology Bulletin*, 20 (2009), 23–8.

39 L. Wittgenstein, *Philosophical Investigations*, 4th rev. edn, trans. G. E. M. Anscombe, P. M. S. Hacker and J. Schulte (Chichester, W. Sussex: Wiley-Blackwell, 2009) [original work published in 1953].

40 See especially T. S. Kuhn, 'Possible worlds in the history of science', in J. Conant and J. Haugeland (eds.), *The Road Since Structure* (Chicago, IL: University of Chicago Press, 2000), pp. 58–89 [original work published in 1989].

illustrated maps resulted from the exaptation of a pre-existing cartographic lexicon. Before there were maps, therefore, there were names for places that reflected not only their location in space but also their social use. But then how can this be made consistent with our updated view of the biological turn?

From a Dawkinsian perspective, both language and maps are an extension of the human phenotype; an artefact of genes selected for the reproductive advantages they provided to ancestors now long dead. From a Gouldian perspective, however, mappish phenomena become something more: they can be understood as having been built upon (i.e. exapted from) an evolutionarily older system for abstracting world-logics. In other words, despite there being many kinds of *langue*, they must all therefore derive their deep grammar from an inherited adaptation: the brain's pre-linguistic action-oriented order-system, exapted and ultimately used both for communication and for mapping (and for music, etc.).[41] Thus, although there are uncountably many possibilities for the production of meaning, the implication is that the *deep structure* underlying representation-in-general has a universal physiological basis and that this inherited biological predisposition is made manifest and shaped to form particulars through use in social interaction.[42]

This provides a sketch of a reasonable brain-based hypothesis describing the cause of Smail's conflicting cartographic *paroles*: although they are similarly constrained, different groups have different histories, vocabularies, cultures and intentions. But, more usefully, it can also be used to approach Hunt's goal of producing a history from within: if there is a grammar of meaningful interaction, then statements *perceived* as ungrammatical will push one's interlocutor *off the shared map*. And indeed, such an experience – if we follow the found-connection between

41 This is how I read Koechlin and Jubault's review of the neurophysiology underlying the bilateral cortical areas that, in the left hemisphere, is occupied in Broca's area by language and, in the right, by music: E. Koechlin and T. Jubault, 'Broca's area and the hierarchical organization of human behavior', *Neuron*, 50 (2006), 963–74; see also A. Patel, 'Language, music, syntax and the brain', *Nature Neuroscience*, 6 (2003), 674–81. This interpretation is supported by simulations run by Christiansen, Chater and Reali, which led to the conclusion that early humans' ability 'to language' evolved from a pre-existing biological substrate that was exapted for a new use: M. Christiansen, N. Chater and F. Reali, 'Restrictions on biological adaptation in language evolution', *Proceedings of the National Academy of Sciences*, 106 (2009), pp. 1015–20. Although not relevant to historians, strictly speaking, the response to Hunt's and Smail's appeals to neuroscience suggests that a minimum amount of due diligence on the brain side is necessary here.

42 This then also seems to synthesize the two major competitive proposals. On the one hand: M. Hauser, N. Chomsky and W. Fitch, 'The faculty of language: what is it, who has it, and how did it evolve?' *Science*, 298 (2002), 1569–79. And, on the other: M. Tomasello, *Constructing a Language: a Usage-Based Theory of Language Acquisition* (Cambridge, MA: Harvard University Press, 2003).

maps, language and music – has a *what-it-is-like-ness* with which we are all familiar: dissonance ('evil').[43] In this, however, we have come to the limit of what can be 'read out'. To go further, we will have to leave the Hunt–Smail lineage and instead engage with the problem Hunt inherits from Kuhn: *what is the sharing of meaning, as the external shaper of 'the experience of revolution', but viewed from the perspective of the brains that make it?*

Enter neurophilosophy

The attempt to bring the brain into history can be compared to a similar project that has since been largely successful in philosophy: in 1986, Patricia Smith Churchland introduced an extended argument about the brain's relevance to discussions of the mind in an attempt to eliminate the implicit folk psychology that had to that point dominated philosophy. This book, *Neurophilosophy*, has since become a classic.[44] Yet it does not provide a method that would be useful to historians; nor does it really explain what meaning *is*. Instead, it lays out the foundations for a new paradigm in philosophy, albeit one with obvious parallels to the ideal to which Hunt appeals.

Churchland, like Hunt and Smail, claims that bringing in the brain will be useful to the extent that it will allow us to ask useful questions. But this is not the only reason to do it, as Smail explained:

> The [brain's] relevance to history is less obvious [than it is to culture], since very few hypotheses deriving from neuropsychology could ever be testable in a historical context. But that's not the point. The point is that historians habitually think with psychology anyway. We are prone to making unguarded assumptions about the psychological states of the people we find in our sources ... Whole works can be shaped by psychological assumptions ... Historians have to make psychological assumptions.[45]

In other words, Smail's drive towards neurohistory is an attempt to address *historians'* implicit folk psychology. Despite this parallel, however, it is clear that many of the ideas of neurophilosophy – indeed, much of neuroscience and its advances – are irrelevant to the historian's task. We need to extract the bits that are not.

43 Peterson, *Maps of Meaning*. See also J. B. Peterson and J. L. Flanders, 'Complexity management theory: motivation for ideological rigidity and social conflict', *Cortext*, 38 (2002), 429–458.

44 P. Smith Churchland, *Neurophilosophy: Toward a Unified Science of the Mind/Brain* (Cambridge, MA: Bradford/MIT Press, 1986).

45 Smail, *On Deep History*, pp. 159–60.

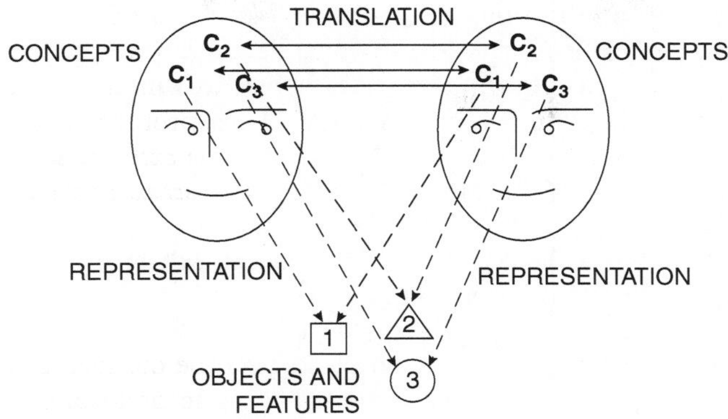

Figure 3.1. 'What is the relation that maps identical conceptual frameworks across individuals?', reproduced from Paul Churchland, 'Neurosemantics: On the Mapping of Minds and the Portrayal of Worlds', in *Neurophilosophy at Work* (Cambridge University Press, 2007), p. 127. Reprinted with author's permission

Neurophilosophy moved a lot closer to providing what historians would need, methodologically, when Paul Churchland built upon the new approach to examine 'meaning'.[46] Indeed, his work in 'neurosemantics' attempts to address the same sort of philosophical problems as those underlying Smail's comparison of the languages informing his imaginary cartographies: if such attempts are to highlight differences accurately, then the mappings must otherwise 'preserve sense, meaning, or semantic identity across the pairings'.[47] Of course, Churchland's purpose goes well beyond what we would need to abstract a neurohistorical method, but – because it allows us to side-step the Kuhnian problem of incommensurability – it will be useful for our larger discussion of Hunt's goal to review some parts of his discussion.[48]

Churchland's goal is to replace the old perspective of the process of meaning-sharing (illustrated in Figure 3.1 by the dashed lines) with a new one derived from his and his collaborators' studies in neurophilosophy (solid lines). In other words, he aims to replace the 'representation'

[46] P. M. Churchland, 'Neurosemantics: on the mapping of minds and the portrayal of worlds', in *Neurophilosophy at Work* (Cambridge University Press, 2007), pp. 126–60.

[47] Churchland, 'Neurosemantics', p. 126.

[48] For Kuhn, incommensurability is an incompatibility of world-views. This can manifest as a language problem, but really it is a problem of conflicting world logics: there is no common factor that can be used to fully translate one world-view into the other. For a more formal definition, as well as a related discussion of how to conceive of conflict between epistemic groups, see J. Burman, 'Convergent plurality'.

of objects with the 'translation' of their meaning. And he does this by examining the idea that, when observing a stimulus, interpreted meaning is a function of concepts that have already been mapped in the networks modelled by the brain's activation patterns.[49]

In other words, neurosemantics is a theory of 'cognitive explanation'. The proposal rests on an argument regarding the identity of the networks constructed in each mind, as a shared concept map, despite their different developmental histories. Meaning can thus be shared without loss or corruption, from his perspective, by the endogenous activation of the features in this shared map: objects in the world are therefore 'read' through the same interpretive lens in each mind (or, more accurately, through the activation of functionally isomorphic networks in each brain). The result, however, is not a commensurability of *structural* brain states; it is rather a commensurability of *functional* semantic states implemented structurally in brains.

Such a perspective supports Hunt's argument about the universalization of human rights, but only if her narrative is reframed to be about the construction of commensurable *mind*-states. Churchland's discussion makes it clear that we cannot make any conclusion, in Hunt's case, regarding the similarity of *brain* states. We can conclude only that it is possible that the new form of reading might have made new connections between semantic (implicative) networks *implemented* in brains; that reading *about feelings* changed how the readers *felt*.[50] Thus, in other words, the readers' brains were made similar in *function*, yet without requiring an equivalently large change in *structure* (i.e., new functional states can be exapted from pre-existing structural causes).

Contrary to first impressions, this does not replicate Descartes' error; separating function from structure is a not a new kind of dualism, since one is a reflection of the other at a different level. Indeed, this perspective has the same effect as what Hunt seeks to achieve: the projected felt-meaning of moral selfness could indeed have expanded to include, in its formerly tight-knit category, all distant Others as a result of the invention of a new vicarious way to feel.

Churchland's contribution to neurohistory, from this perspective, is to support the Kuhnian intuition that the sharing of meaning is tied to

49 Meaning, for Churchland, is thus a function of embodied history.

50 Cf. P. Bal and M. Veltkamp, 'How does fiction reading influence empathy? An experimental investigation on the role of emotional transportation', *PLoS ONE*, 8 (2013), e55341; R. Mar, K. Oatley, M. Djikic and J. Mullin, 'Emotion and narrative fiction: interactive influences before, during, and after reading', *Cognition & Emotion*, 25 (2011), 818–33.; K. Oatley, 'The cognitive science of fiction', *Wiley Interdisciplinary Reviews: Cognitive Science*, 3 (2012), 425–30.

the degree of similarity between the semantic networks implemented by individual brains-in-context. This tells us nothing about *what it was like* to be in that context, of course, but it does give us licence to speak about different groups of people as having had nearly identical experiences so long as it can also be reasonably argued that they had nearly identical semantic maps (i.e. they had similar developmental trajectories in similar contexts). And since *what it was like* for *this* individual is, in large part, indistinguishable – historically – from the experience of any other person in the same group, Churchland's neurosemantic model also thereby justifies broadening our use of evidence in ascribing feeling prosopographically: any context-consistent description of *what it was like* for one person in the category (cf. 'thought collective') will probably do as an approximation for a description of someone else's feeling. Where this does not apply, however, is as follows: (*a*) when that second individual is categorically different; and (*b*) when the context changes, such that the relevant someone (or something) *becomes dissonant* relative to their previous categorical state. Then the narratives need to change, shifting perhaps to a Bachelard-style historiography: searching for 'ruptures', especially of the sort where previously central members have been ejected from their home group (or come to be called 'apostate' and 'heretic').

Despite all of this, however, I suspect that bringing the brain into history will involve much more than did its earlier introduction into philosophy. In this case, it is not so obvious an importation. As a result, the choice of name – 'neurohistory' – may turn out to be an unfortunate one: the use of this prefix sets off too many alarms among the group of sceptics generated by the very success of the Churchlands' programme. Yet it seems clear that the problems with which Hunt and Smail are engaging also go well beyond simply adding 'the brain' to 'history'. This is a different sort of venture than it appears. Or rather, it could be.

History from within

Hunt's call for revolution encourages historians to tell stories of situated, feeling selves. Here, however, we have also been led to the conclusion that there is no distinct *'what it was like'-ness* except for that provided by our shared maps; no knowable historical self beyond what we can infer from embodied, contextually situated neurophysiology. Hunt's sought-after new paradigm, and her endorsement of Smail, can therefore be understood simply as calling for the broadening of how we use evidence in *approximating* feeling across *groups of individuals* in order to ask new kinds of questions.

To extract a sense of *what it was like to be*, the neurohistorian must first place the relevant historical self in context. This is the standard method of cultural history.[51] Once this is accomplished, it then becomes possible – following Kuhn, Wittgenstein and the neurosemantic model – to treat *groups* of individuals-in-context *as if* they would have near-identical orienting responses.[52] In this way, in other words, we can treat them as if they all belong to the same 'feeling collective'. Categorical groupings of evidence can then be constructed; the documentation of feeling (*via* diary entries, letters, court documents, etc.) read from one historical author's hand into the minds of others in the same rigorously reconstructed evidentiary category.[53] This can then afford new insights, which might lead to new questions and new projects.

These sketches of method do not yet achieve Hunt's and Smail's hopes of a history built from a new kind of evidence. But they do allow for some new uses of the old kinds of evidence. From this perspective, for example, the quality of experience is shaped not only by what is known, but also by its consistency with the dominant group aesthetic; by ideas, but also by what is fashionable given the extant 'moral economy'; in

[51] I recognize that it may be controversial to link the two together, neurohistory and cultural history. Yet this is fully consistent with Smail's intent. As a result, I think his comments are worth including: 'A neurohistory is a deep cultural history, offering a way out of the increasingly sterile presentism that constrains the historical imagination' (*On Deep History*, p. 156). That cultural history includes an implicit presentism follows as a result of drawing inferences from the historian's projecting of their folk-psychological notions through reconstructed context. (There is no such thing as a historicist folk-psychology.) Of course, critics will recognize that neuroscience is not historicist either. Its addition to the historian's toolbox simply constrains intuition in a way that fits the present aesthetic. Again, here is Smail's view: 'A neurohistorical approach does not change the objects of study. What it offers is a new interpretive framework' (*ibid.*, p. 185).

[52] D. L. Smail, 'Psychotropy and the patterns of power in human history', in E. Russel (ed.), *Environment, Culture, and the Brain: New Explorations in Neurohistory* (Munich, Germany: Rachel Carson Center, 2012), pp. 43–53. See also Peterson, *Maps of Meaning*, pp. 51–61.

[53] Again, this might be seen as controversial. Here, though, is Smail on the use of categories: 'Comparison cannot take place without broad categories, so to deny the utility of such categories is to deny that there is much point to writing a deep history. For any deep history to succeed, the use of such categories is a necessary evil' (*On Deep History*, p. 197). The challenge, for the historian who chooses to take this approach, will therefore be to avoid constructing misleading categories; see I. Hacking, 'Kinds of people: moving targets', *Proceedings of the British Academy*, 151 (2007), 285–318, on 'human kinds'. Indeed, Thomas Teo suggests that such a misreading of evidence can have more harmful implications than simple miscommunication; he suggests that when categories are constructed of the Other which include negative consequences, then the result can be 'epistemological violence'. This is an important caveat for those who would follow such an approach. T. Teo, 'From speculation to epistemological violence in psychology: a critical-hermeneutic reconstruction', *Theory & Psychology*, 18 (2008), 47–67.

short, by 'norms'.[54] And, in helping to diagnose the dissonances that separate groupings, non-documentary evidence *can* play a role: different kinds of potsherd can provide evidence of a separation between groupings by proving the existence of different aesthetics.

The result might seem to some like a gloss of Michel Foucault's '*épistémè*'.[55] Indeed, Jean Piaget described Foucault's epistemological theory as providing a more general view than Kuhn's.[56] In this connection, however, Hunt is clear: even as she follows Kuhn, what she seeks also goes beyond Foucault.

> Although Foucault gave subjectivity an historical dimension ... he, like many social and cultural historians, always construed historical meaning in cultural and linguistic, that is, collective terms. He portrayed subjectivity as the virtually automatic outgrowth of culture and discourse. He left virtually no space for a willing, desiring individual to shape his or her own destiny, in short, little space for the self as active agent. It is not surprising, therefore, that the many historians inspired by Foucault have fastened on the body, not on the self, even though Foucault himself argued that the body became the subject of regulation because it provided access to the self.[57]

In other words, Hunt can be understood to be seeking a way to speak about the *regulation of the 'meaning-full' self*. Her call therefore leads in the familiar *neo*-Foucauldian direction of power and 'govern-mentality', but from the perspective of individual experience in shared contexts.[58]

Final thoughts

The result of all this is necessarily a psychological project, even while it is historical and neuroscientific. From one perspective, therefore, doing a 'history from within' is an attempt to examine the possible ways of being a self.[59] From another, it is about the ways in which experience can be

54 L. Daston, 'The moral economy of science', *Osiris* 10 (1995), 2–24; Burman, 'Updating the Baldwin Effect'.

55 M. Foucault, *The Order of Things: an Archaeology of the Human Sciences* (New York: Vintage, 1970).

56 J. Piaget, *Structuralism* (trans. C. Maschler) (London: Routledge and Kegan Paul, 1971); see also the discussion in Burman, 'Piaget no "remedy" for Kuhn'.

57 L. Hunt, 'Psychology, psychoanalysis, and historical thought', in L. Kramer and S. Maza (eds.) *A Companion to Western Historical Thought* (Malden, MA: Blackwell, 2002), p. 347.

58 N. Rose, *Inventing our Selves: Psychology, Power, and Personhood* (New York: Cambridge University Press, 1996). Rose and Abi-Rached, *Neuro: The New Brain Sciences and the Management of the Mind.* See also K. D. Markman, T. Proulx, and M. J. Lindberg (eds.), *The Psychology of Meaning* (Washington, DC: American Psychological Association, 2013).

59 Hacking, 'Kinds of people'.

shared across the members of a group.[60] The next step in its evolution, however, will almost certainly be to determine the grammar of experience that sits upon the logic of shared feeling; the question, how to get from groupings to shared aesthetics.

My impression, when I began revising this chapter, was that Jaak Panksepp had provided the basis for this in his 'affective neuroscience'.[61] However, I am not convinced that there is no looping downward completion at work that could serve to reshape the implications afforded by the affective categories that he has identified. Still, though, this cannot be the end of the project: for if death is the 'undiscovered country', as Hamlet suggested, then what is neurohistory but a 'cultural neuroscience' of the past? And if this is the case, then the journey has only just begun. Just as there are insights to be gained by examining the parallels to neurophilosophy, so too will there be insights from cultural neuroscience.[62]

Just because we may not be able to know *what it was like* to be *in* another's group, we can reasonably expect the members of *that group* to know *what it was like*. Furthermore, we can expect the members of the group to react appropriately, even if we do not know what the rules are that they're following. Thus, we might suggest that the task of the neurohistorian is to reconstruct the context in which a coherent logic of feeling can be read across a grouping of individuals. Beyond providing a history of a group's ideas (of their *paradeigma*), this would then also give the neurohistorian a degree of access to their shared aesthetic (*aisthánomai* or, perhaps, *asithesis*). From this, it would then also be possible to set expectations regarding reactions to novel phenomena and unexpected change, which might in turn afford new questions. That said, of course, grouping people in order to access their 'experience' is not new.[63] Only the justification here is new, although perhaps the resulting groupings will also be tighter.

60 K. J. Gergen and M. M. Gergen (eds.), *Historical Social Psychology* (Hillsdale, NJ: Lawrence Erlbaum, 1984).

61 See, most accessibly, J. Panksepp and L. Biven, *The Archaeology of Mind: Neuroevolutionary Origins of Human Emotion* (New York: Norton, 2012).

62 See especially J. Chiao (ed.), *Cultural Neuroscience: Cultural Influences on Brain Function* (Amsterdam: Elsevier, 2009).

63 See E. P. Thompson, *The Making of the English Working Class* (London: V. Gollancz, 1963).

4 The successes and obstacles to the interdisciplinary marriage of psychology and history

Paul H. Elovitz

Knowledge of human motivation has increased enormously as a result of the application of psychology to history, political science and other disciplines. Extensive methodologies have been developed and an enormous psychohistorical literature has been written and published. Yet the comfortable relationship that psychology and history should enjoy usually is absent in academia for a variety of reasons. Professional historians view overt psychodynamic approaches as reductionist and are inclined to think that everyday psychology is sufficient for their work. Academic psychologists, who in America mostly have been defensive about protecting their prerogatives, consider psychoanalysis, upon which psychohistory is overwhelmingly based, to be unscientific and therefore not worthy of consideration. The promise of disciplinary cooperation leading to greater insight into the human condition has been realized in the United States, mostly as a result of the openness of individual historians, psychoanalysts and colleagues from many different disciplines rather than strictly in academic psychology and history. Thus, the enormous body of psychohistorical knowledge is an interdisciplinary accomplishment, not the fruit of cooperative labours of psychology and history departments. This chapter is the story of the marriage of psychology and history, with the leading advocates of this marriage having lost most of the battles and yet winning the war through the dissemination of their concepts.[1]

In the last century, psychology has been applied to history and historical personages to become a part of American consciousness to the point where the language of psychology permeates society. For example, the words and concepts of anxiety, ego, empathy, guilt, id, identity, denial, masochism, narcissism, neurosis, obsessive-compulsiveness, paranoia, post-traumatic stress disorder (PTSD), repression, sadism, superego

1 For reading this chapter and making helpful editorial suggestions, I want to thank Professors David Beisel and Peter Petschauer, as well as Nicole Alliegro and Devin McGinley. Also, my appreciation goes to the innumerable psychohistorical colleagues and students I have worked with in the past four-and-one-half decades.

and the unconscious are everyday terms. Increasing numbers of individuals are exposed to therapies, or are trying to raise their children based on what was said on television by child psychologists. The language of self-help groups borrowed from therapies so permeates our society that there are innumerable references to people or groups 'being in denial', for example. In a culture increasingly laden with psychological terms, the notion of applying psychology to society and history seems commonsensical. When students and the average layperson first encounter the words 'psycho' and 'history' together, they ask, what is it? Then, they usually answer: 'Oh, that makes perfect sense; what a good idea!' To the average individual, the merger of psychology and history is an exciting possibility, but most American academic history and psychology departments have been either lukewarm or hostile to this form of interdisciplinary scholarship. Nevertheless, the insights of the merger are regularly used in writing biography, normally without attribution to this breakthrough. Thus the ideas, methodology and terminology of psychohistory are often adopted without being acknowledged or even while defaming the field. The principles of this work include listening carefully to all of the evidence surrounding a particular topic, event or issue, including evidence of its unconscious aspects. Very much like history, psychohistory concerns itself with beginnings and alterations: both history and psychoanalysis share a concern for origins and a desire to explain decisive turning points in the lives of individuals – famous ones, in the case of history. Psychohistorians focus on childhood, coping mechanisms (the mechanisms of psychic defence), creativity, dreams, group dynamics (and fantasies), psychobiography, psychopathography, psychopolitics, psychoanthropology and trauma. Some classic studies are Alexander and Juliette George, *Woodrow Wilson and Colonel House: a Personality Study*, Erik H. Erikson, *Young Man Luther*, and Robert Jay Lifton, *Death in Life: Survivors of Hiroshima*.[2]

Obstacles to the successful integration of history and psychology go beyond the lack of receptivity in history and psychology departments. They include awe of those with clinical or other psychological expertise and a tendency to overuse technical terminology. So it was with Robert Waite in his *The Psychopathic God: Adolf Hitler*; with Lloyd deMause's claim that psychohistory is a science in 'The Independence of Psychohistory'; with a political bias by Justin Frank leading to the pathologizing of George W.

[2] A. George and J. George, *Woodrow Wilson and Colonel House: a Personality Study* (New York: Dover Publications, 1964); E. H. Erikson, *Young Man Luther* (New York: Norton, 1958); and R. J. Lifton, *Death in Life: Survivors of Hiroshima* (Charlotte, NC: University of North Carolina Press, 1968).

Bush; and with a lack of knowledge of and respect for the expertise of either history or psychology.[3] Experienced practitioners of psychological history are sometimes impatient with discussing theoretical questions and problems of interdisciplinarity because they want to see colleagues focused on their application, doing the challenging work of combining academic disciplines and publishing. Obstacles to the successful marriage of these two disciplines can be overcome by doing good work: writing carefully researched and well-argued papers without much technical terminology. This chapter concentrates on the history of psychohistory in the light of the themes of this book.

Some early steps in applying psychology to history, politics and society

The growing interest in and development of the field of psychology in the late nineteenth century led some scholars in the beginning of the twentieth to apply it to history and society. The American historian James Harvey Robinson called for a 'new history' that drew on economics, psychology and other developing disciplines in order to move beyond describing events and explain the progress of humanity. Robinson was an associate editor of the *American Historical Review* (1912–20) and later president of the American Historical Association (AHA), who was repeatedly cited by various advocates of psychological history as a supporter.

Even before Sigmund Freud arrived in the United States to deliver his famous lectures at Clark University in 1909, elements of American society had opened themselves up to the idea of the unconscious and psychotherapy. The 'Boston School' mostly led the way in this process. James Jackson Putnam and Morton Prince were two of its major figures. Then, in the period between 1904 and 1909, popular and medical interest in psychotherapy became intense, partly as a result of the publication of European texts and Pierre Janet's American lectures in 1904 and 1906.

Putnam eventually practised psychoanalysis, while Prince benefited from Freud's work even as he maintained an independent position. Prince, a Boston neurologist and professor of nervous diseases at the Tufts College Medical School, specialized in dissociative disorder and made a

[3] R. Waite, *The Psychopathic God: Adolf Hitler* (New York: Basic Books, 1977); L. deMause, 'The independence of psychohistory: a symposium', *The History of Childhood Quarterly: The Journal of Psychohistory*, 3 (Fall 1975), 163–200. Richard Lyman's critique of deMause on pp. 184–90 provides an appreciation of deMause's contributions with thoughtful critiques of his tendency to overstate his case on a number of occasions. For George W. Bush see J. A. Frank, *Bush on the Couch: Inside the Mind of the President* (New York: HarperCollins, 2004).

name for himself with his 1905 volume, *The Dissociation of Personality*, and the establishment of the *Journal of Abnormal Psychology* the next year. Neither his study of Roosevelt nor that of the Kaiser is a fully fledged psychobiography or work of political psychology.[4] Yet both studies are fledgling efforts to bring the new field of depth psychology to the public's attention as a valuable instrument for understanding how political leaders' emotional expression represents their unconscious conflicts.

Developments in the Freud circle

The early practitioners of applied psychoanalysis were members of the Freud circle. They were mostly European physicians, psychiatrists and psychoanalysts steeped in history, which led them to use historical examples in their work. An added incentive to move in this direction was that analysis was developing in a tight-knit, mostly Jewish community in which many individuals knew each other. Attributing diagnoses and behaviour to historical figures was a way of deflecting attention from colleagues (or their spouses) who might also be analysands (patients) in training to become analysts. The four volumes of the *Minutes of the Vienna Psychoanalytic Society* reveal a great deal of interest in expanding the psychodynamic paradigm but less in details of psychobiography and psychohistory.[5] The physician Isidor Isaak Sadger (1867–1942) wrote pathographies of poets and others that focused on the effects of disease on the lives of historical personages, stressing failures and faults. They were simplistic and subject to considerable criticism in the Freud group, which in turn may have prompted Freud, Jones and others to write more in-depth psychoanalytic biographies.

In the four years after Freud's return from America, scholars associated with him, mostly in Vienna, published many psychoanalytic articles of well-known personages. These included Sadger on Lenau and von Kleist; Ernest Jones on Shakespeare as revealed in *Hamlet*, von Kleist, the artist Del Sarto and Louis Bonaparte; Oskar Pfister on Count von Zinzendorf and Margareta Ebner; Karl Abraham on Giovanni Segantini (1911) and Amenhotep IV (1913); Max Graf on Richard Wagner, Edward Hitschmann on Schopenauer, and Ludwig Jekels on Napoleon I.[6] Although today one might consider these studies

[4] M. Prince, *The Psychology of the Kaiser: a Study of His Sentiments and His Obsession* (Boston, MA: R. G. Badger, 1915). See also 'Roosevelt as analyzed by the new psychology', *New York Times Magazine* (24 March 1912), SM1–2.

[5] See H. Nunberg and E. Federn (eds.), *Minutes of the Vienna Psychoanalytic Society*, vol. I: *1906–1908* (Madison, CT: International Universities Press, 1962), pp. 256–69.

[6] I. Sadger, *Aus Dem Liebesleben Nicolaus Lenaus* (Leipzig: Franz Deuticke, 1909); I. Sadger, *Heinrich Von Kleist: Eine Pathographisch-Psychologische Studie* (J. F. Bergmann, 1910); E. Jones, *Essays in Applied Psycho-Analysis* (London: The International Psycho-analytic

poorly researched, some were valuable applications of psychoanalytic studies to history and society. *Imago*, a psychoanalytic journal established by Freud, became a ready medium for many of these scholars.

Freud's endeavours in psychohistory and psychobiography were quite evocative, but flawed as history. In 1910, he wrote *Leonardo Da Vinci and a Memory of His Childhood*, spelling out his concept of psychobiography.[7] Alan Elms, a rare American academic psychologist who openly admired Freud, pointed out his strengths as a psychoanalytic historian, arguing that Freud was innovative in a variety of different ways.[8] These included the systematic use of motivational theory to probe a subject, the utilization of psychoanalytic techniques to interpret biographical data, the move beyond the psychological limitations and failures of the subject to focus on his or her positive characteristics and achievements, the establishment of significant guidelines in conducting psychohistorical research, and in providing guidelines for psychohistorical study. Among Freud's other excursions into psychobiography were '*The Moses of Michelangelo*', Goethe's childhood, Dostoevsky's gambling and '*Moses and Monotheism*'.[9] Because the founder of psychoanalysis did not understand Egyptian history and Moses' life, he could have saved himself a considerable amount of criticism if he had stayed with his original title, 'The Man Moses: a Historical Novel'. Elms pointed out the extent to which 'Sigmund

Press, 1923); O. Pfister, *Die Frömmigkeit des Grafen Ludwig von Zinzendorf* (Leipzig and Vienna: Deuticke, 1910); O. Pfister, 'Hysterie und Mistik bei Margareta Ebner (1291–1351)', *Zentralblatt Für Psychoanalyse*, 1 (1910); K. Abraham, 'Giovanni Segantini: a psycho-analytical study', in C. Hilda and M. D. Abraham (eds.), *Clinical Papers and Essays on Psycho-Analysis* (London: The Hogarth Press and the Institute of Psychoanalysis, 1955); K. Abraham, 'Amenhotep IV. Psycho-analytical contributions towards the understanding of his personality and of the monotheistic cult of Aton', in C. Hilda and M. D. Abraham (eds.), *Clinical Papers and Essays on Psycho-Analysis* (London: The Hogarth Press and the Institute of Psychoanalysis, 1955), pp. 262–91; M. Graf, *Richard Wagner im 'Fliegenden Holländer': Ein Beitrag zur Psychologie künstlerischen Schaffens* (Leipzig and Vienna: F. Deuticke, 1911); E. Hitschmann, *Great Men: Psychoanalytic Studies* (International Universities Press, 1956); L. Jekels, 'Der Wendepunkt im Leben Napoleons I', *Imago*, 3 (1914), 313–81.

[7] S. Freud, *Leonardo Da Vinci and a Memory of His Childhood* (London: Routledge & Kegan Paul, 1957).

[8] A. C. Elms, 'Sigmund Freud, psychohistorian', in J. A. Weiner and J. W. Anderson (eds.), *Psychoanalysis and History* (Hillsdale, NJ: Analytic Press, 2003), pp. 65–78. In contrast to clinical psychologists who treat patients, academic psychologists have not been very open to Freudian ideas.

[9] S. Freud, 'The Moses of Michelangelo', in J. Strachey (ed. and trans.), *The Standard Edition [SE] of the Complete Psychological Works of Sigmund Freud*, vol. XIII (London: Hogarth Press), pp. 209–38; S. Freud, 'A childhood recollection from *Dichtung und Wahrheit*', *SE*, vol. XVII, pp. 145–56; S. Freud, 'Dostoyevsky and parricide', *SE*, vol. XXI, pp. 175–96; S. Freud, 'Moses and monotheism', *SE*, vol. XXIII, pp. 3–137.

Freud always regarded his own psychohistories with serious reservations, and he repeatedly apologized for their flaws'.[10]

Smith, Clark, Barnes and two emigrés in America

Preserved Smith deserves to be designated as America's first fully fledged psychobiographer for his article, 'Luther's Early Development in the Light of Psycho-analysis', published in 1913.[11] In this essay, he used his expertise as a Reformation historian and a detailed knowledge of Freud's writing to explore Luther's childhood, personality, obsession with the devil and struggles with sexual desire. While this study is exceptional for the period, subsequently Smith did not write explicit psychohistory. All the same, as Elizabeth Wirth Marvick suggests, he 'had integrated psychoanalytic hypothesis into his perspectives'.[12]

Psychiatrists, neurologists and physicians with an interest in applying psychology were less subject to peer pressure from writers in their own field than historians, as was the case with Preserved Smith. For these other professionals, it was an opportunity to show the historical importance of medical knowledge and demonstrate their erudition, while to colleagues of professional historians, it often appeared that they simply fit their data into a Procrustean bed. Leon Pierce Clark, a New York neurologist who in the first decade of the twentieth century had a type of conversion experience to psychoanalysis, wrote his first essay in 1908. Subsequently, he applied psychoanalysis to epilepsy, genius, Greek art and famous individuals.[13] By the early 1920s, Clark began using the terms 'psychobiography' (at first sometimes with a hyphen) and 'psychohistory'. His writings were accessible to the layperson because he usually avoided technical language, as seen in his *Napoleon: Self-Destroyed*.[14] Apparently without much original research, Clark successfully described the childhood, genius, grandiosity, identification with his mother, extreme narcissism and self-defeating quality of the French emperor.

[10] Elms, 'Freud, psychohistorian', p. 77.

[11] P. Smith, 'Luther's development in the light of psycho-analysis', *American Journal of Psychology*, 24 (1913), 360–77.

[12] E. W. Marvick and P. H. Elovitz, 'America's first psychobiographer: Preserved Smith and his insights on Luther', *Clio's Psyche*, 17 (2010), 22–8. In designating America's first psychobiographer, priority was given to Smith rather than Prince because of his greater depth of knowledge, sophistication, and the fact that he published in a journal rather than a newspaper.

[13] He wrote about Alexander the Great, Caesar, Leonardo da Vinci, Dostoevsky, Napoleon, Lincoln, Michelangelo, and Akhenaton. See E. W. Marvick and P. H. Elovitz, 'L. Pierce Clark: an early psychobiographer', *Clio's Psyche*, 17 (2010), 10–17.

[14] L. P. Clark, *Napoleon: Self-Destroyed* (New York: J. Cape & H. Smith, 1929).

As a young historian, Harry Elmer Barnes began publishing about the application of psychology to history right after the First World War.[15] Barnes' definition of psychology was broad; he started with Aristotle, the Stoics and Cicero before moving on to John Locke, David Hume and Adam Smith. Eventually he came to the unconscious and Freud.

The growth of applied psychoanalysis and psychology during the twentieth century is a significant development in intellectual history. Thus, for example, in William Gilmore's helpful 1984 survey, *Psychohistorical Inquiry: a Comprehensive Research Bibliography*, one finds three entries for the first decade of the century, six for the second decade, eighteen for the 1920s, seven for the 1930s and eighteen for the 1940s.[16] Some authors' names became well known by the 1940s, including Erik Erikson, Erich Fromm, Karl Menninger, Geoffrey Gorer and Abraham Kardiner. Others, such as the economic historian Sydney Ratner, ventured into psychological history in the 1941 article, 'The Historian's Approach to Psychology', but quickly moved on to other issues.[17]

There is no doubt that the influx of European psychoanalysts and other refugees of Nazism who had been influenced by psychodynamic thought had a huge impact in the United States. Among these refugees were psychoanalysts and others interested in applying psychology to history. The aforementioned Erik Erikson and Erich Fromm were German-born psychoanalysts who both wrote major studies in the field. In 1941, Fromm came out with *Escape from Freedom* and two years later with 'On the Problem of German Characterology', while in 1942 Erikson wrote 'Hitler's Imagery and German Youth'.[18] Erikson's 1958 *Young Man Luther* led to his being widely viewed as the father of psychohistory. This characterization never sat well with Fromm; he in turn wrote and sold millions of books, including *Man for Himself: an Inquiry*

15 H. E. Barnes, 'Psychology and history: some reasons for predicting their more active cooperation in the future', *American Journal of Psychology*, 30 (1919), 337–76; H. E. Barnes, 'Some reflections on the possible service of analytical psychology to history', *Psychoanalytic Review*, 8 (1921), 22–37.

16 W. Gilmore, *Psychohistorical Inquiry: a Comprehensive Research Bibliography* (New York: Garland, 1984). The structure of both this book and its index makes a definitive count difficult. W. J. Gilmore, in his invaluable bibliography, missed a fair number of sources and was inclined to include some that are dubious as psychohistorical or psychological. Clearly a new bibliography is needed for our field. W. M. Runyan, *Life Histories and Psychobiography: Explorations in Theory and Method* (New York: Oxford University Press, 1984), pp. 193–5, has a historical sketch of some value.

17 S. Ratner, 'The historian's approach to psychology', *Journal of the History of Ideas*, 2 (1941), 95–109.

18 E. Fromm, 'On the problems of German characterology', *Transactions of the New York Academy of Sciences*, 5 (1943), 79–83; E. H. Erikson, 'Hitler's imagery and German youth', *Psychiatry: Journal for the Study of Interpersonal Processes*, 5 (1942), 475–93.

into the Psychology of Ethics, *The Art of Loving* and *The Anatomy of Human Destructiveness*.[19]

The blossoming of psychoanalysis in the United States and the burgeoning of psychohistory

In the two decades after the Second World War, depth psychology and a profound concern for psychosocial issues became well established in the United States. Freud's character and special contributions were hailed among intellectual leaders and in many books, including Phillip Rieff's *Freud: the Mind of the Moralist*.[20] Hollywood cinema glorified the role of psychoanalysts, and it became stylish in certain circles to be analysed. Isaac Asimov's (1920–92) fantasy psychohistory had a science fiction psychohistorian predict precise events hundreds of years into the future, thus contributing to an exaggerated popular belief in the predictive power of analysis along with the common perception in academia that psychohistory is a fantasy.[21] But the newly created Pentagon hired analysts to engage in classified psychological studies of leaders and potential leaders around the world, just as the head of the Office of Strategic Services had hired analysts during the Second World War, resulting in the subsequently declassified study of Hitler that predicted his suicide.[22] The Iron Curtain under Stalin kept data on the Soviet Union from flowing to the West, but it did not inhibit numerous psychological studies of Soviet society that helped fill the informational vacuum. For example, Nathan Leites used psychoanalytic principles in writing *The Operational Code of the Politburo* (1951) and *A Study of Bolshevism* (1953), as did Geoffrey Gorer in *The People of Great Russia: a Psychological Study* (1949) and other work.

Starting in the 1950s and gaining momentum in the 1960s and 1970s, the integration of psychology and history came into its own; the creation of anthologies, articles, books, journals, local, national and international groups, college courses and the training of academics in psychoanalysis

[19] L. J. Friedman, *The Lives of Erich Fromm: Love's Prophet* (New York: Columbia University Press, 2013). Friedman is the noted psychobiographer of both Erik H. Erikson and the Menningers.

[20] P. Rieff, *Freud: the Mind of the Moralist* (Garden City, NY: Anchor Books, 1959). See also P. Rieff, *The Triumph of the Therapeutic: Uses of Faith after Freud* (New York: Harper & Row, 1966).

[21] The first use of the term 'psychohistory' is incorrectly and usually attributed to Asimov, even by psychohistorians such as R. J. Lifton, *Witness to an Extreme Century: a Memoir* (New York: Free Press, 2011), 76fn. The science fiction author, scientist, and polymath Asimov claimed to know nothing of psychology even though his second wife was both a psychiatrist and psychoanalyst.

[22] W. Langer, *The Mind of Adolf Hitler: the Secret Wartime Report* (New York: Basic Books, 1972).

dramatically increased. Some leaders of the historical profession embraced it, but few leaders of academic psychology departments did so. In the 1950s, some fine and inspiring psychobiography and psychohistory was being written, including Brown on the psychoanalytic meaning of history and the above-mentioned volumes by Erikson on Luther and the Georges on Wilson.[23] While none of these books were the work of historians, they inspired some members of this profession. A major breakthrough came in 1957 when William L. Langer, a distinguished Harvard University diplomatic historian and scholar of Europe, in his Presidential Address to the American Historical Association declared the application of psychoanalysis to history to be 'the next assignment' that he called upon younger historians to accept.

In the print version of this well-footnoted speech, Langer referred to psychoanalysis twenty-five times and Freud thirty-five times, crediting Freud with doing the most for creating the intellectual spirit of the era and becoming dominant in psychiatry. He saw the application of psychoanalysis to history as one 'of the many lacunae in our knowledge'. He urged his profession to risk taking flights 'into the unknown, even though some of them may prove wide of the mark' because, like natural scientists, a lot can be learned from mistakes and with persistence greater facility can be achieved.[24] Applying modern psychology to history would open the way to understand the irrational. Just as 'traditional political-military history' had been augmented by economic, intellectual, scientific and social knowledge, so the benefits of psychoanalysis needed to be added. Compared to psychoanalysis, which he refers to at one point as depth psychology, 'the homespun, common-sense psychological interpretations of past historians' appear as 'woefully inadequate' and even 'naïve'.[25] Although many in the audience grumbled at Langer's advocacy of applying the new psychology in history, a number of younger historians took up the cause, especially in the following twenty years. Some historians heeded his call to go into training at psychoanalytic institutes, as had 'for many years young scholars in anthropology, sociology, religion, literature, education and other fields'.[26]

The enthusiasm for applying psychoanalysis to history was reflected by an enormous increase in publications during the 1960s. These included Harold Lasswell's *Psychopathology and Politics*, Robert Jay Lifton's *Death*

[23] N. O. Brown, *Life Against Death: the Psychoanalytical Meaning of History* (Middletown, CT: Wesleyan University Press, 1959).

[24] W. L. Langer, 'The next assignment', *The American Historical Review*, 63 (1958), 284.

[25] Langer, 'The next assignment', p. 287.

[26] Langer, 'The next assignment', p. 303.

in Life: Survivors of Hiroshima and Revolutionary Immortality: Mao Tse-Tung and the Chinese Cultural Revolution, Lucian Pye's *Politics, Personality and Nation Building: Burma's Search for Identity*, Bruce Mazlish's *Psychoanalysis and History*, Erik Erikson's *Gandhi's Truth*, Rudolph Binion's *Frau Lou: Nietzsche's Wayward Disciple*, Frank Manuel's *A Portrait of Sir Isaac Newton* and Peter Loewenberg's *Decoding the Past: the Psychohistorical Approach*.[27] Five of these authors were historians, two political scientists, one a psychologist, the best known a psychoanalyst and the most prolific a psychiatrist.[28]

Psychohistorical articles began to appear in mainstream journals. The prestigious *American Historical Review*, under the editorship of Robert K. Webb (1968–75) and to a lesser extent under Otto Pflanze (1977–85), published some explicitly psychohistorical articles, including two by Peter Loewenberg in 1971 on Heinrich Himmler and Nazi youth.[29] Psychobiographical articles continued to be published in *American Imago*, *The Psychoanalytic Quarterly*, *The Psychoanalytic Study of the Child*, *The Annual of Psychoanalysis* and a variety of other journals. The *Journal of Interdisciplinary History* began publication in 1970 and printed psychohistorical articles until about 1980. Next, a number of publications specializing in psychohistory started in 1972 with the mimeographed *Newsletter of the Group for the Use of Psychology in History* that became a fully fledged quarterly journal by 1978 but ceased publication in 1999. In 1973, *The History of Childhood Quarterly: the Journal of Psychohistory* (later *The Journal of Psychohistory*) began publication as a substantial quarterly. The editor reported that in the 1980s it had 8,000 subscribers. *Political Psychology*, the journal of the International Society

27 H. Lasswell, *Psychopathology and Politics* (New York: Viking Press, 1960); R. J. Lifton, *Death in Life: Survivors of Hiroshima* (New York: Random House, 1968); R. J. Lifton, *Revolutionary Immortality: Mao Tse-Tung and the Chinese Cultural Revolution* (New York: Random House, 1968); L. Pye, *Politics, Personality, and Nation Building: Burma's Search for Identity* (New Haven, CT: Yale University Press, 1962); B. Mazlish (ed.), *Psychoanalysis and History* (Englewood Cliffs, NJ: Prentice-Hall, 1963); E. Erikson, *Gandhi's Truth: On the Origins of Militant Nonviolence* (New York: Norton, 1969); R. Binion, *Frau Lou: Nietzsche's Wayward Disciple* (Princeton, NJ: Princeton University Press, 1968); F. Manuel, *A Portrait of Sir Isaac Newton* (Boston, MA: Belknap Press of Harvard University Press, 1968); and P. Loewenberg, *Decoding the Past: the Psychohistorical Approach* (Berkeley: University of California Press, 1969).

28 Other notable contributions were R. J. Lifton, *Thought Reform and the Psychology of Totalism: a Study of 'Brainwashing' in China* (New York: Norton, 1961); L. Pye, *The Spirit of Chinese Politics: a Psychocultural Study of the Authority Crisis in Political Development* (Cambridge, MA: MIT Press, 1968); K. Keniston, *Young Radicals: Notes on Committed Youth* (New York: Harcourt, Brace & World, 1968); and A. Mitzman, *The Iron Cage: an Historical Interpretation of Max Weber* (New York: Knopf, 1969).

29 P. Loewenberg, 'The unsuccessful adolescence of Heinrich Himmler', *The American Historical Review*, 76 (1971), 612–41; P. Loewenberg, 'The psychohistorical origins of the Nazi youth cohort', *The American Historical Review*, 76 (1971), 1457–502.

for Political Psychology (ISPP), came into existence in 1979 and continues to thrive.[30]

However, the greatest dissemination of psychological ideas applied to history did not come through these journals but through articles and books that adopted them, often without acknowledging or, perhaps, realizing it. In *Stalin: a Biography*, Robert Service makes many references to personality traits and psychological states without much sophistication or indication of having read specific psychological studies of the Soviet leader.[31] In a pre-Freudian era, this psychological emphasis would not have been present. Ian Kershaw's 875-page *Hitler 1889–1936: Hubris* has numerous psychological interpretations without psychoanalysis, psychohistory, or psychology appearing in the index.[32] In his bibliography and notes, he demonstrates some awareness of individual psychohistorical studies, which he rejects, although it is clear to both me and David R. Beisel, a veteran psychohistorian who has published a book on Nazi foreign policy, that his interpretation is influenced by the numerous psychohistorical studies of the Nazi leader.[33]

Organizing the psychological study of society: conflicting conceptions of the field

Groups for applied psychoanalysis proliferated from New York to Boston, Buffalo, Los Angeles and beyond. Interested parties from all disciplines gathered with clinicians as part of this enormous expansion of applied psychoanalysis. The *New York Times* reported in 1971 on a weekend meeting at the Graduate Center of the City University of New York of forty leading historians debating the integration of psychology and history. Although the participants were quite divided, psychohistory was being organized on an ad-hoc basis.[34]

The first psychohistory organization, the Group for the Study of Psychohistorical Process, came together around Robert Jay Lifton's

30 Readership of the *Journal of Psychohistory* fell below a thousand in the twenty-first century, although it still maintains a circulation larger than any psychohistorical journal and most academic journals. Additional journals are *Clio's Psyche* (1994–); *Mind and Human Interaction* (1989–2005); *The Psychohistory News* (1978–); *Mentalities/Mentalitiés* (1981–2011); *Or le temps: Revue Française de Psychohistorie* (1994–2000); *Psicologica Politica* (1990–); *Journal for the Psychoanalysis of Culture and Society* (1995–); *Psychoanalysis and History* (1999–); and *Gesellschaft für Psychohistorie und Politische Psychologie* (1993–).

31 R. Service, *Stalin: a Biography* (Cambridge, MA: Belknap Press of Harvard University Press, 2005).

32 I. Kershaw, *Hitler 1889–1936 Hubris* (New York: W. W. Norton, 2000).

33 D. R. Beisel, *The Suicidal Embrace: Hitler, the Allies, and the Origins of the Second World War* (Nyack, NY: Circumstantial Productions, 2003).

34 I. Shenker, 'Meeting explores history from psychologist's view', *New York Times* (26 August 1971), 37.

seminar tables in the renovated hut outside his summer home in Wellfleet on Cape Cod and still meets every year in the fall for a three-day conference. Lifton (a psychiatrist), Kenneth Keniston (a psychologist) and Bruce Mazlish (a historian) came together in 1966 around Erik Erikson and brought in an amazing array of leading intellectuals. Throughout the years, these meetings have included well-known figures such as Norman Birnbaum, Robert Coles, Wendy Doninger, Kai Erikson, Carol and Jim Gilligan, Doris Kearns Goodwin, Stuart Hampshire, Norman Mailer, Steven Marcus, David Riesman (who helped with planning), Philip Rieff and Richard Sennett. The American Academy of Arts and Sciences funded the early Wellfleet meetings with the expectation that it would become a well-organized group and, ultimately, 'a training center for psychohistorical work'. Key members of the group, most especially Lifton, rejected this agenda in favour of 'presentations that were speculative, probing, and freewheeling'.[35] One could argue that this decision lessened the role of psychohistory in academia.

After 'three years or so', Lifton simply referred to 'his' gatherings as the 'Wellfleet meetings' and subsequently published the edited *Explorations in Psychohistory: the Wellfleet Papers*.[36] Although he, like his friend and mentor Erik Erikson, was ambivalent about using the word 'psychohistory', he considers himself to be a psychohistorian. Despite the ambivalence of some prominent contributors to the psychodynamic understanding of society, colleagues were coming together in large numbers to discuss it.

In 1976, the first national conference of psychohistorians was held at Stockton State College in New Jersey. Erikson sent his best wishes but, typically, did not attend. There was much debate over the relationship of psychohistory to history, political science, psychology, psychoanalysis, psychiatry, sociology and other disciplines. Robert Jay Lifton admonished this author that he should not make his scheduled presentation on Democratic presidential candidate Jimmy Carter because he considered it unethical to write about a living person without their written permission, which he correctly presumed was not obtained.[37] The pathologizing of Republican presidential candidate Barry Goldwater in 1964, based on a survey sent to psychiatrists who had had no direct contact with him or special expertise in applying their discipline to biography, had led the

[35] Lifton, *Witness to an Extreme Century*, p. 346.

[36] R. J. Lifton with E. Olson (eds.), *Explorations in Psychohistory: the Wellfleet Papers* (New York: Simon & Schuster, 1974), p. 13.

[37] Psychohistorian Bruce Mazlish did in fact get permission to publish from Carter, but this came at the cost of publically endorsing his candidacy for president, which is not a good precedent for psychobiographers. B. Mazlish and E. Diamond, 'Thrice-born: a psychohistory of Jimmy Carter's "Rebirth"', *New York Magazine* (30 August 1976).

American Psychiatric Association (APA) to prohibit its members from writing about living people without their expressed permission. While the author, who is not a psychiatrist, gave the presentation anyway, such divisions among psychohistorians became apparent even then.

The leadership of the APA wanted the public to view their members as scientific clinicians, healers and researchers, not as partisans who use their special knowledge for the purposes of political psychopathologizing. Because in 1964 many psychiatrists were fearful of Senator Goldwater's threat to use nuclear weapons in the struggle against communism in Vietnam, 19.5 per cent of the 12,356 APA members who were sent the questionnaire regarding the mental health of the Republican presidential candidate overwhelmingly characterized him as unbalanced. Embarrassed by this assessment of over 2,400 of its members, the APA designed its stringent ethical guidelines. Regrettably, this meant that member psychiatrists were effectively banned from writing about political candidates and living people unless it suited the needs of the subject.[38] Thus, in voting for president the educated public was denied the insights of all psychiatrists, including those who were ready to do serious psychobiographical work on the candidates. Fortunately, this restriction impacted only a minority of those interested in this endeavour, because most were historians, independent scholars, journalists, political scientists and psychoanalysts.

Psychohistory blossomed as an organized field in the 1970s in the United States with the establishment of a variety of organizations. The new groups included the Group for the Use of Psychology in History (GUPH, 1972–), which now meets sporadically at the annual American Historical Association conference. Lloyd deMause's Institute for Psychohistory held its first summer workshop in July 1975. The day-long meeting was so inspiring that two participants suggested that, rather than meeting annually, the Institute hold Saturday meetings every month or two; the members did so for the next seven years. The International Psychohistorical Association (IPA, 1977–) held its first annual conference in 1978, and a week later, the International Society for Political Psychology (ISPP, 1977–) met for the first time and went on to become the largest and most internationally effective of these groups.[39]

[38] S. Renshon, *The Psychological Assessment of Presidential Candidates* (New York: New York University Press, 1996), p. 126.

[39] The ISPP, IPA and GUPH have been joined by a variety of other organizations, including the Bay Area Psychobiography Working Group (early 1990s–); the Center for the Study of Mind and Human Interaction (CSMHI, 1987–2005); the Psychohistory Forum (1983–); the Group for the Psychohistorical Study of Film (1989–2008); the University of California Interdisciplinary Psychoanalytic Consortium (1991–); and the Association for the Psychoanalysis of Culture and Society (APCS, 1995–). The IPA has annual

Avowed psychohistorians have been divided between those who declare their field to be a science and those who see it as an art form. Very few have argued for psychohistory as both a science and as a separate discipline, with Lloyd deMause being the outstanding exception. DeMause had pioneered in the history and evolution of childhood when he declared in 'The Independence of Psychohistory' that psychohistory is 'the science of historical motivation', which is separate from history because it is 'predictive' and 'stands or falls on the clarity and testability of its concepts'.[40] To develop his conception of psychohistory as a science, he founded the Institute for Psychohistory (1972) and the International Psychohistorical Association (1977–), edited and published the *Journal of Psychohistory* (1973–), published a number of books in the 1970s and 1980s under the imprint of the Psychohistory Press, and wrote or edited a number of books including *The Emotional Life of Nations*.[41] To this day, his version of psychohistory maintains a dominant online presence. These endeavours were aimed at using deMause's considerable energy and talents as a successful businessman publishing automotive newsletters to create and build a separate discipline of psychohistory.

By contrast, Robert Jay Lifton refused to turn the Wellfleet meetings into a formal programme. He once told this author, 'I am not too keen on the word "psychohistory" as a noun. I like the adjective "psychohistorical" better because it suggests a direction rather than a complete discipline which I am not sure we have or want to have.' It is interesting to note that the psychohistory of both men was influenced by their involuntary service during the Korean War. Lifton began the development of his research method by interviewing former American prisoners of war who identified with the ideology of their communist captors, and deMause often said his commitment to understanding the history of children and improving their lives stemmed from the orphaned children hiding under bridges in Korea.[42] In practice, deMause and Lifton mostly ignored each other's endeavours.

meetings in New York City. The ISPP, the most international and least psychoanalytically based of the larger groups, has members from numerous groups but the dominant ones are psychology and political science. The Association for the Psychoanalysis of Culture and Society membership is drawn from clinical work, educators, literature, film, sociology, history, political science, in about that order. In recent years it has met annually at Rutgers University for a two- or three-day meeting that has increasingly been attracting Europeans as well as colleagues from across the United States. The other groups have more frequent, regional, small-group meetings.

40 L. deMause, *The Foundations of Psychohistory* (New York: Creative Roots, 1982), pp. 84–104.

41 L. deMause, *The Emotional Life of Nations* (New York: Other Press, 2002).

42 The early editorial board of deMause's *Journal of Psychohistory* included a broad range of psychohistorians, including John Demos, Peter Loewenberg and Bruce Mazlish. However, within several years these and some other prominent colleagues withdrew

Struggles against psychohistory and within psychohistory

William Langer was not naive about the objections to the interdisciplinary marriage of history and psychoanalysis commonly held by the colleagues who elected him as AHA president. He spelled out many of their criticisms in his 1957 Presidential Address. They include a 'certain uneasiness' based on a suspicion of new ideas, because historians, like some other scholars, tend to be suspicious of methodological novelty. Unlike natural scientists in general, he said, historians are not inclined to 'learn a lot from our mistakes' by viewing failure as a step in the process of achieving knowledge. As a group, historians have maintained 'an almost completely negative attitude towards the teachings of psychoanalysis'. Historians, Langer suggested, 'as disciples of Thucydides, have habitually thought of themselves as psychologists in their own right' and consequently indulge 'freely in psychological interpretation'. Many historians fear the loss of 'the humanistic appreciation of personality' by the adoption of what they see as a biological, deterministic and conjectural psychoanalysis. He also noted the strong reluctance 'to recognize and deal with unconscious motives and irrational forces'.[43]

These statements show that, in spite of the progress made in building a community of scholars and a body of literature merging history and psychology, the approach has been met with intense resistance. The resistance was so intense within history that Joseph Dowling of Lehigh University, an advocate of psychological history, wrote in 1972 that 'history ... has remained relatively immune to the influence of psychoanalytic concepts' and that 'whatever advances are being made to bring the two disciplines [psychology and history] together are the work of non-historians'.[44] Five years later, Bruce Mazlish wrote in the *Psychohistory Review* 'of the enormous expansion of psychohistory'. How did these contradictions evolve and how accurate were their varying perceptions?

The basis of these conflicting reports and the intense opposition to the open and organized integration of psychology into history does indeed merit closer examination. Much of the opposition centred on

their names because they were not comfortable with deMause's approach. More historians identified with the *Psychohistory Review* than the *Journal*, and Lifton later disdained deMause's approach as 'cultism'. The historians resigning from the editorial board, and many of their colleagues, objected to the claim that psychohistory is a separate discipline as well as to deMause's way of doing psychohistory.

43 Langer, 'The next assignment', pp. 284–86.

44 J. A. Dowling, 'Psychoanalysis and history: problems and applications', *The Psychoanalytic Review*, 59 (1972), 433–34.

the argument that dead people, unlike the living, cannot be analysed. Dowling's pessimism is perhaps understandable, given the incredible difference between the vision expressed by William Langer and the reality within the historical profession. Mazlish, a historian at the Massachusetts Institute of Technology (MIT), was well aware of the intense criticism because he was working (unsuccessfully) to dispute it in the *New York Review of Books*, as discussed below. However, in addition to the momentum gained by the creation of psychohistorical journals and organizations, he was more optimistic about the application of Freudian principles to the study of history, since 'many historians were now playing with the approach and, even more, all historians were now conscious of the necessity of looking at subjects with psychoanalytic ideas in mind, even if not voiced openly'.[45]

Some colleagues, such as Peter Gay and Richard J. Hofstadter, were examples of psychological historians who stayed in the 'closet'. After building an international reputation, Gay eventually came 'out of the closet', but he never encouraged his doctoral students to be open about their psychological interests, lest it hurt their careers.[46] While most of Gay's works reflect the emphasis of psychohistorians on emotion, identity and sexuality, later in his career he wrote books on explicitly psychoanalytic subjects. Most notable are *Freud for Historians* and *Godless Jew: Freud, Atheism, and the Making of Psychoanalysis*.[47] Hofstadter's essay on 'The Paranoid Style in American Politics' was well received and has been cited many times, including in a number of places on the Op-Ed page of the *New York Times*, but his early death meant that he did not have contact with the organized field of psychohistory.[48]

In contrast to Gay, who wrote an undelivered lecture on having history graduate students at Yale trained in psychoanalysis, Peter Loewenberg implemented this dual training at UCLA. Loewenberg's history doctoral students had the option of studying in a psychoanalytic institute. Unfortunately, because few historians were hired in the 1970s and 1980s, and because of the long-standing prejudice against psychohistory, most of his students encountered difficulties obtaining professorships. Indeed, unlike economic, social and intellectual history, psychological history did not become firmly ensconced in graduate programmes. Still, there was

[45] Mazlish, 30 January 2013, pers. corr. by email to the author.

[46] D. Felix, P. Elovitz and B. Lentz, 'The psychoanalytically informed historian: Peter Gay', *Clio's Psyche*, 4 (1997), 66. P. Gay complained that his *Freud for Historians* (New York: Oxford University Press, 1985) was read neither by historians nor psychoanalysts.

[47] P. Gay, *Freud for Historians*; P. Gay, *A Godless Jew: Freud, Atheism, and the Making of Psychoanalysis* (New Haven, CT: Yale University Press, 1987).

[48] R. Hofstadter, *The Paranoid Style in American Politics, and Other Essays* (Cambridge, MA: Harvard University Press, 1964).

less resistance to hiring psychohistorians at some well-known institutions such as Brandeis, Wesleyan, Williams and in the California University system. The eminent historian H. Stuart Hughes, who had encouraged Richard Schoenberg's creation of the first psychohistory newsletter in 1972, moved to California because of professional prejudice at Harvard against his wife, Judith Hughes, who had just earned her doctoral degree in European history and who went on to train in psychoanalysis and write psychohistory.

Peter Loewenberg did yeoman service for psychological history. He was a key person in passing the 1977 California Research Psychoanalyst Law, which made it possible for professors from many disciplines trained in psychoanalysis to practise analysis, and in 1992 coming together with colleagues to create the University of California Interdisciplinary Psychoanalytic Consortium, which meets annually. The sense of academic community among these colleagues from history, literature, sociology, anthropology and other disciplines helps them deal with criticism of their psychoanalytic approach.

The struggle for and against psychohistory was sometimes centred at Columbia University in New York City. Many prominent exponents trained or taught there, as did outstanding critics of the field. Rudolph Binion, a psychohistorian for his entire distinguished career, trained at Columbia and taught there for three years before resigning, mostly because of differences over his *Frau Lou: Nietzsche's Wayward Disciple* – a brilliant book that he considered flawed.[49] He spent the bulk of his career at Brandeis University, where Frank Manuel, a historian of ideas and an early psychohistorian, also taught twice. But Jacques Barzun was an influential and outspoken critic of psychohistory. In *Clio and the Doctors: History, Psycho-History and Quanto-History*, he severely criticized the field, as well as the movement to quantify history, suggesting that the psychology of Pascal, rather than Freud, was sufficient for historians.[50] Lloyd deMause quit Columbia's Political Science Department in disgust after an administrator named Herbert Deane told him he could not write an openly psychohistorical doctoral dissertation. Nevertheless, psychodynamic approaches found their way into other Columbia dissertations in a less overt manner.

[49] R. Binion, *Frau Lou: Nietzsche's Wayward Disciple* (Princeton, NJ: Princeton University Press, 1968). See also D. Hayden, 'Rudolph Binion's traumatic encounter with Frau Lau', *Clio's Psyche*, 18, 2 (2011), 209–15. When Binion died over 40 years later, a half dozen students from his few years at Columbia wrote tributes. See the September 2011 'Binion memorial issue' of *Clio's Psyche*.

[50] J. Barzun, *Clio and the Doctors: History, Psycho-History and Quanto-History* (Chicago, IL: University of Chicago Press, 1974).

However much Barzun, David F. Stannard, Columbia University administrator Deane, and many others attempted to stop the integration of psychology and history, they were doomed to fail. Even while they denounced the messengers of disciplinary integration, the message was being accepted, however haphazardly. In the same breath that they denounced a psychological approach, they continued to use some psychological terms. This is best described as 'killing the messenger while taking the message'. To be sure, the victory of the psychosocial approach is partial, more outside academia than in it, where unfavourable comments on psychoanalysis and psychohistory often go unchallenged.

Despite the attacks, psychohistory was advancing. At the first IPA Conference in New York in 1978, almost all presenters were academics, mostly historians. However, open support within academia subsequently declined for several reasons. 'History's Reckless Psychologizing' was the title of the denunciation in the prestigious *Chronicle of Higher Education.*[51] In 1980 Stannard made his name as a debunker by writing a scalding attack on the field in *Shrinking History: On Freud and the Failure of Psychohistory.*[52] Frederick Crews, who started out applying psychoanalysis to literary figures, became a caustic critic of the field as well and was given free rein to do this in the pages of the *New York Review of Books.* The *Review* either attacked Freud and psychohistory or ignored the psychohistorical content of the books under review. Negative reactions to deMause, the most productive psychohistorical organizer and an active author, were also a factor. His ideas about fantasy analysis and the foetal origins of history were simply too extreme for all but a few academics. In addition, there were sometimes complaints that he was insufficiently diplomatic, as when he wrote that any hundred historians would give less than one per cent of their space to motivation.[53]

Areas of recent greatest interest

Psychohistory has produced some exceptional work, especially biographical studies, the area of greatest development in the marriage of history and psychology. Earlier psychobiographies of individuals such as Darwin, Freud, Jefferson, Lincoln, Napoleon and Poe were followed

[51] K. S. Lynn, 'History's reckless psychologizing', *Chronicle of Higher Education* (16 January 1978), 48. See Gay, *Freud for Historians*, pp. 14–33, for a discussion of many of the attacks on psychohistory and Freud.

[52] D. Stannard, *Shrinking History: On Freud and the Failure of Psychohistory* (New York: Oxford University Press, 1980).

[53] L. deMause, 'Independence of psychohistory', p. 165. See 'Comments' by Barbara Tuchman and Richard Lyman following.

in the 1970s and 1980s by path-breaking publications on Carter, Hitler, leading Nazis and Nixon. The quality of some studies is high, but others readily slipped into psychopathologizing for political purposes, especially when it came to Richard Nixon. Publishers sometimes solicited psychohistorical books of this nature, as in the case of the New York psychoanalyst David Abrahamsen's *Nixon vs. Nixon: an Emotional Tragedy* (1977) and Gilmore's *Psychohistorical Inquiry* (1984).[54]

As children of the late nineteenth century, both Freudian psychology and professional history claimed to be scientific. However, academic psychologists, increasingly leaning towards behaviourism and working in the laboratory, saw these fields as unscientific. At Harvard University, partly for reasons of personality, the Psychology Department split into two with those working in the more humanistic, subjective tradition of psychology forming Social Relations with cultural anthropologists and sociologists, and the 'hard scientists' dominating the Department of Psychology.[55] Gradually, clinical programmes came into existence for graduate psychologists and social workers at larger universities, enabling them to work with patients and train clinicians. A large number of, if not most, students entering psychology in the twenty-first century are more interested in helping people cure their psychological maladies rather than doing laboratory experiments. However, psychologists with an overwhelming desire to study biographies had a very difficult time establishing their credentials within psychology departments, though some, following in the tradition of Henry Murray, persisted and published valuable work. Alan Elms and William McKinley Runyan are two such individuals who want to create a 'historicized psychology'.[56] A number of their students, such as William Todd Schultz, editor of the *Handbook of Psychobiography*, are following in their footsteps.[57]

Applied psychohistory has been a most fruitful area of interdisciplinary integration. The 'why' of war, violence and enemy formation has been examined in depth using psychoanalysis, history and allied disciplines.

[54] D. Abrahamsen, *Nixon vs. Nixon: an Emotional Tragedy* (New York: Farrar, Straus & Giroux, 1977); W. J. Gilmore-Lehne and W. J. Gilmore, *Psychohistorical Inquiry: a Comprehensive Research Bibliography* (New York: Garland, 1984).

[55] I. Nicholson, 'From the Book of Mormon to the operational definition: the existential project of S.S. Stevens', in W. T. Schultz (ed.), *Handbook of Psychobiography* (New York: Oxford University Press, 2005), pp. 294–6.

[56] W. M. Runyan, 'From the study of lives and psychohistory to historicizing psychology: a conceptual journey', in J. Winer and J. Anderson (eds.), *Psychoanalysis and History* (Hillsdale, NJ: Analytic Press, 2003), pp. 119–32. As a graduate psychology student at Harvard interested in biography, a prominent professor invited Runyan to leave the programme since he considered psychobiography to be a waste of time.

[57] W. T. Schultz (ed.), *The Handbook of Psychobiography* (New York: Oxford University Press, 2005).

Robert Jay Lifton, Vamik Volkan and Charles B. Strozier published extensively on these subjects and built communities of scholars, clinicians and practitioners to further the process of peacemaking. Lifton left his Sterling Professorship of Psychiatry at Yale to found and head The Center for the Study of Violence and Human Survival at John Jay College of CUNY (1985–2003). There, among many others, peacemakers from the United Nations met with therapists, historians, political scientists and psychologists to deepen their understanding of the difficult problems they faced. Since his retirement, his younger colleague, the historian/psychoanalyst Strozier, transformed this institution into the Center on Terrorism to help police and firefighters develop a psychosocial approach to their work.

At the University of Virginia, Volkan, a psychiatric professor and psychoanalyst, created and headed the Center for Mind and Human Interaction (1987–2002), where he brought diplomats and policy-makers together, along with clinicians and political psychologists, to focus on issues of violence. He also took a proactive approach by travelling to trouble spots, notably within the former Soviet Union, to help defuse the hatred of the Other. His journal, *Mind and Human Interaction: Windows Between History, Culture, Politics, and Psychoanalysis* (1987–2003), used psychodynamic language.

Unlike academic psychologists, psychiatrists have played a key role in psychohistorical achievement. The psychoanalyst and Harvard psychiatrist John Mack won a Pulitzer Prize for his 1998 *A Prince of Our Disorder: the Life of T. E. Lawrence*; he later suffered academic condemnation for accepting as reality some subjects claiming to have been abducted by aliens.[58] Ralph Colp made his living providing psychiatric services to graduate students at Columbia University and in private practice, while devoting a lifetime of scholarship to Charles Darwin and developing the psychohistorical paradigm. He was an impeccable primary source scholar, a quality seldom exhibited by others who have not been trained as researchers.

Sources and methodology requirements for good work and greater scholarly acceptance

In his famous 1957 address, William L. Langer warned historians against leaving the field of applied psychoanalysis to the 'untrained popular

[58] J. Mack, *A Prince of Our Disorder: the Life of T. E. Lawrence* (Cambridge, MA: Harvard University Press, 1998).

biographer'.[59] Certainly many who have engaged in psychobiography, especially non-historians, have been careless in their treatment of sources with unfortunate consequences. To do their best work, psychobiographers must rely on primary sources even more so than most historians and other scholars. The reason is that a researcher must seek nuances in his or her subjects' childhoods, behaviours, emotions and personalities – these are givens in which polite society and more traditional scholars find little to no interest or skill in examining. Here are two examples from this author's own research.

During a speech aimed at demonstrating that Richard Nixon was effectively running the country during the Watergate Crisis despite the scandal, the President declared, 'Your thoroughly discredited President ... [stumbling] ... I mean Congress'. Regrettably, the *New York Times* printed his speech – as released by the White House – without this most revealing Freudian slip that, psychohistorians would argue, reflected Nixon's unconscious fear of being caught, and perhaps his wish to be exposed. Likewise, the varied sources for the life of the nineteenth-century British industrialist and inventor James Naysmith provide invaluable information for the psychobiographer. His autobiography, business papers and parliamentary testimony are all-important, but most unique is the initial 1839 series of sketches in his workbook of his most important invention, the steam hammer, which he called 'my thumping baby' in his autobiography. The main sketch shows a man, with the initials JN, creating a powerful steam hammer that appears to come right out of his body from the area of his penis. Smaller sketches around it show a human transforming into a machine. There is also a devilish-looking creature about to cut off the machine head of the man. The drawing may suggest Naysmith experienced his invention of the extremely large and powerful steam hammer as a manifestation of his sexual prowess and the threat of beheading in the act of transformation as a reflection of the anxiety about the invention.

Dreams can also be a valuable source of information for the psychobiographer as well as for the psychoanalyst, but unfortunately there is considerable resistance to their use.[60] Clues as to the fears, hopes and fantasies of Peter the Great of Russia, Humphry Davy, Abraham Lincoln, Osama bin Laden, Woodrow Wilson, Lyndon Johnson and many others can be found in recorded accounts of their dreams. Psychoanalysts and

[59] Langer, 'The next assignment', p. 288.

[60] J. L. Shneidman, 'On the nature of psychohistorical evidence', *Journal of Psychohistory*, 16 (1984), 205–12. After attending a historical dream workshop, Shneidman came to accept the value of probing the dreams of historical figures.

most historians often correctly point out that deceased people may not be able to free-associate to their dreams, but this does not necessarily obviate their value for the biographer. Records often survive about the dreamer's thinking at a particular period of life. Quite importantly, psychobiographers need to probe their own dreams in search of unconscious thoughts and feelings about their subjects. For example, a dream one psychobiographer had of being President Carter's therapist revealed a concern for the president's self-defeating tendencies, as well as the desire to help him overcome these inclinations. The more scholars understand about their own unconscious motivations in researching and writing about a subject, the more conscious choices they have, making for better results.

A central issue in psychohistory is methodology. How does one approach a subject psychohistorically? The first answer is to focus on initial experiences – that is, childhood. First experiences are vital because people are likely to repeat patterns developed early in life: 'The child is the father of the man.' For example, Richard Nixon, whose childhood was marked by injury, abandonment and the death of two of his brothers, declared *Resurrection* to have been his favourite book in college and devoted much of his life to resurrecting his political career after his loss to Kennedy in 1960 and his reputation after his Watergate disgrace.

Psychohistorical methodology has many components. A key element is to examine and probe the difference between conscious and unconscious intention. Changes in emotion need to be listened for and examined carefully. A central issue is how individuals deal with trauma and loss. The mechanisms of defence they use to protect themselves from the pain of reality are of the utmost significance in psychobiographical work. Coping mechanisms, a less clinical and more positive term than defence mechanisms, draw attention to psychic defences in themselves being neither good nor bad. Denial, for example, may be a necessary ingredient to help a person through a major trauma. An individual who did not deny or suppress anger and grief felt upon the loss of loved ones, say of a father or wife in the same concentration camp, would be at much greater risk of death at the hands of the guards who severely punished any signs of anger.

The empathetic approach to psychobiography views the subject matter and the sources of a character in an open, non-critical manner. This means focusing on the person as an individual, avoiding pathological terminology and minimizing the use of psychoanalytic or psychological terms. It means literally trying to walk in the subject's shoes, immersing oneself in the evidence and trying to determine how she or he felt and thought at a given moment of time. The individual's childhood, family background, personality, life traumas and patterns of coping need to be considered carefully. In working to accomplish this sensitivity, the training and practice as a psychoanalyst have been more powerful influences on the scholarship of this author than his graduate training in history and political science.

An invaluable tool for the psychobiographer is disciplined subjectivity: carefully monitoring one's own feelings in researching the subject to find useful clues. Psychoanalytic biography benefits enormously from the psychoanalyst/biographer's experience of personal psychoanalysis, psychoanalytic practice and supervision by more experienced analysts, as well as on the theories generated by psychoanalysis. These can be transformational, opening up new avenues of investigation and changing older ones. When well-analysed psychobiographers and other scholars in tune with their feelings use disciplined subjectivity carefully, they greatly enhance their work; clinicians can then apply a non-judgemental approach to the biographical subject. The process de-emphasizes theory and pathological terminology; on the occasions when clinical terms are applied, they are put forth tentatively rather than presented as the scientific truth, sanctified by medical fact. This research methodology focuses on the careful choice of words and, whenever practical, lets the subject's words speak for themselves. Scholars must be immersed in the subject's childhood, personality, family background, life crises, coping devices and study the individual's patterns of successes and failures carefully. Thus, scholars read and reread memoirs of childhood, transcripts of speeches and other documents with great care. This methodology of political psychobiography also requires careful listening to facts and emotions, in what psychoanalyst Theodore Reik called 'listening with the third ear'.[61] But caution is well advised. Biographers develop positive and negative feelings for the subject in a process called countertransference – the feelings held towards the subject. These feelings must be monitored closely, which is possible because the psychobiographer communicates with himself or herself, as well as to the audience. Like the analyst, the biographer must be careful to avoid using countertransference as a cloak for narcissistic self-justification. Throughout the entire process, the feelings of a psychobiographer must also be monitored carefully and continuously. Erik Erikson and Robert Jay Lifton are the best-known advocates of this approach.

Different approaches to psychohistory make for different methodologies. Lifton created an interview technique that enabled him to engage

[61] T. Reik, *Listening with the Third Ear* (New York: Farrar, Straus & Giroux, 1983).

in path-breaking and excellent research.[62] Lloyd deMause ambitiously developed a method of fantasy analysis as a way of tracking the unconscious intention of large groups in society. It is a methodology with real potential, but it also raises the question of how one separates the world-view and unconscious projections of the fantasy analyst from the varied and complex emotions and viewpoints of the group. Some have used it to draw speculative and unwarranted conclusions.

A very different approach to that of the majority of psychobiographers who use considerable technical terminology is taken by the journal *Clio's Psyche*. Its goal is to encourage a psychohistory emphasizing adaptability, childhood, creativity, empathy, innovation, personality, psychobiography and overcoming trauma. Just as the psychoanalyst does not normally use technical psychological terminology with a patient, this journal seeks to keep psychological concepts and theories in mind, but avoids them in the analysis where possible. The advantages of this approach include making psychohistory accessible to a larger audience drawn from many fields and disassociating psychohistory from pathology. As long as it is associated with the Hitlers, Stalins and Nixons of the world and is seen as mainly a brush with which to tar the despised, rather than to understand all human beings, then the marriage of psychology and history will not gain full academic respectability.

To do valuable work and to ultimately be accepted in the general intellectual community, advocates of the merger of psychology and history must both be open to new approaches and maintain a high standard of professional rigour. This is an important but not an easy balance to establish and maintain.

Conclusion

While the Freud bashing and attacks continue, psychological history remains alive and well in America and even among individuals in academia. This enables them to gain some of the insights of the field, without subjecting themselves to the criticism associated with an approach that history and psychology departments have inclined to dismiss out of hand.

More important than the creation of specific organizations dedicated to the spread of psychological and psychodynamic ideas has been the wider diffusion of these ideas in our society. The primary reason the combination of psychology and history has good prospects is that psychoanalytic,

[62] See C. Strozier and M. Flynn, 'The Lifton Method', *Psychohistory Review* (Winter 1992), 131–44 and the Robert Jay Lifton *Festschrift*, *Clio's Psyche*, 19 (2012), 177–88.

psychological, psychohistorical and therapeutic concepts permeate all aspects of our world – transforming the ways we see it. What was called 'psychobabble' forty years ago is now part of the everyday thinking of most Americans, even if critics continue to use this denigrating word.

Because historically there has been a close relationship between psychoanalysis and psychohistory, in our age of biological determinism, managed care, miracle drugs and neurobiology, many psychoanalytic practices have been diminished in size – with some authors foreseeing the death of psychoanalysis. They are wrong. There has been an enormous proliferation of psychoanalytic institutes and an opening of these private organizations to candidates from various backgrounds; the number of analysts has increased considerably. Psychoanalysis offers a unique healing, as well as an intellectual experience. Though the ideal career for graduates of these institutes has been full-time individual analytic practice, most certified analysts have always maintained other institutional affiliations or do other kinds of psychotherapy as well as psychoanalysis, with the impact of an analytic experience often affecting their other work. The current difficulties practitioners experience being reimbursed from third parties, or Health Management Organizations, has reduced the number of candidates, but most institutes continue to train future analysts.

Yet, even in the extraordinarily unlikely event that psychoanalysis would cease to be a valued treatment modality, it seems likely it will hold its own as an intellectual discipline. Its value 'as a humane 21st-century worldview', 'an investigative research method', and 'a mode of perceiving human interactions, data, events, and behaviors' is spelled out with great clarity by Peter Loewenberg.[63] Psychohistory, as mentioned above, has taken on a life of its own; while enriched by clinical practice, this is not a requirement for its continued growth and success.

The psychohistorical torch has been burning for over a century and has strengthened our knowledge of the individual and society. This erudition can deepen and make more meaningful the valuable scholarship of psychology and history academic departments. The benefit of exploring this invaluable paradigm is a deeper, more profound knowledge of the people of our society. They include a deeper understanding of creativity and its roots as well as of the dangerous, disclaimed aspects of the human condition associated with individual and societal self-destructive tendencies. Despite some disappointments, the psychological study of culture, current events, biography, history and society has a bright future, as a

[63] 'Dual training: professional and personal insights', in P. H. Elovitz (ed.), *Psychohistorical Explanations: the Best of the Journal Clio's Psyche* (Franklin Lakes, NJ: The Psychohistory Forum, 2011), p. 7.

result of public acceptance, a vast body of scholarship, and the development of a variety of professional organizations and journals. It is perhaps fitting to close with the words of the Pulitzer Prize-winning journalist and popular historian Barbara Tuchman: 'Every thoughtful historian is a psychohistorian.'[64]

[64] B. Tuchman, 'Comment' on Lloyd deMause, 'The independence of psychohistory', *The History of Childhood Quarterly*, 3 (Fall 1975), 184.

5 Questioning interdisciplinarity: history, social psychology and the theory of social representations

Ivana Marková

During the last two centuries, traditional sciences, such as chemistry, physics and biology, opened up their borders to accommodate newly emerging disciplines, for example biochemistry, biophysics, quantum information processing, statistical mechanics, among many others.[1] It has become apparent that a combination of knowledge from different disciplines can lead to the solution of problems and to new inventions that traditional disciplines were unable to make. As a result, the quest for interdisciplinarity has also become widespread throughout human and social sciences in the hope that bringing together knowledge from diverse fields would lead to new ideas and coping with acute human and social challenges. While some disciplines, such as social anthropology and sociolinguistics, have achieved their new unions relatively easily, the editors of this volume show that history and social psychology have remained uncomfortable companions in the long-standing climate of mutual suspicion. The editors pose fundamental questions in relation to opening an interdisciplinary dialogue between these two scholarly fields.

Yet, what do we mean by 'interdisciplinarity' with respect to social psychology and history? We can suggest at least two answers. First, social psychology and history could be interdisciplinary in the sense that they might combine knowledge from both disciplines about a specific subject matter. For example, the emergence of HIV/AIDS in the 1980s has led to extensive social psychological explorations of attitudes, social representations, knowledge and the perception of risk of this condition. Knowledge of venereal diseases like syphilis, which caused an epidemic in the nineteenth century, or of plague in the Middle Ages, often served as a historical and socio-political contexts of that research and as a background or a stage (as in the theatre) for psychological investigation. In this way

[1] This chapter is an edited and slightly changed version of an article published in the special issue on History and Psychology in the journal *Integrative Psychological and Behavioral Science*, December 2012, under the title 'Method and explanation in history and in social representations'.

it became possible to compare and contrast the spread of infectious diseases on the basis of knowledge from both psychology and history, and to construct a comprehensive understanding of the phenomenon of HIV/AIDS founded on an interdisciplinary approach.[2]

Second, social psychology and history can be understood as interdisciplinary not only in the sense that they combine knowledge from both disciplines, but also in the sense that they are underlain by a common epistemology to the extent that social psychological knowledge is historical and historical knowledge is social psychological. This is a totally different matter from the former kind of interdisciplinarity, and it is this latter sense to which I wish to draw attention in this chapter.

Common concerns of history and social psychology

What could be common epistemological concerns of historians and social psychologists, if any, when they study historical and social psychological phenomena, respectively? Casual inspection of literature in these two disciplines shows that, at least in the past, they were both preoccupied with the question as to whether research methods by means of which they acquire knowledge about phenomena in their respective disciplines strengthen their scientific status. With respect to history, Isaiah Berlin expressed his concern in the article on the concept of scientific history. There he asked: 'Is history … a science, as, let us say, physics or biology or psychology are sciences?'[3] He maintained that this and related questions have occupied philosophically minded historians from at least the beginning of the nineteenth century. He reminded readers that in the seventeenth century Descartes rejected history as a serious study in the *Discourse on the Method*.[4] Nevertheless, a number of historians have tried to show that history is just as respectable a science as natural sciences, because, like natural sciences, *it studies facts*. In contrast, other scholars claim that despite studying facts, history 'is poorly endowed with or even lacks the ability to predict, one of the important things that separates science from other forms of learning'.[5]

[2] A. M. Brandt, *No Magic Bullet* (Oxford University Press, 1987); S. Sontag, *AIDS and Its Metaphors* (New York: Farrar, Strauss & Giroux, 1989).

[3] I. Berlin, 'History and theory: the concept of scientific history', in A. V. Riasanovsky and B. Riznik (eds.), *Generalizations in Historical Writings* (Philadelphia: University of Pennsylvania Press, 1963), p. 61.

[4] R. Descartes, 'Discourse on the method', in E. S. Haldane and G. R. T. Ross (eds. and trans.) *Philosophical Works of Descartes* (New York: Dover Publications, 1637/1955), vol. I, pp. 84–5.

[5] I. Rothschild, 'Induction, deduction and the scientific method', The Society for the Study of Reproduction (2006), www.ssr.org/Documents/2006–01–04Induction2.pdf, p. 3; see

If we turn to social psychology, in his classic paper on 'Social Psychology as History', Kenneth Gergen raised similar issues.[6] He pointed out that natural sciences aim to determine general natural laws through systematic studies by means of observation and experimentation. Social psychology, in its attempt to be a science, makes an effort to establish *facts* in order to discover general laws of human behaviour and interaction. If universal principles of human behaviour could be ascertained, above all through experimentation, it might be possible to decrease social conflict, reduce a number of cases of mental illness, and create social conditions in which society as a whole would benefit. The philosopher Bertrand Russell, too, expressed this view when he envisaged that it might even be possible to develop 'a mathematics of human behaviour as precise as the mathematics of machines'.[7]

Research in social psychology today (e.g. social cognition, attribution processes, influence theories, the theory of identity, intergroup conflict, among others) is based on hierarchical and mechanistic epistemologies. They start from what the researcher considers to be elements of reality (e.g. categories like male and female, Protestant and Catholic) and they choose variables that presumably interact with these elements (e.g. poverty and richness, trust and distrust, etc.). If historical and socio-political contexts are at all considered to be part of research, it is usually as a background or a stage rather than as a context that is interdependent with the phenomenon under study. Let us consider, as an example, a study that explored temporal distancing as a determinant of the perception of a just world, published in the *European Journal of Social Psychology*.[8] Participants (introductory psychology students) were randomly assigned to read, online, a vignette about a victim in the near past (the victim was abused last year) or a vignette about a victim in the distant past (five years ago), and make a judgement about blaming the aggressor. In this case, the context (i.e. the vignette) serves as a background, or an independent variable, that is, 'near past' or 'distant past'. Context is not treated as a historical event in which the content, circumstances of the assault, the participant's personal experience, his/her psychological background play any role and are mutually interdependent. In this particular experiment participants are treated or classified as subjects without history and

also B. C. Shafer, 'History, not art, not science, but history: meanings and uses of history', *Pacific Historical Review*, 29 (1960), 159–70.

6 K. J. Gergen, 'Social psychology as history', *Journal of Personality and Social Psychology*, 26 (1973), 309–20.

7 B. Russell, *Our Knowledge of the External World* (New York: Menton Books, 1956), p. 142.

8 R. H. Warner, M. J. Vandeursen and A. R. D. Pope, 'Temporal distance as a determinant of just world strategy', *European Journal of Social Psychology*, 42 (2012), 276–84.

culture, as undifferentiated and undefined. All that matters here is the researchers' hypothesis about the effect of 'near past' and 'distant past' and attributing these categories, quite mechanically, to social reality.

Induction, deduction and abduction in history and social psychology

If a discipline aims to be a science, what does it imply? A commonly held point of view in social sciences, and in social psychology specifically, defines a discipline as a science if it uses inductive and/or deductive methods in studying phenomena in question because these methods, it is believed, will enable the generalization of findings. Stating this very simply, *induction* involves aggregating data from individual instances, averaging them by using statistical methods, and computing probabilities with which data can be generalized to populations. As Salvatore and Valsiner remind us in their critical comments, consensual acceptance of aggregating implies the possibility of generalization, and 'inductive generalization has become *the* generalization, then the way of doing science – the ground and the guarantee of the social role of the scientists' (the authors' emphasis).[9] But this perspective encourages pure empiricism and ignores any epistemological questions about presuppositions on which empiricism is based.[10]

Inductive generalization is complemented by deduction, that is, by making inferences from a set of presumed facts and by formulating predictions on the basis of these, and so apparently being capable of establishing links between causes and effects. One infers conclusions from propositions (e.g. syllogistic reasoning) or from signs that apparently indicate causes (e.g. footprints of animals or humans signify their presence in a given location, smoke signifies fire, etc.). While it is usually assumed that induction and deduction are principal scientific methods, some philosophers of science make further specifications, for example, by proposing empirical falsification or by suggesting hypothetic-deductive methods.[11] However, despite these specifications and proposed alternatives, the aim of the great part of the philosophy of science remains unchanged: 'objective knowledge' and abstract concepts must be pursued

[9] S. Salvatore and J. Valsiner, 'Between the general and the unique: overcoming the nomothetic versus idiographic opposition', *Theory & Psychology*, 20 (2010), 821.

[10] I. Marková, *Paradigms, Thought and Language* (Chichester and New York: Wiley, 1982).

[11] See, for example, C. G. Hempel, *Philosophy of Natural Science* (Englewood Cliffs, NJ: Prentice-Hall, 1966); K. R. Popper, *An Objective Knowledge: an Evolutionary Approach* (Oxford: Clarendon Press, 1979); P. Godfrey-Smith, *Theory and Reality* (Chicago, IL: University of Chicago Press, 2003).

by logical and formalistic thinking. In view of this, let us explore whether inductive and deductive methods apply to our two disciplines, history and social psychology.

If we consider history, Berlin argued that history is neither an inductive nor deductive science.[12] It cannot specify any logical rules that would be applicable to particular situations or historical events. Each event is unique and it takes place in a particular time and space. The study of unique events and their specificity distinguishes history as a discipline from natural sciences. Historians attempt 'to capture the unique pattern and peculiar characteristics of its particular subject; not to be an X-ray which eliminates all but what a great many subjects have in common'.[13] Drawing attention to these issues, Berlin emphasises that misguided attempts to transform history into a natural science have not been always clearly acknowledged and, as a result, the difference between natural sciences and history has been disregarded. Historical thinking 'is much more like the operation of common sense, where we weave together various logically independent concepts and general propositions, and bring them to bear on a given situation as best we can'.[14] This capacity of weaving together concepts and propositions is guided by intuition and/or judgement, which are features of natural, rather than formalistic thinking.

In contrast to history, social psychology does largely aim at inductive generalization. It treats populations as aggregates of independent individuals rather than as groups in which individuals are related to one another in terms of social psychological features.[15] In other words, independent individuals are considered as belonging to rigid categories like males, females, democrats, conservatives, Americans or Europeans and no thought is given to whether such categories share any characteristics of groups. Instead, categories are treated *as if* they are empirically vital for the study of dependent variables, which researchers a priori determine as relevant to their preconceived ideas.[16] Such relations between independent and dependent variables are confirmed or disconfirmed by means of experimental manipulations or questionnaires. In order to expand their findings, researchers multiply their studies by choosing still other categories or subcategories of humans (e.g. women under 20 years of age, men who are Catholics) or objects; this enables researchers to make claims about seemingly general findings, and about universal laws of behaviour.

[12] Berlin, 'History and theory', pp. 78–9.
[13] *Ibid.*, p. 91. [14] *Ibid.*, p. 78.
[15] S. Moscovici, and I. Marková, *The Making of Modern Social Psychology: the Hidden Story of How an International Social Science was Created* (Cambridge: Polity Press, 2006).
[16] Salvatore and Valsiner, 'Between the general and the unique'.

In contrast to most theories in social psychology, the epistemology of the theory of social representations is akin to that of history. The theory of social representations was first formulated in 1961 by Serge Moscovici in his classic book *La Psychoanalyse: son image et son public.*[17] In choosing a unique historical event in France in the 1950s, that is, the circulation of ideas and activities in relation to Freud's psychoanalysis in the press and public discourse, Moscovici explored how psychoanalysis was transformed from a purely professional and scientific endeavour into a phenomenon that infiltrated everyday thinking. Moscovici studied different kinds of discourses of various social groups, their percolation into reports of the mass media and everyday activities. He showed that these transformations of scientific and professional knowledge into social representations were enriched in and through different kinds of knowing, such as common sense, collective memories, conscious and unconscious beliefs, myths and metaphors. Moscovici's study suggested that common-sense language and different forms of thinking guided the ways of organizing relations between various kinds of participants, like those between parents and children, or professionals and lay people. For example, his study has shown the importance of naming people and objects. Giving someone or something a name generates new kinds of social representations in relation to those persons or objects. For example, Moscovici showed that with the mere addition of the qualifier 'American', the term 'psychoanalysis', which was originally associated with a certain representation (e.g. psychoanalysis as a therapy), was transformed into a new representation, 'American psychoanalysis', which had an ideological and negative meaning. Names turn ideas into social realities; equally, ideas transform meanings of names and fix them in those realities. These transformations and fixations do not take place in a vacuum. Communication and daily activities are underlain by experience, traditions, customs, folk-knowledge and historical narratives.

The theory of social representations is underlain by the epistemology of common sense. It explores the formation and transformation of common-sense knowledge and beliefs of unique social phenomena in specific socio-political and historical situations. Like historical events, phenomena studied in social representations are unique. Their uniqueness is given by the fact that historical, political, cultural and social circumstances are just as important for studying social representations, as are the data obtained from participants and objects of representing. The

[17] S. Moscovici, *La Psychanalyse: son image et son public*, 2nd edn (Paris: Presses Universitaires De France, 1976), translated by D. Macey as: *Psychoanalysis: Its Image and Its Public* (Cambridge: Polity Press, 2008).

relevant features of the field in which social representations are embedded, and the data about participants and objects of representations are interdependent; they define and transform one another. For example, if we take the case of social representations of psychoanalysis in France in the 1950s, the influence of political power of the Communist Party and of the Catholic Church reflected themselves in citizens' thinking and communications about psychoanalysis. Within such patterns of interdependence between the political power of the Communist Party and the Catholic Church in citizens' thinking, all components exert a mutual influence on one another, and they jointly generate new patterns of knowledge, beliefs and images of the object of representation. Following the publication of *La Psychanalyse*, social representing has been studied in various social, political, health-related and other kinds of fields that have preoccupied the minds and discourses of the general public. For instance, Jodelet explored social representations of madness in a specific and economically deprived French region, Doise traced the origin of normative social representations of human rights as general principles or articles of the Declaration of Human Rights in communication and human interactions, Marková and Wilkie have explored myths and images of HIV/AIDS in the British press during the epidemic in 1980, and so on.[18] All these studies built on common-sense ideas of people that formed substantive features of social representations in question. Like in history, the study of unique phenomena using the perspective of social representations is unsuitable for the application of inductive and/or deductive methods resulting in statistical tables or correlations as was the case in the study based on vignettes mentioned above. Instead, analyses of data in social representations bring together different kinds of knowledge; the theory considers their transformation, and relies on various forms of natural, rather than formalistic, thought. Different kinds of knowledge, beliefs and images are encountered in and through lived social experience. Practical wisdom and common-sense knowledge relate the theory of social representations with language and communication, with images, values and collective visions about which humans communicate: 'It is these features – their specificity and their creativity within collective life – that make social representations different' from other concepts in social sciences.[19]

[18] D. Jodelet, *Madness and Social Representations*. Trans. T. Pownall, ed. G. Duveen (London: Harvester Wheatsheaf, 1989/1991); W. Doise, *Human Rights as Social Representations* (London: Routledge, 2002); I. Marková and P. Wilkie, 'Concepts, representations, and social change: the phenomenon of AIDS', *Journal for the Theory of Social Behaviour*, 17 (1987), 398–409.

[19] Moscovici, *Psychoanalysis: Its Image and Its Public*, p. 10.

Examples of common-sense thinking in relation to social representations bring us to the ideas of the American pragmatic philosopher Charles Sanders Peirce. For Peirce, common sense results from the traditional experience of mankind, steered more by sentiments than by formalistic logic. Common sense is the safest guide in life and it implies faith in instinct and imagination.[20]

Peirce thought that induction and deduction are not methods of discovery: they are simply methods of validation or methods of proof based on the similarity of cases. Instead, the method of discovery is abduction (called also retroduction, hypothesis, hypothetic inference, presumption), which, nevertheless, we must treat cautiously. Peirce was developing and changing his ideas about abduction throughout all his life, and his early views (before the year 1900) on abductive inferences, considerably differ from his later views (after the year 1900). It is in his later work that abduction became much more clearly characterized as a form of innovation based on imagination or on what he called instinctive thinking. It is the latter concept of Peirce's abduction to which I am referring in this chapter. In 'Scientific imagination' Peirce argues that when a researcher passionately desires to know the truth, 'his first effort will be to imagine what that truth can be'.[21] While imagination must be restrained, its absence does not lead to any creative thoughts. In his very long letter of 22 June 1911 to his friend and mathematician J. H. Kehler, Peirce labours his views on abduction: 'A scientific inquiry must usually, if not always, begin with Retroduction. An Induction can hardly be sound or at least is to be suspected unless it has been preceded by a Retroactive reasoning.'[22] He considers retroduction – which he also calls abduction – to be the most important kind of reasoning 'because it is the only kind of reasoning that opens up new ground' and he is no longer convinced that abduction can be assigned any logical form.[23] Humans must trust their power to getting the truth because it is all they have to guide them; abduction 'depends on our hope, sooner or later, to guess at the conditions under which a given phenomenon presents itself'.[24]

Let us take a concrete example of using abductive thinking. In her 2011 Ph.D. thesis on sexual and reproductive health among indigenous

[20] C. S. Peirce, *Collected Papers of Charles Sanders Peirce*. Vols. I–VI, ed. C. Hartshorne and P. Weiss, 1931–1935. Vols. VII–VIII, ed. Arthur W. Burks, 1958 (Cambridge, MA: Harvard University Press), 4.658.

[21] Peirce, *Collected Papers*, vol. I, p. 46.

[22] C. S. Peirce *The New Elements of Mathematics*, ed. C. Eisele, vol. III/I, *Mathematical Miscellanea. Letter to Kehler, 22 June 1911* (The Hague and Paris: Mouton, 1976), p. 178.

[23] Peirce, *The New Elements of Mathematics*, p. 206.

[24] *Ibid.*, p. 206.

young Mexicans, Jacqueline Priego Hernández explored their social representations of sexual health in two different contexts, rural and urban. She introduced a theoretical model of typologies of knowledge that she then tested in her work. Having analysed her empirical data from focus groups, she found that the model would have to be modified by bringing in an additional knowledge generated in an interview. Although she did not discuss her model in terms of Peirce's ideas on abduction, she followed Peirce's way of thinking. Like Peirce, she did not start with the search for facts. Instead, phenomena were in front of her and her task was to devise a theory to make sense of them or to explain them.[25] In the Peircean way of thinking, this can be achieved by observing the whole event and devising a preliminary theory by means of intuition (or what Peirce would call instinct). Such a preliminary theory of knowledge merely suggests that something may or may not be the case.[26] In using intuitive knowledge or a preliminary theory, the researcher must be prepared to discard or to change it if it proves to be irrelevant. This was also the case in Priego Hernández's study: in view of her empirical findings, she reconceptualized her model to fit her data.

It could be argued that in inductive research, too, the researcher starts with a preliminary theory. Even if he or she starts explicitly with the collection of data, this is guided by some ideas and goals of exploration. While this is true, the epistemology of inductive thinking treats fragments or elements of phenomena as units that, themselves, are considered to be stable statistical variables.

In contrast, the epistemology based on abduction is concerned with the whole event in its relation to the context in which it is embedded.[27] But what is 'the whole event'? Does it include everything in the world? Certainly it does not. As stated above, the researcher constructs his or her preliminary theory of the interdependence between the data and the contexts within which they are embedded. Such a preliminary theory could be based on the researcher's knowledge of history, culture, own experience, findings of others, and so on. In other words, the epistemology of abductive thinking is *relational*; the assumption of interdependence between phenomena and their contexts has fundamental implications for generalization of a totally different kind than that of induction (see below).

The concept of the later form of Peircean abduction is adopted by Salvatore and Valsiner in their analysis of single case studies: '*In the*

[25] Peirce, *Collected Papers*, 5.145 [26] *Ibid.*, 5.171; also 6.475 and 8.238.

[27] F. Cornish, *Journal of Health Psychology*, 9 (2004), 281–94; S. Jovchelovitch, *Knowledge in Context: Representations, Community and Culture* (London: Routledge, 2007).

abductive logic, theory and evidence are circularly bonded within an open-ended cycle.'[28] The authors identify several types of dynamic interactions between the evidence, its local modelling and the general theory of mediation.[29] Their types of dynamic interactions focus on discovery enabling the researcher to model the local exemplar, elaborating the theory to facilitate generalization, widening the domain of application of the general theory to new phenomena, and differentiating the study of the exemplar from new cases. This procedure conceptually develops Peirce's concept of abduction as a method of discovery, and suggests ways by means of which a researcher, when not satisfied with his/her model, may abandon it and suggest a new one.

The style of thinking emphasizing intuition and common-sense knowledge has evoked considerable criticism from scientifically minded social scientists as being subjectivist and arbitrary. However, defendants of common-sense and intuitive thinking have argued that the study of single events is not less rigorous than inductive studies. It simply follows a different procedure, and it has its own logic that has to be respected. It reflects the study of social reality as conceived by ordinary knowers rather than the study of abstract and preconceived variables.[30]

In view of the discussion indicating that induction and deduction are not suitable methods either in the work of historians or in that of students of social representations, let us consider the following: what scientific status, if any, can these disciplines claim? And how is abduction used in these two disciplines?

Let us take Berlin's interesting observation concerning the inference connectors in propositions, like 'because' or 'therefore'. In communications of knowledge, for example in textbooks of natural sciences, the links between individual propositions are logically ordered, one proposition following from the other. Berlin notes that even if the inference connectors like 'because' and 'therefore' are not used to combine such propositions, the cause/effect links are still obvious owing to the established logical steps that determine the inner structure of propositions implying links between them. In contrast, history texts use a great deal of connectors like 'events took their inevitable course', 'small wonder if', 'thereupon', and so on. Without such connectors, Berlin argues, the text

[28] Salvatore and Valsiner, 'Between the general and the unique', p. 828, the authors' emphasis.

[29] J. Valsiner, 'Process structure of semiotic mediation in human development', *Human Development*, 44 (2001), 84–97.

[30] D. T. Campbell, 'Degrees of freedom and the case study', *Comparative Political Studies*, 8 (1975), 178–191; C. Geertz, *After the Fact: Two Countries, Four Decades, One Anthropologist* (Cambridge, MA: Harvard University Press, 1995); and B. Flyvbjerg, 'Five misunderstandings about case-study research', *Qualitative Inquiry*, 12 (2006), 219–45.

would be much less smooth or even ambiguous, because at times there seems to be no great logical relation between propositions. He observes that connectors 'because', 'therefore', and the like, have different meanings in natural and human sciences. In inductive inferences, the logical connector 'because' implies that one piece of evidence provides the same results as in another case; when something is considered true, one can generalize from that case to another one. For example: 'It was minus 10 degrees. The lake was frozen.' In contrast, in the formation of knowledge using abduction, 'because' infers the common-sense understanding or the recognition that a given activity is part of a superordinated activity, or of a pattern of activity that is generally understood, remembered or that can be imagined. For example: 'It was minus 10 degrees. Thus it was not surprizing that Napoleon's army suffered.'

Both Peirce and Berlin indicate that abductive understanding is provisional; we can make mistakes, and we may substitute one explanation for another one. However, this way of thinking is different from inductive reasoning, and inductive reasoning cannot substitute abductive reasoning. When we understand something, it is not because we think inductively, but because we apply common-sense knowledge. We choose to put together fragments that fit and make sense: 'When, in fact, I am successful in this – when the fragments seem to me to fit – we call this an explanation; when in fact they do fit, I am called rational; if they fit badly ... I am called irrational ... if they do not fit at all, I am called mad.'[31] Historical events, we can see, are interwoven from disparate ingredients that researchers structure into a coherent story, and they imagine how the story may correspond to social reality as they know it. As Peirce puts it, abduction means 'examining a mass of facts and in allowing these facts to suggest a theory'.[32]

If we turn to the theory of social representations, its basic presupposition is common-sense thinking – the thinking of daily life that uses knowledge shared by social groups; it prioritizes human interactions and relations and these, by definition, take diverse forms. Owing to social circumstances, common-sense thinking forces humans to take up their own positions and defend them; it is thinking that judges, evaluates, criticizes and makes proposals for action. Common-sense thinking uses knowledge and beliefs generated by the established cultural and historical experiences and it makes inferences on the basis of these. An individual may be using a plurality of modes of thought; and different professionals approach the analysis of a problem-situation in different ways. They use diverse meanings, or we could say with Bakhtin, different languages to speak about 'the same' problem.

[31] Berlin, 'History and theory', p. 97. [32] Peirce, *Collected Papers*, 8.209.

In sum, both the history and the theory of social representations explore unique or single events and conceive of them as complex phenomena interdependent with their social, political, demographic and otherwise, contexts. The consideration of uniqueness of a historical event or of a social phenomenon is a specific epistemological feature of our two disciplines.

Generalization in history and social representations

As scholarly disciplines, history and the theory of social representations aspire at making general claims about their findings. If by nature of their research approaches they do not adopt inductive generalization, what kind of generalization is available to them?

Epistemologically, both history and the theory of social representations treat historical events and social phenomena, respectively, as dynamic, systemic and unique, interdependent with the situation/context. One needs to ask, nevertheless, what is meant by situation/context and what aspects of the situation/context form the interdependent relation with the historical event or with the social phenomenon under study. In order to answer this question we need to ask in addition: what is the problem that the researcher explores? How is the problem defined? Surely for each problem different aspects of the context are relevant and certainly not all of them are pertinent to the problem concerned. Some aspects of the context participants of the study actively select or deselect. For example, although the Freudian model of psychoanalysis centres on the concept of libido, the surprising finding in Moscovici's study of psychoanalysis was the absence of the concept of libido in subjects' spontaneous comments. Moscovici argued that the dominant values of society at the time of his research rejected sexual drives as major psychological forces.[33] Developing Moscovici's arguments, Jesuino takes an epistemic approach, looking beyond the data and searching for hidden meanings of a representation: 'The figurative nucleus uncovered by Moscovici is not obvious but rather grounded in the data.'[34] Such approach, like in Peirce's abduction, explains how the fragmented data 'in the present case the hundreds of answers provided by the respondents, could be internally articulated and structured'.[35] Moreover, the search for hidden meanings may also point to the fact of the (re)emergence of the suppressed *libido* in subjects' recognition of the word and in their judgements of language meanings, rather than expressing it spontaneously:

33 Moscovici, *Psychoanalysis: Its Image and Its Public*, p. 63.

34 J. C. Jesuino, 'Linking science to common sense', *Journal for the Theory of Social Behaviour*, 38 (2008), 396.

35 *Ibid.*, p. 396.

'Moscovici observes that the libido disappears from the social representation of psychoanalysis, rather as though, according to his interpretation, it were incompatible with social norms.'[36] Jodelet, too, draws attention to the selection of contextual features in the formation of social representations.[37] She emphasizes that it is not that all elements of the context would be selected by lay people in representing the clinical state of the mentally ill patients in her study. For example, she found that sexuality, affectivity and willpower were missing in villagers' representations of mentally ill patients. There is a general anthropological finding showing that people select elements that form a meaningful pattern in terms of traditions and common-sense thinking. With respect to Jodelet's own study, it was the traits of the close personal contact, which in daily interactions of people with and without mental illness were prohibited by fears of the group, and these prohibitions became part of the villagers' representations. However, if certain aspects of the context are missing from participants' speech or activities, it does not mean that they are totally absent from their representations. It simply points to the fact that some aspects may affect representations subconsciously; the researcher's task is to search for those aspects of the context that are selected, or deselected, or for signs of those features that are subconsciously present.

In view of this a fundamental question arises: if generalization is the aim of science, including social science, can one make any generalizations from unique cases? If one can generalize, clearly, it must be done in a different way than when inductive methods are used. There is a fundamental difference between inductive studies that are based on aggregation of elements of the data from a number of individual cases and studies of unique phenomena that treat single cases as complexes. In the former, the context in which research takes place is considered as stable. It is not treated as interdependent with the phenomenon under study and does not enter either into the process of knowledge building, or into generalization. In contrast, in studies of unique cases, the context is treated as interdependent with the phenomena under research; it participates in the formation of knowledge and in generalization. As Salvatore and Valsiner put it, in abductive methodology, 'theory and data are circularly connected and the construction of general knowledge is pursued through modelling the local phenomena'.[38] In their analysis, research moves from the logic of the confirmation to the logic of the construction of the knowledge.[39]

[36] D. Lagache, 'Préface à Moscovici' in S. Moscovici, *La Psychanalyse, son image et son public* (Paris: Presses Universitaires de France, 1976), p. 11.

[37] Jodelet, *Madness and Social Representations.*

[38] Salvatore and Valsiner, 'Between the general and the unique', p. 828.

[39] *Ibid.*, p. 828.

We have seen that Peirce, Berlin and Moscovici suggest that the researcher should examine unique events as wholes interdependent with their contexts and not as isolated fragments, and he or she should create a preliminary theory in relation to the event (or phenomenon) so conceived. He or she should test the relevance of the preliminary theory with regard to the observed phenomenon, and pose the question as to whether this theory is generalizable (or transferable) to other unique events (or phenomena). For example, if we take the study of social representations of psychoanalysis, Moscovici did not start his research with collecting the data, but with acute observations of the ways in which psychoanalysis penetrated the daily life of individuals and groups, their language, relationships, images, transforming scientific and professional knowledge into social representations. He postulated a preliminary theory intuitively (remember, it was in the context of specific historical and political conditions in France in the 1950s). Jesuino observes that if Moscovici were to pursue an inductive strategy, he would probably never arrive at the concept of the '*figurative scheme*'.[40] The figurative scheme or a figurative model refers to a scientific theory or otherwise (in Moscovici's case psychoanalytic theory) that is reconstructed in common-sense knowledge. Moscovici specifically points out that 'figure' reproduces the object of representation *selectively* (in contrast to mirroring it in its entirety). I have already pointed above to the selection of features from the context. Representation organizes the figure by impregnating it with visual and metaphoric elements and so creates the semantic network pertinent to that figure. As Moscovici says: 'If I say that the model we have described is figurative that is because it is not just a way of coordinating data, but the product of a coordination that defines every part of representation in concrete terms.'[41] The figurative scheme, Jesuino (2008) comments, has become one of the most important concepts of the theory, influencing the subsequent ways of thinking about social phenomena.

Flyvbjerg emphasizes that unique cases (or single case studies) must be strategically selected in order to bring out their richness and make them most effective for 'analytic generalization' (the term 'analytic generalization' was introduced by Yin in order to differentiate it from inductive or statistical generalization).[42] Flyvbjerg argues that the aim of research is to bring out the greatest possible knowledge of a given phenomenon. In contrast, random or representative samples, aggregation of cases, and averaging of gathered facts cannot provide rich knowledge about the

[40] Jesuino, 'Linking science to common sense'.
[41] Moscovici, *Psychoanalysis: Its Image and Its Public*, p. 66.
[42] Flyvbjerg, 'Five misunderstandings'; R. Yin, *Case Study Research*, 3rd edn (Thousand Oaks, CA: Sage, 2003), pp. 31–3.

phenomenon in question because these methods are not equipped to do so. Rich knowledge is better manifested in extreme or deviant cases than in normal or average cases because it is the extreme or deviant case that gets the point across, sometimes in a dramatic manner. Psychoanalysis was such an extreme case in the sense that it captured social representations during cultural fights that took place in France in the 1950s and early 1960s. Both the Catholic Church and the Communist Party were strong and involved in propaganda and the dissemination of their positions. In this unique historical event it was the co-existence of strong contradictory forces of different institutions (the Communist Party, the Catholic Church, the media), which interacted with common-sense thinking, that generated social representations of psychoanalysis.

If we turn to historical studies, we can find similar patterns of interdependencies as in the study of social representations. Let us take the often-quoted historical example, the study of 'The Peasants of Languedoc' by Roy de Ladurie, a global historical account of the ancient province in the south of France during the period from the Middle Ages until the Enlightenment.[43] Roy de Ladurie's detailed research combined historical geography, demography, psychohistory and economic history among others, in studying the life of peasants. The author selected the relevant social phenomena, the changes in social struggles and consciousness that contributed to the pattern of events over several centuries. He examined all these components in relation to one another as parts of the whole social structure.

The findings from these two unique events, that is, the study of social representations of psychoanalysis in France in the 1950s and early 1960s, and the historical study of peasants in Languedoc, have implications for studies of similar kinds and for generalizations of theories relating to these two pieces of research. Concerning the former, one can pose the question as to whether intellectual polemics, forms of thinking and the clash of new ideas with the established values are transferable to studies of social representations other than those represented by the case of psychoanalysis in France in the late 1950s. With respect to the latter, here again, the theory treating the nature of religious clashes, epidemics of severe illnesses, poverty and economic depression and prosperity, could be transferable to other classes of historical events. The forces that combine contexts in both of these cases with the studied phenomena do not leave any components stable over time, whether they concern the data

[43] E. Le Roy Ladurie, *Les Paysans de Languedoc* (Paris: S.E.V.P.E.N., 1966); published in English as *The Peasants of Languedoc*, trans. J. Day (Urbana and Chicago: University of Illinois Press, 1974).

gathered from participants (interviews, the media) or interpretations from archival materials on the one hand, and the data constituted by the relevant historical, political and social situations on the other.

To sum up: if the researcher presupposes that a science is dynamic, he or she uses different conceptual tools than if he or she holds the presupposition that it is static. This perspective applies to any sciences, whether natural or social. Equally, this holds for those theories of social psychology that do not define their areas of research in terms of making inductive generalizations, that is, generalizing findings from limited samples to populations. In developmental psychology, Piaget discovered the child's operational stages while studying very few cases.[44] It was the sense of reality and intuition that guided his work in in-depth clinical observations and interviews; from these he arrived at discoveries of a general nature. Similarly, Kurt Lewin's discovery of group relations pertaining to democratic and non-democratic thinking did not require representative samples from which to generalize to the population.[45] His experiments pursued the question of the dynamics of interaction between individuals in groups and their social environment. According to Lewin, interactions modelled realities of daily life and a sense of reality was important in his theory: 'The "reality" of that to which the concept refers is established by "doing something with" rather than "looking at", and this reality is independent of certain "subjective" elements of classification.'[46]

Conclusion

Although it has been often repeated that scientific knowledge is formed through inductive and deductive methods, in natural sciences inductive methods are not as prevalent as one might think.[47] Whilst induction and deduction have been discussed since Aristotle, modern inductive methods are the product of positivism and they do not necessarily apply to natural sciences. For example, Einstein remarked that '[T]here is no inductive method which could lead to fundamental concepts in physics. Failure to understand this fact constituted the basic philosophical error of so many investigations in the nineteenth century.'[48] Instead, just like the Italian philosopher of the eighteenth century, Giambattista

[44] J. Piaget, *Origins of Intelligence in the Child* (London: Routledge & Kegan Paul, 1936).

[45] K. Lewin, 'Frontiers in group dynamics', in D. Cartwright (ed.), *Field Theory in Social Science. Selected Theoretical Papers by Kurt Lewin* (London: Tavistock, 1952), pp. 188–237.

[46] Lewin, 'Frontiers in group dynamics', p. 193.

[47] F. Stadler (ed.), *Induction and Deduction in the Sciences* (Dordrecht: Kluwer Academic, 2004).

[48] A. Einstein, *Ideas and Opinions* (New York: Crown, 1954), p. 307.

Vico, Albert Einstein saw concepts and systems of concepts to be human creations. He presented scientific inferences as creative thoughts, very closely connected with intuition, although, he also pointed out that intuition must be viewed as provisional and has to be corrected in and through interaction with the phenomenon under study.[49] Einstein argued that concepts are free inventions of the human mind and cannot be deduced by abstraction, that is, by logical means. Equally, Einstein rejected the point of view that it is the method that should guide the researcher's theoretical accomplishments. He emphasized that theoretical descriptions are not directly dependent upon empirical assertions.[50] Instead, '[s]cience forces us to create new ideas, new theories. Their aim is to break down the wall of contradictions which frequently blocks the way of scientific progress.'[51] The growth of science is characterized by paradoxes, by the postulation of new problems and by invention. For Einstein, Moscovici points out, what was important was 'surprise' arising from invention.[52] Open-ended systems create new conditions for living and interacting. Considering these views, one may wonder why they have not been noticed by social psychologists who persistently aim at a scientific status of their discipline.

In this chapter I have focused on one epistemological feature that is common to history and the theory of social representations: interdependence between the unique event in history or of a social phenomenon in the study of social representations, and their situation/context. There are at least two fundamental implications of this epistemological feature. First, a social phenomenon, which is the subject of study of the theory of social representations, is by definition a historical phenomenon. In this sense, interdisciplinarity is built into the theory's epistemology. The second implication is methodological. Both in history and in the theory of social representations we deal with unique phenomena, which can be appropriately explored using abduction and single case studies.

We need to conclude that owing to the nature of our two disciplines and their epistemologies, there does not exist – and very likely will not be found – a strong predictive theory of history and the theory of social

[49] See Schilpp, P. A. (ed.), *Albert Einstein: Philosopher-Scientist* (London: Cambridge University Press, 1949).

[50] *Ibid.*, p. 674.

[51] A. Einstein and L. Infeld, *The Evolution of Physics* (London: Cambridge University Press, 1938/1961), p. 264.

[52] S. Moscovici, 'La Relativité a cent ans', 2007, available at www.serge-moscovici.fr/documents/Relativite.pdf [accessed 9 March 2013]; on this issue see also Schilpp (ed.), *Albert Einstein*, Einstein and Infeld, *The Evolution of Physics*, and S. Moscovici, 'The discovery of group polarization', in D. Granberg and G. Sarup (eds.), *Social Judgement and Intergroup Relations* (New York: Springer, 1992), pp. 107–27.

representations. Humans live in concrete conditions and their actions, passions, intentions and thinking is context-dependent. Thus, while some elements of context remain similar over history and cultures, and allow for some weaker forms of prediction, any strong prediction would mean a conception of the context as independent of human agency and this simply is meaningless. In his later work, Donald Campbell, just like Charles Sanders Peirce, explained that common-sense thinking is all that humans have in pursuing knowledge. It is not dependable and it is noisy and fallible – but it is all they have. Predictive and universal theories do not make sense in the study of human affairs, but it is the exploration of social phenomena itself that forces researchers to revise their theories and hypotheses if they do not fit their findings.

In history, in social representations and in culture, phenomena do not appear arbitrarily; they are part of superordinated phenomena that characterize a particular epoch. The Czech-French writer Milan Kundera presents an anecdote from music, showing that Beethoven could write a certain piece at a particular time but not in another. When we consider painters, we could say the same; Picasso's artistic development at the beginning of his career was a part of a certain culture and what he painted at one time would not be possible at another time. Isaiah Berlin similarly points out that Shakespeare's *Hamlet* could not have been written in the Genghis Khan culture. Single case studies mean not only that one cannot take them out of their context, but that their context is part of the study and, therefore, an integral part of historical or social psychological explanation.

Part II

Empirical dialogues: cognition, affect and the self

6 Redefining historical identities: sexuality, gender and the self

Carolyn J. Dean

The history of sexuality touches on many areas of inquiry, including the history of the family, the history of women and gender, the history of science, in particular scientific psychology, and populations. It also traverses a vast array of methodological approaches. Family historians, for example, measure illegitimacy rates in order to assess the impact of social developments like industrialization on family structures. Historians of women necessarily address sex by analysing how and why states regulate female sexuality by limiting or outlawing access to contraception. The chapter that follows limits its inquiry to works that focus primarily on the centrality of sexuality to modern Western culture. Thus, although historians of pre-modern cultures have contributed much to the history of sexuality, it concentrates for the most part on those works by scholars of the modern period. The chapter asks exactly what historians of *sexuality* investigate. They render central questions that are relatively peripheral in works on family or women's history. Moreover, because historians place sexuality in time and place, historical investigation should help to frame studies in psychoanalysis and psychology that presume a universal human subject whose sexual desires and responses can be measured without reference to context. Indeed many of the questions posed by histories of sexuality, including the works I will discuss, ask how historical forces shape sexuality, and Michel Foucault's work presumes that desire itself is generated historically. Thus how does sex become an object of historical inquiry when it expresses the human body's biological desires? What is the cultural significance of debates and discussions about sex – what does sexuality represent? And in what terms did sexuality become discussable? – how was it linked to selfhood and gender identity, and how was it invested with historical meaning? More recent works address how sexuality is central to definitions of citizenship and impact profoundly social policy, especially for women and sexual minorities. Sexual mores can even become metaphors of other social and cultural forms of belonging. Historian Joan W. Scott, for example, addresses French intellectuals today who argue that a particularly French idea of 'seduction' and heterosexual coupling encourages men to exercise dominance through gallantry if they want to win over women. In their view, gallantry, Scott argues, civilizes society by using sexual difference as armour against an imagined sameness represented by those groups who cannot understand seduction as a means metaphorically of reconciling the differences that inevitably arise in democracies – feminists, 'militant homosexuals', and Muslims who allegedly refuse to play by French rules. Here 'seduction' relies on a rigid gender difference and the subordination of women that sells itself as natural and quintessentially French.[1]

The history of sexuality is a relatively recent area of inquiry in historical thought, and we will trace how it has developed over time, with what foci and questions. It is based on examining, interpreting and incorporating the work of nineteenth-century sexual science and that of Sigmund Freud, the father of 'psychoanalysis'. At the end of the nineteenth century in Europe and the United States, doctors developed elaborate taxonomies of different kinds of sexual desire. They no longer conceived sexual expressions in terms of behaviours in which all sinful or immoral men and women might engage, but as symptoms of different moral characters. Indeed, they constituted 'sexuality' or 'sexual instinct' as objects of scientific inquiry. The Austrian Dr Richard von Krafft-Ebing, the most famous taxonomist of all, published a large book entitled *Psychopathia Sexualis* in 1886 that introduced the terms 'sadist' and 'masochist' into the medical lexicon, and disseminated others, such as 'homosexual'. Krafft-Ebing's classifications thus not only identified specific sorts of desire more precisely, but also redefined self-identity in new terms. Now sexual desire was no longer only a bodily drive that one might resist or indulge, but defined a person's identity, so that, for example, the man who derived pleasure from sexual violence was not simply subject to particularly strong impulses but a creature with a diagnosable psychological condition. Krafft-Ebing's sadists were certain kinds of people with specific histories: they demonstrated their affliction usually at an early age, perhaps by harming animals, and as they grew older they derived sexual pleasure from harming people. Such creatures, according to the doctor, were almost always men whose 'natural' instinct to dominate went awry. Doctors thus no longer conceived sexuality as sexual practices – as vices that might be indulged in by any morally unrestrained person – but as defining a psychic identity whose contours they could map and whose inner life might be analysed and controlled through the

[1] J. W. Scott, *The Fantasy of Feminist History* (Durham, NC: Duke University Press, 2011), pp. 117–40.

scientific investigation of sexual fantasies and behaviours. Hence sadists, masochists, homosexuals, fetishists, necrophiliacs and, finally, 'heterosexuals' appeared in the course of the late nineteenth and early twentieth centuries, objects now of a new science dubbed 'sexology' in 1904 (*Sexualwissenschaft*) by the German Iwan Bloch.

Freud's work radicalized the way sexuality had been imagined throughout the nineteenth and early twentieth centuries. In his *Three Essays on the Theory of Sexuality* (1905) Freud argued that sexuality is a 'psychical' representation of the body's sexual energy so that sexuality could not be reduced to bodily drives.[2] As he argued eventually, the link between the sexual aim (the desire to 'discharge' libidinal energy) and the sexual object (whom or what one desires) was shaped by unconscious fantasies generated by the infant's relationship with its parents rather than by a purely biological drive to procreate. There was thus no longer any 'natural' or necessary relationship between desire and procreation, as had been assumed by the majority of late nineteenth-century sexologists. Freud thus argued that too much sexual repression was problematic, that sex was absolutely central to understanding the human psyche, and that psychoanalysis could help regulate sexual behaviour in healthy ways. He thus insisted on a more or less ideal trajectory of human sexual development culminating in normative heterosexuality and gender roles. Though it was now a struggle to become sexually normal – one's sexual drives were shaped by a process he termed the 'Oedipus complex' – it was desirable and might be achieved through the intervention of psychoanalytic techniques.

How was this allegedly scientific work a touchstone for the history of sexuality? Sexuality was now central to identity, and Freud, in popularized versions, a common reference. Still, so-called histories of sex appealed primarily to a male audience who sought erotic stimulation until the 1960s. Such works masqueraded as serious anthropological studies of other cultures, or as medical tracts aimed ostensibly at educating sexually naive male readers about how to avoid the perils of venereal disease. To be sure, medical literature on sex gained legitimacy as sexual science became increasingly respectable in the inter-war period (1918–39), and inter-war artists, political radicals and liberal reformers often insisted on sexual freedom. But it was not until the 1960s that works calling themselves 'history' about sex and unrelated to matters medical or 'hygienic' – as reformers and writers euphemistically referred to the effects of proper and moderate sex – gained currency and respectability.

[2] S. Freud, *Three Essays on the Theory of Sexuality*, trans. J. Strachey (New York: Basic Books, 1975), p. 34.

Numerous histories of erotica published in those years aimed at liberating sex from the constraints imposed on its expression by moralists, but they also sought to titillate readers. Informed by Freud's emphasis on the importance of sexuality with little of his complexity, they – Montgomery Hyde's 1964 *History of Pornography*, for example – recount an epic struggle between sexual liberation and repression in which increasing numbers of enlightened readers recognize the centrality of sex to human creative expression. Hyde embraced an argument made more modestly in the inter-war period: he asserted that 'Obscenity and pornography are ugly phantoms which will disappear in the morning light when we rehabilitate sex and eroticism', meaning that repression was a dark force obstructing the development of natural, healthy sexuality.[3] Repression led not only to the proliferation of pornography, of which the healthy individual would have no need, but to a world in which men and women would confuse their so-called natural roles and seek to imitate each other. When they spoke of 'history', then, critics who scorned censorship meant a clash between the joyous triumph of human self-understanding and the sinister forces of repression, between those who would leave nature unfettered and those who would shackle her, between those who would liberate the human soul and those who would deform it. Attitudes to sex in a given culture measured the progress of humankind.

Such critics, as well as doctors and moralists, all believed that sexuality, like masculinity and femininity, was outside history – a natural force to be repressed, regulated, liberated, or channelled by social institutions but not in any conceivable way the *product* of human history. Still, to the extent they equated sexual 'liberation' with the progress of culture and civilization, they suggested that sexual norms reflect shifts in historical development. Indeed, the first work to relate sexuality to specific historical formations was published in 1964: in the path-breaking *The Other Victorians: a Study of Pornography and Sexuality in Mid-Nineteenth Century England*, the literary critic Steven Marcus claimed that his study was born by melding his interest in the history of culture and ideas about the self with those of social and behavioural scientists fascinated by the empirical study of sexuality.[4]

The Other Victorians assumes that the Victorians relentlessly repressed sexuality, but links prohibitions on sexual expression to the historical experience of modernity: 'as an urban, capitalist, industrial middle-class

[3] M. Hyde, *The History of Pornography* (New York: Heinemann, 1964), p. 204.

[4] S. Marcus, *The Other Victorians: a Study of Pornography and Sexuality in Mid-Nineteenth Century England* (New York: Norton, 1985). The period is dubbed 'Victorian' after Queen Victoria of Great Britain, who assumed the throne in 1837 and is usually believed to personify the spirit of that era.

world was being created … the whole style of sexual life was considerably modified. By a variety of social means which correspond to the psychological processes of isolation, distancing, denial and even repression, a separate and insulated sphere in which sexuality was to be confined was brought into existence.'[5] That is, sexual repression was necessary and particularly acute at a historical moment (the late eighteenth and nineteenth centuries) when social advancement required the reconstruction and disciplining of the human body and mind. Though Marcus does not elaborate, we presume he refers to new concepts of time introduced by work discipline and industrial capitalism, as well as new spatial divisions between the world of work and of the home first articulated at the end of the eighteenth century. In this context, sex, as he puts it, was not just a problem but 'problematical', because its power to compel and distract posed a threat to the demands of social discipline.[6]

Marcus thus does not judge sexual repression to be necessarily good or bad but understands it as symptomatic of different stages of historical and social development. For example, in his view, pornography is a symptom of repression, the 'price we pay for social advancement'.[7] Medical men in the Victorian period disseminated fantastical treatises meant to instil fear of sexual pleasure and thereby ensure social discipline. In so doing, they generated an equally fantastical world of pornography as its antithesis – an anxiety-free world of sexual plenty rather than scarcity. Similarly, Marcus argues, the more upper-class society demands restraint in outward appearance, the more a Victorian gentleman (whose memoirs Marcus analyses) lives an unrestrained 'secret life' – a 'pornographic' world of easy, frequent and exploitative sex split off from the world of Victorian propriety. Doctors, pornographers and gentlemen alike describe sex either in a moral vocabulary of condemnation or in a pornographic language in which sex is always good and gratifying to all, in which women (doctors said) are either 'not troubled by sexual feeling' or (pornographers insisted) sexually hungry. According to Marcus, the Victorian period represents one stage in intellectual and social development that will eventually be surpassed by more open and rational attitudes to sexuality, marked particularly by the work of Sigmund Freud. Marcus' work mirrored Freud's views that repression was necessary for social discipline but that its social costs should be controlled rather than condemned.

The Other Victorians thus offered a sophisticated, historicized analysis of sexuality. Methodologically speaking, Marcus asked that we focus on how properly to characterize attitudes towards sex and seek

[5] *Ibid.*, p. 283. [6] *Ibid.*, p. 2. [7] *Ibid.*, p. 262.

to reconstruct the sexual organization of society and sexual experiences among persons in the past. He asked how the meanings and expressions of sex are constructed by culture, and also suggested implicitly that sex was a proper object of historical inquiry by demonstrating that sexuality intersects private and public experience – that sexual fantasies exist not only in a realm split off from public discussion but mark 'official' medical discourse about sex as well. He asks how pornography, medical treatises, popular works about sex, diaries, journals and erotic literature more generally constitute cultural expressions of sexuality, male or female, though he uses male sexuality as his only model. In this important book, Marcus defined the questions and analytical parameters of much of the history of sexuality as it was to be written – in improved and modified form – for the next twenty years.

In particular, Marcus' work articulated self-consciously the ideology of historical progress as well as the centrality of male sexuality that underlay the histories of sexuality published in the 1960s and 1970s. For modern sexual history recounts the birth and development of the middle-class male self: 'Every man who grows up', he wrote, 'must pass through such a phase in his existence, and I can see no reason for supposing that our society, in the history of its own life, should not have to pass through such a phase as well.'[8] Modern sexual history unfolds away from the distorting lens of repression towards a more enlightened era, and thus towards clarity about matters sexual. Marcus, like most liberal writers and scholars of those decades, believed that sexual attitudes measure human progress, and thus believed that sexuality expresses something essential and essentially spiritual about human beings.

Marcus' work was thus the most distinguished instance of an ideology that tied sexual repression and enlightenment to historical progress. In this vision, the Victorian period emblematizes the effects of sexual repression, including the proliferation of pornography and 'secret' lives, shame and guilt that writers and scholars since the beginning of the twentieth century sought to reverse. Marcus the literary critic relied on Freud, especially in his view that the progressive development of civilized man requires increased sexual discipline. But Freud's work was limited in its influence on historians, except to the extent that he rendered sexuality a central problem in Western culture. Indeed, institutionalized psychoanalysis, in spite of the far more complex views of its founder, insisted on the pathology of homosexuality until very recently. And those historians who flirted briefly with 'psychohistory' in the 1970s also emphasized the normative developmental model in order to explain irrational forces

[8] *Ibid.*, p. 286.

in human history, and they were eventually rebuked by most historians for relying on a timeless psychological theory that did not meet the evidentiary standards of most historical research.[9] Freud's timeless psyche posed a dilemma for historians who study social change, and while relying on neurology, he could not demonstrate empirically the existence of the unconscious, and, from most historians' perspectives, was thus insufficiently 'scientific'.

Freud's work, nonetheless, influenced the historian Peter Gay, though for reasons discussed he shied away from calling himself a psycho-historian.[10] In 1984, Gay took aim at the limits of Marcus' implicit use of Freud. He claimed that Marcus' study had 'immortalized smug twentieth-century condescension' about the Victorians' ostensibly prudish attitudes to sex and, in particular, immortalized 'respectable women's sexual anesthesia'.[11] He argued that Marcus mistakenly took the so-called 'official discourse' of Victorian sexuality at its word, particularly in reference to female sexuality, and consequently overemphasized the modern rupture with a repressive Victorian past. Gay thus adds Marcus' name to the pantheon of 'anti-Victorians' – sexologists Havelock Ellis and, later, William Masters and Virginia Johnson – who saw themselves rebelling against the so-called strictures of Victorian moral imperatives, both past and present.

This argument against Marcus forms the basis for two very different repudiations of his generation's portrait of Victorian sexuality. One group of historians, represented by Peter Gay and numerous others, including Carl Degler, Martha Vicinus and Carroll Smith-Rosenberg, seeks to revise the popular image of the Victorian past touted by Marcus and others, insisting that official views of sexuality were not necessarily reflected in private life. Though their analyses differ, these historians generally argue that even official Victorian views were not as monolithic or as homogenous as Marcus made them out to be.

This challenge to Marcus focused on female sexuality, which Marcus had all but ignored. The emerging field of women's history heavily influenced this challenge because it addressed not only women's experience, but also the regulation of and debates about female sexuality (about prostitution, birth control and abortion, to name only a few). Historians began to trace the lives of women who rebelled against Victorian propriety and

[9] For more on psychohistory, see Scott, *The Fantasy of Feminist History*, pp. 1–6; and L. Hunt, 'Psychology, psychoanalysis, and historical thought', *A Companion to Western Historical Thought* (Oxford: Blackwell, 2001), pp. 337–56.

[10] Hunt, 'Psychology, psychoanalysis, and historical thought', p. 340.

[11] P. Gay, *The Bourgeois Experience, Victoria to Freud*, vol. I: *Education of the Senses* (New York: Oxford University Press, 1984), p. 468.

those who happily carved themselves out niches within it – *pace* Marcus, who ignored women's voices entirely and with little evidence, claimed that most women simply accepted men's stereotypes of female sexuality. But more dramatically, as Gay argues, 'To define the nature of female sexuality was to do nothing less than to define the nature of marriage itself and to supply instructive clues to the quality of bourgeois communions.'[12] Marcus argued that sexuality became 'problematical' in the nineteenth century; Gay and others argue that women symbolized the problematic nature of sex. Whether women were fundamentally maternal or sexually passionate determined not only their fitness for different social roles, but also shaped ideas about their marital obligations. This debate about women's 'nature' suggests that Victorians were far more ambivalent than repressive concerning matters sexual.

Drawing on surveys, correspondence, diaries and literary sources, revisionist historians paint a generally positive picture of middle-class Victorian sexuality in which sex is not necessarily repressed but an expression of human joy and intimacy, particularly in married life. Victorian men and women understood sex, Gay and Degler argue, to be the cornerstone of married relationships, affording mutual pleasure and enhancing intimacy. They use new sources to demonstrate that Victorian women enjoyed sex, repudiating the Victorian stereotype of the sexually passive, unresponsive women for whom sexual desire was inspired by the thought of childbearing. Gay and Degler do not deny the existence of sexual ignorance, abuse and other reminders of the bleaker world that Marcus paints. But in this revisionist interpretation, the Victorians rather than the 'moderns' – meaning those doctors, writers and thinkers who insisted on the virtues of sex and sex education – are the real paragons of enlightenment and progress. Victorians recognized the centrality of sex and sought to integrate eroticism and love into their lives such that binding, equal, loving relationships flourished.

This revision of standard concepts of Victorian sexuality moves the idea that sex is essential to self-fulfilment back in time. It thus challenges that teleological ascent of sexual attitudes from darkness towards light, and repression towards liberation, that characterized dominant modes of historical thinking about sexuality. In the revisionist view, the history of sexuality thus does not represent the unfolding of a pre-established script and it is not a phase in society's 'life'. Instead, that history is born of a struggle waged between middle-class culture and the sexual desires that threatened to undermine its moral imperatives and ideals, one that Victorian men and women engaged in constantly and in varied ways.

[12] Gay, *The Bourgeois Experience*, vol. I, p. 145.

How, revisionists ask, did new attitudes towards the self – the necessity of disciplining mind and body in the interests of progress – shape and give meaning to middle-class men's and women's experiences of their bodies and their sexual unions? For if Victorians, and Victorian women in particular, enjoyed sex, then they did so ideally within the parameters of spiritual unions they believed legitimated their sexual pleasure and marked them as constrained, 'civilized' people.

Many other historians nuance this unabashedly positive reinterpretation of the Victorian period: they insist that it is difficult to know whether medical treatises and other educational texts were prescriptive or descriptive, and note also that evidence about women's sexual passion is in large part anecdotal, gleaned from sources that may not be representative. Some too have argued that conclusions about female sexuality must be tempered by the reality of women's subordinate political and social position, and that Gay's celebration of women's pleasure gives such realities short shrift. Many revisionists presume, for example, that sexual intimacy and sexual secrets defined the essence of private life, a human need for intimacy, comfort and discretion that appear to be part of the natural order of things. And yet the very categories of the public and private are historical fictions (if lived realities) first developed in the late eighteenth and the early nineteenth centuries, and cemented women's subordination by naturalizing their place in the private realm, away from the nasty world of politics and commerce reserved for men. What, we might ask, is the relationship between this subordination and women's private sexual fulfilment? What is the relation between women's exclusion from political and social power and their ostensible private happiness?

In 1976 the French philosopher-historian Michel Foucault published a path-breaking book entitled *The History of Sexuality: an Introduction*, which dramatically departed from all extant histories of sexuality.[13] In a direct reference to Marcus, Foucault titled the first part 'We "Other Victorians"', and sought to debunk Marcus' characterization of Victorian sexuality. Foucault claims that the Victorians did not repress their sexual desires in the interests of human progress, but spoke incessantly about sex: during the Victorian period, he wrote, there was 'an institutional incitement to speak about [sex]'.[14]

Like the revisionists, then, Foucault repudiates the idea that the Victorians were sexually repressed. Yet any similarity is superficial, for Foucault takes

[13] The French title is *La Volonté de savoir* (Paris: Gallimard, 1976). This was the first in a series, of which Foucault completed three volumes before his untimely death in 1984.

[14] M. Foucault, *History of Sexuality*, vol. I (New York: Vintage), p. 18.

issue with two interrelated assumptions that inform all prior strains of thought about the history of sexuality, in spite of their differences: that sexuality is a gauge of human enlightenment; and that sex is a biological force shaped by culture. Foucault argues that by the end of the eighteenth century, sex became central to the life and death of nation-states dependent on the regulation and maintenance of healthy populations. Population experts, legislators and doctors, among others, began to develop statistical norms meant to define ideally hygienic, restrained sexual behaviour best suited to capitalist demands for productive workers. The newly powerful middle-class all over Europe sought to create a symbolic 'sexual body' in its own image, no longer defined genealogically after the 'bloodlines' that determined status in feudal societies, but fashioned after an efficient, productive and measurable body mapped out by experts.

Like Marcus, Foucault conceives modern sexual opinion as formed within the experience of modernity – of the time and space of factories, cities, of economically and militarily competitive nations, of a rising middle-class. But unlike Marcus, Foucault repudiates the idea that the Victorian middle-class repressed sex. And unlike Gay, he also repudiates the idea that sexual pleasure within proper boundaries is necessarily a mark of civilized happiness. He rejects Freud outright for having transformed sex into *the* deep secret of Western culture. Instead, he argued that demography, psychology and psychoanalysis, medicine, law and pedagogy – disciplines he termed 'technologies of sex' – *produced* sex in the interests of the powers whose aims they served. In Foucault's paradoxical view, all talk of sex had the effect of regulating sexual expression, and all provocations of erotic desire (whether the fantastical imaginings of Victorian doctors, pornographic literature, or the quiet intimacy of bourgeois unions) regulated and controlled it. Culture does not thus constrain sexual desire 'unnaturally', and hence deform or distort it, nor does it provide an ideal forum, as Gay insists does bourgeois marriage, for its expression. Foucault claims instead that sexuality is not an instinct imposed upon, shaped, or channelled by culture; it has no imaginable life apart from politics and culture and is an idea constituted by and within power relations. He puts it this way: 'Now, it is precisely this idea of sex *in itself* that we cannot accept without examination. Is sex really the anchorage point that supports the manifestations of sexuality, or is it not rather a complex idea that was formed inside the deployment of sexuality?'[15]

Thus repudiating any clear distinction between desire and culture, Foucault claims famously that 'we must not think that by saying yes to sex, one says no to power; on the contrary'.[16] This force Foucault calls

[15] Foucault, *History of Sexuality*, vol. I, p. 152. [16] *Ibid.*, p. 157.

'power' is not unitary: it does not reside in the state and it is not something possessed by anyone. It is the omnipresent and intangible condition of all social relations. Sex is a 'discourse of power': it is no longer a force to be harnessed or repressed by culture but is the effect of these technologies of sex that have no clear origin or cause though they are related to the interests of ruling elites. Those technologies produce normal and abnormal individuals, and the nineteenth-century science of sexology as well as psychoanalysis simply represent the increasing differentiation of human beings along this continuum: the 'science' of sexuality is itself one more technology that rationalizes and regulates populations.

Foucault reinterprets the history of sexual science or 'sexology' in this vein. He argues that these terms were not objective, scientific categories, but ones aimed at defining and regulating new kinds of people now deemed 'normal' or 'deviant'. He deemed psychoanalysis a particularly sinister mode of social regulation because of its emphasis on sexual confession as a source of sexual knowledge and, inevitably, of the analyst's power over the patient.

In this vision, sexuality marks the self in crucial ways – indeed it is the very crux of identity – but its modes of expression over time no longer mark human enlightenment. Instead, sexuality exemplifies the discipline of bodies and minds rather than a force that disrupts social order and must be properly domesticated. If sex is now worth dying for, as Foucault claims, it is not because of something intrinsic in the experience of sexual pleasure, but because power relations have constituted sex in order to discipline us; they have rendered sex the 'mirage', he says, in which we see ourselves reflected. 'Sex', then, 'is historically subordinate to sexuality. We must not place sex on the side of reality, and sexuality on that of confused ideas and illusions: sexuality is a very real historical formation; it is what gave rise to the notion of sex, as a speculative element necessary to its operation.'[17] That is, all this time we have been speaking as if the pleasures of the flesh were the 'real' experience with which we invest an illusory, dreamy, 'confused' cultural meaning we call 'sexuality'. But it turns out that sex is just another expression of the way in which the body, seemingly beyond culture and history, is invested with power, with 'sexuality'. In thus arguing, Foucault addressed the perennial problem of how 'sex' could be a 'psychical representation' and a bodily drive at once.

Foucault's work repudiated the basic presumptions of the history of sexuality as it had been written (and was to be, since the revisionists wrote before and after Foucault's work was published), and laid out a

[17] *Ibid.*, p. 157.

provocative new narrative about the meaning of modern sexuality, particularly its disciplinary function. Though his work is highly controversial, it remains perhaps the single most important contribution to the field and a crucial point of reference. Most scholars in the history of sexuality address his work implicitly or explicitly and take as their own point of departure many of Foucault's insights. To summarize them: the experience of sexuality is utterly mutable and never fixed, never explicable in terms of normative criteria that presume what sexual fulfilment means, what 'healthy' sex is, and so on; so-called perverse identities and perversions (and normalcy) were invented at the end of the nineteenth century; talk about sex proliferated rather than waned in the course of that century because sex was not a repressed drive but constituted as one more power relation; sexuality was a means of regulating and disciplining populations.

We might summarize the work that Foucault's ideas generated by saying that studies now more than ever focus on how sexuality symbolizes social relations of power between men and women, between doctors and patients, and between the state and society. Foucault's greatest influence was arguably not methodological, but lay in his substantive shift of focus away from self-liberation to social discipline, and especially from sexual repression to sexual regulation. In other words, though historians generally accept his contention that sexual desire involves serious questions of power relations and discipline, they seek ways to historicize Foucault's insights by reference to precise social formations rather than to an ill-defined 'power'. James Grantham Turner writes that Foucault 'abolished all existing methods of combining sex and history', but that he 'did not solve the problem of how to put these insights into practice'.[18] Thomas Laqueur notes that 'I have no interest in denying the reality of sex ... But I want to show on the basis of historical evidence that almost everything one wants to *say* about sex – however sex is understood – already has in it a claim about gender. Sex ... is explicable only within the context of battles over gender and power.'[19]

Laqueur, one among a prolific group of historians, thus defines the field of the history of sexuality as it has unfolded since Foucault: it is now arguably the history of the regulation of the body's pleasures, understood as inseparable from 'claims about gender' and often also from claims about race and class ideology. This emphasis on gender derived in part

[18] J. G. Turner (ed.), *Sexuality and Gender in Early Modern Europe* (Cambridge University Press, 1993), p. xv.

[19] T. Laqueur, *Making Sex: Body and Gender from the Greeks to Freud* (Cambridge, MA: Harvard University Press, 1990), p. 11.

from broader developments within the historical discipline itself, as historians moved away from a focus on women's experience to another emphasis on how masculinity and femininity signified usually unequal power relations. In 1986, Joan W. Scott published a path-breaking article in the *American Historical Review* entitled 'Gender: a Useful Category of Historical Analysis' that built upon but also challenged the premises of over a decade of scholarship on women's experience. Scott argued that while women's history was primarily descriptive, gender history addresses 'dominant disciplinary concepts', thus challenging the very premises of historical analysis. In other words, using gender, the historian not only includes women in the history of events, but reinterprets those events: gender history does not only analyse women's experiences in the spheres they occupy (the family, the private sphere) but 'is a primary way of signifying relationships of power'. Gender not only describes the culturally imposed attributes of the female sex, but also explains social interaction more generally, so that even areas marked by women's absence – high politics, for example – legitimate and define themselves through the celebration of masculine attributes and the exclusion of feminine ones.[20] Gender in this sense is not a descriptive term but a category of analysis: 'man' and 'woman' are not fixed categories but culturally constructed meanings attributed to sexed bodies that change over time.

The history of sexuality merged with this new approach to the history of women that has by now been extended to explore even political and intellectual history. Since culture prescribed the relationship between gender and sexed bodies, then the relationship between gender and sexuality was culturally constructed rather than timeless and fixed. Thus it was possible to conceive sexual practices as shaped but not determined by gender and to analyse the relationship between them. Since gender not only described sexed bodies but 'relationships of power', it described how sexuality was embedded in those relationships. By insisting that sexuality be understood in relationship to gender, then, many historians sought to extend Foucault's insights in new directions as well as to historicize the changing relationship between gender and power neglected by historians who gave women's inequality short shrift. Moreover, the new emphasis on gender proved an important corrective to Foucault, who neglected it almost entirely. As historians of sexuality increasingly recognized, in so doing he neglected one of the fundamental ways in which sexuality is invested with political and cultural meaning.

[20] J. Scott, *Gender and the Politics of History* (New York: Columbia University Press, 1988), pp. 30 and 42.

Sexuality, after all, had always been defined in relation to gender in a way that presumed and naturalized social inequities. Dr Krafft-Ebing gauged normal and perverse sexual behaviour by reference to whether or not it signified masculinity in men or femininity in women. Hence sadism was a 'normal' male instinct gone awry, and masochism represented the pathological triumph of femininity in men but was an intrinsic part of women's constitution. He also defined homosexuality first and foremost as gender deviance, insisting that men attracted to other men had 'feminine' souls and that women who desired women had 'masculine' ones. Moreover, female sexuality, as we have seen, was inextricably tied to cultural ideas about women's proper gender role.

Many historians take the relationship between gender and sexuality as their central theme. Laqueur's 1990 *Making Sex: Body and Gender from the Greeks to Freud* makes perhaps the most sweeping claims about how literate, professional (mostly medical) men constructed the relationship between sexuality and gender to justify male domination. In a study that spans two thousand years of medical discussion about human biology, Laqueur argues that our concept of the body and its pleasures is inseparable from changing notions of masculinity and femininity. He claims that until the eighteenth century, a 'one-sex' model predominated in which women's bodies were understood to be inferior versions of men, their genitalia inverted versions of men's own. The female body was less perfect than the male, and this difference illustrated an extra-corporeal metaphysical hierarchy. By the end of the eighteenth century, when Enlightenment claims about human liberty and equality did not inherently exclude women, men justified their dominance by turning to nature: the 'two-sex' model of gender difference tied ideas about proper modes of sexual expression to women's fundamentally different 'nature', leading to the presumption that women were intrinsically more nurturing and less sexually needy than men. As Laqueur puts it: 'Sometime in the eighteenth century, sex as we know it was invented.' That is, 'the two-sex model *was not* manifest in new knowledge about the body and its functions', but '*was* produced through endless microconfrontations over power in the public and private spheres'.[21]

In short, historians of sexuality now often seek to understand the formation of sexual norms by reference to changing gender ideals and, increasingly, to ideas about race. Their work spans Antiquity through the Renaissance to the present. These recent emphases within the history of sexuality (including the relationship between gender and sexuality as well as the nature of Foucault's influence) are developed in subtle and

21 Laqueur, *Making Sex*, pp. 149 and 192.

important ways in gay, lesbian and 'queer' history. Recall that Foucault suggested that sexual deviance was an important means by which populations were labelled healthy or pathological and thus controlled; sexology and psychoanalysis, he insisted, were two different discourses by which doctors exercised such control. While taking up Foucault's notion that deviance is a form of regulation (rather than an 'objective' description of the workings of the mind and body), these historians also reject his insistence that this regulation is all pervasive. Their work links sexuality to power by historicizing the relation between sexuality and gender, but also demonstrates that sexual practices and sexual identities often did not correspond to normative gender roles. In an influential 1984 essay about historical shifts in the social organization of sexuality, Gayle Rubin wrested sexual identity away from gender identity, arguing that too often feminist scholars conflated women's sexuality with gender ideals and thus inadvertently reiterated stereotypes of women's intrinsically more 'passive' or less forceful sexuality.[22] George Chauncey's work on the making of a gay male culture in New York between 1890 and 1940 demonstrates how men used gender roles self-consciously, flexibly and often with tremendous creativity to define identity as well as to ward off public hostility by presenting themselves as effeminate and unthreatening.[23]

Moreover, such works also show that sexual subcultures offered resistance to social discipline and that deviant sexual identity in particular sometimes became central to *affirmative* definitions of self. Though Foucault had said that sexual identities might become the locus of new self-definitions, he insisted that such identities constituted a 'reverse discourse', or the redeployment of power, which somehow constituted new identities to regulate. Most social histories of those condemned for sexual deviance assume implicitly that sexuality is always normatively constituted and thus always socially regulated. Yet they also insist in different ways that sexual deviants use a variety of strategies to combat social marginality and create communities that protect them from the political and psychological consequences of oppression. By putting Foucault's insights into 'practice' – by focusing in detailed ways on communities and voices to analyse how individuals constructed and experienced their sexuality – they counter his bleak vision of a world always in thrall to 'power'.

Thus historians have written the internal histories of communities – including narratives about how those communities formed, how gay

[22] G. Rubin, 'Thinking sex: notes for a radical theory of the politics of sexuality', in C. Vance (ed.), *Pleasure and Danger: Exploring Female Sexuality* (Boston, MA: Routledge & Kegan Paul, 1984), pp. 267–319.

[23] G. Chauncey, *Gay New York: Gender, Urban Culture, and the Making of the Gay Male World, 1890–1940* (New York: Basic Books, 1994).

men and lesbians began to identify themselves as such, and how external pressure and discrimination shaped that identification. Works such as Georges Chauncey's *Gay New York: Gender, Urban Culture, and the Making of a Gay World, 1890–1940*, Lillian Faderman's *Odd Girls and Twilight Lovers*, and Jeffrey Merrick and Bryant T. Ragan's *Homosexuality in Modern France*, among others, demonstrate the existence of vibrant subcultures, clearly constituted within but not absolutely constricted by dominant sexual and political culture.[24] And though such histories tend to be overwhelmingly focused on the late nineteenth and early twentieth centuries, when medical men and legislators first recognized homosexuality as an identity category, historians have increasingly moved into the more distant past.

Emma Donoghue's *Passions Between Women: British Lesbian Culture 1668–1801*, Alan Bray's *Homosexuality in Renaissance England* and Maurice Lever's *Les Bûchers de Sodome* seek to identify sexual subcultures before the 'invention' of homosexuality.[25] In contrast to modern historians of sexuality, they interpret meanings ascribed to sexuality and sexual preference in the pre-modern period before the self was so inextricably tied to sexual identity. Thus, for example, in Ancient Greece, gender identity defined the meaning of sexual practices: an upper-class man could have sexual relations with a person of any gender as long as his partner was literally female or symbolically 'feminine' – of unequal rank or age. So-called 'sodomites' in the early modern period were not seen as objects of analysis, or as creatures apart – though accounts tell us that contemporaries often equated same-sex practices with cross-gender identifications. They were immoral men with particular tastes and might be punished for their transgressions with death.

Starting in the nineteenth century, historians, writers, medical men and others tied sexuality to self-definition.[26] The histories that trace this development all presume or render problematic that link, assigning it a negative or positive meaning. Since Foucault demonstrated the *naïveté* implicit in the connection between sexual freedom and human

[24] *Ibid.*; L. Faderman, *Odd Girls and Twilight Lovers: a History of Lesbian Life in Twentieth-Century America* (New York: Columbia University Press, 1991); J. Merrick and B. T. Ragan (eds.), *Homosexuality in Modern France* (Oxford University Press, 1996).

[25] E. Donoghue, *Passions Between Women: British Lesbian Culture 1668–1801* (New York: Harper Perennial, 1996); A. Bray, *Homosexuality in Renaissance England* (New York: Columbia University Press, 1996); M. Lever, *Les Bûchers de Sodome* (Paris: Fayard, 1985).

[26] Foucault's posthumously published work turned to an interest in self-making in Ancient Greece. See in particular his discussion of men's self-making and the role of marriage. M. Foucault, *The History of Sexuality*, vol. II: *the Use of Pleasure*, trans. R. Hurley (New York: Vintage, 1990), pp. 158–9.

enlightenment first drawn by anti-Victorians more generally, most historians have found it difficult to celebrate sexual liberation in an unqualified manner. And as historians demonstrated that sexual freedom meant very different things for women and men, they historicized the link between sexual identity, gender identity and the self – the relationship between sexuality and self was now always a historical product contingent on a wide variety of factors that could never be captured by the opposition between freedom and repression.

At the same time, as Peter Cryle and Christopher Forth have pointed out, some historians' work conceals an anti-historical claim that sexuality has always been at the heart of 'moral, social, and political discourse'.[27] Jeffrey Weeks – one of Cryle's and Forth's targets – argues that the Victorians sought above all to control male lust and male sexuality, asserting that sexual regulation helped consolidate normative constructions of (restrained, self-possessed) masculinity and thus stigmatized so-called gender deviants. And yet, as Cryle and Forth note, true as these accounts may be, 'understanding how sexuality came to be located at the center of human life means understanding what had to be ... pushed aside to make room ... for this new concept'. Inspired by Foucault, they call for sophisticated assessments of how sexuality came to be so central to Western culture and particularly how it is linked to a 'wide range of representations, practices and experiences connected to discourses about race, gender and other vectors of difference'.[28] This kind of history should not presume that sexuality was central, but should investigate its centrality.

And indeed, another set of historians tries to do just that. These include several historians who work on the fin-de-siècle and inter-war period. They also emphasize the instability and fluidity of sexual identities and selves over time and often focus on how sexuality helps constitute citizenship. For example, in *Sexing the Citizen*, Judith Surkis demonstrates how the construction of sexual difference in France grounded republican visions of sociality. She focuses on how medical professionals, politicians, academics, and the elite responsible for the fashioning of productive and 'civilized' Frenchmen under a new regime of universal male suffrage rendered the married and ideally reproductive heterosexual couple central to their vision of a just and ordered polity. The married couple thus served as the guarantor and sign of social order by binding individuals productively to social norms – hence the centrality of discourses of

[27] P. Cryle and C. E. Forth, *Sexuality at the Fin de Siècle: the Making of a 'Central Problem'* (Newark: University of Delaware Press, 2008), p. 12.

[28] *Ibid.*, pp. 14–15.

sexuality.[29] For her part, Tracie Matysik argues that we must understand various inter-war German reformers' and psychoanalysts' efforts to define female sexuality coherently as evidence of a moral subject always in the making and never fully contained by regulation. The instability of efforts to define femininity and female sexuality, she claims, is symbolic of the absence of a stable moral subject central to citizenship then in the course of being constituted.[30]

Historians of sexuality now address these tensions between positive and negative interpretations of our basic cultural presumption that sexuality is in some fundamental way about selfhood. Debates in the field centre implicitly and sometimes explicitly around these tensions, accounting for a split between a more theoretically informed history of the sort exemplified by Surkis, Matysik and Cryle, and the history of sexuality as written by social historians who seek less to demonstrate the instability of all normative frameworks (including the centrality of sexuality) than to bring to life the sexual experiences of persons in the past. Notions about selfhood and its relation to sexuality often determine distinctions between these approaches: theoretically informed historians emphasize more the constraints implicit in sexual identity formations, while others tend to insist on the importance of historical actors' own visions and experiences. Most important, in the thirty odd years since Marcus first made sexuality a respectable area of inquiry, the field has flourished, developing and challenging all the assumptions with which Marcus began. However it is interpreted, the history of sexuality is now a history of the generation and regulation of knowledge about gendered and racially marked human beings; it is about the increasing significance of sex in defining what is most significant, knowable and discussable about men and women and often defines what constitutes feminine and masculine identities; and it is about how sex symbolizes social order and disorder, in particular anxieties about the erosion of hierarchies based on gender as well as class, race and even religion. Now most inquirers can agree that the link between sexuality and the self is historically contingent and its meaning culturally invested; that sexual identity never exhausts the self and yet always constrains it, that sexuality may express a free or private self and yet is never, in spite of all our illusions, simply free or private.

[29] J. Surkis, *Sexing the Citizen: Morality and Masculinity in France, 1870–1920* (Ithaca, NY: Cornell University Press, 2006).

[30] T. Matysik, *Reforming the Moral Subject: Ethics and Sexuality in Central Europe, 1890–1930* (Ithaca, NY: Cornell University Press, 2008).

7 The affective turn: historicizing the emotions

Rob Boddice

This chapter is a contribution to the debate about how to 'do' the history of emotions. It explores how contemporary understandings of emotions are influencing historical narratives and the scope for historical revision wrought by the 'affective turn'.[1] The chapter is divided into five sections. The first examines how historians have engaged with the work of psychologists, anthropologists and neuroscientists in seeking to define emotions. The second section sets out how various historians have envisaged a history of emotions, looking at methodologies employed to enable the historian to chart continuities and changes over time. This specifically centres on the questions of 'emotionology' or emotional style, emotion and power, the concept of an 'emotional community' or 'regime' and emotional 'suffering'. These concepts, which form the mainstay of history-of-emotions jargon, are explicated and directed towards a discussion of the most important concept that the history of emotions has created: 'emotives'. The third section deals extensively with William Reddy's concept of 'emotives' as a way of describing the process of translation that takes place between culture and body in order to form emotional expressions, or in Reddy's terms 'utterances'. Central to the notion of 'emotives' is the idea that humans always fail in their efforts, at least to some degree, to match feeling states to conventional modes of emotional expression. The more complete the match, the greater the continuity in emotional regime; the greater the failure, especially if experienced by many people at the same time, the more likely this is to drive historical change. The fourth section digs deeper into the question of emotive

[1] The 'affective turn' has been proclaimed by J. Moscoso in *Pain: a Cultural History* (Basingstoke, Hants.: Palgrave Macmillan, 2012); Colin Jones wrote of an 'emotional turn' in the history of medicine: 'The emotional turn in the history of medicine and the view from Queen Mary University of London', *Social History of Medicine* (virtual issue, 'Emotions, Health, and Well-being', 2012, www.oxfordjournals.org/our_journals/sochis/historyofemotions.pdf [accessed 17 September 2012]. The affective turn has also been proclaimed in sociology, but historians have not taken their inspiration from these methods. See P. T. Clough and J. Halley (eds.), *The Affective Turn: Theorizing the Social* (Durham, NC: Duke University Press, 2007).

failure, exploring a late nineteenth-century case study of what might happen under extreme cases of emotional uncertainty, where conventions of emotional expression and perceptions of inward feelings are most jarringly out of sync. Using the evolutionary psychology of Darwin, and the encounter with it of T. H. Huxley, commonly known as 'Darwin's bulldog' for his fierce defence of Darwinism, and George John Romanes, Darwin's young disciple, I explore how evolutionary scientists sought to renegotiate how they should feel and how they should act in the light of new understandings of the historical development of emotions. I posit here the potential for a history of 'emotional crisis', and demonstrate the possibilities for a re-imagining of social and cultural history from the point of view of emotional displacement. The final section builds on this theoretical point in its discussion of the emotions as the basis for moral action, and as a vital clue in beginning to approach the history of morality. Suggesting that the current historiography constitutes something of a loose canon, I argue that history-of-emotions jargon can be replaced by Lorraine Daston's concept of 'moral economies' – collective psychologies that encompass not only feeling but also *doing* – which combines the explanatory power of the 'emotional regime', the 'emotional community' and the 'emotionology' of a society with a way of identifying how these things had a direct bearing on everyday bodily and social practices.

Making emotions accessible to the historian

In a key intervention, Ute Frevert claims that emotions both have a history and *make* history. Not only do emotions come and go, necessitating detailed enquiry into their particular histories, but also they are 'embedded into social and cultural environments', and as such they help define, direct and change societies.[2] As Barbara Rosenwein points out, noting the difficulty of looking for emotions in historical sources, 'To assume that our emotions were also the emotions of the past is to be utterly unhistorical.'[3] Together, these assertions mark what is at stake in the history of emotions. They also have the necessary effect of destabilizing *a priori* knowledge of our own emotions. An implicit criticism raised by historians of emotions is that, unlike almost every other branch of history where Whiggish teleology has been rejected for historicism, emotions have been treated by historians as matter of fact, unworthy of critical reflection.

[2] U. Frevert, *Emotions in History – Lost and Found* (Budapest: Central European University Press, 2011), pp. 205–19, esp. p. 219.

[3] J. Plamper, 'The history of emotions: an interview with William Reddy, Barbara Rosenwein, and Peter Stearns', *History and Theory*, 49 (2010), 253.

Love, hate, anger, pity, sympathy, grief: all these emotions have *seemed* instantly accessible to the historian, because the historian knows from personal experience the meaning of these feelings. It is precisely this assumption that the history of emotions challenges, asking, instead, what if similar feelings used to mean something different? And if there was a change in the meaning of feelings, how did this change happen? Frevert's assertion, therefore, that emotions have a history, gives way to the central task of historians of emotions: to understand what emotions are and have been, how and why emotions change, and what that change means.

Unlike historians' brief dalliance with psychohistory – a largely Freudian endeavour that retains a few notable proponents – the history of emotions seems to have found a sure footing within the discipline of history, and its approach is making enough of an impact that some are declaring an 'affective turn'.[4] A number of self-styled history-of-emotions monographs and edited volumes have provided the intellectual impetus.[5] Three significant centres of research in the history of emotions are already well established, in Berlin, London, and across five Australian universities. Much of what happens in the history-of-emotions world is collated, packaged, and disseminated by the project *Les Émotions au Moyen Âge* (EMMA), responsibility for which is shared by the Université d'Aix-Marseille and the Université du Québec à Montréal. There are now three book series dedicated to the history of emotions, at the University of Illinois Press, Oxford University Press and Palgrave Macmillan. To complement all of this there have been recent special issues of journals dedicated to the topic, and new journals

[4] The most distinguished adherent to psychohistory is Peter Gay, whose monumental study of the *Bourgeois Experience, Victoria to Freud* over five volumes marks the high point of the approach. But by the time of the publication of the final volume in 1998 Gay was a rare survivor of a defunct sub-discipline. Other notable scholars in this field include: E. Erikson, whose *Young Man Luther: a Study in Psychoanalysis and History* (New York: W. W. Norton, 1958) defined the field; L. Roper, *Oedipus and the Devil: Witchcraft, Religion and Sexuality in Early Modern Europe* (London: Routledge, 1994); and T. Crosby, *The Two Mr. Gladstones: a Study in Psychology and History* (New Haven, CT: Yale University Press, 1997).

[5] P. Stearns, *American Fear: the Causes and Consequences of High Anxiety* (New York: Routledge, 2006); P. Stearns, *Battleground of Desire: the Struggle for Self-Control in Modern America* (New York University Press, 1999); P. Stearns and J. Lewis (eds.), *An Emotional History of the United States* (New York University Press, 1998); W. Reddy, *The Navigation of Feeling: a Framework for the History of Emotions* (Cambridge University Press, 2001); Frevert, *Emotions in History*; B. Rosenwein (ed.), *Anger's Past: the Social Uses of an Emotion in the Middle Ages* (Ithaca, NY: Cornell University Press:1998); B. Rosenwein, *Emotional Communities in the Early Middle Ages* (Ithaca, NY: Cornell University Press, 2006); J. Bourke, *Fear: a Cultural History* (London: Virago, 2005); T. Dixon, *From Passions to Emotions: the Creation of a Secular Psychological Category* (Cambridge University Press, 2003); T. Dixon, *The Invention of Altruism: Making Moral Meanings in Victorian Britain* (Oxford University Press, 2008).

(*Journal of the History and Philosophy of Emotions*; *Passions in Context*) entirely devoted to it.[6]

Despite the institutional presence of the history of emotions, much of the scholarship emanating from it has concerned the fundamental question, what are emotions? Here historians entered into a difficult but rewarding conversation with cognitive and developmental psychologists and neuroscientists.[7] At the root of these conversations was a sense of unease with the prevalent notion that there were universal emotions (and accompanying expressions) irrespective of culture. The work of Paul Ekman in particular has provided historians with a significant corpus to bring down.[8] In Ekman and Friesen's classic 1971 intervention, 'Constants across Cultures in the Face and Emotion', they argued for the compelling evidence that 'the association between particular facial muscular patterns and discrete emotions is universal', downplaying the role of culture in marking out differences in the expression and experience of emotions. The shortcomings of the evidence, the methodology and the argument have been well documented.[9] But Ekman and Friesen themselves ended that essay with a number of concessions that went some way to undermining their own position. For, they insisted, their argument did not 'imply the absence of cultural differences in the face and emotion', since 'cultural differences will be manifest in the circumstances which elicit an emotion, in the action consequences of an emotion, and in the display rules which govern the management of facial behaviour in particular social settings'. Their final words referred to 'cultural differences in the antecedent and consequent events' of emotions, and to cultural 'differences in attitudes about particular emotions'.[10] To have conceded all this might have suggested that similar expressions across cultures would tell only little about the emotions themselves. But once historians pointed to historical differences in the ways in which emotions

6 B. Gammerl (ed.), *Emotional Styles – Concepts and Challenges*, special issue of *Rethinking History*, 16 (2012); U. Frevert and A. Schmidt (eds.), *Geschichte, Emotionen und visuelle Medien*, special issue of *Geschichte und Gesellschaft*, 37 (2011); U. Frevert (ed.), *Geschichte der Gefühle*, special issue of *Geschichte und Gesellschaft*, 35 (2009).

7 See, for example, J. C. Wood, 'A change of perspective: integrating evolutionary psychology into the historiography of violence', *British Journal of Criminology*, 51 (2011), 479–98.

8 P. Ekman and W. Friesen, 'Constants across cultures in the face and emotion', *Journal of Personality and Social Psychology*, 17 (1971), 124–9; P. Ekman and W. Friesen, *Pictures of Facial Affect* (Palo Alto, CA: Consulting Psychologists Press, 1976); P. Ekman, *Emotions Revealed: Recognizing Faces and Feelings to Improve Communication and Emotional Life* (New York: Times Books, 2003).

9 For a summary, see B. H. Rosenwein, 'Problems and methods in the history of emotions', *Passions in Context*, 1 (2010), 1–32, at 5–7.

10 Ekman and Friesen, 'Constants across cultures', p. 129.

were represented, even in the ways in which emotions themselves were conceptualized (as passions, e.g., centred in the heart, the spleen, and only latterly in the brain), the whole notion of universality began to collapse in on itself. What happiness, love, hate, anger, or anguish mean, how they are constituted, and how they *feel*, cannot be reduced to an expression. Where a smiling face leads to us to conclude that happiness is occurring we are duped by the red herring of representation without context. Clifford Geertz's playful riff on how to spot the difference between a twitch, a wink and a burlesqued wink – especially if you are not party to the context in which the nictitation takes place – should have brought down the universalist house of cards at once.[11] But in a striking introduction to a new edition of Charles Darwin's *The Expression of Emotions in Man and Animals*, Ekman suggested that 'the intellectual climate had changed', becoming more closely aligned with Darwin's universalism, against the vivid imaginations of 'cultural relativists or social constructionists'. Ekman threw a bone to culture, where it concerned 'our attempts to manage our emotions, our attitudes about our emotions and our representations of them verbally', but he continued to insist that 'expressions do show universality'.[12]

Historians since the cultural turn have a well-schooled scepticism about anything deemed built-in, universal, transhistorical, or 'natural'. When turning to emotions, they inevitably applied their culturally deconstructive tools to the universalist claims of evolutionary biologists, anthropologists, psychologists and neuroscientists alike.

The emotions considered from the point of view of the historian constitute a problem of the same order as that imagined by Sartre when considering the emotions from the point of view of the phenomenologist. The problem Sartre imagined was how psychology might look for the meaning of emotions beyond physical phenomena through the interrogation of consciousness. He informed psychologists that 'emotion *does not exist*, considered as a physical phenomenon, for a body cannot be emotional, not being able to attribute a meaning to its own manifestations'. The question that Sartre thought ought to motivate psychologists was 'what does emotion *signify*?', and through this question psychology itself would be transformed or abandoned.[13] The historian also looks for the significance of emotions, but rather through culture than through

[11] C. Geertz, 'Thick description: toward an interpretive theory of culture', *The Interpretation of Cultures* (New York: Basic Books, 1973), pp. 6–12.

[12] P. Ekman, 'Introduction to the Third Edition', in C. Darwin, *The Expression of the Emotions in Man and Animals*, 3rd edn (London: HarperCollins, 1998), p. xxxv.

[13] J.-P. Sartre, *Sketch for a Theory of the Emotions*, trans. Philip Mairet (London: Routledge, 2002), pp. 11–14, esp. p. 10.

consciousness. In fact it is in the relation between culture and consciousness that the significance of emotions lies.

It is precisely this challenge that historians of emotions have taken to contemporary neuroscientists in an effort meaningfully to engage with emotion scientists. The temptation of neuroscience is to revert to a we-can-find-it-all-in-the-brain approach, attempting to demonstrate that certain emotions are hard wired, or to isolate the process by which empathy works (via 'mirror neurons'), and so forth. Two examples will suffice: Jaak Panksepp asserts that 'Modern evidence suggests that anger emerges from the neurodynamics of subcortical circuits we share homologously with other animals ... The more we understand about these circuits, the more we will understand the fundamental nature of anger itself'; Rizzolatti and Sinigaglia argue that 'The instantaneous understanding of the emotions of others, rendered possible by the emotional mirror neuron system, is a necessary condition for the empathy which lies at the root of most of our more complex inter-individual relationships'.[14] That the metaphor of 'wiring' or 'circuitry' is itself historical, and that 'empathy' as a concept did not exist before the twentieth century ought to give neuroscientists pause in their attempts at 'finding' emotions or the mechanisms by which they work, attempts that were given great impetus by early twentieth-century physiological experimentalism.[15] The finding of hard-wired emotions will always arouse the scepticism of the historian, since the historian proceeds with the assumption that the meaning of all emotions in context is cultural and historical.[16] But against this strain, which some have dismissed as neo-phrenology, ascribing universalist significance to areas that light up, or to specific regions of the brain, neuroscientists and evolutionary biologists are also exploring the ways in which culture can alter the ways in which the brain works – how

[14] J. Panksepp, *Affective Neuroscience: the Foundations of Human and Animal Emotions* (New York: Oxford University Press, 1998), p. 187, in a chapter on 'The neurobiological sources of rage and anger'; G. Rizzolatti and C. Sinigaglia, *Mirrors in the Brain: How Our Minds Share Actions and Emotions*, trans. Frances Anderson (Oxford University Press, 2006), pp. 190–1. For a view of why mirror neurons are useless without socialization see B. M. Hood, *The Self Illusion: How the Social Brain Creates Identity* (Oxford University Press, 2012), pp. 63–70.

[15] For early twentieth-century 'finding' of emotions in the body, see Otniel Dror, 'The affect of experiment: the turn to emotions in Anglo-American physiology, 1900–1940', *Isis*, 90 (1999), 205–37; for a review of the current debates concerning empathy, encompassing developmental psychology, philosophy, cultural studies, neuroscience and anthropology (but not history), see E.-M. Engelen and B. Röttger-Rössler, 'Current disciplinary and interdisciplinary debates on empathy', *Emotion Review*, 4 (2012), 3–8; for the early usages and meanings of 'empathy' see C. Burdett, 'Is empathy the end of sentimentality', *Journal of Victorian Culture*, 16 (2011), 259–74.

[16] Plamper, 'The history of emotions', p. 239.

learned emotional practices have a biological effect on the body.[17] This insight adds grist to the historian's mill in the effort to demonstrate that culture directly affects the experience of emotions, and that affects are themselves the result of a body's being dynamically, or 'plastically', to put it in the terms of evolutionary biologists, in a culture.[18] A common joke runs that neuroscientists of emotions are perhaps the largest body of researchers who cannot define the thing they are researching. Indeed, that definition is partly the goal of their research. Historians have a rare opportunity here to reach out to and assist the cutting edge of science, where their insights might help interpret the fMRI and PET images of neuropsychologists, and where in turn historians can benefit from psychological sciences that are increasingly culturally, not to say temporally, aware.[19]

What should historians do with emotions?

Historians have set about making sense of the emotional body, or the emotional individual, by placing it in a broader context of emotional conventions at the level of culture, the scale of which is determined by context. One might talk of an emotional culture of the home or family, of the urban street, of a social or professional organization, or of a national society. There is general agreement amongst historians of emotions that agents belong to many cultural contexts at any given time, and that they 'navigate' between emotional conventions, causing concomitant shifts in their affective behaviour.[20]

There are currently competing analytical approaches to interpreting these emotional contexts. Barbara Rosenwein devised the concept of 'emotional communities' to make sense of the emotional cultural

17 For one notable critic, see W. R. Uttal, *The New Phrenology: the Limits of Localizing Cognitive Processes in the Brain* (Cambridge, MA: The MIT Press, 2003); On the relationship of biology and culture, see, for example, P. W. Turke, 'Which humans behave adaptively, and why does it matter?', *Ethology and Sociobiology*, 11 (1990), pp. 315, 321. See also R. Turner and C. Whitehead, 'How collective representations can change the structure of the brain', *Journal of Consciousness Studies*, 15 (2008), 43–57.

18 E. Jablonka and M. J. Lamb, *Evolution in Four Dimensions: Genetic, Epigenetic, Behavioral, and Symbolic Variation in the History of Life* (Cambridge, MA: MIT Press, 2005), pp. 76–8.

19 B. Rosenwein has called for just this: 'The uses of biology: a response to J. Carter Wood's "The limits of culture"', *Cultural and Social History*, 4 (2007), 553–8. Developmental psychologists are becoming increasingly aware of the importance of context. See in particular R. K. Silbereisen and X. Chen (eds.), *Social Change and Human Development: Concepts and Results* (London: Sage, 2010). fMRI is functional magnetic resonance imaging; PET is positron emission tomography.

20 The concept of 'navigation' belongs to Reddy, and is best exemplified in his seminal work, *The Navigation of Feeling*.

conventions that define why emotional expressions seem to change from place to place and over time. She defined emotional communities as:

> precisely the same as social communities – families, neighbourhoods, parliaments, guilds, monasteries, parish church membership – but the researcher looking at them seeks above all to uncover systems of feeling: what these communities (and the individuals within them) define and assess as valuable or harmful to them; the evaluations that they make about others' emotions; the nature of the affective bonds between people that they recognize; and the modes of emotional expression that they expect, encourage, tolerate and deplore.[21]

Rosenwein is clear that an individual always belongs to more than one 'emotional community' at a time, and can move between them. She stresses the competing influences within individuals, depending on changing contextual circumstances, but she has asserted that movement between one 'community' and another depends on the 'new emotional community's norms' not being 'radically different from the original'.[22] Rosenwein uses this concept not to determine how people actually felt, but rather to explore normative codes of affective expression. In so doing, she developed Peter and Carol Stearns' pioneering intervention in the history of emotions in which they introduced the concept of 'emotionology' to 'distinguish the collective emotional standards of a society from the emotional experiences of individuals and groups'.[23] Central to Rosenwein's work is that such 'emotional standards' are constructed at various levels of society, and in differently configured and interrelated groups. Rosenwein is not interested in emotional 'authenticity' so much as in cultural standards of emotional responses and the reasons behind historical change in those standards.[24] In advocating the study of 'emotional communities' Rosenwein has thus frequently aligned herself against William Reddy's conceptual understanding of the 'emotional community' as an 'emotional regime'.[25]

Rosenwein is uncomfortable with 'emotional regimes' because she assumes the concept only to work where a given 'emotional community' 'dominates the norms and texts of a large part of society', which ties it closely to the nation state and therefore to the modern period. While it

21 B. H. Rosenwein, 'Worrying about emotions in history', *American Historical Review*, 107 (2002), 842.

22 Rosenwein, 'Worrying about emotions in history', pp. 842–3; Plamper, 'The history of emotions', p. 256.

23 P. N. Stearns and C. Z. Stearns, 'Emotionology: Clarifying the history of emotions and emotional standards', *American Historical Review*, 90 (1985), 813.

24 Rosenwein, 'Problems and methods', p. 21.

25 Rosenwein, 'Problems and methods', pp. 22–3; Plamper, 'The history of emotions', pp. 255–6. See also Peter Stearns' differentiation of culture and experience in *ibid.*, p. 262.

is true that the 'emotional regime' emphasises the power structure of an 'emotional community', it has been objected by Reddy himself that 'regime' does not necessarily only relate to societal-level governance (be it political, cultural, or bodily). On the contrary, according to Reddy, a 'regime' exists wherever 'the sum of the penalties and exclusions adds up to a coherent structure, and the issue of conformity becomes defining for the individual'.[26] An emotional regime might therefore be mapped onto all the examples Rosenwein gives of 'emotional communities', but her caveat that navigation between different 'communities' is limited seems to dissolve. One can imagine radically differentiated emotional contexts between which an individual can successfully navigate, where not only structures of penalties and exclusions, but also cultural practices, limit affective behaviour in starkly contrasting ways. In my own work I have examined just such radical oppositions, between the Victorian physiological laboratory (the site of vivisection) and the domestic parlour, and between scientific and religious communities, for example. It has been possible, without sensing any contradiction (that to a contemporary reader might seem obvious) to have been an animal lover and active animal protector, a hunter of animals and a practising physiologist, vivisecting animals in the name of humanity.[27]

Whether we settle on the 'emotional regime' or the 'emotional community', or something else (see the fifth section), historians generally agree that a central element of the cultural contextualization of affective experience concerns power. Who gets to decide the conventions for emotional expression, thereby influencing how actors strive to feel? How have historical actors conformed or responded to, resisted and changed those conventions? The use of emotions and affective behaviour as vehicles for better understanding the history of power and violence has been explicit in the formation of a historiography of the emotions. According to Joanna Bourke, 'emotions ... mediate between the individual and the social. They are about power relations. Emotions lead to a negotiation of the boundaries between self and other or one community and another'.[28] Meanwhile, William Reddy has asserted that the 'core issue' of the his-

[26] Plamper, 'The history of emotions', p. 243.

[27] R. Boddice, 'Vivisecting major: a Victorian gentleman scientist defends animal experimentation, 1876–1885', *Isis*, 102 (2011), 215–37; R. Boddice, 'Species of compassion: Aesthetics, anaesthetics and pain in the physiological laboratory', *19: Interdisciplinary Studies in the Long Nineteenth Century*, 15 (2012), available at www.19.bbk.ac.uk/index.php/19/article/view/628 [accessed 9 March 2013].

[28] J. Bourke, 'Fear and anxiety: Writing about emotion in modern history', *History Workshop Journal*, 55 (2003), 124.

tory of emotions concerns 'effortful self-management (and its failures) in relation to political power'.[29]

Power dynamics can be defined, for example, by tacit exclusions according to class, race, gender, sexuality, or national identity biases, or by any number of configurations thereof. Reddy in particular has explored the emotional consequences of being unable to conform to conventions of emotional expression. As the distance between conventions of expression and inward feeling grows, so a sense of 'emotional suffering' grows along with it. Emotional sufferers may find 'refuge' in subcultural contexts where different conventions allow for more successful 'emotives' (see below). Reddy himself describes elements of late *ancien régime* France in precisely these terms, contrasting the stern emotional style of public life with the sentimentality of the theatre as emotional 'refuge'. It is this tension that drives historical change, for where the members of an emotional 'refuge' find the numbers, the momentum, or the precise political conditions, this community can break out and assume a dominant position, supplant the previous 'regime' and install its own conventions as both 'natural' and hegemonic.[30]

Emotives: a process of failure

All of this brings us back to the question, what is an emotion? For if the emotions are to be taken as not only fundamental to the individual human experience, but also as the cause and effect of human culture and historical change within cultures, then we need a precise set of tools for approaching the emotions historically. While rejecting an appeal to universal human emotions in the tradition of Darwin and Ekman, which assumes that emotions can be understood at face value (literally as a common value of the face), it is, nevertheless, in expressions that historians have found their method. Historians understand that value is historical, that facial expressions signify different meanings at different times, and that, correspondingly, the individual experience is reflected by or related to those changing meanings.[31] Turning Ekman's assertions on their head, historians look for differences in expressions (not just facial, but also linguistic and gestural expressions) across space and time, and even where they find sameness, they look contextually to find nuances in meaning. This also involves the rejection of 'basic' emotions – the six

[29] Plamper, 'The history of emotions', pp. 248–9.

[30] Reddy, *Navigation of Feeling*. See the discussion in Plamper, 'The history of emotions', pp. 241, 247 and in Rosenwein, 'Problems and methods', p. 22.

[31] Plamper, 'The history of emotions', 254–5; Rosenwein, 'Problems and methods', 6; Moscoso, *Pain*, pp. 9–18.

emotions that Ekman identified as being fundamental to humanity (happiness, sadness, disgust, surprise, anger, fear) – for if we set out to look for examples of contemporary emotions in the past, we are certain only to find anachronisms.

There is an acknowledgment in this emphasis on expression that the body cannot be written out of the story.[32] The history of emotions cannot be reduced to cultural constructs and textual analysis because emotional experience is always translated by and through the body. As bodily practices, emotions clearly have certain physiological anchors. To understand emotions in history, therefore, the historian needs to be able to coordinate the cultural with the physical, the meaning of emotion with bodily functions.[33] Historians of emotion might agree with John Carter Wood that from 'an evolutionary psychological perspective, the importance of social construction to human [biological] life both enables and results from our inhabiting what has been referred to as "the cognitive niche", a species-typical way of life that requires a unique degree of reliance upon information and socially imparted knowledge'.[34] Peter and Carol Stearns acknowledged this relation in the mid 1980s, noting the likelihood that 'emotionological change will normally have some bearing on emotional experience' of the body.[35] To serve this joint need William Reddy conceptualized the 'emotive', reducing cultural and biological understandings of the emotions to one process. More than any other concept, 'emotives' emphasize what Carter Wood has referred to as the 'common ground' of 'biological and cultural approaches to behaviour and thought'.[36]

An 'emotive', succinctly defined, is an affective utterance – an expression not limited to acts of speech – that represents an individual's attempt to translate inward feelings through cultural conventions in order to try to match the two. 'Emotives' emphasize the effort – the 'emotion work' – that an individual carries out in order to fit in with a given context. This emphasis on effort, context and translation helps make sense of the feeling of 'emotional suffering' described above. Every emotive is a 'failure' and a source of 'suffering' to some extent, since inward feelings can never be 'authentically' expressed. The greater the distance is between inward feelings and conventions of expression, the more acute the 'emotional suffering'. In Reddy's own terms, emotive 'failure' leads to the 'discovery

[32] For a clear expression of this, see W. Reddy, 'Against constructionism: the historical ethnography of emotions', *Current Anthropology*, 38 (1997), 327–51.

[33] See M. Scheer, 'Are emotions a kind of practice (and is that what makes them have a history)? A Bourdieuian approach to understanding emotion', *History and Theory*, 51 (2012), 193–220.

[34] Wood, 'A change of perspective', p. 486.

[35] Stearns and Stearns, 'Emotionology', p. 829.

[36] Wood, 'A change of perspective', p. 486.

of something unexpected about one's own feelings'. In other words, emotives feed back on to the body.

Reddy is not going so far as to say that naming emotions, uttering them, tells a body how to respond, how to feel, but he does maintain that utterances do things to bodies and, in turn, bodies do things to utterances.[37] Central to this process is a continual striving to make meaning out of sensory input, to add signification to stimulation. The more people make meanings associated with given states, the more readily accessible those meanings become, leading to the appearance of effortlessness: a seemingly natural accord of emotion and expression. But since these utterances of emotions are made in conformity to cultural norms that are associated with and imposed by collective practices – variable according to the context in which a person finds him- or herself – there is always scope for the 'natural' emotion to feel out of joint. A context changes, an organization breaks down, a family dysfunctions, a government falls, a taboo loosens: the emotional subject no longer knows how to utter – how to 'emote' – correctly. The effort of emoting suddenly emerges anew, though it was there all along. If the change in convention is complex, occurs over a prolonged period, and seems important to an individual's sense of self, then we may have cause to identify an 'emotional crisis'. Arlie Russell Hochschild described something like this, where there 'is a change in the relation of feeling rule to feeling and a lack of clarity about what the rule actually is … Feelings and frames are deconventionalised, but not yet reconventionalised. We may, like the marginal man, say, "'I don't know how I should feel".'[38]

Emotional uncertainty has a rich history, but as yet it has been underexplored. The following is a small case study that provides some insight into how one might approach the 'emotional crisis' historically.

Emotional crisis

In 1874 a young George John Romanes mused that a man of prayer 'has loved to think' of God as a 'guiding influence', 'an influence which in human form and with human lips has declared, that man is to Him of all that is on earth immeasurably the dearest charge; that there is no word, no thought, of ours which escapes His loving care'. In a vigorous defence of Christian prayer, Romanes put a rhetorical question to an

[37] See G. Colombetti, 'What language does to feelings', *Journal of Consciousness Studies*, 16 (2009), 4–26.

[38] A. R. Hochschild, 'Emotion work, feeling rules, and social structure', *American Journal of Sociology*, 85 (1979), 567–8.

imagined scientist reader: 'Are we to relinquish this great and hallowed creed, merely for the sake of an empty figment of the intellect, which can have no substantially valid reason for its support?'[39] Romanes' own path to science was just beginning. The following years would see him become perhaps the most prominent of Charles Darwin's disciples, one of the first comparative psychologists, a physiologist and an evolutionary theorist. His scientific apprenticeship would cause him to reverse his prior defence of the belief in God.[40]

Although it is true, as Thomas Dixon reminds us, that 'the application of scientific method and commitment to Christianity were by no means mutually exclusive', that is not to say it was a mere matter of course to make them mutually agree.[41] Romanes struggled perhaps more than most. In 1878 Romanes thoroughly, but anonymously, examined theism as a scientist and found materialist objections on every level. Now convinced by the path of science, Romanes was, nevertheless, disquieted by it. He accepted his own conclusions with the 'utmost sorrow', and declared his own 'lively perception' of 'the ruination of individual happiness' that a materialist view necessarily brought about. Romanes set himself the task to 'stifle all belief of the kind which I conceive to be the noblest, and to discipline my intellect with regard to this matter into an attitude of the purest scepticism'. A scientist he would be, which meant not just a set of professional practices, but a reorientation of the self. Never mind that 'with this virtual negation of God the universe ... has lost its soul of loveliness', for a man's scientific principles entailed that he adhere to and live by them.[42]

Romanes was not alone in making emotional control a predominant theme of evolutionary science as it charted the development of those 'civilized' emotions considered to be the foundation of morality. So far as humanity had come, the evolution of emotions, especially sympathy, had encouraged social cohesion and progress. At the high point of Victorian ambition, or perhaps conceit, the evolutionists attempted to justify their own superiority via natural-law narratives of racial fitness, masculine intellect and a species-specific distinction of sympathetic disposition. Positioning themselves at the intellectual avant-garde, Darwin, Spencer

[39] G. J. Romanes, *Christian Prayer and General Laws, being the Burney Prize Essay for the Year 1873, With an Appendix, the Physical Efficacy of Prayer* (London: Macmillan, 1874), p. 124.

[40] For Romanes see R. J. Richards, *Darwin and the Emergence of Evolutionary Theories of Mind and Behavior* (Chicago: University of Chicago Press, 1987), pp. 332–53; Boddice, 'Vivisecting major'.

[41] Dixon, *From Passions to Emotions*, p. 23.

[42] Physicus [G. J. Romanes], *A Candid Examination of Theism* (London: Trübner, Ludgate Hill, 1878), pp. 113–14.

and their followers imagined themselves as the progenitors of the next stage in human evolution, ushering in a science-led species where those sympathetic instincts that had served humanity so well would be subjected to human will, and to rational abstraction, allowing an even greater emotional – and therefore moral – development.[43]

There were a number of reasons why emotional control was deemed to be necessary. Romanes eloquently summed up one of these reasons, which he might have described as a purely sentimental attachment to an irrational but accepted norm, in his account of religious belief. A process of emotional distancing was necessary in order to be able to see the moral errors that stemmed from this sentimentalism. An emotional response was subjected to abstract considerations of what constituted the greatest good, and in the process of deliberation – an internal conversation between that which was felt and that which was known – a new feeling, and a new moral course, could be reached.[44]

Emerging scientific practices that scandalized polite society provided further reasons to push this model of emotional control for moral betterment. The growth, from the 1870s, of experimentation on living animals was frequently justified by the physiologists who did it, as well as by the evolutionary scientists (including Darwin) who made use of the results, in terms of its great moral purpose. Humanity would reap enormous advantages through the gains to knowledge that vivisection would provide, particularly in the field of medical science. Yet physiologists could not easily rid themselves of the stigma of the butcher, a perceived callousness that marked them as morally cold. It was common colloquial knowledge that butchers would not be called to jury service because of their hardened hearts, but otherwise they performed a necessary service. Scientists, however, claimed for themselves positions of authority and influence in a reforming society, and this struck fear into the hearts of traditional moralists.[45] So physiologists invoked the emotional control of the surgeon – the equanimity of the physician – to claim that their lack of sentimental response during the performance of vivisection was necessary for the greater good of humanity. But this callousness was only a temporary, situational disposition in themselves. Their own

[43] R. Boddice, 'The manly mind? Re-visiting the Victorian "Sex in Brain" debate', *Gender and History*, 23 (2011), 321–40;

[44] C. Darwin, *The Descent of Man and Selection in Relation to Sex*, 2nd edn (London: Penguin, 2004), pp. 122–60. Key passages in this regard at pp. 133, 147 and 149; H. Spencer, 'Morals and moral sentiments', *Fortnightly Review*, 52 (1871), 419–32, esp. 432.

[45] See, for example, F. P. Cobbe, *Darwinism in Morals and Other Essays* (London: Williams & Norgate, 1872).

humanity was preserved through their advanced and conscious decision not to react to the sight of the opened body, or to the sight of blood.[46]

Yet just as Romanes struggled with his emotional loss in consigning religion to the domain of the irrational, so other scientists could not make themselves feel what they felt they ought to feel in the laboratory. Whereas Romanes himself had no problem experimenting on animals, T. H. Huxley (who had no problem with giving up religion) could not bring himself to perform vivisections, even though he supported the practice and used the results. If it was to him a 'disagreeable' practice, he nevertheless found anti-vivisectionists to be afflicted with a 'venomous sentim[ent]ality & inhuman tenderness'. They placed a false notion of humanity in the way of medical advance 'as long as poodles are happy'.[47] Though he could not himself vivisect in the laboratory, in principle Huxley thought it necessary to put 'natural sympathy aside, to try to get to the rights and wrongs of the business from a higher point of view, namely, that of humanity, which is often very different from that of emotional sentiment'.[48]

The point being illustrated here is that even the most ardent advocates of a new set of cultural feeling rules could not always manage to follow them all the time, and that this led to inward feelings of sorrow, doubt and confusion. The new feeling rules were opposed to the old ones; yet they emerged out of, and were contextually related to them. As Thomas Dixon has observed, Darwin's 'moral categories were the long-established ones of British moral philosophy', bearing the 'indelible stamp of its eighteenth-century British origins'.[49] The confusion, unsurprisingly, can be found locked into Darwin's most elegant summary of the evolution of emotions in the *Descent of Man* (1871).[50] Would not a truly rationalized sympathy make a point of avoiding the preservation of the 'weak' for the good of society as a whole? Although much of Darwin's text points the way for the eugenic ideas that would be created in his name, Darwin himself could not endorse such a path. Certainly, 'the surgeon may harden himself whilst performing an operation, for he knows that he is acting for the good of his patient'. Likewise, the vivisectionist could reassure himself with the contribution he would make to the store of knowledge. Yet 'intentionally to neglect the weak and helpless' would

46 Boddice, 'Species of compassion'.

47 Quoted in S. Catlett, 'Huxley, Hutton and the "White Rage": a debate on vivisection at the metaphysical society', *Archives of Natural History*, 11 (1983), 185.

48 Leonard Huxley (ed.), *Life and Letters of Thomas Henry Huxley*, 2 vols. (London: Macmillan, 1900), vol. I, p. 436 [letter of 1890].

49 Dixon, *Invention of Altruism*, p. 133.

50 See note 44.

herald a 'deterioration in the noblest part of our nature'. To that end, Darwin chose to 'bear the undoubtedly bad effects of the weak surviving and propagating their kind', even if it meant the decline of civilization.[51] One can scarcely avoid the poignancy of the word 'noble' in this passage, when put into the light of Romanes' 1878 work. For while Romanes felt himself unable to preserve his 'noblest beliefs' in the light of Darwin's works, Darwin himself fought to keep his 'noblest part', despite the overwhelming force of his argument.

Evolutionary scientists lived in two connected but increasingly incommensurate worlds, distinguished by stark differences in their affective norms: that of the (professional) scientist and that of the predominant culture of polite society. As Darwin and his peers developed their expressions of an evolutionary model of the emotions and of morality, so the difficulty of navigating between these worlds must have increased. As the emotive process became more acute – a greater amount of failure occurring between inward feelings and novel feeling rules – so the feeling of 'emotional crisis' in certain contexts must have grown. The power dynamic of this imbalance is crucial in determining whether 'emotional crisis' leads to continuity or change. Where the new feeling rules have the authority of public opinion; where they are implicitly folded into formal rules, regulations and policies; where they are practised frequently and increasingly in public and private life, then gradually the 'crisis' is eased as repetition of the emotive process affects inward feelings, bringing them closer to the feeling rules. The implicit need to reduce emotive failure facilitates the building and reinforcement of the structures – the perceived 'naturalness' – of new conventions. It was precisely because evolutionary scientists understood morality to have an emotional basis that they projected a future for human evolution in which the emotions could successfully be taken in hand, mastered, and the moral action delayed and filtered through an understanding of the requirements of the greater good. This is not to say that emotions would be written out of the picture by a superior reason, but rather that emotions themselves were engaged in a dialogue with rational abstractions, removed from the surface, slowed down, refined. The result, they foresaw, would give rise to the appearance of greater equanimity in moral subjects, who would no any longer react immediately to emotional impulses.[52] Emotions – especially sympathy – would remain as the basis of morality, but they would not act freely without the agency of the human

[51] Darwin, *Descent of Man*, pp. 90, 159–60.

[52] Two classic practical statements to this effect are T. L. Brunton, 'Vivisection and the use of remedies', *Nineteenth Century*, 11 (1882), 479–87, and W. Osler, 'Aequanimitas', *Aequanimitas, with other Addresses to Medical Students and Practitioners of Medicine*, 2nd edn (Philadelphia, PA: P. Blakiston's Son., 1925), pp. 3–11.

who felt them. Indeed, this evolution could be sped up by public opinion. The individuals of a civilized society could become more moral by literally changing the way they felt.

Conclusion: emotions and morality

It should by now be clear that historians of emotions have neither settled on a common language or approach, nor programmatically defined their relationship to other emotion sciences. So long as that is the case, it cannot claim to have the status of a metanarrative, and perhaps it is as well that the fluidity of intellectual exchange is not substituted for theoretical orthodoxy. When Reddy projected the future for the history of emotions as a discipline, he was explicit that this was 'not something to be added to existing fields', but rather a 'way of doing' history *per se*.[53] With methodologies and terminologies lacking uniformity, the history of emotions is at present a cluster of different ways of doing history. While this perhaps risks the appearance of being only a loose canon, esoteric and obscure to historians outside of the history of emotions, a discipline that is defined by the intellectual richness of its exchanges, both with emotion sciences, and within the history of emotions itself, is a sign of rude health.

Yet, if there is an emphasis on *doing* history, there is also an emphasis on what historical actors *did*, and not only on what they felt or affected. History, ultimately, finds ways to make sense of *what happened*, and that ties historians to questions of practice and morality. What emerges from my story of Darwinists struggling with Darwinian emotional conventions is that their struggle directly affected their daily practices as scientists, men, and members of various communities, as well as affecting their own understanding of who they were. Darwin's and Spencer's accounts of the history and evolution of the emotions were aimed at finding natural-law explanations of Victorian morality, and positing a future for the evolution of morals. Conventions of emotional expression define not just what is acceptable in a given context, but also what is proscribed. The inappropriateness of an emotional expression is understood in terms of the immorality of an action. This implicit connection, between emotions and morality, has been strongly asserted among philosophers from Hume and Smith down to Jesse Prinz today.[54]

The conceptual apparatus of the history of emotions suggests this link, but does not provide a clear way of investigating it. But as far back as 1995, Lorraine Daston put forward a scheme for precisely this approach

[53] Plamper, 'History of emotions', p. 249.
[54] J. Prinz, *The Emotional Construction of Morals* (Oxford University Press, 2007).

in her article on 'The Moral Economy of Science'. Daston defined 'moral economy' as 'a web of affect-saturated values that stand and function in well-defined relationship to one another', referring to 'the psychological and the normative', and deriving its 'stability and integrity' from 'its ties to activities'.[55] Moral economies bind individuals to a collective psychology in which reason is always bound with emotion, and where emotion itself is defined by social and bodily practices. There have been some echoes of this among historians of emotion, but there is much left to do. Paul White called for a return to an 'emotional economy of science' that suggests 'ways in which the emotions might be studied as objects and as agents integral to scientific *practice*: the principles of observation, experiment, and theory and, reciprocally, the practices of the self', and Ute Frevert details the 'historical economy of emotions', 'enacting and reacting to cultural, social, economic and political challenges'.[56] The attraction of this category of analysis lies in its capacity to incorporate the advances made by the history of emotions described in this chapter, and to take them further. A 'moral economy' not only describes an 'emotional community' of any size or order, but it also examines what people do, individually and collectively, in it, because of it, or in spite of it. It allows us a way to judge, without anachronism, what constituted moral action in a given context. Moreover, we can easily imagine multiple 'moral economies' and the 'navigation' of individuals between them. Here the emphasis on practice within a 'moral economy' explains the ability of historical actors to move with great freedom – though not without the risk of 'emotional crisis' – between radically different contexts. Each 'moral economy' has, at its heart, a power structure (a 'regime') that defines the normative, both in terms of feeling and doing. The historian therefore charts where 'emotives' begin to fail acutely according to where normative practices are performed only with difficulty, or not at all. Huxley's aversion to vivisection and Romanes' reluctant atheism are cases in point. It is in the emphasis on what was *done*, or *not done*, that the historian can confidently claim that emotions both have and make history.

Cultural conventions of emotional expression determine the parameters of affective behaviour. The history of emotions is concerned with the power dynamics that determine who, or what, gets to determine these conventions. This lays bare, according to different scholars, the

[55] L. Daston, 'The moral economy of science', *Osiris*, 2nd series, 10 (1995), 4–5. The idea, though not the terminology, was developed in Daston and Peter Galison's book, *Objectivity* (New York: Zone Books, 2007), esp. pp. 40–1.

[56] P. White, 'Introduction to "Focus: the emotional economy of science"', *Isis*, 100 (2009), 793; Frevert, *Emotions in History*, 6–12, esp. 12.

'emotionology' of a society, an 'emotional community', or the 'emotional regime'. Emotions are defined by and through their expression in a cultural context, as a process of negotiation with inner feelings. This process – always to some degree a failure – of reconciliation between emotional utterances and feelings is an 'emotive'. When 'emotive' failure becomes acute there is an 'emotional crisis'. A 'moral economy' encapsulates these history-of-emotions concepts, allowing for an understanding of not only collective feelings, but also of collective practices, and causes of emotional and moral change over time.

Taken together, the insights of the 'affective turn' in historical practice are surely of value to a developmental psychology that is increasingly contextually aware, and to a neuropsychology that is increasingly culturally aware. Moreover, historians of emotion would surely benefit from a richer relationship with such psychologists in enhancing their own understandings of emotions in bodies, groups and societies, and in bringing to bear contemporary advances in the understanding of how emotions *work* on historical interpretations of what emotions *mean*.

8 The role of cognitive orientation in the foreign policies and interpersonal understandings of Neville Chamberlain, Winston Churchill and Franklin Delano Roosevelt, 1937–1941

Mark E. Blum

> Different people perceive that which happens in the world differently, so that if many people describe an event, each would attend to something in particular – if all were to perceive the situation properly. The cause of the difference is due partly to the place and positioning of our body which differs with everyone; partly to various associations with the subject, and partly to individual differences in selecting objects to attend to. It is generally accepted that there can only be one correct representation for each object and that if there are some differences in description, then one must be completely right and the other completely wrong. This principle is not in accordance with other general truths or with the more exact perceptions of our soul.
>
> (Johann Martin Chladenius, 1742)[1]

> It is not things that disturb men, but their judgements about things.
>
> (Epictetus)[2]

> *Whereas a fixed delimitation was not possible for lived experiences, this could be found for expressions and objectifications* ... This indirect procedure that uses expressions (to reconstitute lived time) has to some extent been applied by Brentano and Husserl.
>
> (Wilhelm Dilthey, *c.*1907–08)[3]

Neville Chamberlain in his notoriety as an 'appeaser' of anti-democratic dictators – Hitler, Mussolini and Stalin – has become an icon for misread history and the failure to confront emergent danger to a society. This

[1] J. M. Chladenius, 'On the interpretation of historical books and accounts', in K. Mueller-Vollmer (ed.), *The Hermeneutics Reader* (New York: Continuum, 1989), p. 65.

[2] As quoted by L. Sterne, *Tristram Shandy* (New York: W.W. Norton, 1980), p. 1.

[3] W. Dilthey, 'Fragments for a poetics', in R. A. Makkreel and F. Rodi (eds.), *Poetry and Experience*, (Princeton, NJ: Princeton University Press, 1985), p. 229. The German original is in Dilthey's 'Fragmente zur Poetik, Strukturpsychologie', in *Die Geistige Welt, Einleitung in die Philosophie des Lebens, Gesammelte Schriften VI* (Göttingen: Vandenhoeck & Ruprecht, 1958), p. 318.

reputation was enhanced by Winston Churchill's aggressive attacks on Chamberlain's foreign policy views when the latter was the Conservative British prime minister between May 1937 and September 1939. Churchill was a fellow Conservative who was impatient with what he saw as the vacillating policies of Chamberlain towards the dictators, month after month, meeting after meeting, giving them 'the benefit of the doubt', and hoping an accord could stick that would give Europe, indeed the world, 'peace in our time'. Churchill was proven correct in his reading of Hitler's motives, in particular. After the Second World War began in September 1939, Chamberlain was compelled to include Churchill in his cabinet to keep unity within the party. In September 1939 Churchill was named First Lord of the Admiralty. This move only underscored the view within the allied West of Churchill's correct understanding of history, and Chamberlain's disastrously mistaken policy of appeasement. Churchill's assertive demand for total war against Germany and its allies again eclipsed a continuing cautious policy by Chamberlain. Chamberlain saw a short war of attrition, and hesitated to commit British forces to any decisive battle where all was on the line.[4] As Churchill became First Lord of the Admiralty, he was immediately contacted by US President Franklin Delano Roosevelt. President Roosevelt by-passed the normal courtesies between national leaders in his contact with Churchill regarding the conduct of foreign policy. Ordinarily, such communication between executive authorities of differing nations is channelled through the diplomatic hierarchy. Roosevelt reminded Churchill of their mutual biographies as leaders of naval policy in the First World War, inviting a direct and continuing correspondence.[5] Roosevelt, too, had long prepared for a world war between democracy and the dictatorships that were emerging in the 1930s. Churchill was viewed by Roosevelt as one who would facilitate a joint strategy to defeat Germany and its allies. When Churchill replaced Chamberlain as the British prime minister in May of 1940, the way seemed cleared for both to bring their combined forces into battle against the fascist nations.

In truth, the policy decisions between May of 1940 and the entry of the United States into the war against Japan and Germany on 8 and 11 December 1941, respectively, were never of a unity between Churchill and Roosevelt. Each of them saw the transpiring of events, and consequently what each nation could ask of the other, differently. American

[4] G. Stewart, *Churchill, Chamberlain and the Battle for the Tory Party* (London: Phoenix, 1999), pp. 387–9.

[5] See J. P. Lash, *The Partnership That Save the West, Roosevelt and Churchill, 1939–1941* (New York: W. W. Norton, 1976), 23–4.

isolationism, a history of suspicion regarding the self-interest of each country, differing geographical interests and day-to-day politics is the ground on which these differences are ordinarily explained. I will demonstrate a historiographical instrument of interpretation that places into the foreground different lifelong mindsets that were foundational for the nature of the conflicts or accords in point of view between Churchill, Roosevelt and Chamberlain. Regardless of political issues or any other content, a cognitive-orientation in each man that characterized how any event would be configured, construed and acted upon, will be seen as more foundational for the foreign policy perspectives and the interpersonal understandings. As Epictetus held, 'it is the judgments about things' that are primary in how we conceive and interrelate among others in the midst of the things of our in-common situations. The judgemental styles of Chamberlain, Churchill and Roosevelt, as well as any of us, are understood as lifelong cognitive orientations that condition all personal and interpersonal experience.

A cognitive orientation is the frame of perceiving, judging, and one's consequent praxis, that is formed by the construction from the data of experience. The cognitive orientation as a framework of perceiving and judging can be construed as what transpires as an 'event' to the beholder, that is the predication of a totality that links all the phases of what one attends. This frame of perceiving is the basis of higher levels of reflective judgement, upon one's own life experience or reflection upon the past experiences of others. I will call this an 'event-structure' as I go on in this chapter. The 'event-structure' is created by language – both the non-verbal percept and the verbal grammar by which we articulate our perception. An event is constructed through language and through how experience is configured as a totality, in the parts that make it up, how they are conjoined, and how that totality is combined with the actions and issues that give us as sense of the history of ourselves or others. Cognitive orientation has been studied as a logical process of ordering the parts and wholes of experience since Chladenius and his contemporaries in the early eighteenth century. This line of inquiry has acquired the philosophical designation of 'phenomenology', and the psychology of personal attention, its attendant interest, conation, attitude and praxis is understood as 'phenomenological psychology'. Phenomenological psychology differs from other schools of interpretative psychology into motivation, interest, attitude and praxis in that it begins with a focus upon the style of grammatical expression, seeing this style as developing before reflective consciousness at a level of immediate perception, that is in the 'phenomenon' which is articulated.

My method relies on the thought and writings of Wilhelm Dilthey (1833–1911), a late mentor of his, Edmund Husserl (1859–1938), the descendants of Dilthey and Husserl in the 1930s through the 1950s, such as Emil Staiger (1908–87), as well as contemporary linguists who have engaged in 'stylistics', the study of the nuanced meanings generated by differing proclivities among individuals in their use of grammar.[6] My own studies have shown a lifelong consistency in cognitive orientation among historical figures of different centuries – among them leading Tudor political personalities, the framers of the American Constitution and a score of nineteenth- and twentieth-century minds, studies which I have coupled with the exploration of contemporary adolescents – in order to show the existence and persistence of cognitive orientation as the key factor in comprehending one's own life experience and historical events over time.[7] I will demonstrate a 'context-free' cognitive orientation persistent in the judgements of Chamberlain, Churchill and Roosevelt, and in doing so move beyond the exploration of the political contexts of their mutual relations which dominates existing historical inquiries into their lives and political careers. 'Context-free' cognitive orientation that hinges upon pre-reflective language constructions has been widely studied in cognitive science.[8] Stylistics as a path into this issue has received less attention. Determining a consistency in judgemental styles as an avenue for comprehending the historical personality in his or her praxis is not a return to the 'great man in history' theory. Rather it recognizes that all persons have inherent styles of judgement that condition their personal and interpersonal activity in its style of judgement and action. One of the elements retarding this approach is the 'juridical' model of objective reality – that there is one best answer based on facts. While cultural differences that condition personal expression have allowed for diversity in judgement within in-common states of affairs, these studies are as a rule averse to the hypothesis of context-free differences in individual judgement that hinge on a pre-reflective, inherent style of judgement that

[6] See Dilthey's use of grammatical analysis, for example, in comprehending the mindset of Goethe and Hölderlin in *Poetry and Experience* (Princeton, NJ: Princeton University Press, 1985), pp. 235–379. For Husserl's reflections on the differentiated effects of grammatical construction on cognitive orientation, see *Logical Investigations*, vol. II, trans. J. N. Findlay (London: Routledge & Kegan Paul, 1970), especially Investigation III ('On the theory of parts and wholes') and Investigation V ('On intentional experiences and their contents'. See also Emil Staiger, *Die Zeit Als Einbildungskraft des Dichters* (Zürich: Max Niehans Verlag, 1939).

[7] See M. E. Blum, *Continuity, Quantum, Continuum, and Dialectic: the Foundational Logics of Western Historical Thinking* (New York: Peter Lang, 2006).

[8] See, for example, T. Wasow, 'Grammatical theory', in M. I. Posner (ed.), *Foundations of Grammatical Science* (Cambridge, MA: MIT Press, 1990), pp. 161–206.

underlies any cultural learning.[9] Phenomenological analysis of judgemental artefacts – the grammar of personal expression – gives evidence that any in-common state-of-affairs has multiple ways of being perceived. To be sure, there enters into the semantics and rhetoric of the person a cultural bias conditioned by educational and societal influences; nonetheless, one can determine the individually persistent, context-free style within his or her discourse.[10] The 'context-free' style of judgement differs in fundamental and more nuanced ways among individuals over a career of thought and action. I will demonstrate this in 1937 through 1941 with Chamberlain, Churchill and Roosevelt.

Chladenius' insight of what I will call the 'multiple objectivities' of historical reality – each individual being objectively correct as they address the same universe of facts, even as they differ on the selection and interpretation of these facts – have their foundation in the styles of judgement each person brings to the facts at hand. The style of judgement is found in the grammatical proclivities articulated by an individual that can be tracked in their constancy from early adolescence, when the well-formed sentence is first mastered, through one's career of thought.[11] Word choice, phrase and clause ordering and the consequent rhetorical development of an argument, signal this lifelong cognitive orientation. I will examine the cognitive orientation of Chamberlain, Churchill and Roosevelt by dissecting and deliberating upon the grammatical patterns that inhered in each of their sentential judgements. I will show how these persistent

[9] See, for example, R. G. D'Andrade, 'Cultural cognition' in M. I. Posner (ed.) *Foundations of Grammatical Science* (Cambridge, MA: MIT Press, 1990), pp. 795–830. For a counterpoint with the 'context-free' notions of linguistic development that accepts many of its findings, but stresses cultural determination of language expression in its differences among persons, see M. Tomasello, 'Cognitive linguistics', in W. Bechtel and G. Graham (eds.), *A Companion to Cognitive Science* (Malden, MA: Blackwell, 1998), pp. 477–87.

[10] See my studies of Austrian and German individuals as they are affected by rhetorical norms of their society and generation, which illustrates the difference between what is individually inherent over a lifetime of thought, and what is societally conditioned in discourse; compare, for instance, the individual event-structure depicted in Max Weber, discussed in M. E. Blum, 'Breaks or continuity in Sombart's work: a linguistic analysis', in J. G. Backhaus (ed.), *Werner Sombart (1863–1941) Social Scientist*, vol. III (Marburg: Metropolis Verlag, 1996) with my study of the influence of Germanic norms of thought in Mark E. Blum, 'Contrasting historical-logical narrative conventions in Germany and Austria and their influence upon inquiry and explanation in the arts and the sciences: an example from the economic inquiries of Gustav Schmoller, Max Weber, Carl Menger and Ludwig von Mises', in J. G. Backhaus (ed.), *Political Economy, Linguistics and Culture, Crossing Bridges* (New York: Springer Verlag, 2008), pp. 59–100.

[11] See C. Chomsky, *The Acquisition of Syntax in Children from 5 to 10* (Cambridge, MA: M.I.T., 1969), 1. Jean Piaget's stage of 'formal reasoning' corresponds to the maturation of this syntactical ability; see J. Piaget, *The Construction of Reality in the Child* (New York: Basic Books, 1954). My research into children aged 12 and 13 years is valuable in seeing the presence and ideational effects of a cognitive orientation; Blum, *Continuity, Quantum, Continuum*, pp. 439–75.

patterns generated not only how the men viewed the events they helped to shape, but how the shaping itself – the 'event-structure' taken on by the grammatical construction of what is attended – shaped the articulation of the men's vision, conditioning the decisions and relations each man fostered. Moreover, I will review the reception, by each of the three figures, of the other's characteristic actions and understandings, illustrating how their cognitive orientations were conditioned and influenced by each other.

First, I will introduce the kind of mutual misunderstanding that can arise when two minds have radically differing cognitive orientations, focusing on Chamberlain and Churchill. In illustrating the conception that each man had of the other, and how their respective cognitive orientations functioned in their policies, I will introduce a philosophical-linguistic distinction derived from Immanuel Kant – the difference between an aggregative and a quantum manner of constructing an event. I will then proceed to offer a more thorough epistemology of my historiographical methodology and detail the grammatical indicators of the aggregative or quantum cognitive orientations. Having done so, I will take up the policies and relationships between Chamberlain, Churchill and Roosevelt over the several years leading to the Second World War within the framework of the aggregative–quantum distinction of cognitive orientation. Finally I will offer a concluding understanding of the gain provided by stylistic analyses into the judgemental processes of historical persons for the field of history.

Cognitive orientations of Neville Chamberlain and Winston Churchill

Neville Chamberlain wrote of Winston Churchill in 1928 that 'it is comic how he flounders directly we get to the difficult details. His part is to brush in broad splashes of paint with highlights and deep shadows. Accuracy of drawing is beyond his ken.'[12] Chamberlain's complaint was in response to Churchill's recommendation as Chancellor of the Exchequer that the rates imposed on industry and agriculture by local government be removed, and the resulting shortfall in revenues which had supported local governmental expenditures, particularly those associated with the Poor Law, be compensated by block grants from central government raised through new taxes on petrol. While Chamberlain, as

[12] Quotation taken from D. Dilks, *Neville Chamberlain*, vol. I, *Pioneering and reform, 1869–1929* (Cambridge University Press, 1984), p. 546; cited from a letter of Neville Chamberlain to his wife, 25 January 1928.

Minister of Health, agreed that growth in the national economy must be spurred by alleviation of taxes on agriculture and industry, he found Churchill's negation of rates that had been determined by the local communities, and the substituting of a new national tax, too broadly sweeping a policy. Chamberlain's perspective demanded a more incrementally specific address community by community. He saw the difficulties in dealing with local governments whose diverse situations required a differentiated set of operative relations between the central government, the industries and agriculture – as these private enterprises existed in local conditions.[13] Churchill, on the other hand, viewed a reorientation of rates and taxes as a measure that addressed in a comprehensive manner the totality of Britain's economic condition.[14] As Dilks characterized the cognitive orientations of the two men with regard to this issue: 'Churchill believed that Chamberlain had too narrow a vision, and Chamberlain that ... Churchill's conceptions were too vague and slapdash.'[15] In speaking of this issue, and the contrasting views of Churchill and Chamberlain, the historian Graham Stewart brings out that Chamberlain 'noted that Churchill was the opposite to himself' because of his neglect of the difficult details.

Normally, a common-sense or a more sophisticated historical address of this difference in cognitive orientation to the issue at hand between Chamberlain and Churchill would satisfy itself with a description of the motivating policy preferences, or perhaps, by long-standing values, political exigencies, or other topical influences upon the judgement at hand. A deeper explanation could be a depiction of personal character. Personal character or 'personality' has been recognized as a ground that influences judgement and consequent action throughout human history. The determination of 'personality' or 'personal character' is ordinarily a subjective assessment with criteria that comes from the manner within a cultural period of judging the attitudes and actions of an individual. Contemporary schools of psychology that probe both the organic and cultural causation of personality offer evidential bases of character that can rise beyond the limitations of the subjective knowing of a time. The phenomenological psychological method that I bring to the study of personal character in this chapter can augment existing schools of psychology in its search for the causal scientific rigour in standardizing knowledge of personality. My approach, which stems from the traditional focus of phenomenology and stylistics, both of which are concerned in

[13] D. Dilks, *Neville Chamberlain*, vol. I: *Pioneering and Reform, 1869–1929* (Cambridge University Press, 1984), p. 547.
[14] *Ibid.*, pp. 535–6. [15] *Ibid.*, p. 534.

their examination of judgement in the semantics and syntax of representation, focuses upon enduring grammatical patterns of judgement that have distinct implications for the thought and action of the person.

Kant described two fundamental cognitive orientations in the formulation of the part–whole structures that constitute a state-of-affairs in thought – the aggregative and the quantum.[16] A 'state-of-affairs in thought' is any predication of a time, place, or manner; in short, 'how things are'. The 'quantum' and the 'aggregative' of fundamental differences in the cognitive construction of any 'state-of-affairs'. Kant explains the difference by an account of how 'thirteen thalers' are perceived by the aggregative thinker 'through repetition of an ever-ceasing synthesis' of each individual coin. The aggregative cognitive orientation is incremental, stressing isolated wholes, such as each coin. Separateness is the dominant cognition, that is, 'the ever-ceasing synthesis' that isolates each person, place, and thing in its own time, place and manner. The quantum cognitive orientation, on the other hand, is the immediate perception of the totality constituted by the thirteen thalers, 'a mark of fine silver'. Kant terms this quantum whole 'a continuous magnitude, in which no part is the smallest, and in which every part can constitute a piece of coin that always contains material for still smaller pieces'.[17] Interdependence is the rule in the quantum cognitive orientation. The 'continuous magnitude' is the whole or totality that is the summative organization of all other entities. Persons, places and things share a time, place and manner; differences among the parts are of lesser moment than what conjoins them. The aggregative, as I will demonstrate, is the cognitive orientation of Neville Chamberlain's incremental, 'detailed' construction; the quantum is the cognitive orientation of Churchill in its striving to see each part within its role of the whole that comprehends it. Franklin Delano Roosevelt will share a quantum orientation with Churchill.

Interpersonal understanding is affected by one's inherent cognitive orientation, just as we have read in the above reaction of Chamberlain to Churchill and of Churchill to Chamberlain over the issue and approach to rates. A quantum thinker will insist upon a cooperation in the service of the overarching 'continuous magnitude', which he or she sees as guiding every decision; the aggregative thinker will insist upon a give and take of positions that incrementally take up the specific facts at hand, as Kant puts it 'the pieces of money', rather than the 'silver standard', which is a more abstract measure.[18] Churchill's semantics offer a

[16] I. Kant, *Critique of Pure Reason*, trans. N. Kemp Smith (New York: Macmillan, 1968, 204 [A 170, B 212].

[17] *Ibid.*, p. 204. [18] *Ibid.*, p. 204.

quantum characterization of the needed acquiescence of Chamberlain in a letter to him regarding his rate plan. Churchill asserts that each of them must pull with equal energy on the 'shafts', if the 'cart' of a common purpose was to be 'dragged ... up the hill'.[19] Chamberlain in his reply to Churchill offers an aggregative semantics. He said that the two might be 'in tandem', but that each of them was positioned differently insofar as their authority and function – it was he that was in the shafts and Churchill who was the leader. If the two were to work effectively together it required 'give and take on both sides' as each aspect of the issue at hand was addressed.[20]

The 'appeasement' which made Neville Chamberlain notorious in the history of the West was a policy that can be deemed normal to a diplomat with an aggregative cognitive orientation. 'Appeasement' for Chamberlain was an incremental effort to reach accord and balances – normal diplomacy. Each time and place was distinct in its conditions; each person had his or her own trajectory of interests of that time to consider. On 20 October 1937 Chamberlain used the term 'appeasement' to describe the object of a planned Nine Powers Conference in Brussels to address the Japanese presence in China.[21] For him the term described an intended 'mediation' among the parties invited to the conference in search of a balance of interests, where all parties were to make clear the extent and limit of their positions.[22] Chamberlain's favoured approach to Hitler even earlier in the decade reflected his incremental event-structure, where no overarching concept or telos determined the outcome of the exchange of views in any negotiation. While Chamberlain viewed Hitler as 'the bully of Europe' as early as 1935,[23] his comment upon the diplomatic outreach by the Foreign Secretary John Simon in March of that year, although it failed to reach an accord with Hitler, reflected an event-structure whose configuring pattern Kant termed the 'ever-ceasing synthesis' of each time, place and manner, where the 'this-there' of each distinct occurrence was articulated:

> I feel one ought not to criticize the conversations when one was not there ... but I did regret that the position was not more thoroughly explored in some respects. I never for one moment expected that Hitler would sign the Eastern Pact. He says he can't contemplate fighting alongside Communists against someone else, in consequence of events outside his control. If that be taken as genuine, I don't

[19] Dilks, *Neville Chamberlain*, p. 548.
[20] *Ibid.*, p. 548.
[21] W. R. Rock, *Chamberlain and Roosevelt, British Foreign Policy and the United States, 1937–1940* (Columbus: Ohio State University Press, 1988), p. 42.
[22] *Ibid.*, p. 42.
[23] K. Feiling, *The Life of Neville Chamberlain* (London: Macmillan, 1947), p. 256.

think it's unreasonable. But seeing that the possible antagonists in the East are Germany and Russia, and that they are divided by a band of small States, – the Baltic States, Poland, and Czecho-Slovakia, – I should have thought it was worth while to have explored the possibility of Russia and Germany mutually guaranteeing the western and eastern frontiers of those States.[24]

Winston Churchill's consistent telic purview of Germany's aggressive intentions was a quantum orientation, a Kantian 'continuous magnitude', within which any specific act or policy was to be understood as a 'part of that magnitude'.[25] A 1934 statement suffices to introduce Churchill's quantum event-structure as it takes up the changing states of affairs among the European nations in the inter-war years: 'Germany is rearming. That is the great new fact which rivets the attention of every country in Europe – indeed, in the world – and which throws almost all other issues into the background. Germany is rearming, that mighty power which only a few years ago, within our own experience, fought almost the whole world, and almost conquered.'[26]

Despite the historical consensus that Churchill was right throughout the decade and Chamberlain wrong in their foreign policies, attention to their different cognitive orientation enables us to see the logical bases of the respective event-structures that informed their thinking. There is the necessity for both the aggregative, incremental comprehension of reality as well as the quantum comprehension. Attention to both the aggregative and quantum styles of judgement held, respectively, by individuals who share an in-common situation, enables a historiographical vision of 'multiple objectivities', rather than the law-court understanding of history where one true reality is sought by the best evidence. Determining cognitive orientation with a phenomenological inquiry into a style of grammatical expression enables one to appreciate the conflicting, at times complementing, event-structures brought to any state-of-affairs by differing minds, and thus reveals that historical occurrences are only to be comprehended by attention to multiple perspectives, not solely within the cognitive orientation of one commentator or historical agent.

The distinction between aggregative and quantum cognitive orientation

Historical experience as well as one's interpretation of historical experience is a product of rational consciousness, and consequently of language.

[24] *Ibid.*, p. 256.

[25] Kant, *Critique of Pure Reason*, p. 204 [A 170, B 212].

[26] W. Churchill, *While England Slept: a Survey of World Affairs 1932–1938* (New York: Putnam, 1938), p. 141.

One's cognitive orientation is in itself a language orientation. Moreover, one's cognitive orientation as language is in its processes of judgement, as argued by phenomenological thinkers, the foundation and generator of the human experience of personal time, and through greater abstraction, historical time. The epistemology of consciousness that maintains this understanding of temporal experience from Kant through Husserl, and his descendants, is central to the historiographical hermeneutic that I offer. Discerning the grammatical form of verbal predications enables understanding of how the person experiences and construes 'temporality'. Temporal increments are articulated in a judgement by phrases and clauses, which Husserl calls 'time-stretches', which culminate in a 'temporal concretum', that is the sentential judgement as a whole.[27] A phenomenological understanding of historical experience appreciates that phenomenal time as well as the larger abstractions of societal time are generated by the consciousness of the perceiver. The language of the perceiver constructs the state-of-affairs, that is, event, 'time-stretch' by 'time-stretch'.

Kant's age sought the construction of a univocal objectivity. All laws of thought were universal in all humans. Indeed, such universality has been demonstrated, but the salience of a style within these invariant categories of thinking can also be demonstrated. Edmund Husserl, in an age where the distinctiveness of individual personality was a major concern, recognized that such a personal character of thought existed.[28] From the 1870s into the First World War, creative, cultural minds formulated with an interdisciplinary inquiry that integrated linguistics, literature, psychology and other disciplines a foundation of knowledge that enabled the study of individual character in its individuative complexity. Contributors in this age to the problematic of individual character and its individuative bases in consciousness were legion, but among those who contributed most greatly included Georg Brandes (1842–1927) and Wilhelm Dilthey (1833–1911) who brought an interdisciplinary amalgam of the human sciences to their literary studies and biography; William James (1842–1910) furthered the understanding of the complexity of individual consciousness and thus deepened the culture's need to formulate measures to determine the dimensions and character of the individual personality; Carl Gustav Jung (1875–1961) worked with the grammar of human expression in his depth psychology as he tracked personal individuation; and, the mathematician Gottlob Frege (1848–1925), who

[27] Husserl, *Logical Investigations*, pp. 484–89 and 507–22.

[28] See E. Husserl, *Ideas Pertaining to a Pure Phenomenology and to a Phenomenological Philosophy*, vol. II, trans. R. Rojcewicz and A. Schuwer (Dordrecht: Kluwer Academic Publishers, 1989), pp. 288–293 [Par. 61].

separately, but in a striking parallel to Edmund Husserl (1859–1938), discerned the distinctive paths of 'thought' that differentiated one person's judgement from another at a plane of phenomenological insight that remains fecund.

Husserl saw the science of meanings as necessitating a new inquiry into grammar that can expose the elementary cognitive operations that are conveyed by grammatical expression. Grammar is the handmaiden of thought, and its rules of expression are foundationally, if not in all its mechanisms of articulation, rules that stem from thought. Husserl challenged his contemporaries, and, of course, those who came after, to determine 'the primitive meaning-patterns' that generated the essentially different points of view which were potentially co-present among observers in the in-common state-of-affairs.[29] Determining these patterns leads to the ability of the historical analyst to see 'multiple objectivities' in the reports and action patterns of past lives. Ironically, Husserl's search, which included his own sense of Kant not offering sufficiently refined tools of analysis to capture the 'meaning-patterns', could have been developed by him with attention to the aggregative/quantum distinction of Kant that provides the essential difference in paths of meaning formation in thought. Nuanced differences exist, formed over the evolution of human cognition, but they are traceable to the more foundational difference between the aggregative and the quantum modes of structuring an event in experience in the grammar of cognition.[30]

Normally, determining the consistency or inconsistency of the conceptual preferences and positions of political agents relies upon an ascription of political and social causation. A grammatical analysis questions these causalities as a foundation for cognitive orientation, as it brings to view the deep structural formation of sentential judgements that are beyond the reflective composition of the speaker or even the writer. The pre-reflective formation of judgement through language – be it verbal or non-verbal – is a universally recognized problematic, even as it is challenged among schools of linguistic thought. I argue for Noam Chomsky's understanding as a basis for what I have come to see as a psychogenetic disposition in the person.[31] Let it suffice here to reference a stylistic theoretician who addresses the degree of consciousness of writers who should be the most aware of positing with complete reflective consciousness their own choices of grammar. Louis T. Milic, a contemporary stylistic analyst, stresses that the findings of his research into writers are

[29] Husserl, *Logical Investigations*, pp. 518–19.

[30] Cf. Blum, *Continuity, Quantum, Continuum.* [31] *Ibid.*, pp. 115–23.

that they cannot edit out basic syntactic structures that characterize their prose, occurring as they do at a pre-reflective level of composition.[32]

Philosophers of language have identified grammatical stylistic habits that differentiate how a sentential judgement reflects either the quantum or the aggregative establishment of facts and their organization. The quantum predication is realized with a 'non-dissective' grammar.[33] 'Non-dissective' means that a general state-of-things is communicated by choice of grammar, a state-of-affairs that is more significant than any particular moment of it. As Churchill said in this vein, using the verbal noun predication 'Germany is rearming' to characterize the German activity in relation to the Entente countries since 1918. Verbal nouns are one of the grammatical categories that enable a quantum cognitive orientation. The aggregative predication is realized with a 'dissective' grammar.[34] A 'dissective' grammar stipulates, separates, that is, dissects a state-of-affairs into increments. Chamberlain's characterization of Hitler's foreign policy in 1935 includes the long, punctuated sentence, replete with count-nouns and restrictive, qualifying identifiers – staple grammatical ploys of the careful discriminations of the aggregative thinker: 'But seeing that the possible antagonists in the East are Germany and Russia, and that they are divided by band of small States, – the Baltic States, Poland and Czecho-Slovakia, – I should have thought it was worth while to have explored the possibility of Russia and Germany mutually guaranteeing the western and eastern frontiers of those States.'

Grammatical differences that differentiate the quantum/non-dissective from the aggregative/dissective vision are found in the formation of each semantic and syntactic choice. The quantum cognitive orientation has a preference for non-count and plural nouns, indefinite articles, the weak sense of 'the', or determiners such as 'some', 'many', 'few', 'every', and predicate adjectives that articulate a general condition. Non-restrictive phrases or clauses carry the meaning of the subject into a predication that imparts a generalized, open-ended state-of-affairs. The aggregative cognitive orientation prefers definite articles, pre-modifying adjectives, adverbs that are specific in terms of time, place and manner, and count and proper nouns. Restrictive phrases or clauses stipulate a quality or a particular condition of time, place, or manner.

32 L. T. Milic, 'Rhetorical choice and stylistic option: the conscious and unconscious poles', *Literary Style: a Symposium*, ed. S. Chatman (London: Oxford University, 1971), p. 82.

33 See E. Hirsch, *Essence and Identity in Identity and Individuation*, ed. M. K. Munitz (New York University Press, 1971), pp. 45ff.

34 See N. Goodman, *The Structure of Appearance* (Indianapolis, IN: Bobbs-Merrill, 1951), pp. 54ff.

Cognitive orientation and political decision making: Chamberlain, Churchill and Roosevelt

Arthur Schlesinger, in characterizing Franklin Delano Roosevelt's New Deal Years observed that the complaint most made of him was his 'weakness for postponement. Yet his caution was always within an assumption of constant advance'.[35] Roosevelt was a 'morphological' thinker, a quantum cognitive orientation that saw each decision as contributing further to a continuing line of value and action, as an oak tree develops from the acorn over a lifetime.[36] Caution was central to his movement of thought in its inherent form in that the morphological mind weighs what will contribute to on-going values, habits, or any continuous magnitude taken up by consciousness. The sentential judgements of the morphological mind will include several phrases and/or clauses that are not metonymically selected in characterizing a state-of-affairs. Rather, they can seem arbitrary in their order – denoting a logic of selection that is personal in its deliberation of what is considered judicious in determining the completion of a thought. Caution was also necessary, given his value priorities, within the isolationist sentiment of the United States, if he was to realize the assertive protection of human liberty that he felt was necessary in the face of developing fascist aggression in the years 1937–41. The morphological mind seeks to comprehend all persons, places and things in its breadth of understanding, and attends each and every person, place and thing in its character – listening and observing. As a politician, Roosevelt was masterful in thus judging the mood of his potential constituencies. Distinctions are made and positions rejected, but this is a deliberative process.

Franklin Delano Roosevelt cleaved to several broad political-social values that became identified in his own policies as the bases of his decision making throughout the critical pre-war years for the United States of 1937–41. Known as the 'four freedoms' when they were articulated to Congress on 6 January 1941, in his State of the Union Address, their presence in his domestic and foreign policies since his entry into politics, even before the First World War, can be discerned. As articulated in the State of the Union Address, they had been the basis of decisions since

[35] Cited in J. P. Lash, *Roosevelt and Churchill, 1939–1941, The Partnership That Saved the West* (New York: W.W. Norton, 1976), p. 302.

[36] There are two major sub-types of the quantum orientation – the pure quantum, which Churchill reflected, and the morphological, which was Roosevelt's perspective. Two subtypes of the aggregative are found, that of continuity and that of the continuum; see Mark E. Blum, *Continuity, Quantum, Continuum, and Dialectic: the Foundational Logics of Western Historical Thinking*.

he began his interactions with Neville Chamberlain in 1937, and subsequently with Winston Churchill:

> In the future days, which we seek to make secure, we look forward to a world founded upon four essential human freedoms.
>
> The first is freedom of speech and expression – everywhere in the world.
>
> The second is freedom of every person to worship God in his own way – everywhere in the world.
>
> The third is freedom from want – which, translated into world terms, means economic understandings which will secure to every nation a healthy peacetime life for its inhabitants – everywhere in the world.
>
> The fourth is freedom from fear – which, translated into world terms, means a world-wide reduction of armaments to such a point and in such a thorough fashion that no nation will be in a position to commit an act of physical aggression against any neighbor – anywhere in the world.
>
> That is no vision of a distant millennium. It is a definite basis for a kind of world attainable in our own time and generation.[37]

As Roosevelt develops his vision of the world that will govern his foreign policy between 1937 and 1941, each of the sentences which articulate the four freedoms is constructed with a non-dissective grammar. The non-restrictive adverbial phrases 'everywhere in the world' or 'anywhere in the world', the indefinite determiner 'every', and, the plural nouns that broaden membership potentially to everyone without qualification. [38] Even the numbering of one through four has the semantic function of allowing an understanding of the equal standing or sequencing of the other freedoms in status.[39] The fourth freedom seems to create a specific condition; yet attention to the verbal noun phrase 'world-wide reduction' generates the non-dissective quantum state-of-affairs. And, the adverbial phrase 'to such a point' typifies the morphological quantum vision of the non-dissective stage of development – phases or stages central to the thought of the morphological mind.

Nonetheless, for Roosevelt, the 'indefinite' was a 'definite' goal for which pragmatic choices were made, even as these plans seemed ambiguous to an aggregative thinker. Roosevelt began and ended his 'four freedoms' State of the Union message with these sentences that were a hallmark of the morphological mind in their potential futurity, a transitional present, emerging out of a tangible past: 'In the future days, which we seek to make secure, we look forward to a world founded upon

[37] F. D. Roosevelt, *The Public Papers and Addresses of Franklin D. Roosevelt*, vol. IX (New York: Macmillan, 1941), p. 672.

[38] See R. Quirk *et al.*, *A Comprehensive Grammar of the English Language* (London: Longman, 1986), pp. 253–57 and 1239–44.

[39] *Ibid.*, pp. 530–3.

four essential human freedoms ... That is no vision of a distant millennium. It is a definite basis for a kind of world attainable in our own time and generation'. Roosevelt's entry to the major foreign policy issue that engaged him and Churchill between 1937 and 1941, that of preparation for a possible war with Hitler and other fascist leaders, began with his 'Quarantine Speech' of 5 October 1937. In this speech, the broad metaphor of 'quarantine' was formulated as a policy to counter the aggressors like Germany, Italy and Japan. The world had become 'interdependent', and the 'contagion' of becoming aggressive either for gain or for defence was spreading.[40] Here one can see the quantum construction operative in Roosevelt's thought. No specific measures were offered in the speech, only the general principle that would serve as Roosevelt's quantum perspective over the next four years which ended the speech: 'America hates war. America hopes for peace. Therefore, America actively engages in the search for peace.'[41] When quizzed the next day in a press conference about the speech, and asked if he had 'economic sanctions' in mind, Roosevelt responded by referring to the last sentence of his speech the day before, stating that 'sanctions is a terrible word to use. I can't tell you what the methods will be.'[42] Both Chamberlain and Roosevelt's own advisors were troubled by the vagueness, the non-specificity of his policy. Harold Ickes called it 'highly suggestive but obviously lacking in specifics'.[43] Chamberlain thought it very vague in essentials, adding 'Now they jump in, without saying a word to us beforehand and without knowing what they mean to do.'[44] The London *Times* characterized the speech as 'an attitude without a program', to which Roosevelt responded, 'It is an attitude, and it does not outline a program; but it says we are looking for a program.'[45]

On 12 October 1937, Roosevelt called for 'mediation' with the aggressors to be realized within a Nine-Power Conference that had been proposed with the urging of Chamberlain in the weeks before the Quarantine Speech. Chamberlain was irked as 'mediation' was a term he preferred – 'which was exactly my idea', linking it to person to person diplomacy in what he called the true purpose of the proposed Conference, that of 'appeasement' – appeasement being the meeting of a specific interest with an appropriate means of reaching an accord with it in mind.[46] As an aggregative thinker who eschewed overarching concepts, Chamberlain

[40] F. D. Roosevelt, *The Public Papers and Addresses of Franklin D. Roosevelt*, vol. VI (New York: Macmillan, 1941), pp. 409–10.

[41] *Ibid.*, p. 411. [42] *Ibid.*, p. 423.

[43] Rock, *Chamberlain and Roosevelt*, p. 34. [44] *Ibid.*, p. 35.

[45] Roosevelt, *The Public Papers*, p. 423.

[46] Rock, *Chamberlain and Roosevelt*, p. 42.

saw actuality as being shaped by personal interaction on a one-to-one basis. Indeed, some of his discomfort with Roosevelt was in the latter's taking a personal action that was uninvited, thus interfering with his own self-image as problem solver whose personal agency was being compromised.[47] As an aggregative thinker, the reality of interpersonal communication was limited to the specific issue of a distinct time, place and manner. One needed autonomy in decision making for this praxis where one was not beholden to the abstractions that governed the quantum cognitive orientation. Thus 'mediation' was a semantic term that underscored that 'appeasement' was to be seen as an action to prevent war in a proactive manner. 'Mediation' was the means of facilitating the often shifting nature of achieving 'appeasement'. Chamberlain's aggregative mind with its stress on specific actions in relation to individual persons at definite times, places and manners, can be seen, for example, in a letter sent to an American on 16 January 1938 that speaks of his intentions towards Hitler and Mussolini, as well as the US president. All his thoughts are formulated as individuals being the alpha and omega of events:

> (1) It is indeed the human side of the dictators that makes them dangerous, but on the other hand, it is the side on which they can be approached with the greatest hope of a successful issue. (2) I am about to enter upon a fresh attempt to reach a reasonable understanding with both Germany and Italy, and I am by no means unhopeful of getting results. (3) I have an idea that when we have done a certain amount of spade-work here we may want help from [the] U.S.A. (4) In such an event a friendly and sympathetic President might be able to give just the fresh stimulus we required, and I feel sure that the American people would feel proud if they could be brought in to share the final establishment of peace.[48]

Understanding the structure of any one of these sentences will give us the sentential form of the aggregative thinker. In sentence (1) the noun 'side' asks us to see in the 'human' dimension the unspoken other dimensions that may exist to complete person – such as 'the political' or 'the seeker of power'. Although somewhat metaphorical in its deliberation – one might call his play on 'side' a metonymic metaphor – the dissective specificity is communicated with the count noun 'side' set off with restrictive determiners and phrases, delimiting the purview to individualized human actions that take place within a unity of time, place and manner. Sentence (2) creates the dissective image of his 'about ... to enter' a specific attempt that suggests 'mediation', that is, the restrictive verbal noun phrase 'a reasonable understanding with ...'. Sentence (3) begins

[47] Stewart, *Churchill, Chamberlain and the Battle for the Tory Party*, p. 285.
[48] Feiling, *The Life of Neville Chamberlain*, p. 324.

with the dissective 'I have an idea', which is to ask for 'help from [the] U.S.A.'. Sentence (4) maintains this specific person to person-centred narrative. The 'friendly and sympathetic President', encouraged by the previous 'spade-work' of sentence (3) (again a metonymical metaphor as presented by the guiding activity of Chamberlain) may well contribute the dissective response of 'the fresh stimulus'.

Winston Churchill did not have the interpersonal patience bred by such a perspective to be a one-on-one politician or diplomat. Churchill consulted only his own conscience as it squared with the principles within whose quantum context he saw himself as operating.[49] The quantum-based thinker – either the pure, as Churchill, or the morphological, as Roosevelt – sees how and why a person represents a broader issue, value, or state-of-affairs. The morphological quantum thinker, as Roosevelt, will listen carefully to the perspectives of each and all as he determines the actuality of the perceived quantum state-of-affairs that will govern his cognitive orientation. The quantum that governs the sentential judgement of the morphological thinker is changing gradually, constantly, as it develops in the experience of the world. The pure quantum thinker, as Churchill, has a cognitive orientation that is not developmental. While his governing ideas or principles can be informed, they do not change in their essential meanings. Churchill tends to consult deeply rooted ideas that endure in their clarity over time. Each thought or action is in the service of the immediacy of this recognizable quantum over the life of his discourse. As Churchill wrote in this vein in a eulogy for his former political adversary Neville Chamberlain:

> The only guide to a man is his conscience, the only shield to his memory is the rectitude and sincerity of his actions. It is very imprudent to walk through life without this shield, because we are so often mocked by the failure of our hopes and the upsetting of our calculations; but with this shield, however the fates may play, we march always in the ranks of honour.[50]

It seems to me quite appropriate that Roosevelt's first note to Churchill that opened a cooperative understanding as early as 11 September 1939, when Churchill was the newly appointed First Lord of the Admiralty, was to locate the two of them within an in-common context that gave them kinship – the Navy Department and the Admiralty in the First World War. Churchill as what I call a 'pure quantum' thinker was more reserved, realizing that his every action instantiated the role and station which was his setting. He took pains to point out in his response that he

[49] Cf. Stewart, *Churchill, Chamberlain and the Battle for the Tory Party*, esp. pp. 42–3 and 448.

[50] *Ibid.*, p. 448.

had the permission of Prime Minister Chamberlain. Churchill always deeply respected the continuing presence of his party in its tenets, always acting within the scope of the norms and practices possible within his inherited contexts. His change of context, as in his becoming a Liberal, and then his later return to the Conservatives, was influenced by quantum principles that defined him and that he felt dictated these moves. Where Roosevelt would see a decision and engagement as furthering in some part an emergent quantum, Churchill saw the quantum expressed in its full character immediately by an action. For Roosevelt, present reality was always of the part of a past that initiated the quantum in question, an emergent present that was a part of the quantum in transition, and a potential future that was forming from the parts that were sustained. For Churchill, reality was always fully the scope and breadth of what was occurring. Past, present and future were wholly there to be discerned in that present.

Churchill's cooperative career with Roosevelt from the inception of his being prime minister in 1940 through the close conjunction in the carrying out of their common aims after Pearl Harbor on 7 December 1941 reflect the distinctive difference between the sense of an emergent quantum that changes over time (Roosevelt) or a quantum that is fixed in its purpose and functions (Churchill). An exchange that exemplifies this interesting differentiation of cognitive orientation occurs on 30 November 1941:

> It seems to me that one important method remains unused in averting war between Japan and our two countries, namely a plain declaration, secret or public as may be thought best, that any further act of aggression by Japan will lead immediately to the gravest consequence … We would, of course, make a similar declaration or share in a joint declaration, and in an case arrangements are being made to synchronize our actions with yours.[51]

Churchill assumes that Roosevelt, if in a genuine partnership with Britain, can act in the tandem of identical accord. He misreads Roosevelt's sense of a past, present and emergent future in the differences of the history of American foreign policy. The morphological thinker, such as Roosevelt, will attend differentiated voices that help him generate his sense of a shared, but evolving quantum effort. Joseph P. Lash comments after this citation that Roosevelt had long been contemplating the inevitability of a war with Japan, and did not relish the possibility that a Japanese attack on English colonies in the Pacific might compel him to declare a war that had not yet resulted from an attack on American soil. Churchill did not

[51] J. P. Lash, *Roosevelt and Churchill, 1939–1941: the Partnership That Saved the West* (New York: W.W. Norton, 1976), p. 475.

see the differentiated motives in his insistence on the need 'to synchronize our actions with yours'.

Conclusion

Stylistic analysis enables us to determine the enduring cognitive orientations of political persons, but also ordinary individuals in society, from the age of adolescence when a well-formed sentence can first be written. For political or social historians, or for cultural historians, historians of idea, or any school of historical inquiry that takes up individual biography, stylistic analysis enables one to analyse the effects of cognitive orientation upon idea and action, upon interpersonal relationships, and thus, to comprehend individual understanding and choice at a more individually primary level than the accustomed political, social, or even common sense (i.e. ordinary language) biographical methods of determining cultural causation. From the grammar of a culture as the individual matures certain syntactical forms and semantics are preferred that accommodate either the aggregative or the quantum event-structures. The aggregative and the quantum cognitive orientation not only generate a perspective on experience, but also in this perspectival focus carry attitudes and inclinations for the person in his praxis among others. I have demonstrated this in my analyses of Chamberlain, Churchill and Roosevelt.

Nonetheless, there is always a political, social, or biographical causation that involves institutions of society, class and the interactions of family, friends and strangers as the contextually unavoidable matrix for the maturation and formal and informal education of the individual. These overlapping contexts of life are the 'content', which becomes the lifelong 'menu' for life choices. A historical work of any individual must take up these contexts, for one's interests, motivations and actions are always towards this content. One's cognitive orientation, however, is 'how' we address these persisting contents, and to a large extent 'why' we think and act within their purview as we do.

Stylistic inquiry into cognitive orientation will only show why and how two persons who are both democratic, republican or monarchists formulate such shared ideas and values in a manner that can be contrasted, and why these shared ideas, values and consequent actions are so formulated. Moreover, in examining 'why' certain ideas and actions occur in the historical individual, other psychologies can complement the approach to cognitive orientation that I pursue. Cognitive orientation has many differing epistemological understandings and accompanying psychologies. Carl Gustav Jung's notion of mental functions, such a thinking, feeling, intuition and sensation, provide a fecund source of reflection upon how a person interacts with others. Certainly, pathologies studied by Freud and others in the Freudian school can be used to examine biographical issues, such as that of power and its abuse – a historical topic one meets in any political-social inquiry.

Finally, cognitive orientation, with my method based upon stylistics or other psychologically informed methods, is to be used by the historian only after a thorough understanding of the society in which the persons live, in terms of cultural norms as well as the generational changes experienced by persons in that society or societies. Without comprehending what is at issue in a society, psychological issues cannot adequately assist historical interpretation. In a longer work, I might have developed a section on isolationism in American ideation that contributed to Roosevelt's hesitation to join Churchill in an earlier declaration of war. Moreover, there are personal reasons that bias certain courses of judgement, such as the family relations between the Churchills and the Chamberlains in the parents of Winston and Neville. To bring those lingering resentments and points of family honour into an essay on the men's mutual understandings would be required in a longer work on the men themselves.

Yet, finally, the historiographical method that I present that discerns cognitive orientation from grammatical analysis, exposing the enduring style of thought of an individual and its implications, is a method that I see as always complementary to any study of the individual in history.

9 Self-esteem before William James: phrenology's forgotten faculty

George Turner, Susan Condor and Alan Collins

It has been suggested that the self represents 'one of the most actively researched topics in all of psychology'.[1] Consequently, it is not surprising that a good deal of work in the history of psychology has focused on matters relating to self and identity.[2] What is surprising, however, is that none of these accounts has paid any specific attention to the construct of *self-esteem*. As Nicholas Emler has noted: 'Few ideas in the human sciences have ever achieved the level of attention that has been lavished upon the notion of self-esteem.'[3] In psychological research, self-esteem is now commonly used as a predictor variable, an outcome variable and as a mediating variable.[4] At the turn of the millennium, Matthew Whoolery and Judson Stelter reported that nearly 17,000 articles and dissertations with the term 'self-esteem' in the title or abstract had been published in the previous twenty-five years.[5]

1 R. Baumeister, *The Self in Social Psychology* (Abingdon: Psychology Press, 1999), p. 1.

2 R. Baumeister, 'How the self became a problem', *Journal of Personality and Social Psychology*, 52 (1987), 163–76; P. Cushman, 'Why the self is empty: toward a historically situated psychology. *American Psychologist*, 45 (1990), 599–611; J. Fosshage, 'Some key features in the evolution of self psychology and psychoanalysis', *Annals of the New York Academy of Sciences*, 1159 (2009), 1–18; K. Gergen, 'The self: colonization in psychology and society', in M. Ash and T. Sturm (eds.), *Psychology's Territories: Historical and Contemporary Perspectives* (Mahwah, NJ: Lawrence Erlbaum, 2007), pp. 149–67; R. D. Logan, 'Historical change in the prevailing sense of self', in K. M. Yardley and T. Honess (eds.), *Self and Identity: Psychosocial Perspectives* (Oxford: John Wiley & Sons, 1987), pp. 13–26; N. Rose, 'Assembling the modern self', in R. Porter (ed.), *Rewriting the Self: Histories from the Renaissance to the Present* (London: Routledge, 1997), pp. 224–48; N. Rose, *Inventing Ourselves: Psychology, Power and Personhood* (Cambridge University Press, 1998); N. Rose, *Governing the Soul: the Shaping of the Private Self* (London: Free Association Books, 1999); Q. Wang and N. Chowdhary, 'The self', in K. Pawlik and G. d'Ydewalle (eds.), *Psychological Concepts: An International Historical Perspective* (New York: Psychology Press, 2006), pp. 325–58.

3 N. Emler, *Self-Esteem: the Costs and Causes of Low Self-Worth* (York: Joseph Rowntree Foundation, 2001), p. 2.

4 J. D. Brown, K. A. Dutton and K. E. Cook, 'From the top down: self-esteem and self evaluation', *Cognition and Emotion*, 15 (2001), 615–31.

5 M. L. Whoolery and J. Stelter, 'Deconstructing self-esteem', Lecture presented to the Annual Convention of the American Psychological Association in San Francisco, CA,

Self-esteem is evidently a popular topic of contemporary social psychology theory and research, but interest in the subject also crosses sub-disciplinary boundaries. In recent years (2010–12) articles with 'self-esteem' in the title have been published in specialist journals in developmental psychology, educational psychology, health psychology, organizational psychology, sports psychology, evolutionary psychology, cognitive psychology, clinical psychology, biological psychology and neuroscience, as well as in journals in social psychology and personality psychology. Of course, *self-esteem* is not simply a technical term confined to the reified universe of the human sciences.[6] It is also, as Roy Baumeister and colleagues note, a 'household word' and the subject of numerous self-help books and therapeutic programmes.[7]

In one of the few historical accounts to focus specifically on the construct of self-esteem, Steven Ward suggested that the term 'first entered the discourse of the human sciences in the late nineteenth century', and that 'the first reference to self-esteem in psychology can be found in William James' *Principles of Psychology*'.[8] Similarly, conventional academic wisdom has long attributed psychologists' current interest in self-esteem to William James' writings on the self. Most authors have also been inclined to assume that common-sense understandings of self-esteem have followed from its formal psychological use. Some authors have gone even further, in attributing responsibility to William James for coining the term.[9] This kind of account can be quite easily refuted: the term 'self-esteem' dates back to at least the seventeenth century. The *Oxford English Dictionary* gives the first written record as 1657, but even earlier examples can be identified.[10] It is interesting to note that etymologists have been inclined to attribute the popularization of the term 'self-esteem' not to William James'

August 2001. Available online at www.whoolery.com/psychology/self-esteem.htm [accessed 7 March 2013].

[6] S. Moscovici, 'On social representations', in J. P. Forgas (ed.), *Social Cognition* (New York: Academic Press, 1981), pp. 181–209; S. Moscovici, 'The phenomenon of social representations', in R. M. Farr and S. Moscovici (eds.), *Social Representations* (Cambridge University Press, 1984), pp. 3–69.

[7] R. F. Baumeister, J. D. Campbell, J. I. Krueger and K. D. Vohs, 'Does high self-esteem cause better performance, interpersonal success, happiness, or healthier lifestyles?' *Psychological Science in the Public Interest*, 4 (2003), 1.

[8] S. Ward, 'Filling the world with self-esteem: a social history of truth-making', *Canadian Journal of Sociology*, 21 (1996), 1, 5; W. James, *Principles of Psychology* (New York: Henry Holt, 1890).

[9] For example C. Mruk, 'Self-esteem', in W. E. Craighead and C. B. Nemeroff (eds.), *Corsini Encyclopedia of Psychology*, 4th edn (Hoboken, NJ: Wiley, 2010), vol. VI, pp. 1536–40.

[10] *Oxford English Dictionary*, 2nd edn, eds. Simpson and E. Weiner (Oxford: Clarendon Press, 1989); E. Pickering, 'Unidentified first use of self-esteem: Milton's *An Apology for Smectymnuus* (1642)', *Notes & Queries*, 55 (2008), 287–89.

Principles of Psychology, but to psychological work on phrenology published half a century earlier.[11]

Phrenology has been a topic of considerable interest to historians of science, who have debated its political, cultural and scientific significance.[12] It has also been treated as crucial to the emergence of the human sciences, and particularly to sciences concerned with individual differences.[13] Despite this intense scrutiny, to our knowledge, nothing has been written on the relations between phrenology and self-esteem. This chapter represents an initial attempt to chart this relationship. Specifically, we will be asking how the term 'self-esteem' was used in phrenology, and whether there is any evidence to suggest that this may have impacted upon common-sense understandings.

The adoption of self-esteem in phrenology

Phrenology was introduced by Franz Joseph Gall in the late eighteenth century, with the first published account appearing in 1798. The movement became very popular throughout Europe and North America during the first half of the nineteenth century. Although phrenology was most fashionable between about 1820 and 1840, Roger Cooter described it as 'the nineteenth century's most popular and popularized "science" and one of its most fecund in the period preceding Darwin'.[14] Erwin Ackerknecht argued that Gall had as great an impact on nineteenth-century thought as Freud had on twentieth-century understandings of the human condition.[15]

Gall, a Viennese physician (1758–1825), believed that the mind was composed of multiple, distinct, innate faculties each of which had their own seat or 'organ' in the brain and that the size of these organs reflected their power. Moreover, 'where the internal and external plates of the skull are parallel, we may infer the form of the brain from the outward

[11] See Online Etymology Dictionary, www.etymonline.com [accessed 7 March 2013].

[12] G. N. Cantor, 'The Edinburgh phrenology debate: 1803–1828', *Annals of Science*, 32 (1975), 1195–212; R. Cooter, *The Cultural Meaning of Popular Science: Phrenology and the Organisation of Consent in Nineteenth Century Britain* (Cambridge University Press, 1984); S. Shapin, 'Homo Phrenologicus: anthropological perspectives on an historical problem', in B. S. Barnes and S. Shapin (eds.), *Natural Order: Historical Studies of Scientific Culture* (London: Sage, 1979), pp. 41–71; J. van Wyhe, *Phrenology and the Origins of Victorian Scientific Notation* (Aldershot: Ashgate, 2004).

[13] R. Smith, *Fontana History of the Human Sciences* (Waukegan, IL: Fontana Press, 1997).

[14] Cooter, *The Cultural Meaning of Popular Science*, p. 2.

[15] E. Ackerknecht, *Medicine at the Paris Hospital 1794–1848* (Baltimore, MD: The Johns Hopkins University Press, 1967); see also J. van Wyhe, 'The authority of human nature: the schadellehre of Joseph Gall', *British Journal for the History of Science*, 35 (2002), 17–24.

shape of the skull'.[16] Generally, phrenologists ignored the caveat about the plates being parallel, and claimed they could assess the power of the underlying organs by measuring the exact shape of the head.

Initially, the study of phrenology was confined to Gall and his disciple Johann Spurzheim. However, thanks mainly to Spurzheim's efforts, it was established in both Britain and the United States by the early 1820s: the Edinburgh Phrenological Society was established in 1820 and the Philadelphia Phrenological Society in 1822. Phrenology was always highly controversial. Supporters claimed it was 'the only true science of mind'.[17] Equally vociferous opponents characterized it as 'just a piece of thorough quackery from beginning to end' and 'a pseudo-science of the present day'.[18]

Evidence suggests that the adoption of the term 'self-esteem' in the phrenology literature occurred in a number of stages. First, apparently following a meeting with a beggar who said he was too proud to work, Gall noted a bump on the back of the head to which he gave a series of names: *orgueil*, *fierté* and *hauteur* in French and *Stolz*, *Hochmut* and *Herrschsucht* in German. At the time, these terms were variously translated as pride, bossiness, arrogance and haughtiness.[19] Subsequently, Spurzheim, described this bump as *the organ of self-love*, in the first edition of his book *The Physiological System of Drs Gall and Spurzheim*.[20] However, in the second edition, Spurzheim renamed the bump as *the organ of self-esteem*.[21] This change of name happened over the space of a few months: Spurzheim wrote the preface to the first edition in December 1814 and the preface to the second edition in June 1815. The change does not appear to have arisen from a difference in translation, as the prefaces reveal that Spurzheim wrote both editions in English. In the second edition of his book Spurzheim also changed the names of four further organs. In subsequent works, Spurzheim consistently favoured the term '*self-esteem*' over the term '*self-love*'.[22]

16 C. W. Hufeland, *Some Account of Dr Gall's New Theory of Physiology* (London: Longman, Hurst, Rees & Orme, 1807), 41.

17 See van Wyhe, *Phrenology*, p. 70.

18 *The Edinburgh Review* (June 1815), p. 227; F. Magendie, *An Elementary Treatise on Human Physiology*, 5th edn, trans. J. Revere (New York: Harper, 1843), p. 150.

19 For example N. G. Dufief, *A New Universal and Pronouncing Dictionary of the French and English* (Philadelphia, PA: T. & G. Palmer, 1810).

20 J. G. Spurzheim, *The Physiognomical System of Drs Gall and Spurzheim*, 1st edn (London: Baldwin, Cradock & Joy, 1815), p. 404.

21 J. G. Spurzheim, *The Physiognomical System of Drs Gall and Spurzheim*, 2nd edn (London: Baldwin, Cradock & Joy, 1815), p. 332.

22 For example J. C. Spurzheim, *Phrenology or, The Doctrine of the Mind,* 3rd edn. (London: Charles Knight, 1825); J. C. Spurzheim, *The Anatomy of the Brain* (London: S. Highley, 1826).

Many other phrenologists adopted Spurzheim's revised list of organs, including *self-esteem*. Notable among them was George Combe who used the term in his immensely popular and influential *The Constitution of Man* (1828), which sold 300,000 copies and which, according to at least one writer, had more influence on nineteenth-century thought than Darwin's *Origin of Species*.[23] By the late 1820s, the organ that Gall had referred to as pride, arrogance and haughtiness, and Spurzheim had initially called self-love, had become firmly established as self-esteem. While the term 'self-love' continued to be used alongside self-esteem, for George Combe and many others the organ and faculty in question were generally referred to as self-esteem.[24]

A modern-day reader can easily be struck by parallels between some of the original phrenological writing on self-esteem and more recent psychological approaches. For example, Combe's account of situations in which the organ of self-esteem is 'too small' appears to modern eyes remarkably similar to current psychological arguments concerning the dangers of 'low self-esteem': 'In such a case, the individual wants confidence, and a due sense of his own importance. He has no reliance upon himself; if the public or his superiors frown, he is unable to pursue even a virtuous course, through diffidence of his own judgment.'[25]

Combe's account also prefigured contemporary concerns about the potentially maladaptive aspects of the self-presentational strategy known as 'sandbagging', that is, a feigned demonstration of inability:

> Dr Adam Smith, in his *Theory of Moral Sentiments*, remarks, that it is better, upon the whole, to have too much, than too little, of this feeling; because if we pretend to more than we are entitled to, the world will give us credit for at least what we possess; whereas, if we pretend to less, we shall be taken at our word, and mankind will rarely have the justice to raise us to the true level.[26]

Excess was also damaging Combe's description of the abuses occasioned by self-esteem when 'possessed in an inordinate degree, and indulged

[23] G. Combe, *Constitution of Man* (Edinburgh: John Anderson, 1828).

[24] For example H. Lundie, *The Phrenological Mirror: Or, Delineation Book* (London: Chapman & Hall, 1844); O. S. Fowler, and L. N. Fowler, *New Illustrated Self-Instructor in Phrenology* (New York: Fowler & Wells, 1869).

[25] G. Combe, *A System of Phrenology*, 5th edn (Edinburgh: Maclachlan & Stewart, 1853), p. 344; for an example of a recent account of self-esteem, see Baumeister *et al.*, 'Does high self-esteem cause better performance?'.

[26] Combe, *A System of Phrenology*, p. 344; for literature on 'sandbagging' see B. Gibson, 'Sandbagging as a self-presentational strategy: claiming to be less than you are', *Personality and Social Psychology Bulletin*, 26 (2000), 56–70; J. Shepperd and K. Kwavnick, 'Maladaptive image maintenance', in R. M. Kowalski and M. Leary (eds.), *The Social Psychology of Emotional and Behavioral Problems* (Washington, DC: American Psychological Association, 1999), pp. 249–77.

without restraint from the higher faculties' predated Isidor Sadger's psychoanalytic account of extreme egoism and Freud's (1914) better-known *On Narcissism: an Introduction* by sixty years:

> [A] great development of the organ, with deficiency of the moral powers, produces arrogance, conceit, pride, egotism, and selfishness. The first thought of persons so endowed is, how the thing proposed will *affect* themselves; they see the world and all its interests only through the medium of self. When it is very large, and Love of Approbation small, it prompts the individual to erect himself into a standard of manners and morals. He measures himself by himself, and contemns the opinions of all who differ from him ... I have seen individuals mistake the impulses of the sentiment under discussion for the inspiration of genius, and utter common-place observations with a solemnity and emphasis suitable only to concentrated wisdom ... In short, when the organ is inordinately large, it communicates to the individual a high sentiment of his own importance, and leads him to believe that whatever he does or says is admirable, because it proceeds from *him*. It inspires him with magnificent notions of his own respectability, and prompts him, on comparing himself with others, to depreciate them, in order to raise himself in the scale of comparative excellence ... Persons who are fond of discussing the characters of their acquaintances, and feel the tendency to vituperate rather than to praise them, who are vexed when they are elevated, and pleased when they are humbled, will be found to have this organ large. It is the comparison with self, and a secret satisfaction at fancied superiority, that gives pleasure in this practice. Envy is the result of Self-Esteem, offended by the excellencies or superior happiness of others, and calling up Destructiveness to hate them.[27]

Did phrenology popularize self-esteem?

The undoubted popularity of phrenology in the early nineteenth century and the incorporation of self-esteem into the set of faculties it proposed, makes it plausible that phrenology provided a crucial impetus to the growth in popularity of self-esteem as a psychological term. If this is the case, we might expect to find the use of the term in the nineteenth

[27] Combe, *A System of Phrenology*, pp. 344–5; I. Sadger, I. 'Psychiatrisch-Neurologisches in psychoanalytischer Beleuchtung', *Zentralblatt für das Gesamigebiet der Medizin und ihrer Hilfswissenschflen* (1908), pp. 7–8; S. Freud, 'On narcissism: an introduction', in J. Sandler, E. Person, and P. Fonagy (eds.), *Freud's 'On Narcissism: An Introduction'* (New Haven, CT: Yale University Press, 1991). Conventionally, historical accounts have dated the origins of the idea of extreme egotism or narcissism as a character trait even later, typically attributing this perspective to R. Wälder, 'The psychoses: their mechanisms and accessibility to influence', *International Journal of Psychoanalysis*, 6 (1925), 259–81. See, for example, K. N. Levy, W. D. Ellison and J. S. Reynoso, 'A historical review of narcissism and narcissistic personality', in W. K. Campbell and J. D. Miller (eds.), *The Handbook of Narcissism and Narcissistic Personality Disorder: Theoretical Approaches, Empirical Findings, and Treatment* (New York: Wiley, 2011), pp. 3–13.

century to follow the rise in popularity of phrenology. In order to test this idea, we used the Google Books n-grams corpus.[28] The n-gram data for books in American English (1800–99) indicate that the use of the term 'phrenology' reached its peak in 1838, a finding that is consistent with historical accounts of the rise and subsequent decline in the popularity of the perspective. However, use of the term 'self-esteem' (entered as 'self esteem' to avoid confusion with self minus esteem) peaked earlier, in 1823. Moreover, as books began to refer more often to phrenology, use of the term 'self-esteem' started to decline. British English books (1800–99) show a similar pattern with use of the term 'self-esteem' peaking in 1807, and 'phrenology' peaking in 1839.

One limitation of the Google Books n-gram corpus is that it cannot tell us about the ways in which words may have been used in other types of written texts. In an attempt to correct this, Google Books produced their English One Million sample based on a collection of works that includes pamphlets, periodicals and newspapers. When the terms 'phrenology' and 'self-esteem' were entered into this corpus for the period from 1800 to 1899, the n-gram results followed the same pattern: the use of the terms 'self-esteem' reached its peak (1810) before 'phrenology' (1839). Of course, none of this need imply that phrenological perspectives on self-esteem did not affect the way the term was used, and it is to this issue that we now turn.

Phrenological and common-sense views of self-esteem

The way in which phrenology contributed to the available meanings associated with the term '*self-esteem*' is suggested by the two thesaurus classes given for the term in the *Oxford English Dictionary*.

The first class begins with the mind: 'the mind > emotion or feeling > pride > self esteem > [noun] > self-esteem (1657)'. In this convention of use, self-esteem is a mental state closely akin to pride; for example:

rooting out of Pride and selfe esteeme from their minds[29]

A proud minde is a high minde in conceit, self-esteem, and carnal-aspiring.[30]

In contrast, the second class involves the body: the external world > the living world > body > nervous system > cerebrospinal axis > brain > [noun] > faculties of > self-esteem (1815). The reference to 1815 is,

[28] Cf. S. Konrath and P. A. Anderson, 'A century of self-esteem', in S. De Wals and K. Meszaros (eds.), *Handbook on Psychology of Self-Esteem* (Hauppauge, NY: Nova Science, 2011), pp. 1–19.

[29] O. Torsellino, *The Admirable Life of St. Francis Xavier* (Paris: At the English College Press, 1632), p. 516.

[30] R. Baxter, *The Saints Everlasting Rest* (London: Underhill & Tyton, 1650), p. 657.

in fact, for Spurzheim's book, *The Physiological System of Drs Gall and Spurzheim*.

Although the phrenologists may have associated self-esteem with a new set of meanings, they did not necessarily do so at the expense of alternative understandings. Indeed, the fact that self-esteem was related to pride, its status as a feeling, and its existence in the mind were all accepted by phrenology. Phrenologists usually classified self-esteem as a 'sentiment' and generally supposed the brain to be the seat of the mind, a view that was increasingly widely accepted by the mid nineteenth century.[31]

As Roger Cooter noted, one general intellectual legacy of phrenology was that it 'established in the public mind the notion that human behaviour was capable of classification and measure'.[32] However, as the following examples from Early English Books Online illustrate, the idea that self-esteem may exist as some form of quantity also predated phrenology by several hundred years:

> Some pride and self-esteem will remain and be stirring in us, do what we can.[33]

> Those 'who have the smallest knowledge, and Faith, and Love and the greatest self-esteem or spiritual pride' will not be close to God.[34]

Given that Spurzheim selected the term 'self-esteem' to denote one of phrenology's faculties, and given that the term appears to have pre-existed phrenology, just what connotations did the term have in the early nineteenth century? In order to investigate the meanings associated with the term '*self-esteem*' before phrenology become popular, Google Books Advanced was searched for the period 1800 to 1809 (full view, in English, all content and given in order of relevance). The first fifty uses of the term, excluding duplicates, were examined in context. Thematic analysis revealed three interconnected and often co-occurring formulations. In eleven instances (22 per cent of the sample) self-esteem was treated as a flexible mindset:

> self-contempt, and self-esteem, are the immediate punishment and reward with which it [our conscience] sanctions its will.[35]

> if I abase and cast off all self-esteem and (as I am) account myself as dust [thou Lord] wilt be favourable to me[36]

31 For example Spurzheim, *The Physiognomical System*, p. 405; see also van Wyhe, 'The authority of human nature', p. 22.
32 Cooter, *The Cultural Meaning of Popular Science*, p. 271.
33 Baxter, *The Saints Everlasting Rest*, p. 252.
34 J. Howe, *The Blessedness of the Righteous Discoursed from Psalm 17,15* (London: Samuel Thomson, 1686), Image 8.
35 C. de Villers, 'Philosophy of Kant', *The Edinburgh Review*, 2 (1803), 262.
36 Thomas a Kempis, cited by J. Kendall, *An Abstract of That Excellent Treatise 'The Imitation of Christ by Thomas a Kempis'* (London: William Phillips, 1804), p. 122.

Soon are the haughty habits of command,
And self-esteem, and scorn acquired[37]

In sixteen cases (32 per cent of the sample) references to self-esteem occurred in the context of a normative argument concerning more or less appropriate bases for self-evaluation:

she who only finds her self-esteem
In others' admiration, begs an alms,
Depends on others for her daily food,
And is the very servant of her slaves.[38]

Self-esteem grounded on external advantages, or gifts of fortune is pride. When it is grounded upon a vain conceit of inward worth we do not profit.[39]

rational conduct contributes to happiness ... by giving a justly founded self- esteem.[40]

In six instances (12 per cent of the sample), references to self-esteem were associated with injunctions concerning ethical self-government:

O! then renounce that impious self-esteem,
That aims to trace the secrets of the skies[41]

I have endeavoured to ... stifle the very first suggestions of self-esteem; to establish my mind in tranquillity, and overvalue nothing in my own or in another's possession.[42]

You know the Emperor Alexander ... he returned with self-esteem; he had not succeeded but he had done his duty.[43]

None of these formulations would have been easy to reconcile with phrenology at the start of the nineteenth century. Gall believed that psychological traits were innate and fixed.[44] Consequently, it would have made no sense for him to consider issues such as the proper basis of self-esteem, or to hold an individual responsible for his or her own sense of self-esteem. However, later phrenologists, including Combe, believed

[37] J. West, *The Mother: a Poem in Five Books* (London: Longman, Hurst, Rees & Orme 1809), p. 34.

[38] R. Baille, *A Series of Plays*, 5th edn (London: Longman, Hurst, Rees & Orme, 1800), vol. I, p. 109.

[39] T. Reid and D. Stewart, *Essays on the Powers of the Human Mind* (Edinburgh: Bell & Bradfute,1803), p. 300.

[40] H. Kames, *Sketches of the History of Man* (Glasgow: J. Mennons & Son, 1802), vol. IV, p. 42.

[41] J. Evans, *A Sketch of Dominations of the Christian World*, 11th edn (London: Crosby, 1807), p. 290.

[42] A. Chalmers, *The British Essayists*, Vol. III (London: J. Johnson, 1808), p. 119.

[43] G. Vasa, *Letter in Anticipation on Politics, Commerce and Finance During the Present Crisis* (London: Glindon, 1808), p. 189.

[44] van Wyhe, 'The authority of human nature'.

that the effect of organs could be changed either by counteracting their effect by stirring up other organs, or by changing the power of the organ permanently. This latter course was seen as analogous to exercising a muscle to strengthen it.[45] By accepting that organs such as self-esteem could change, later phrenologists were able to introduce notions of personal responsibility into their system.

Later phrenologists were also inclined to believe that a given organ, such as self-esteem, could have both positive and negative aspects. As we have already noted, Combe associated self-esteem with both self-respect and personal dignity (its *uses*) and with conceit and selfishness (its *abuses*). One consequence of this change in perspective was that it was now harder to use phrenology to give a clear-cut character reading. For Gall (around 1800) a prominent bump of self-esteem had meant the owner was proud, bossy, arrogant and haughty. However, for Combe (around 1830) the same bump indicated either that the individual was suffering from pride, disdain and overweening conceit, or that they were displaying the virtues of self-respect, independence and personal dignity (depending on the organ's usage) or even that the individual had a propensity to pride but was working hard, and perhaps successfully, to 'offset the undesirable hyper-development' by stirring up other organs, such as Benevolence, 'into greater activity'.[46]

However, there remained three main differences between the way in which self-esteem was understood in the later phrenological literature, and the way in which the term was generally used in other writing. First, phrenology adopted a particular perspective on the methods by which an individual might govern his or her own propensity to self-esteem. Specifically, this involved working with other innate organs, enlarging some through exercise and counteracting some through the actions of other organs. Second, phrenologists were inclined to assume that any changes to the organ of self-esteem required considerable effort and time. In this respect, their accounts were incompatible with literary accounts which often presented self-esteem as potentially fragile and volatile:

> heart-broken at the sudden loss of his self-esteem, Philip buried his face in his hands and groaned aloud.[47]

Finally, phrenology associated the faculty of self-esteem with a physical presence, an organ that was both tangible and objectively measurable through the bump it created in the skull. Non-technical uses of the term,

[45] See M. S. Staum, *Labelling People* (Montreal: McGill University Press, 2003).

[46] S. Shapin, 'Phrenological knowledge and the social structure of early nineteenth century Edinburgh', *Annals of Science*, 32, (1975), 232.

[47] J. McNair Wright, *Almost a Priest* (Philadelphia, PA: McKinney and Martin, 1870), p. 274.

in contrast, did not necessarily assume that self-esteem corresponded directly with some physiological organ.

Self-esteem in literary fiction

One further way to assess the wider impact of the new phrenological views is to investigate how self-esteem was referred to in a very different kind of writing – literary fiction. Previous writers have considered some of the ways in which psychological ideas were communicated in nineteenth-century literature, and it is relatively easy to demonstrate that nineteenth-century authors of popular fiction from both sides of the Atlantic were familiar with phrenology and were inclined to presume a similar awareness on the part of their readers.[48] Writers of fiction often made passing references to phrenology, or used phrenological terminology.[49] For example:

CHARLES DICKENS: 'Strong phrenological development of the organ of firmness, in Mr. Murdstone and his sister, sir.' [*David Copperfield*][50]

CHARLOTTE BRONTË: I suppose I have a considerable organ of Veneration, for I retain yet the sense of admiring awe with which my eyes traced her steps. [*Jane Eyre*][51]

MARK TWAIN: She [Tom's aunt] was a subscriber for all those 'Health' periodicals and phrenological frauds. [*Tom Sawyer*][52]

However, even those authors who were demonstrably aware of phrenology did not appear especially inclined to use or to mention the approach in relation to self-esteem. For example, Charles Dickens used the term 'self-esteem' on at least eight occasions.[53] However, he never referred to self-esteem as a bump or an organ. Similarly, Charlotte Brontë used the term 'self-esteem' in both *Jane Eyre* and *Shirley*, but in neither of

48 R. Rylance, *Victorian Psychology and British Culture* (Oxford University Press, 2000); S. Shuttleworth, *George Eliot and Nineteenth-Century Science: the Make-Believe of a Beginning* (Cambridge University Press, 1984); S. Shuttleworth, *Charlotte Brontë and Victorian Psychology*, vol. VII (Cambridge University Press, 1996); see also P. Labenz, 'On common knowledge in conversation', *Semiotica*, 188 (2012), 121–37.

49 John van Wyhe, the author of the website 'The History of Phrenology on the Web', lists eighty-two fiction writers who he claims have been influenced by Phrenology and, even then, he argues there are many more to be discovered (see www.historyofphrenology.org.uk/literature.html [accessed 8 March 2013]).

50 C. Dickens, *The Personal History of David Copperfield* (London: Bradbury, 1850), p. 245.

51 C. Brontë, *Jane Eyre: an Autobiography* (London: Smith, Elder, 1847), p. 50.

52 M. Twain, *The Adventures of Tom Sawyer* (Hartford, CT: The American Publishing Company, 1876), p. 108.

53 These included *The Old Curiosity Shop* (New York: D. Appleton, 1868), p. 299; *The Life and Adventures of Martin Chuzzlewit* (London: Chapman, 1866), p. 178; *Barnaby Rudge* (Boston, MA: Tichnar & Fields, 1868), p. 181; and, his weekly journals, *Household Words* and *All Year Round*.

these books does her use of the term appear to reflect the influence of phrenology:

I thought so too; and my self-esteem being wounded by the false charge [pettiness], I answered promptly, 'I never cried for such a thing in my life'. [*Jane Eyre*][54]

She hinted, that if I did not make an effort to quell my 'ungodly discontent', to cease 'murmuring against God's appointment' and to cultivate the profound humility befitting my station, my mind would very likely 'go to pieces' on the rock that has wrecked most of my sisterhood – morbid self-esteem. [*Shirley*][55]

In order to assess the general impact of phrenology on the manner in which the term 'self-esteem' was used throughout the nineteenth century, a sample of literature containing the term was obtained from Google Books Advanced (fiction, all books, all content in English and given in order of relevance for each decade). Any reference to self-esteem as a bump or organ, the skull, or to measurement with callipers was taken to demonstrate the influence of phrenology. The first examples given from all the available books and journals (up to a maximum of fifty) were considered.

The only decade in which there was evidence of even a modest influence of phrenology on literary references to self-esteem was the 1860s, in which case four instances were identified, of which two appeared ironic:

I know where the bump of self-esteem lies, because … it was pointed out to me one day … On the head of some particular person who was set down immediately as a conceited booby … I don't think he is conceited.[56]

There it is, in fact: that confounded bump of self-esteem does it all, and has more imprudent matches to answer for than all the occipital protuberances that ever scared poor Harriet Martineau.[57]

More generally, it was apparent that (in this sample at least) self-esteem was still overwhelmingly being treated by authors as a feeling or passion rather than as a physical quantity:

But Mr. Downes had gradually, and against his will, arrived at a doubt most humiliating to his self-esteem, and to a higher and better feeling than mere self-esteem.[58]

54 Brontë, *Jane Eyre*, p. 24.

55 C. Brontë, *Shirley* (London: Smith, Elder, 1849), p. 247.

56 E. Sewell, *A Glimpse of the World*, vol. II (London: Longman, Green, Longman, Roberts & Green, 1863), 151.

57 C. J. Lever, *Charles O'Malley, The Irish Dragon* (London: Chapman & Hall, 1866), 149. Martineau was a well-known Victorian reformer.

58 K. S. Macquoid, *Patty*, vol. II (London: Macmillan,1871), p. 241.

Partly from the aggressive nature of the passion of self-esteem, never satisfied if, with each day, it has not made further inroad.[59]

Self-esteem was sometimes personified: it could be 'humiliated' (see above), 'soothed', 'flattered' and 'comforted' or, alternatively, 'tormented', 'wounded' or even 'mortified':

A short visit to Fairford, on his way back to Cambridge, renewed his aspirings and comforted his self-esteem.[60]

This systematical persuasion of superiority occasionally broke out into little petulancies, which did not fail grievously to wound my kind friend's self-esteem.[61]

In sum, many fiction writers in the nineteenth century were aware of phrenology, and used the term 'self-esteem'. However, there is little evidence to suggest that their understandings of self-esteem had been influenced by phrenology.

Non-fiction references to self-esteem

It might not come as a surprise that nineteenth-century writers of fiction would be predisposed to treat self-esteem as a feeling rather than as a faculty or an organ. After all, feelings (particularly volatile feelings) are more typically the stuff of fiction than is the functional organization of the brain. How, then, did writers of non-fiction refer to self-esteem? In order to explore this issue, we used Google Books Advanced (all books, all content in English given in order of relevance) and selected the first examples given from all the available books and journals (up to a maximum of fifty). The selected sources were then classified into three categories: (1) Works closely associated with phrenology, specifically works on cerebral physiology, physiognomy or mesmerism; (2) Other works specifically about the human body (e.g. medicine); (3) All the remaining works, including works on philosophy, religion, education and so on.

This analysis indicated that only in the 1840s and 1850s was there any evidence of a phrenological view of self-esteem spreading beyond its 'home'. Even then, its impact was modest and generally confined to works on topics closely related to phrenology. So, of the five instances of references to self-esteem influenced by a phrenological view identified in work published in the 1840s, three were in articles on cerebral physiology, one was on mesmerism and one on medicine.

59 C. J. Lever, *One of Them* (London: Chapman & Hall, 1861), p. 471.

60 C. G. Frances, *The Banker's Wife or Court and City* (New York: Harper & Brothers, 1843), p. 19.

61 W. Godwin, *Fleetwood or, the New Man of Feeling* (London: Richard Bentley, 1832), p. 7.

The phrenological view of self-esteem was generally confined to closely associated topics, but even here it was sometimes questioned, if not ridiculed. For example, one of the three articles on cerebral physiology identified in the 1840s sample consisted of a barrage of questions about the phrenological view: 'What is the function of that particular packet of medullary fibres, entitled the organ of Self-esteem? Is self-esteem some particular motion of these fibres; and if so, what sort of motion? Is self-esteem the product or the cause of the motion?' [62]

Similarly, the only example of work adopting the phrenological view of self-esteem from Category 3 (works in philosophy, education, religion, etc.) was explicitly critical of it. In *Phoenixiana; or, Sketches and Burlesques*, the author having learnt he has a self-esteem of ½ (on a scale of 0 to 12) then suggests (as 'figures won't lie') that, in future, when asked say about his health he should answer something like, 'Thank you, I'm 52 [out of 100] today' or, when feeling under the weather, 'I'm 13, I'm obliged to you'.[63]

The fact that technical phrenological understandings of self-esteem were not simply absorbed by other authors was indicated by the fact that writers who did allude to phrenological perspectives were often inclined to refer explicitly to the source of these views, suggesting the adoption of an ironic distance:

> Conceit, my Lord is the infirmity of little minds, proceeding from an abuse of what phrenologists term the organ of self-esteem.[64]

> When vainglory besets us, we must hold, if we are phrenologists, that there is a molecular stirrage and activity of brain-particles beneath a certain bump of 'self-esteem'.[65]

> Phrenologically speaking ... his firmness, self-esteem, approbativeness and hope were large.[66]

Finally it should be remembered that the alternative view of self-esteem (as a feeling in the mind: class one in the *OED* classification) remained dominant in this non-fiction sample. For example, in the influential *Popular Science Monthly*, between its start in 1872 and the end of the century, self-esteem was mentioned thirteen times in nine editions.

[62] J. H. Green, *Vital Dynamics. The Hunterian Oration before the Royal College of Surgeons in London (14th Feb. 1840)* (London: William Pickering, 1840), p. 67.

[63] G. H. Derby, *Phoenixiana, or, Sketches and Burlesques* (New York: D. Appleton, 1856), pp. 37–8.

[64] *Monthly Repository* (January 1829), p. 575.

[65] *Popular Science Monthly*, vol. XIV (1879), p. 478.

[66] O. Dyer, *Great Senators of the United States* (New York: R. Bonner and Sons, 1889), 316.

Of these, only once was it used in its phrenological sense, as a 'bump'.[67] Even this single example did not represent an effort on the part of the author to promote phrenology. On the contrary, the author argued the conclusions of the phrenologists were those from which 'physiology simply retires in unspoken distain'.[68]

Concluding comments

In this chapter we have shown how, contrary to popular assumption, there existed a psychology of self-esteem many decades before William James used the term in his *Principles of Psychology*. In fact, far more detailed accounts of the faculty of self-esteem can be found in the writings of phrenologists like Combe than were ever produced by William James.

In recent years, several historians of psychology have considered the relationship between the technical language of psychology and the everyday language that we use to describe ourselves and others.[69] These relationships are not straightforward or consistent. Self-esteem is one of many psychological terms that had a long history prior to there being any recognizable discipline of psychology. Such lexical items cannot be completely shorn of their everyday meanings as they entered into use as technical terms. As we have seen, when phrenologists described the faculty of self-esteem, they adopted some aspects of the existing common-sense use of the term. However, they also introduced some new assumptions. In particular, the phrenological view identified self-esteem with an organ of the brain that was tangible, relatively fixed and objectively measurable. Consequently, phrenologists were inclined to discuss normative issues primarily as a matter of quantity, with potential problems or vices being associated with the condition of possessing too small, or too large, an organ of self-esteem.

Notwithstanding widespread awareness of the phrenology movement by writers in the nineteenth century, there is little evidence to suggest that phrenology's account of the faculty of self-esteem popularized the use of the term outside the discipline, nor that it influenced the way in which self-esteem was generally understood.[70] In fact, one incidental

[67] *Popular Science*, vol. XIV (1879), p. 478.

[68] *Ibid.*, p. 479.

[69] K. Danziger, *Naming the Mind: How Psychology Found its Language* (London: Sage, 1997); G. Richards, *On Psychological Language and the Physiomorphic Basis of Human Nature* (London: Routledge, 1989); R. Smith, *Inhibition: History and Meaning in the Sciences of Mind and Brain* (Berkeley: University of California Press, 1992).

[70] It is, of course, possible that the everyday meanings of terms like 'self-esteem', 'attitude', 'intelligence' and 'memory' were very subtly changed following their transformation in the technical literatures of psychology and the professional practices of psychologists (see

finding to arise from our inspection of uses of the term 'self-esteem' in other forms of literature is the extent to which authors who were aware of the phrenology movement often adopted an ironic, dismissive or even overtly critical stance towards it. In recent years, historians of science have challenged the diffusionist view that in the popularization of science knowledge passes from experts to the wider public in a relatively unproblematic manner.[71] In contrast, most existing work on the popularization of psychology has overlooked the possibility that the lay public can actively resist 'expert' knowledge.[72]

In the second half of the nineteenth century phrenology declined dramatically in popularity, and so too did the phrenological view of self-esteem. However, this may not be the end of the story. While the growth of phrenology may have had only a limited and short-term effect on understandings of self-esteem, at least amongst English language writers, in the nineteenth century, it is possible that phrenology may have had a longer-term impact. For example, it has already been noted that phrenology 'established in the public mind [both] the notion that human behavior was capable of classification' and, equally important, that it was capable of 'measure'.[73] Further research might reveal whether there was any a direct or indirect connection between the nineteenth-century phrenologists' concern with self-esteem as physical, localized and measurable, and the kinds of perspective which are now commonly adopted in twenty-first-century psychology.

Danziger, *Naming the Mind*; also K. Danziger, *Marking the Mind: a History of Memory* (Cambridge University Press, 2008). Demonstrating such changes is no easy task and lies beyond the scope of this chapter.

71 R. Cooter and S. Pumfrey, 'Separate spheres and public places: reflections on the history of science popularization and science in popular culture', *History of Science*, 32 (1994), 237–67; A. Daum, 'Varieties of popular science and the transformations of public knowledge: Some historical reflections', *Isis*, 100 (2009), 319–332; J. Secord, 'Knowledge in transit', *Isis*, 95 (2004), 654–72.

72 A notable exception is M. Thomson, *Psychological Subjects: Identity, Culture, and Health in Twentieth-Century Britain* (Oxford University Press, 2006).

73 Cooter, *The Cultural Meaning of Popular Science*, p. 271. The possibility remains, of course, that the phrenological view of self-esteem may have had a larger, and more enduring, impact in Continental Europe.

Part III

Empirical dialogues: prejudice, ideology, stereotypes and national character

10 Two histories of prejudice

Kevin Durrheim

In his classic historical study entitled 'From "race psychology" to "studies in prejudice"', Franz Samelson identified a dramatic thematic reversal in the way psychologists studied race.[1] In the 1920s, 'most psychologists believed in the existence of mental differences between races; by 1940, they were searching for the sources of "irrational prejudice"'.[2] This same impulse to study prejudice spread throughout the liberal social sciences and intensified after the Second World War but the rhetorical and material context had changed considerably. Early conceptualizations of prejudice in psychology were designed to undermine the biological theories of categorical race differences that prevailed at the time and that underpinned legislative segregation and racial inequality of the Jim Crow system in the American South. After the racist genocide of the Holocaust and after the social and material transformations of the Civil Rights era in the United States, the kinds of 'prejudice' that remained as objects of psychological concern were fundamentally changed. Attention moved from crude and explicit forms of biological racism to subtle, modern, new, neo, symbolic, cultural and colour-blind racism.[3]

[1] I would like to thank Colin Leach for his comments on an earlier version of this chapter.

[2] F. Samelson, 'From "race psychology" to "studies in prejudice": some observations on the thematic reversal in social psychology', *Journal of the History of the Behavioral Sciences*, 14 (1978), 265.

[3] J. Duckitt, 'The development and validation of a Subtle Racism Scale in South Africa', *South African Journal of Psychology*, 21 (1991), 233–39; J. B. McConahay, 'Modern racism, ambivalence, and the Modern Racism Scale', in J. F. Dovidio and S. L. Gaertner (eds.), *Prejudice, Discrimination, and Racism* (Orlando, FL: Academic Press, 1986), pp. 91–125; M. Barker, *The New Racism: Conservatives and the Ideology of the Tribe* (London: Junction Books, 1981); E. Balibar, 'Is there a neo-racism?', in E. Balibar and I. Wallerstein (eds.), *Race, Nation, Class: Ambiguous Identities* (London: Verso, 1991), pp. 17–28; D. O. Sears, 'Symbolic racism', in P. A. Katz and D. A. Taylor (eds.), *Eliminating Racism: Profiles in Controversy* (New York: Plenum, 1988), pp. 53–84; H. A. Giroux, 'Living dangerously: identity politics and the new cultural racism: towards a critical pedagogy of representation', *Cultural Studies.* 7 (1993), 1–27; E. Bonilla-Silva, *Racism Without Racists*, 2nd edn (Lanham: Rowman & Littlefield, 2006).

This chapter tells two histories of prejudice. The first is a history of how social psychologists have conceptualized prejudice as a property of mind, a psychological condition that results in distorted views and negative perceptions. This meta-theory has informed a series of attempts to look beyond the changing expressions of prejudice to theorize and measure the underlying psychological condition. This has been a quest to define and measure prejudice without history, outside the influence and reach of its social context.

The second history is an account of prejudice in context. It seeks to understand how changing social contexts shape and are shaped by historically embedded forms of prejudice expression. Social psychologists have often sought to understand such change by way of a rather crude distinction between 'old-fashioned' and 'modern' racism. They have also attempted to map the new language of racism, describing its primary tropes, theme and modes of expression or to develop measurement scales with items that reflect these new themes and concerns.[4] Formulations of new racism have always been controversial, with critics arguing that racism has in fact changed very little. This second history is exemplified by an account of how prejudiced racial expression has changed in South Africa following the demise of apartheid.

Set alongside each other, these histories reveal the orientation to history that predominates in mainstream social psychology. In their quest for a tool to judge historically bounded expressions, social psychologists have conceived of a prejudiced mind outside of history, but in so doing, they have failed to appreciate how mind is itself a product of history.

The history of prejudice I: the quest for a theory and measure of the prejudiced mind

Gordon W. Allport introduced *The Nature of Prejudice* by contrasting the anti-Semitism of an hotelier who refuses to accommodate a Mr Greenberg with the decision of an anthropologist not to allow his family to enter an American Indian village where cases of tuberculosis had been identified.[5] What differentiated these two acts of racial segregation was the underlying psychological motive of prejudice. According to Allport, the hotelier was anti-Semitic whereas the anthropologist 'had

[4] M. Wetherell and J. Potter, *Mapping the Language of Racism: Discourse and the Legitimation of Exploitation* (Herts.: Harvester Wheatsheaf, 1992); C. Tarman and D. O. Sears, 'The conceptualisation and measurement of symbolic racism', *The Journal of Politics.* 67 (2005), 731–61.

[5] G. W. Allport, *The Nature of Prejudice* (Garden City, NY: Doubleday, 1954).

no generally negative attitude toward the Indians'.[6] This example shows how psychologists could use their theories of prejudice to judge whether events were racist or not. The psychological mark of prejudice identified racism.

Although Allport acknowledged the role that cognition played in shaping universal patterns of overgeneralization and in-group bias, it was to personality dynamics that he looked to find the sources of irrational prejudice. Personality was the site at which social norms and other historical and economic factors became proximal forces where people harboured within themselves 'habits, or expectancies, or mental sets, or attitudes'.[7] Because prejudice was 'more than an incident' in people's lives, Allport suggested that it was 'often lockstitched into the very fabric of personality'.[8] It was this lockstitching of prejudice into personality that Allport believed distinguished the rational racial discrimination of the anthropologist from the anti-Semitism of the hotelier. Racism was the result of irrational personalities and prejudiced attitudes which psychologists could measure and use to judge whether particular instances of discrimination were genuinely racist or not.

Allport's foundational text on prejudice was written at a time when many Americans explicitly defended racial segregation and inequality and people presumably said things such as 'Negroes are stupid, dirty, and inferior'.[9] Early measurement scales could thus include items that were unambiguously racist to measure these underlying prejudiced attitudes. These included crude stereotypes, the belief in the constitutional inferiority of black people, and support for segregation and unequal service provision. In his South African research, for example, Pettigrew included in his attitude scale the item 'I wish someone would kill them all' – to which 40 per cent of his white sample agreed regarding their Indian compatriots![10]

As the years and decades passed, fewer and fewer Americans (and South Africans, Australians, Europeans and others) were willing to endorse such crudely racist attitudes and stereotypes, prompting speculation about whether racism was in decline.[11] Liberal California was

[6] *Ibid.*, p. 5.

[7] G. W. Allport, 'Prejudice: is it social or personal?' *Journal of Social Issues*, 18 (1962), 123.

[8] Allport, *The Nature of Prejudice*, p. 408. [9] *Ibid.*, p. 20.

[10] T. Pettigrew, 'Social distance attitudes of South African students', *Social Forces*, 38 (1960), 246–53.

[11] See H. Schuman, C. Steeh, L. Bobo and M. Krysan, *Racial Attitudes in America: Trends and Interpretations*, Rev. edn (Cambridge, MA: Harvard University Press, 1997); M. Karlins, T. Coffman and G. Walters, 'On the fading of social stereotypes: Studies in three generations of college students', *Journal of Personality and Social Psychology*, 13 (1969), 1–16.

way ahead of most of the USA in rejecting racism and so Sears and Kinder were struck by the fact that the 1969 mayoralty campaign in Los Angeles was contested along racial lines, with the majority of whites supporting the conservative white incumbent (Sam Yorty) against a liberal black city councilman (Tom Bradley).[12] This mismatch between their unprejudiced and politically liberal attitudes and their seemingly racist and conservative voting behaviour had major implications for the Allportian theory of prejudice. How did these racist attitudes, beliefs and behaviours escape the lockstitching of the liberal non-prejudiced personalities 'as measured by the traditional standards of agreement with generalized principles of egalitarianism and rejection of simple-minded racial stereotypes?'[13]

Kinder and Sears suggested that a new form of prejudice had emerged.[14] Symbolic racism was still prejudice in the Allportian terms of personality-based antipathy and faulty generalization, but this had broken free of crude 'old-fashioned' beliefs of the past and had become 'conjoined' with 'traditional American values'.[15] By this theory, Sears and Kinder were able to reapply the lockstitch to the fraying edges of American racism, using the psychological thread of prejudice to stitch firmly together new antagonisms about blacks 'pushing too hard', resentments about reverse discrimination, and denials of continuing discrimination.[16] Their measure of symbolic racism could thus be used in the same way as earlier instruments to make judgements about which individuals, behaviours or beliefs were racist and which not. This was to be done by identifying the underlying psychological mark of prejudice. Symbolic racism researchers were thus able to demonstrate that a raft of attitudes that supported desegregation and equality in principle but that opposed concrete strategies through which desegregation was implemented – such as busing and racial quotas – were indeed racist.

Symbolic racism theory came under a scathing attack from Sniderman and Tetlock, who argued that it reduced 'legitimate political disagreements' about affirmative action to 'mere outbursts of racism'.[17] The

12 D. O. Sears and D. R. Kinder, 'Racial tensions and voting in Los Angeles', in W. Z. Hirsch (ed.), *Los Angeles: Viability and Prospects for Metropolitan Leadership* (New York: Praeger, 1971).

13 *Ibid.*, p.16.

14 D. R. Kinder and D. O. Sears, 'Prejudice and politics: symbolic racism versus racial threats to the good life', *Journal of Personality and Social Psychology*, 40 (1981), 414–31.

15 D. R. Kinder (1986) 'The continuing American dilemma: white resistance to racial change: 40 years after Myrdal', *Journal of Social Issues*, 42 (1986), 151–71.

16 D. O. Sears, 'Symbolic racism'.

17 P. M. Sniderman and P. E. Tetlock, 'Symbolic racism: problems of motive attribution in political debate', *Journal of Social Issues*, 42 (1986), 148; see also P. M. Sniderman and

problem was that Sears, Kinder and their colleagues had included items about busing and racial quotas in their measure of symbolic racism and had thus gratuitously equated opposition to affirmative action with racial prejudice. Sniderman and Tetlock argued that operationalizing symbolic racism in these terms was a political rather than scientific act because it amounted to attributing racist motives to conservative beliefs – and once it was done, it was not possible to use these measures – which now confounded racism and conservatism – to study, empirically, the relation between the two.

This criticism exposes a more general challenge to social psychological research on racial prejudice. Political bias in the items of racism scales is a potential threat to all measures that predefine racism in terms of particular (ideologically loaded and historically specific) attitude statements, and is not peculiar to symbolic racism. Sniderman and Tetlock recommend building measures of genuine prejudice from 'agreed-on sign(s) of racism' such as crude stereotyping, but they concede that even this would be contestable as it makes *a-priori* links between racist motives and particular political and ideological beliefs.[18] This criticism of symbolic racism made visible an inherent circularity in the Allportian tradition whereby racism is defined in psychological terms as behaviour and beliefs that are motivated by prejudice, but where prejudice could only be identified by particular beliefs and behaviours that are assumed to be racist.[19] Racism then depends (politically) on where researchers set the bar of prejudice. Sniderman and Tetlock insist on setting it high – focusing on clear instances of crude racist beliefs – but Kinder, Sears and colleagues argue that these are precisely the kinds of expression that are avoided in subtle or covert racism today. It is not possible to escape the circularity by empirical research because a particular (historical, ideological and political) conception of racism is built into the measures of prejudice.

Particular historical conditions were necessary for this problem to become manifest. In an earlier age the self-presentational demands and social desirability constraints of the normative climate did not require the kind of subtle or symbolic expressions that would later be associated with racism. If anything, as La Pierre's famous study showed, white Americans in the 1930s presented themselves as more racist in public

P. E. Tetlock, 'Reflections on American Racism', in E. Cashmore and J. Jennings (eds.), *Racism: Essential Readings* (London: Sage, 2001), pp. 217–26.

18 Sniderman and Tetlock, 'Symbolic racism', p. 146.

19 See K. Durrheim and J. Dixon, 'Attitudes and the fiber of everyday life: the discourse of racial evaluation and the lived experience of desegregation', *American Psychologist*, 59 (2004), 626–36.

than in private.[20] Although the normative climate had already begun to change by the time Allport produced *The Nature of Prejudice*, by the 1970s there were strong social pressures against endorsing explicitly racist stereotypes and beliefs.[21] In any case, such crude beliefs were no longer needed because new symbolic racist attitudes or laissez-faire ideologies had emerged to shape the political concerns of the time.[22]

It is not surprising then that during the 1970s researchers sought to develop forms of attitude measurement that would be free of social desirability responses. Sigall and Page's bogus pipeline was an early attempt to measure racial attitudes 'relatively distortion free, as more honest, and as "truer" than rating-condition responses'.[23] This was done by strapping participants into a machine that they were told 'provides a direct physiological measure' of race attitudes, and then asking them to report, not their attitudes, but the score they thought the machine would give.[24] By these arts of indirection, Sigall and Page showed that the 'stereotype ascribed to Negroes [was] more favorable under rating than under bogus pipeline conditions', especially for traits, such as intelligent, honest, stupid and unreliable, that 'carried a relatively large amount of affective loading'.[25]

The bogus pipeline never really took off as a measure of prejudice, and it was not until 1983 that Gaertner and McLaughlin could announce the emergence of 'a truly nonreactive measure'.[26] Cognitive measures of associative strength made it possible for the first time in history to split the social and psychological aspects of prejudiced responding. As Gaertner and McLaughlin saw it, stereotypes were 'in part, a collection of associations that link the target group to a set of descriptive characteristics'.[27] This was the cognitive or psychological part of prejudice. The other part was the social aspect that came into being when such traits were *ascribed* to the group in the forms of utterances or responses. Such ascriptions had audiences – including the individual speakers

[20] R. T. La Pierre, 'Attitudes versus actions', *Social Forces*, 13 (1934), 230–37.

[21] I. Katz, 'Gordon Allport's *The Nature of Prejudice*', *Political Psychology*, 12 (1991), 125–57.

[22] J. B. McConahay, 'Self-interest versus racial attitudes as correlates of anti-busing attitudes in Louisville: is it the buses or the blacks?', *Journal of Politics*, 40 (1982), 692–729; D. O. Sears, 'Symbolic racism'; L. Bobo, J. R. Kluegel and R. A. Smith, 'Laissez-faire racism: the crystallization of a kinder, gentler, antiblack ideology', in S. A. Tuch and J. K. Martin (eds.), *Racial Attitudes in the 1990s: Continuity and Change* (Santa Barbara, CA: Praeger, 1997), pp. 15–42.

[23] H. Sigall and R. Page, 'Current stereotypes: a little fading, a little faking', *Journal of Personality and Social Psychology*, 18 (1971), 254.

[24] *Ibid.*, p. 248. [25] Ibid., pp. 247, 252.

[26] S. L. Gaertner and J. P. McLaughlin, 'Racial stereotypes: associations and ascriptions of positive and negative characteristics', *Social Psychology Quarterly*, 46 (1983), 23.

[27] *Ibid.*

themselves – and were thus subject to accountability and other social and interpersonal concerns. The major advance of implicit measurement was its ability to apparently tap into the psychological part of the stereotype independently of the social part.

A number of techniques have been developed that measure prejudice indirectly. For example, one version of the Implicit Association Test (IAT) asks respondents to judge (as quickly as possible) whether photographs that flash up on the a computer screen depict 'black' or 'white' faces and whether the words that flash up (e.g. love, joy, hate, agony) are 'good' or 'bad'.[28] In different trials, respondents must indicate whether the photo or word is either 'black' or 'good', 'black' or 'bad', 'white' or 'good', or 'white' or 'bad'. Prejudice is evident when people respond faster when black faces are paired with bad words and white faces are paired with good words, than in the other conditions. Faster responses reflect stronger mental associations between black people and bad traits and white people with good traits than vice versa.

Associative strength measures of prejudice have been taken up by social psychologists with great enthusiasm.[29] It is now common practice to include implicit measures in prejudice research alongside self-reports. These attempts to eliminate the social aspects of self-reported prejudice in two ways. First, rather than asking participants whether they endorse a stereotype or belief, they are asked to perform a judgement task such as deciding whether a word is meaningful or nonsense, or indicating whether one or more words or images is 'good' or 'bad' or belongs to the category 'black' or 'white'. Reaction times (most typically) or other features of the performance are used as the dependent variable, under the assumption that shorter reaction times indicate a stronger cognitive association between categories and traits. These underlying mental associations are thus measured without asking respondents to endorse attitudes, thereby eliminating the social desirability forces that accompany such beliefs about race.[30] A second, temporal, dimension of measurement

[28] See the 'Project Implicit' website at https://implicit.harvard.edu/implicit/ [accessed 8 March 2013].

[29] For examples see J. F. Dovidio, K. Kawakami, C. Johnson, B. Johnson and A. Howard, 'On the nature of prejudice: automatic and controlled processes', *Journal of Experimental Social Psychology*, 33 (1997), 510–40; R.H. Fazio, J. R. Jackson, B. C. Dunton and C. J. Williams, 'Variability in automatic activation as an unobtrusive measure of racial attitudes: a bona fide pipeline', *Journal of Personality and Social Psychology*, 69 (1995), 1013–27; T. Wilson, S. Lindsey, and T. Y. Schooler, 'A model of dual attitudes', *Psychological Review*, 107 (2000), 101–26; B. Wittenbrink, C. Judd and B. Park, 'Evidence for racial prejudice at the implicit level and its relationship with questionnaire measures', *Journal of Personality and Social Psychology*, 72 (1997), 262–74.

[30] P. G. Devine, E. A. Plant, D. M. Amodio, E. Harmon-Jones and S. L. Vance, 'The regulation of explicit and implicit race bias: the role of motivations to respond without

ensures that the responses are below the threshold of conscious awareness. Participants are either required to answer as quickly as possible, or the stimuli are flashed on the screen so quickly that they leave only subliminal impressions. In this way, the measures eliminate the possibility of reactive responding which could arise if participants moderate their responses due to themselves being their own audience.[31]

Implicit racism measures isolated the psychological mark of prejudice by solving the two intractable problems that had confronted the social psychology of prejudice. First, these measures were unconfounded by particular (ideological and political) belief contents that had so concerned Sniderman and Tetlock. They thus allow researchers to circumnavigate the circularity in defining racism as prejudiced beliefs but measuring prejudice by beliefs that were assumed to be racist. In addition, by not requiring participants to endorse attitudes and by capturing responses outside the awareness of an external or internal audience, implicit prejudice measures could be presumed to be unaffected by self-presentational and social desirability demands. Thus Fazio, Dunton and Williams celebrated their implicit prejudice measure as a 'bona fide pipeline': 'the technique we are proposing provides an estimate of the participants' attitudes without ever asking them to consider their attitudes. That is, we try to 'get inside the head' of the participant. In this respect, the technique represents a potentially bona fide, not bogus, pipeline.'[32]

In shifting from self-report to implicit measures, the meaning of prejudice had been reformulated. In the old personality model, judgements of racism were grounded in the theory that instances were lockstitched into personality. Racism was part of a more general pattern of individual response that was motivated by antipathy and faulty generalization. Implicit prejudice theory adopts a cognitive explanation of the psychological thread of prejudice. It is mental associations that link categories to responses. Bargh describes an automatic process as an if–then relation, explaining that 'If certain conditions hold in the cognitive environment, then the process in question will run to completion.'[33] Once the implicit prejudice measure confirms a mental association of 'black' people and

prejudice', *Journal of Personality and Social Psychology*, 82 (2002), 835–48; but see A. Karpinski and J. L. Hilton, 'Attitudes and the Implicit Association Test', *Journal of Personality and Social Psychology*, 81 (2001), 774–8.

31 B. Wittenbrink, C. Judd and B. Park, 'Evidence for racial prejudice at the implicit level'.

32 R. H. Fazio, J. R. Jackson, B. C. Dunton and C. J. Williams, 'Variability in automatic activation as an unobtrusive measure of racial attitudes', p. 1014.

33 J. A. Bargh, 'Automaticity in social psychology', in E. T. Higgins and A. W. Kruglanski (eds.), *Social Psychology: Handbook of Basic Principles* (New York: Guilford Press, 1997), p. 177; see also M. R. Banaji, K. Lemm and S. Carpenter, 'The social unconscious', in

'bad' traits in an individual mind, we know that when this individual encounters a black person, the automatic process will run to completion, making these negative stereotypes available to be acted on.[34]

In many respects, implicit prejudice theory and techniques constitute a high point of the idea that racism could be defined as behaviour that is stamped with the psychological mark of prejudice. The dream of isolating the mental signature of prejudice was finally realized. This, however, did not put an end to contestations about the politics or psychology of prejudice. Echoing the critique of symbolic racism two decades earlier, Arkes and Tetlock accused implicit prejudice researchers of making political and value-laden attributions of racism in cases that did not satisfy the Allportian conditions of antipathy and faulty generalization.[35] Their basic problem with the paradigm was precisely the same foundational achievement that Gaertner and McLaughlin had so celebrated: prejudice was attributed to individuals without asking them to endorse any attitudes. By itself, this psychological element was not sufficient to make judgements of racism because it is only reasonable to hold people 'morally accountable for the views they endorse'.[36]

Converging lines of evidence showed that implicit prejudice was often unrelated to the kinds of prejudice, racism and discrimination that people endorsed or accountably manifested in everyday life. In addition to the finding that implicit and self-report measures sometimes correlated weakly, implicit prejudice appeared to predict automatic responses such as blinking but not deliberative talk and behaviour; and implicit measures branded unlikely candidates as racists, including anti-racist activists.[37] Given the apparent irrelevance of implicit prejudice to the racism of everyday life, it is not surprising that reticence was expressed about

A. Tesser and N. Schwartz (eds.), *Blackwell Handbook of Social Psychology: Intraindividual Processes* (Oxford: Blackwell Publisher, 2001), pp. 134–58.

34 J. A. Bargh, M. Chen and L. Burrows, 'Automaticity of social behavior: direct effects of trait construct and stereotype activation on action', *Journal of Personality and Social Psychology*, 71 (1996), 230–44.

35 H. R. Arkes and P.E. Tetlock, 'Attributions of implicit prejudice, or 'Would Jesse Jackson "fail" the Implicit Association Test?', *Psychological Inquiry*, 15 (2004), 257–78.

36 *Ibid.*, p. 260.

37 W. Hofmann, B. Gawronski, T. Gschwendner, H. Le and M. Schmitt, 'A meta-analysis on the correlation between the Implicit Association Test and explicit self-report measures', *Personality and Social Psychology Bulletin*, 31 (2005), 1369–85; B. A. Nosek, 'Moderators of the relationship between implicit and explicit evaluation', *Journal of Experimental Psychology*, 134 (2005), 565–84; J. F. Dovidio, K. Kawakami, C. Johnson, B. Johnson and A. Howard, 'On the nature of prejudice: automatic and controlled processes'; J. F. Dovidio, S. L. Gaertner and K. Kawakami, 'Implicit and explicit prejudice and interracial interaction', *Journal of Personality and Social Psychology*, 82 (2002), 62–8; J. T. Jost, M. R. Banaji and B. A. Nosek, 'A decade of system justification theory: accumulated

using implicit measures for such tasks as screening police officers or job applicants.[38]

Parsing off the social dimension of prejudice by means of implicit measurement had left remaining a psychological dimension that was divorced from the reality of prejudice as it was manifest in the fibre of everyday life.[39] Arkes and Tetlock recommend a return to an Allportian understanding of racism – but they will inevitably re-encounter the challenges with that project as described above. Sixty years of research in the social psychology of prejudice suggest that the goal of isolating a psychological signature of racism may be unattainable. This certainly seems to be the conclusion that Tetlock and Arkes reach when they say that the question of what constitutes racial prejudice is, 'at root, not just a psychological one. It is a deeply political one that requires us to make moral judgements of which aspects of public opinion (implicit or explicit) deserve our censure.'[40]

The history of prejudice II: a changing world of inequality

In contrast to the old-fashioned racism of the past, theorists have proposed that new racism rejects crude racial stereotypes, the belief in racial superiority and *de jure* segregation. Nonetheless, it has still been considered to be racism because it is perturbed about (cultural) differences between groups, it endorses preferential segregation, it supports equality in principle while opposing attempts to implement equality, and it expresses racial prejudice in subtle, covert ways or implicit ways.[41] The existence of this pattern of new racism has been supported by researchers working in quantitative and qualitative traditions; and it has been observed in diverse Western societies, including the United States, the United Kingdom and other countries in Western Europe, and in the former British colonies of Australia, New Zealand and South Africa.[42]

evidence of conscious and unconscious bolstering of the status quo', *Political Psychology*, 25 (2004), 881–920.

38 M. R. Banaji, 'See no bias', *The Washington Post Magazine* (23 January2005).

39 K. Durrheim and J. Dixon, 'Attitudes and the fiber of everyday life'.

40 P. E. Tetlock and H. R. Arkes, 'The implicit prejudice exchange: Islands of consensus in a sea of controversy', *Psychological Inquiry*, 15 (2004), 311–12.

41 Dovidio, Gaertner and Kawakami, 'Implicit and explicit prejudice and interracial interaction'; Balibar, 'Is there a neo-racism?'; D. T. Goldberg, 'The new segregation', *Race and Society*, 1 (1998), 15–32; L. Bobo, 'Whites' opposition to busing: Symbolic Racism or Realistic Group Conflict?', *Journal of Personality and Social Psychology*, 45 (1983), 1196–210.

42 For quantitative research see D. O. Sears and P. J. Henry, 'Over thirty years later: a contemporary look at Symbolic Racism', *Advances in Experimental Social Psychology*, 37

The emergence of new racism has been attributed to historical factors and changed social norms. The genetic science increasingly challenged the credibility of biological theories of race and the popular association of racism with the Holocaust made explicit racism stigmatizing.[43] Many theorists attribute the emergence of new racism to the civil rights victories of the 1950s and 1960s, which eliminated explicitly racist policy and legislation and instituted various forms of affirmative action in the United States.[44] By the end of the twentieth century, racial segregation and discrimination were outlawed in all western democracies and in many places policies had been implemented to achieve equality in practice by means of affirmative action. Perhaps the most dramatic change occurred in South Africa, which was not only the last country to relinquish segregation and institutionalized white supremacy, but which saw political power shift to a black majority government who could ensure that affirmative action was implemented.

Colin Leach has cautioned against embracing the concept of new racism uncritically.[45] He argues that the distinction between old and new racism is temporally 'empty' both because beliefs associated with new racism were widely prevalent before the achievement of *de jure* racial equality and because the beliefs associated with old-fashioned racism persist. Myrdal's monumental investigation does suggest that ambivalence about racism predates the modern racism era.[46] Likewise, social desirability concerns were apparent before modern racism research. For example, Adorno *et al.* recognized the need to circumvent 'some of the

(2005), 95–150; for qualitative research see Wetherell and Potter, *Mapping the Language of Racism*. For the USA see M. Omi and H. Winant, *Racial Formation in the United States: From the 1960s to the 1990s*, rev. edn (New York: Routledge, 1994); for the UK, Barker, *The New Racism*; for Western Europe, T. Pettigrew and R. W. Meertens, 'Subtle and blatant prejudice in Western Europe', *European Journal of Social Psychology*, 25 (1995), 57–75; Australia, M. Augoustinos, K. Tuffin and M. Rapley, 'Genocide or failure to gel? Racism, history and nationalism in Australian talk', *Discourse and Society*, 10 (1999), 351–87; for New Zealand, Wetherell and Potter, *Mapping the Language of Racism*; for South Africa, N. Singh-Pillay and S. J. Collings, 'Racism on a South African campus: a survey of students' experiences and attitudes', *Social Behaviour and Personality*, 32 (2004), 607–18.

43 R. Lewontin, 'Are the races different?', in D. Gill and L. Levidos (eds.), *Anti-Racist Science Teaching* (London: Free Association Books, 1987); P. Hervik, 'Anthropological perspectives on the new racism in Europe', *Ethnos*, 69 (2004), 149–55.

44 H. Winant, 'Racism today: continuity and change in the post-civil rights era', *Ethnic and Racial Studies*, 21 (1998), 755–66.

45 C. Leach, 'Against the notion of a "new racism"', *Journal of Community & Applied Social Psychology*, 15 (2005), 432–45. See also S. Pehrson and C. Leach, 'Beyond "old" and "new": for a social psychology of racism', in J. Dixon and M. Levine (eds.), *Beyond Prejudice* (Cambridge University Press, 2012), pp. 120–38.

46 G. Myrdal, *An American Dilemma: the Negro Problem and Modern Democracy* (New York: Harper & Row, 1944).

defenses which people employ when asked to express themselves with respect to "race issues"'; and they thus developed the F-scale to 'measure prejudice without appearing to have this aim and without mentioning the name of any minority group'.[47]

So the question remains about how racial prejudice may have changed in the wake of political and legislative transformations of the twentieth century. Leach recommends that social psychologists study how racial attitudes are related to the 'operation of group inequality'.[48] The aim of this section is to present a very brief history of prejudice in these terms, showing how changing race attitudes in the South Africa are related to ongoing practices of segregation and white privilege.

Leach's concern with how the 'psychology of racism relates to the social reality of racial inequality' is not new.[49] The tradition of scholarship initiated by Blumer (1958) has been keenly interested in how racial attitudes and beliefs reflect an ideology that seeks to preserve the social order and the dominant group's sense of position and entitlement in that order.[50] Jackman and Muha, for example, place social reality at the centre of their theory: 'Dominant groups develop such an ideology without contrivance: it flows naturally from their side of experience as they seek to impose a sense of order on the pattern of social relations and to persuade both themselves and their subordinates that the current organization of relationships is appropriate and equitable.'[51]

Unlike the social psychological work reviewed in the previous section, which sought to place prejudice firmly in the mind, this approach places prejudice firmly in social history and the reality of intergroup relations. Prejudice is the product of the kinds of social relations that exist in a society at a particular time. However, to say that the prejudiced attitudes and beliefs 'flow naturally' from participation in an unequal social order begs the question of how this happens. The discussion that follows will propose three ways in which prejudice features as both an outcome and a productive force in changing worlds of racial inequality. The focus on concrete patterns of 'social relations' recommended by Jackman and Muha will be done with reference to social change in South Africa, and

47 T. W. Adorno, E. Frenkel-Brunswik, D. J. Levinson and N. Sanford, *The Authoritarian Personality* (New York: Harper, 1950), p. 222.
48 Leach, 'Against the notion of a "new racism"', p. 442.
49 *Ibid.*, p. 442.
50 H. Blumer, 'Race prejudice as sense of group position', *The Pacific Sociological Review*, 1 (1958), 3–7.
51 M. R. Jackman and M. J. Muha, 'Education and intergroup attitudes: moral enlightenment, superficial democratic commitment, or ideological refinement', *American Sociological Review*, 49 (1984), 759.

in particular to the social relations on a post-apartheid beach studied by Durrheim and Dixon.[52] During the summer holidays of 1999 and 2001 we interviewed fifty-one white and forty-six black beachgoers on a South African beach that had been officially desegregated 10 years earlier. We wanted to learn how the lived experiences of intergroup contact among these beachgoers were shaped by the place of the beach, the kinds of interaction that occurred there, and the 'working models' of contact that the beachgoers developed to explain their interaction.

The extract below comes from a white interviewee who was reflecting on the way Durban had changed as a holiday destination.

> We've been to Durban often. I've stayed, here, I've stayed in Durban about a million times [Kevin – ja] because I played a lot of sport and we always stayed in Durban in hotels and that [Kevin – ja] so I know Durban quite well. But its pitch black. We were there, when was it? Last Monday I think but Jesus! its pitch, pitch, pitch black [Kevin – ja] We were standing on top of the hotel, the Holiday Inn on the thirtieth floor, I said to my son 'You show me one white person on the beach or on the pavement, I'll buy you whatever you want' [Kevin – ja] He came back about half an hour later and said 'God, Dad, there's nobody there' [Kevin – ja] Unfortunately that's how it goes.

These opinions do seem to flow, without contrivance, from the speaker's perspective as a white man caught up in profound historical change from apartheid. By law and by might, Durban's beach used to be strictly 'whites only', but it had become 'pitch black'. His resigned conclusion, 'Unfortunately that's how it goes', suggests that his experience of Durban is indicative of a more general trend whereby the repeal of apartheid laws had seen whites being displaced by blacks. This sentiment was widely shared among the people we interviewed, who complained about being crowded out or pushed off the beach by the influx of blacks who were deemed to have taken over the beach and its amenities.

This interview extract manifests a number of features of new racism. First, it does not rely on explicit race stereotyping or arguments against equal treatment or even arguments against the principle of racial integration. The problem is not about desegregation per se, or with contact with one to two black people, but the practical consequences that followed political change and the repeal of apartheid. There is a sense, that 'blacks had gotten more than they deserved', which was shared by the white Californian 'symbolic racists' studied by Sears and Kinder in 1971. Implicit or non-deliberative dehumanization characteristic of aversive racism is also evident when, reporting his son's speech, the speaker

[52] K. Durrheim and J. Dixon, *Racial Encounter: the Social Psychology of Contact and Desegregation* (Hove: Routledge, 2005).

equates the absence of whites with 'nobody' being there. The talk also expresses a sense of entitlement to white preserve in Africa and, as such, it articulates a dominant sense of group position.[53] At the same time the talk communicates a sense of location in place and time. The events that unfolded that day on the thirteenth floor of the Holiday Inn were an object lesson in history, infused with local nuance, yearnings, nostalgia and fears that sets it apart from any 'new racism' in the United States, Europe or Australia.

In light of Leach's concerns about empty temporal distinctions between old and new racism, in what way can racial prejudice be said to be new? As Leach argues, we should not expect a sudden discontinuity as the old-fashioned racism of apartheid is replaced by modern racism. Both continuity and discontinuity are evident when one examines the scale items that were used to measure racism in previous eras. For example, Lever's adaption of MacCrone's 'Attitudes towards the native' scale includes items that are so offensive that they would not get past an ethics review committee today, but that nevertheless have resonance with the racism of today.[54] For example, the item 'The black has no right to complain about being called a kaffir' contains a sentiment that is central to symbolic racism, namely that 'blacks are getting too demanding in their push for equal rights'.[55] However, the content of these rights in the context of affirmative action are fundamentally different from this right not to be subjected to racial abuse.

Given these continuities, is it possible to link attitudes to the post-apartheid context so as to trace a history of prejudice in a changing world of racial inequality and exclusion? The first way to appreciate these race attitudes as being new is by considering their novel rhetorical context. Michael Billig has offered a rhetorical theory of attitudes, not as outward expressions of inner subjectivity, but as stances people can take in matters of public controversy.[56] Attitudes, in this view, are not only ways of describing personal reactions to things and events, but are also ways of criticizing some views while justifying others. Attitudes, then, depend on the nature of the controversies of the time and place. We would thus expect racial attitudes to change as history brings new controversies to the fore, displacing controversies of an earlier age. This certainly appears

[53] Blumer, 'Race prejudice'.

[54] H. Lever, 'Measuring the attitudes of whites towards the native', *South African Journal of Science*, 73 (1977), 299–303.

[55] C. Tarman and D. O. Sears, 'The conceptualisation and measurement of symbolic racism', *The Journal of Politics*, 67 (2005), 739.

[56] M. Billig, *Arguing and Thinking: a Rhetorical Approach to Social Psychology*, (Cambridge University Press, 1987); M. Billig, 'The argumentative nature of holding strong views: a case study', *European Journal of Social Psychology*, 19 (1989), 203–23.

to have been the case in the South African transformation. In 1999 beach-goers were expressing attitudes about desegregation in a context where there was no hope of returning to apartheid. The controversy of the time was not about a defence of apartheid; it was about how desegregation was taking place. Controversies about how to implement desegregation policies had replaced the controversies about the principle of separation, justifying or criticizing the view that beachgoers should enjoy 'companionship of their own kind' on racially segregated beaches.[57] Attitudes about how to implement race integration polices could only come to the fore when such policies began to be enacted and then became matters of controversy, contention and debate.

A second reason why new racial attitudes were needed in the post-apartheid context is because they had new work to do in the context of a changing social reality of intergroup relations. From the view of discursive social psychology, attitudes are seen as forms of social action.[58] In addition to being stances in controversy, they have a practical utility in justifying and rationalizing certain forms of conduct. Allport recognized this when he suggested that the attitude 'Negroes are stupid, dirty, and inferior' could help individuals simplify their lives, enacting the policy: 'I simply avoid them one and all.'[59] In a similar vein, the belief in the ineducability of black people justified separate schooling in South Africa and the American South. Categorical attitudes and old-fashioned racism could rationalize categorical rejection of contact and desegregation. But principled attitudes against contact cannot help to regulate conduct in desegregated worlds. In the post-apartheid context it is simply not possible to 'avoid them one and all'. Racial contact, encounter and exchange are inevitable daily occurrences in public contexts, at work, in schools, in shops and on the beaches. Here racial representations that focus on individual differences, culture and class are much more useful in rationalizing a preference-driven 'new segregationism'.[60]

The first two accounts of the historical nature of race attitudes imply that new attitudes flow from the rhetorical and ideological requirements of new social relations: attitudes must adapt to a changing world. This is a changing world in which people's lives are shaped by events such as outbreaks of wars or peace, bombing of cities, forced removals, segregation, desegregation and the end of apartheid. As intergroup attitudes adapt to change, they begin to rationalize new forms of behaviour that

[57] See K. Durrheim and J. Dixon, 'Geographies of racial exclusion: beaches as family spaces', *Ethnic and Racial Studies*, 24 (2001), 433–50.

[58] J. Potter and M. Wetherell, *Discourse and Social Psychology: Beyond Attitudes and Behaviour* (London: Sage, 1987).

[59] Allport, *The Nature of Prejudice*, p. 20.

[60] Goldberg, 'The new segregation'.

collectively constitute the new order of intergroup relationships. This is a third way in which racial attitudes evolve to embed themselves in new forms of intergroup relations, but the direction of the effect is from attitudes to the world rather than the other way round. On the basis of their beach research, Durrheim and Dixon argued that talk and embodied practices were 'articulated' in such a way that they partly produced the social world that was the basis of the attitudes.[61] We might ask, for example, how Durban's beachfront came to be homogenously black as described in the extract above. It was made that way by the manner in which black people and white people used the beach. The attitudes about black people taking over and displacing whites informed decisions of whites to avoid certain beaches while frequenting others, which played a formative role in bringing about the reality of 'displacement' that could then come to be seen as the basis of the attitude.

There are thus three reasons why we might characterize attitudes such as those expressed in the interview extract above as 'new'. They reference new controversies, they justify new forms of behaviour, and this helps to constitute new patterns of (racial) interaction that constitute the new social reality. All this was made possible in South Africa by the monumental socio-political change in which the legislative framework of apartheid was dismantled. Prejudice changed inside a changing world of racial segregation and inequality. Particular forms of prejudice are functional in particular social worlds as prejudice helps to explain and justify the outcomes and individual actions that keep that world in shape. In addition to these rhetorical and practical functions, prejudice thus also serves as a moral and psychological framework for regulating perception of fairness, emotions and behavioural reactions. In so doing, it acquires local nuance and characteristics of its setting.

Conclusion

The two histories of prejudice narrated in this chapter are but one history. They are two counteracting logics that underpin social psychological theory and research. On the one hand, social psychologists have sought to isolate the mental signature of prejudice, outside of history; on the other hand, they have sought indicators of this prejudice in social attitudes and opinions that have been subject to historical change. This allowed them to develop measures that were relevant to current times

[61] K. Durrheim and J. Dixon, 'Studying talk and embodied practices: toward a psychology of materiality of "race relations"', *Journal of Community & Applied Social Psychology*, 15 (2005), 446–60.

but which, as indices of mental prejudice, could also be used in a generally liberal social science agenda, to take sides, making judgements of racism and prejudice.

One way in which researchers have attempted to reconcile these two aspirations is to draw a temporal distinction between old verses new racism, and to use attitudes that had currency in a new context (of, e.g., desegregation, civil rights and affirmative action) to measure new racism. A second strategy has been to use implicit measures that were initially hoped would provide a bona fide pipeline, providing a view of prejudiced minds free from the constraints of social desirability and normative factors that shape opinions in social and historical context.

Both of these approaches have attracted criticism and have been extensively debated in the social psychology literature. The fundamental problem is what counts as racism, and who is to decide. How was it possible to make judgements of prejudice and racism when historically and socially agreed criteria for such judgements were missing? Is support for affirmative action racist? Do automatic – even subliminal – associations between black people and negative traits indicate racism – even among civil rights activists? One solution has been to entrench a divide between implicit, automatic or unconscious forms of prejudice on the one hand and explicit, deliberative and conscious forms on the other. The 'dual process model' maintains that implicit prejudice predicts non-deliberative behaviour, but that explicit prejudice predicts deliberative responding.[62]

But perhaps this approach overdraws a distinction between implicit and explicit forms of prejudice that have proved extraordinarily difficult to separate theoretically or in practice.[63] The historical narratives of this chapter have suggested that it might not be so easy to separate the psychological from the historical or the old from the new. One reason for this is that social psychology is part of history.[64] Social psychologists reflect the concerns and issues of their age when they associate (or disassociate) certain practices, beliefs and communities with prejudice and racism. In addition, their work also served to construct new and authoritative understandings of prejudice and racism. This authority derives from the psychological theory that prejudice is pathological and an enduring feature of certain individual minds. As these ideas 'trickle-down' to form

[62] T. D. Wilson, S. Lindsey and T. Y. Schooler, 'A model of dual attitudes', *Psychological Review*, 107 (2000), 101–26.

[63] J. A. Bargh, 'Automaticity in social psychology', in E. T. Higgins and A. W. Kruglanski (eds.), *Social Psychology: Handbook of Basic Principles* (New York: Guilford Press, 1997), pp. 109–18; J. De Houwer, S. Teige-Mocigemba, A. Spruyt and A. Moors, 'Implicit measures: a normative analysis and review', *Psychological Bulletin*, 135 (2009), 347–68.

[64] K. J. Gergen, 'Social psychology as history', *Journal of Personality and Social Psychology*, 26 (1973), 309–20.

part of the 'social representations' of prejudice and racism, they are used and resisted by people as they express themselves and in criticism and justification, becoming 'skilled at exploiting the rhetorical possibilities of the prejudice problematic'. [65]

From this perspective, new racism can be appreciated not only as a reflection of a new times, but also as a rejection of old-fashioned racism, which social psychologists had helped to make objectionable by mentalizing and pathologizing.[66] Similarly, the naive acts of judgement that formed the basis of implicit measures were soon to take on new meaning as they became recognized as indicators of a prejudiced mental condition. Very soon, such responses became subject to intentional control, situational demands, and even responsive to stereotype threat effects. [67] Prejudice is thus continually changing and adapting in response to new technologies. As soon as the measures have been developed and gain currency as tools with which to diagnose racism, they begin to lose their currency. Early crude measures of racism needed to be replaced with symbolic measures, which in turn needed to be replaced with implicit measures. New measures of prejudice will always be needed when the measures become recognized as such.

Prejudice is also continually adapting to new social and historical circumstances. This chapter has argued that new forms of prejudice are required to regulate concrete forms of intergroup encounter and exchange that new historical circumstances make possible. This is well illustrated in the change from legislative apartheid in South Africa. The new forms of intergroup contact that were capacitated by the repeal of apartheid legislation were to be regulated by new attitudes. These attitudes not only distanced themselves from the crude expressions of the past, but were also directed to explaining and justifying individual participation in new forms of segregation. And when people began interacting with each other in ways that were rendered intelligible by these new attitudes, these emerging forms of prejudice began to constitute the 'new South Africa' in ways that resembled the past. The two histories of prejudice were part of the living fibre of social change.

[65] S. Moscovici, 'Notes towards a description of social representations', *European Journal of Social Psychology*, 18 (1988), 211–50; M. Wetherell, 'The prejudice problematic', in J. Dixon and M. Levine (eds.), *Beyond Prejudice* (Cambridge University Press, 2012), p. 172.

[66] N. Rose, *Governing the Soul: the Shaping of the Private Self* (London: Routledge, 1990).

[67] P. G. Devine, E. A. Plant, D. M. Amodio, E. Harmon-Jones and S. L. Vance, 'The regulation of explicit and implicit race bias'; I. V. Blair, 'The malleability of automatic stereotypes and prejudice', *Personality and Social Psychology Review*, 6 (2002), 242–1; W. Von Hippel, 'Implicit prejudice: pentimento or inquisition', *Psychological Inquiry*, 15 (2004), 302–5.

11 Henri Tajfel, Peretz Bernstein and the history of *Der Antisemitismus*

Michael Billig

In 1923, Fritz Bernstein, a German Jew in his thirties, completed a book about the psychological and sociological roots of anti-Semitism. At the time Bernstein was working as a coffee trader in the Netherlands. He specifically wanted to find a German publisher for his book, but he struggled to find one. As a businessman, he had few connections with the world of academics, and he found that most publishers of that time believed that the topic of anti-Semitism would not attract a wide German readership. The book was eventually published in 1926 by Jüdischer Verlag under the title *Der Antisemitismus als eine Grouppenerscheinung* (literally 'Anti-Semitism as a Group Phenomenon').[1] Jüdischer Verlag was a Jewish publishing house, established in 1902, and, in the main, it published pro-Zionist books, including those by notable writers such as Theodor Herzl, Chaim Weizmann and the poet Hayim Bialik.

The more mainstream publishers had been commercially correct to treat Bernstein's manuscript with caution. They had not overlooked a potential bestseller, for only about three hundred copies were sold in Germany. Bernstein personally bought up the remaining copies to distribute in the Netherlands.[2] The book seemed to fall between potential markets: the title suggested that the work was an academic, sociological tome and so general readers were put off. However, academics in Germany and elsewhere were not going to be impressed by a book that had been written by a businessman and that contained no scholarly footnotes or references. Then, as is the case now, academic specialists tended to look down on amateurs who create their own theories from scratch. On the other hand, any general readers in Germany who were interested in anti-Semitism would have wanted something more dramatic than Bernstein was willing to provide – maybe a tract 'showing' how,

1 F. Bernstein, *Der Antisemitismus als eine Grouppenerscheinung: Versuch einer Soziologie des Judenhasses* (Berlin: Jüdischer Verlag, 1926).

2 B. M. S. van Praag, 'Introduction to the Transaction edition'. In P. F. Bernstein, *The Social Roots of Discrimination: the case of the Jews* (Piscataway, NJ: Transaction, 2009).

throughout history, Jews, by their actions, weaknesses of character and plots to take over the world, had brought misfortunes upon themselves and upon everyone else.

That might have been the end of the story of Bernstein's somewhat obscure book but it was not. The history of his book is worth telling for reasons that will become clearer later. Bernstein emigrated to Palestine in 1936, and unlike many members of his family he escaped the Holocaust. In Palestine, he worked as a journalist, editing the paper *Ha-Boker* ('The Morning'), and he became prominent in Zionist politics. Whereas many Zionist activists of that time were politically on the left, Bernstein was on the right, especially regarding economic issues.[3] His wing of the pre-independence General Zionists was to form the basis for the right-wing Liberal Party. Bernstein was one of the thirty-six signatories of the Declaration of Independence for the new State of Israel in 1948 and he became the minister of trade in the first provisional government. He died in 1970.

Bernstein was a friend of the American Zionist leader, Rabbi Abba Hillel Silver, who persuaded him after the war that his old book on anti-Semitism still carried an important message and should be translated into English. The New York-based Philosophical Library, which specialized in publishing works by European intellectuals such as Sartre, Einstein and de Beauvoir, agreed to publish an English translation. It is hardly surprising that Bernstein, then deeply preoccupied with the politics and security of the new state, had no time to revise his book for the second edition. He realized, however, that the measured tone, which he had adopted while writing in the early 1920s, was no longer suitable. But rather than re-writing the book and making wholesale changes to bring it up to date, he agreed to write a short epilogue. He did this in 1949 although, in the event, Bernstein's epilogue would be published as a prologue when the new edition, appeared in 1951 under the title of *Jew-Hate as a Sociological Problem*. The book was published under the author's Hebrew name – Peretz F. Bernstein.[4]

Bernstein's prologue makes fascinating reading for anyone interested in the relations between social psychological ideas and the passage of history. Not only did Bernstein reflect on the history of his own book and his initial difficulties in finding a publisher but also on the recent history that inevitably made his book belong to earlier, more innocent times. In

[3] S. Sofer, *Zionism and the Foundations of Israeli Diplomacy* (Cambridge University Press, 2009).

[4] P. F. Bernstein, *Jew-Hate as a Sociological Problem* (New York: Philosophical Library, 1951).

addition, Bernstein's prologue touched on the more technical aspects of the relations between psychological (or sociological) understanding and historical understanding. In writing on these matters, Bernstein would be laying the groundwork for his book's most significant brush with the history of academic social psychology. This would occur almost thirty years later, when Henri Tajfel, one of the most important European social psychologists of the post-war years and the inspiration for what would become known as Social Identity Theory (SIT), would write a short appreciation of Bernstein's book.

Bernstein's 1951 prologue

In the prologue for the English edition, Bernstein reflected on his book's 'rather awkward' structure, for in essence *Der Antisemitismus* contained two separate parts.[5] In the first part Bernstein presented a general theory of group hatred and in the second part he discussed the specific issue of anti-Semitism in the light of the general theory outlined in the first part. Bernstein explained in his prologue that he had not wanted to treat anti-Semitism as if it were unique but he wanted to analyse it as an example of more the general phenomenon of group enmity. To do this, he needed to draw upon a suitable sociological or psychological framework that would explain group enmity in general. However, he had been unable to find such a framework, and, as a result, he had invented his own.

The German professors of the time might not have appreciated Bernstein's theorizing, but today his talent for creating innovative social psychological ideas is clear. In the first part, he dismissed the idea that the Jews might be responsible for the strong enmity that they seemed to evoke throughout their history. If hatred of Jews was not the product of Jewish actions, then its source must be sought in other factors, which Bernstein termed 'sociological'. In modern academic terms, we would call these factors 'social psychological', for Bernstein was combining psychological and social aspects. Whether one calls his approach 'sociological' or 'social psychological', one thing was clear: it was not historical. Bernstein was not looking for the causes of anti-Semitism in specific historical circumstances. He was not, for example, explaining mediaeval anti-Semitism in terms of old religious beliefs or twentieth-century anti-Semitism in terms of the insecurities of modern life. Instead, he linked

[5] P. F. Bernstein, *The Social Roots of Discrimination: the case of the Jews* (Piscataway, NJ: Transaction, 2009), p. 7. All quotations from Bernstein's book are taken from the 2009 edition, published by Transaction publishers of Rutgers University, and containing an excellent introduction written by the Dutch economist, Bernard van Praag.

anti-Semitism generally to a very basic, universal condition of human life – the need for humans to live in social groups.

Bernstein's argument was very similar to the frustration–aggression theory, which was originally proposed by group of psychologists from Yale University just before the Second World War and which was to be revised by Leonard Berkowitz in the 1960s and 1970s.[6] In *Der Antisemitismus*, Bernstein noted that we often feel anger that cannot freely express against those who have provoked that anger. Bernstein offered the hypothetical example of a merchant who loses a contract to a business rival but who needs to remain on good terms with that rival. It was a situation that Bernstein would know well as a coffee dealer in Rotterdam, for one of his close business rivals was his own father-in-law. Bernstein postulated that if the merchant, who has lost out to the rival, could not be directly hostile to that rival, nevertheless his anger 'must be vented in some way and in some direction'. This is because 'the outbreak of a hostile feeling cannot be totally suppressed' but instead it 'seeks an outlet'.[7] In consequence the merchant will find other ways to express his feelings of anger – for instance he might find fault with his employees, even provoking them to make mistakes 'in order to find a pretext for ventilating his anger'.[8]

There, in Bernstein's account, written in the early 1920s, is the essence of the frustration–aggression theory, which many years later would be used to provide a scapegoat theory of prejudice. The assumption is that frustration produces anger and that, if this anger cannot be directly expressed against the frustrator, it will not dissipate but will seek another target. The idea can be used as a model of prejudice, whereby a group directs its anger at a scapegoat, who is not the real cause of its frustrations. There were, however, three main differences between Bernstein's account and that which the frustration–aggression theorists would formulate. First, the frustration–aggression theorists would express their ideas in technical, psychological terms; by contrast Bernstein, apart from using some semi-psychoanalytic terms such as 'projection', stuck with non-technical language. Second, the frustration–aggression theorists, as experimental psychologists, tended to cite experimental studies in support of their hypotheses. Bernstein was not bothered with the results

[6] J. Dollard, L. W. Doob, M. N. Miller, O. H. Mowhrer and R. R. Sears, *Frustration and Aggression* (New Haven, CT: Yale University Press, 1939); L. Berkowitz, 'The frustration–aggression hypothesis revisited'. In L. Berkowitz (ed.), *The Roots of Aggression* (New York: Atherton Press, 1969); L. Berkowitz, 'Some determinants of impulsive aggression: the role of mediated associations with reinforcements for aggression', *Psychological Review*, 81 (1974), 165–76.

[7] Bernstein, *The Social Roots of Discrimination*, p. 84.

[8] *Ibid.*, p. 84.

of experimental studies and did not feel that his theory was in need of experimental validation.

The third major difference between Bernstein's work and that of the frustration–aggression theorists is probably the most important, at least with regard to current debates within social psychology. Bernstein did not reduce the problems of group enmity to personal feelings of hostility, as some of the later frustration–aggression theorists would do. Bernstein's own hypothetical example of the merchant suggested that this was the path he might take: the frustrated merchant complained about his ungrateful workers, and this process had been set in motion by the personal accident of his failing to obtain a contract. However, Bernstein argued that prejudices against groups did not originate in the personal vagaries of the hater, for there was something systematic about the phenomenon of group enmity, as compared with interpersonal enmity. Group enmity was, in Bernstein's view, the consequence of the very existence of groups. Living within a group inevitably produces tensions but, in order to preserve the group, there must be restrictions on expressing feelings of anger against fellow members of the group. In consequence, enmity, which could not be expressed internally, would build up within a group; and eventually this reservoir of enmity would be projected onto those outside the group. It was because Bernstein was linking group enmity to the very formation of groups, rather than to the psychology of its individual members, that he considered his approach to be 'sociological'.

In effect, Bernstein was proposing an explanation of group enmity that was universal, in that it applied to all historical ages and to all types of society. He was suggesting that so long as humans lived in groups, then hatred of other groups was inevitable. According to Bernstein, it was important to understand this universal point if one wanted to understand any specific, historically particular, form of group hatred. The structure of *Der Antisemitismus*, as Bernstein wrote in the prologue, reflected the assumption that anti-Semitism was 'a very small, though specific, aspect of a general phenomenon'.[9] He had made this clear in the conclusion of his book, where he had argued that it was 'erroneous' to consider anti-Semitism to be unique, for all the characteristics of anti-Semitism 'can be observed in other group enmities'.[10] Because Jews had lived for centuries as outsiders, it was inevitable that their more powerful neighbours would direct their enmity against them. Jews, therefore, had been convenient targets for all the built-up enmity, but any other group of outsiders would have sufficed.

[9] *Ibid.*, p. 7. [10] *Ibid.*, p. 288.

After the war, Bernstein still defended his strategy of seeking to explain the particular phenomenon of anti-Semitism in terms of general factors. As he wrote in 1949, both parts of his book had been vital, for the general was 'necessary to explain the specific'.[11] He maintained that, in taking this perspective, he had been adopting a scientific approach to the study of anti-Semitism, 'somewhat along the lines practised in scientific research of physical and chemical processes'.[12]

Nowadays, it has become second nature for social psychologists to seek to explain the particular in terms of the general. Experimentalists will declare their scientific credentials and, for them, that means more than using scientific methods (such as experiments): it also means using universal concepts in order to explain specific phenomena. For example, social psychologists tend not to treat anti-Semitism, or Islamophobia or hatred of Romanies as historically specific phenomena, but to treat all as instances of something more general – 'group prejudice'. Social psychologists will then try to formulate general theories of prejudice, which they will apply to the historically specific instances.[13] No matter whether such theories stress the importance of frustration, the effects of identifying with a group or the tendency to exaggerate the differences between groups, social psychologists will assume that these sorts of factors will lead to prejudice, regardless of cultural or historical context. In this regard, the strategy, which the young Bernstein intuitively pursued, has become standard practice within social psychology.

Although Bernstein defended his approach, he also felt, in the aftermath of the war, that it was no longer suitable for analysing anti-Semitism. He began his prologue by stating that he had written his book in 1923 and that it had been published in 1926: 'I mention those dates to explain the painstaking suppression of the emotional moment observed throughout the book.'[14] It was obvious why a researcher might suppress their emotions if they were approaching a topic that touched them personally. If they did not detach themselves, they might become too emotionally bound up in their topic. A Jew, researching anti-Semitism in 1923, needed to step back from their feelings in order to approach their topic in a detached spirit, seeing anti-Semitism, for instance, as an instance of something much more general.

Bernstein, writing in 1949, asserted that during the early 1920s, such an elimination of personal feeling 'was still possible'. By 1951, it had become impossible. The intervening years had brought 'anti-Jewish

[11] *Ibid.*, p. 7. [12] *Ibid.*, pp. 9–10.
[13] See, for example, R. Brown, *Prejudice* (Oxford: Blackwell, 1995).
[14] Bernstein, *The Social Roots of Discrimination*, p. 1.

persecution and mass slaughter to an unprecedented degree of fierceness' and this meant that even the most strenuous attempt at 'scientific detachment would have been in vain'.[15] With the benefit of hindsight his earlier detachment now seemed strange and to persist with it would be, to say the least, inappropriate.

Bernstein's words were precise and significant. They indicated that the balance between the particular and the general – between the sociological and the historical – had fatally shifted. What had changed this balance was not a scientific insight or an empirical finding, but it was the events of history, which had been, to quote his words, 'unprecedented'. Those events would be diminished if they were treated merely as instances of 'group prejudice' or 'projected dislike'. What was unprecedented would then appear as if it had common precedents.

Bernstein was saying that after the Holocaust it was no longer possible to contemplate anti-Semitism as one might have done twenty-five years previously, when a young Jew like himself was innocently unaware of what was about to happen. If, after the war, one treated those events dispassionately, classifying them under general categories like a botanist classifying plants, then one would be displaying a failure of understanding – historical understanding, scientific understanding and, above all, moral understanding. No general category could possibly contain the savage particularity of what happened.

Henri Tajfel and another German edition of Bernstein

If that was the end of the story, Bernstein's book would have remained little more than a passing curiosity. The sales of the post-war English language edition were not good. There were a number of reviews, including several from academics, but overall the book had no impact on either sociology or social psychology – or on public opinion generally. American researchers, examining prejudice and anti-Semitism, preferred to cite the work by Adorno and others into authoritarianism or Kurt Lewin's topological theorizing, which was even more abstract, and certainly much more abstruse, than the first part of Bernstein's book.[16] Post-war social psychologists felt no need to consult the work of an amateur, who a generation earlier had speculated without the methodological benefits of a laboratory and without the disciplinary benefits of a university position.

[15] *Ibid.*, p. 1.

[16] T. W. Adorno, E. Frenkel-Brunswik, D. J. Levinson and R. N. Sanford, *The Authoritarian Personality* (New York: Harper, 1951); K. Lewin, *Principles of Topological Psychology* (New York: McGraw Hill, 1936), K. Lewin, *Resolving Social Conflicts* (New York: Harper & Row, 1948).

This is not a story with a happy ending about a book that, after many years of neglect, was suddenly rediscovered and hailed by experts around the world as a classic work of genius. This has not happened yet and probably never will. If one looks on Google Scholar, one will find that the 1951 edition has only been cited seven times, while the original German edition of 1926 has been cited seventeen times. Even allowing for the incompleteness of Google Scholar, twenty-four citations in 85 years hardly indicates that Bernstein's book has made an impact. And yet there is something odd about this tale of neglect. After it had published the English edition, the Philosophical Library received a letter from one of their other authors, congratulating them for recognizing the value of Bernstein's book and praising it as 'a classical masterwork'.[17] The letter writer was Albert Einstein. How many other social psychological works did Einstein praise as masterpieces? And how many of those have been ignored by virtually all social psychologists?

But there was to be contact with a major social psychologist. Over fifty years after the first edition, *Wissenschaftliche Buchgesellschaft*, an academic German publisher based in Darmstadt, decided that it was time to try for another German edition. The publishers thought that a new edition would benefit from having the backing of a notable academic. So, in May 1977, Rita Orgel wrote to Henri Tajfel on behalf of the publishers, asking him to write a preface for the new edition.[18] Tajfel was Professor of Social Psychology at Bristol University, and one of the major figures in European social psychology, active in establishing the European Association of Experimental Social Psychology.[19] He was pioneering a new way for understanding intergroup relations and group prejudice, concentrating on processes of thinking rather than processes of feeling. As the title to one of Tajfel's most famous papers indicated, he was exploring 'the cognitive aspects of prejudice'.[20] In so doing, he was opposing the frustration–aggression approach, as well as those Freudian approaches that saw normal social life producing reservoirs of repressed aggression which needed to be projected onto outsiders.

It might seem somewhat strange that the publishers should have chosen to approach someone like Tajfel, whose intellectual position was *prima facie* at odds with Bernstein's. Nevertheless, Tajfel immediately

17 Quoted in van Praag, 'Introduction to the Transaction edition', p. xiv.

18 Details of Tajfel's correspondence with the German publishers are contained in the Tajfel archives, the Wellcome Library, London, box PSY/TAJ/1/3/4.

19 S. Moscovici and I. Marková, *The Making of Modern Social Psychology* (Cambridge: Polity Press, 2006).

20 First published in 1969, 'The cognitive aspects of prejudice' is included as a chapter in H. Tajfel, *Human Groups and Social Categories* (Cambridge University Press, 1981).

accepted Orgel's invitation and he asked her whether she could send him a copy of the 1951 English translation, since it would be easier for him to read that version rather than 'rereading' the original German. Tajfel's choice of words implied that he had read Bernstein's book in the original, although he was not to mention this again in his correspondence with the publishers or in the foreword that he eventually wrote.

Problems soon arose between Tajfel and the publishers. Wissenschaftliche Buchgesellschaft had expected Tajfel to write his preface in German, but Tajfel insisted that he would write it in English and that the publishers should pay for the costs of translation – something that the publishers were reluctant to do. Their budget was small, Orgel responded, and they were intending to print only around 300 copies – coincidentally the same number of the first edition that had been sold in Germany. Clearly, the new edition was not expected to fare any better in Germany than the original.

The publishers were also unable to find a copy of the English translation to send to Tajfel, who continued to maintain that he could not start writing his preface until he received one. In February 1978, there was a change of publishers: Wissenschaftliche Buchgesellschaft passed the project onto Jüdische Verlag, who would publish the book under the auspices of the much larger Athenäum publishing company. Once again, only a Jewish publisher could be found to publish *Der Antisemitismus* in Germany. The new publishers also failed to locate an English copy to send Tajfel and, in the end, Athenäum advised him to obtain a copy through his university library. There was to be further wrangling between Tajfel and Athenäum, including arguments about the small fee that Tajfel had been promised for his preface and that the publishers were hoping that he might waive.

In January 1979, Tajfel finally sent the publishers an eight–page manuscript in English, entitled simply 'Foreword'. It actually appeared as an epilogue (*Nachwort*) at the end of the book, when the new edition came out in 1980, the same year in which a Hebrew translation of *Der Antisemitismus* also appeared. This new German edition did not contain Bernstein's 1951 Prologue, which, contrary Tajfel's foreword, had actually been written as an epilogue but was published as a foreword. The new German edition did not attract a wider readership, certainly not the readership that Einstein thought the book deserved.[21]

Despite Tajfel's commendation, the book was hardly noticed by social psychologists. It seems as if the neglect of Bernstein was contagious. Most

[21] P. F. Bernstein, *Der Antisemitismus als eine Grouppenerscheinung: Versuch einer Soziologie des Judenhasses* (Königstein: Jüdischer Verlag, 1980). There was to be a further English language edition in 2009, with yet another title (and curiously one which did not contain the word 'anti-Semitism'), Bernstein, *The Social Roots of Discrimination.*

of Tajfel's other writings, especially those published towards the end of his life, have been richly cited. As far as I am aware, none of Tajfel's students or followers has quoted the preface. Even articles examining Tajfel's ideas in relation to anti-Semitism have not done so.[22] The lack of interest in the short piece is exemplified by the bibliography of Tajfel's writings compiled for the edited volume published in 1996 as a tribute to Tajfel.[23] Tajfel's publications were divided into three categories: 'Intergroup relations', 'Social perception and related topics' and 'Other publications'. The preface was put into 'Other publications', as if to separate it from his writings on the central themes of his social psychological work.

Tajfel often told his students that he came into social psychology in order to understand how genocide was possible. However, none of his technical papers directly approached the topic of genocide in general or the Holocaust in particular.[24] But there, virtually unnoticed amidst 'Other publications', was one of the few papers in which Tajfel discussed, albeit briefly, the issue that was central to his whole work. For anyone wishing to understand Tajfel's thinking, the preface remains an important document. There is an additional reason for discussing it here. Tajfel's preface shows an understanding of the complex relations between history and social psychological theory – an issue about which Tajfel was thinking deeply in the years before his death in 1982.

Henri Tajfel, social identity and history

In recent years, Tajfel's name has become synonymous with 'Social Identity Theory', which is currently one of the most widely used theoretical frameworks in social psychology. Put in over-simplified terms, the theory suggests that people seek to identify with groups that provide them with positive social identities, and that they often achieve such positive identities by distancing themselves from comparable outgroups.[25] Anyone who knows Tajfel only as the formulator of Social Identity Theory might find his Foreword to Bernstein's book somewhat

[22] M. Billig, 'Remembering the particular background of Social Identity Theory', in W. P. Robinson (ed.), *Social Groups and Identities* (Oxford: Butterworth Heinemann, 1996), pp. 337–57.

[23] R. Brown, A. Schipper and N. Wandersleben, 'Bibliography of publications of Henri Tajfel'. W. P. Robinson (ed.), *Social Groups and Identities* (Oxford: Butterworth Heinemann, 1996), pp. 363–70.

[24] M. Billig, 'Henri Tajfel's "Cognitive aspects of prejudice" and the psychology of bigotry', *British Journal of Social Psychology*, 41, (2002), 171–88.

[25] For an early, and non-simplified, version of the theory, see H. Tajfel and J. C. Turner, 'An integrative theory of intergroup conflict', in W. G. Austin and S. Worchel (eds.), *The Social Psychology of Intergroup Relations* (Monterey, CA: Brooks/Cole, 1979).

perplexing. Nowadays, it has become common for social psychologists, along with other social scientists, to package their work into labelled theoretical approaches, typically turning the labels into acronyms in order to promote their approaches.[26] Gerd Gigerenzer has claimed that psychologists treat theories rather like toothbrushes: no one likes to use someone else's.[27] A modern social psychologist who commends an old, forgotten book would be likely to praise it for influencing their own thinking or for being an early, imperfect variety of their own approach. Tajfel, however, did not claim Bernstein to be a social identity theorist *avant la lettre* and, as we shall see, he was not entirely comfortable with the term 'social identity theory'. In any case, Tajfel had much deeper reasons to link himself with Bernstein.

Certainly, Tajfel's approach differed from that proposed by Bernstein, especially since Tajfel believed that it was a serious mistake to explain prejudice against groups in terms of individual feelings of frustration. He criticized the frustration–aggression theory in his important paper 'Experiments in a vacuum', which was included in his book *Human Groups and Social Categories*. In a caustic comment, Tajfel pointed out that the evidence for the frustration-aggression theory came from experiments conducted on frustrated rats or from 'creating ingenious laboratory equivalents of a man berating his wife after having been reprimanded by his boss'; none of these studies, Tajfel continued, 'can be relevant to a confirmation or invalidation of the hypotheses as they might apply to *any* social setting of intergroup relations'.[28]

In his foreword to *Der Antisemitismus*, Tajfel noted that Bernstein also seemed to draw inferences from individual frustration to wider social prejudice. However, Tajfel noted that Bernstein went much further by linking frustration with the structural properties of groups and this was 'something which was never done by the Yale psychologists'.[29] According to Tajfel, Bernstein stressed that what needs to be explained 'is the *collective* phenomenon of hostility between groups which share a common and structured social and historical reality'.[30] That, in Tajfel's view, was one of the reasons why Bernstein so long ago had been able to write 'a book which ... keeps so much of its value today'.[31] Nevertheless, Tajfel was sceptical of Bernstein's

26 M. Billig, *Learn to Write Badly: How to Succeed in the Social Sciences* (Cambridge University Press, 2013).

27 G. Gigerenzer, 'Personal reflections on "Theory and Psychology"'. *Theory & Psychology*, 20 (2010), 733–43.

28 Tajfel, *Human Groups and Social Categories*, p. 20, emphasis in original.

29 Henri Tajfel's 'Foreword', p. 6. Quotations and page numbers are taken from Tajfel's English manuscript for the foreword published as 'Nachwort zur Neuauflage' in Bernstein, *Der Antisemitismus*.

30 *Ibid.*, emphasis in original. 31 *Ibid.*

explanation about the origins of group enmity. Bernstein had assumed that love and hate were two basic emotions and that the 'quantities' of one emotion could be used in the discharge of the other emotion. Tajfel wrote that he 'personally' did not believe that Bernstein's theory would 'stand the test of further advances in the biological and social sciences', although it was 'no better and no worse' than many other theories that biologists and social scientists were proposing.[32]

That leaves a problem: how could Tajfel commend a book whose basic theoretical premise he thought would not stand the test of time and which, in many respects, resembled theories that Tajfel rejected? The very question seems to assume that, when it comes to understanding the social world, formulating theories is more important than sharing a common history. Bernstein and Tajfel were both European Jews who had managed to survive the war. Tajfel had moved from Poland to France two years before the outbreak of the war and, having joined the French army and been captured by German troops, he fortuitously managed to escape death in prisoner-of-war camps.[33]

The underlying point of Tajfel's foreword was not to promote his theoretical position at the expense of Bernstein's but to reflect on the history and the understanding of that history, which they shared. An abstract, universal theory of the sort that Bernstein had proposed in the first part of his book was inappropriate for understanding that history. Tajfel began his foreword with Bernstein's 1951 prologue, which Tajfel describes as an apology, phrased in the form of 'a question as deeply felt as it is desperate: how could anyone have foreseen in 1923 the horror that was to come so soon?'[34] The unimaginable had happened and 'no human endeavour, in art or in science, could ever hope to reflect, understand or explain the enormity of the suffering and of the crimes'.[35] Tajfel recalled watching Charlie Chaplin's film *The Great Dictator* in France around the time that Bernstein must have been writing his preface. He had to leave the cinema, unable to watch Chaplin's 'restrained account' of Nazism. It was no good telling himself that Chaplin, when he made the film before the war, could not have possibly imagined what was to come. Similarly, Bernstein's dispassionate theorizing in 1923 was unbearably inappropriate 'when set against the enormity of what had really happened'.[36]

Tajfel's point was that one cannot blame the young Bernstein or the young Chaplin for failing to predict an unimaginable future, but those with hindsight must treat the past with respect. This means not treating

[32] *Ibid.*, p. 5.

[33] G. Jahoda, 'Henri Tajfel'. In *Oxford Dictionary of National Biography* (Oxford University Press, 2004).

[34] Tajfel, 'Foreword', p. 1. [35] *Ibid.*, p. 1. [36] *Ibid.*, p. 1.

the exceptional moments of history as equivalent to the more mundane, as if all historical events can be fitted into the same general categories. Although Tajfel took up psychology in order to understand how genocide occurred, he never presented his ideas about social identity and the nature of intergroup prejudice as a theory to explain the Holocaust.[37] Indeed, Tajfel developed his theory principally to explain strategies open to groups who have been excluded from power and who, like Black Power activists or feminists, strive to develop a collective, positive identity as a means of changing social reality.[38] This was no oversight. It would be inappropriate to 'explain' the Holocaust, using the same set of terms that 'explain' more ordinary types of group identification, especially those that lead to positive social actions.

Imagine Tajfel, or anyone else, applying the main concepts of social identity theory to explain the Holocaust. For instance, an identity theorist might speculate: the rise of Nazism occurred because the Germans wished to develop their sense of positive identity, and to differentiate themselves from Jews and other non-Aryans, in ways that resemble the ways that participants in a number of laboratory experiments have made their self-identity more positive. The statement in a literal sense might be true, but it would be the sort of truth that is so empty of content that it tells us nothing. Actually, it is a truth that is so beside the point in its triviality that it constitutes an untruth.

Indeed, the Holocaust is one of several historical events that resist explanation, for to 'explain' the Holocaust would be to risk explaining it away. That, in essence, was what Bernstein was saying in 1949 when he reflected how wrong it would have been to adopt once more his earlier dispassionate tone and to treat the Holocaust as just another effect of group formation. Even when writing in 1923, Bernstein was aware of the dangers of explaining the unforgiveable. He wrote that if one tries to enumerate the causative factors behind a crime, one risks diminishing the sense of the guilt that should be attached to the criminal for '*tout comprendre est tout pardonner*'.[39] After the war, that would be unthinkable.

Universal psychology and historical particularity

As a social psychologist Tajfel was never concerned to formulate technically proficient experiments or theories for their own sake and in

[37] See Billig, 'Henri Tajfel's "Cognitive aspects of prejudice"'.

[38] S. D. Reicher, R. Spears, and A. S. Haslam, 'The social identity approach in social psychology', in M. Wetherell and C. T. Mohanty (eds.), *Sage Identities Handbook* (Sage: London, 2010).

[39] Bernstein, *The Social Roots of Discrimination*, p. 98.

the years before his death he was becoming deeply uneasy about the direction that social psychologists were taking. In his important paper 'Experiments in a vacuum', Tajfel argued that social psychology was becoming increasingly trivial. Many social psychologists were conducting petty experiments, often on the assumption that experiments provide 'pure' environments in which theory can be tested. Tajfel argued there can be no 'pure' experiments, for participants will always bring their culture and its history with them into the laboratory. Indeed, far from trying to control that culture and history by vainly trying to create 'pure' environments, social psychologists, according to Tajfel, should be seeking to understand cultural history.

Tajfel stressed that if social psychologists are to produce meaningful theories, then they should try to situate social psychological factors within particular cultural and historical contexts. He gave the example of the art historian E. H. Gombrich, who adapted psychological concepts from the Gestaltists and particularly from Frederic Bartlett. In his book *Art and Illusion*, Gombrich argued that artists used 'stereotypes', with representatives from different artistic schools constructing and employing different visual stereotypes.[40] Tajfel noted that Gombrich could hardly stop there, as if he had solved the problems of art simply by saying that artists used different stereotypes. Historians of art, when studying particular groups of artists, must be familiar with what the artists 'intended to communicate, how they wished to communicate it, and why they chose their particular idioms'.[41]

In short, the historian, whether of art or society, must get down to the particularities of the world; otherwise they will end up with bland generalities. General categories, such as 'stereotypes', 'attributions' or 'group identity', are only valuable if they enable us to see the particular features in new ways. The problem is that social psychologists typically favour the general over the particular. They treat their universal concepts as primary, using the particularities of the world to serve the categories of their theories, rather than vice versa. In their hands, general concepts become greedy concepts, devouring the individual, unique features of the social world. The result is less, not greater, theoretical understanding.

Paradoxically, Tajfel, who is noted for his experimental work, was criticizing experimentalism in ways similar to noted anti-experimentalists like Kenneth Gergen, who argued that all social psychological findings are historical.[42] In fact, some critical theorists today acknowledge Tajfel

[40] E. H. Gombrich, *Art and Illusion* (London: Phaidon, 1960).

[41] Tajfel, *Human Groups and Social Categories*, p. 26.

[42] K. J. Gergen, 'Social psychology as history', *Journal of Personality and Social Psychology*, 26 (1973), 373–83.

as a critical psychologist on the basis of his paper 'Experiments in a vacuum'.[43] On the other hand, many experimentalists have tended to overlook the argument of that paper. In fact, the paper is not even listed in the aforementioned bibliography published in the tribute to Henri Tajfel in 1996.[44]

The philosophy of formulating pure theories of social psychology has been prevalent amongst social identity theorists, who have sought to work out the relations between a widening list of universal variables relating to 'social identity', 'social categorization' and 'social differentiation'.[45] To give just one example of the way that Social Identity Theory is being used to make universal statements, here is a comment from one of the theory's many advocates: 'SIT assumes that we show all kinds of "group" behaviour, such as solidarity within our groups and discrimination against outgroups as part of social identity processes, with the aim to achieve positive social self-esteem and self-enhancement.'[46] It is as if the complexities of the world – 'all kinds' of complexities – are being reduced to the simple, universal motive of achieving positive social self-esteem.

In some of his final writings Tajfel expressed his concern with this sort of development. In the concluding chapter of his edited book *Social Identity and Intergroup Relations*, he tactfully pointed out gaps in the work of his former student John Turner, who was to develop the theory of self-categorization.[47] Turner, in examining how individuals form groups through their sense of self-identity, started with the subjective views of individuals. According to Tajfel, this perspective 'leaves out a preliminary stage that might perhaps be referred to as the pre-history of group formation'.[48] This stage of 'pre-history' was, of course, very much part of a wider history – the history of economic and political relations, as well

43 For example F. P. Colucci and L. Montali, *The origins, characteristics and development of critical psychology in Italy. Annual Review of Critical Psychology*.

44 Brown *et al.*, 'Bibliography of publications of Henri Tajfel'.

45 See, for example, D. Abrams, and M. A. Hogg, *Social Identity Theory* (New York: Springer Verlag, 1990); M. B. Brewer and M. Hewstone (eds.), *Self and Social Identity* (Oxford: Blackwell, 2004); D. Capozza, and R. Brown (eds.), *Social Identity Processes* (London: Sage, 2000); N. Ellemers, R. Spears and B. Doosje (eds.), *Social Identity* (Oxford: Blackwell, 1999).

46 S. Trepte, 'Social identity theory', in J. Bryant and P. Vorderer (eds.), *Psychology of Entertainment* (Mawah, NJ: Lawrence Erlbaum, 2006), p. 256.

47 J. C. Turner, 'Towards a cognitive redefinition of the social group', in H. Tajfel (ed.), *Social Identity and Intergroup Relations* (Cambridge University Press, 1982); J. C. Turner, M. A. Hogg, P. J. Oakes, S. C. Reicher and M. Wetherell, *Rediscovering the Social Group* (Oxford: Blackwell, 1987); Reicher *et al.*, *The Social Identity Approach in Social Psychology.*

48 H. Tajfel (1982). 'Instrumentality, identity and social comparisons'. In H. Tajfel (ed.), *Social Identity and Intergroup Relations* (Cambridge University Press, 1982), pp. 502–3, 10(2013), 596–621.

as the history of myths and beliefs. Tajfel's point was that the decisions that individuals take about their sense of identity should not be separated from this history.

In one of his last writings, Tajfel complained that some social psychologists, including those developing his work, were oversimplifying the history and function of social stereotypes by explaining them in terms of an individual's needs for a positive identity. He wrote that 'the blame must be firmly assigned to an over-extension of what has come to be known as the "social identity" theory'.[49] The use of quotation marks around 'social identity' indicates his discomfort the label and the way it was being used. Here Tajfel was underlining the importance of social myths and their social power. He wrote that questions about social identity are 'to some extent represented in the so-called "social identity" perspective, but social identity is not enough', for issues about identity must be considered in relation to the creation and diffusion of social myths.[50] Tajfel discussed how social myths can be used, in times of conflict to sanction extreme actions. The sort of violence, which would be considered criminal if used against individuals, then becomes acceptable, even demanded, when it is pursued for the sake of the group against its 'enemies'. He added: 'examples are unnecessary for anyone who is familiar with even a small part of the history of the present century'.[51]

Tajfel was hinting at the history that he experienced at first hand and that he described briefly but movingly in the opening pages of *Human Groups and Social Categories*.[52] His remark certainly distances him from those social psychologists who assume that analysts can only trust events that have been created in laboratories under controlled conditions. Regarding his statements about individual and collective violence, Tajfel was not saying 'we must conduct an experiment to see whether this is true'. He knew it was true: the evidence from history was more than sufficient.

History and anti-Semitism

Tajfel's reservations about universal social psychological theories could be applied equally to Bernstein's theory of group enmity. In ascribing the causes of anti-Semitism to group formation Bernstein had been simultaneously explaining too much and too little. In very general terms Bernstein's theory might seem to explain why anti-Semitism existed in Germany during the 1920s, but that theory could not explain why such

49 H. Tajfel, 'Intergroup relations, social myths and social justice in social psychology', in H. Tajfel (ed.), *The Social Dimension*, vol. 2 (Cambridge University Press, 1984), p. 699.

50 *Ibid.*, p. 713. 51 *Ibid.*, p. 708.

52 Tajfel, *Human Groups and Social Categories*, pp. 1ff.

anti-Semitism should have increased in intensity over the following years and resulted in a scale of violence beyond imagining. The existence of social groups – or of social identities or of residues of frustration – cannot possibly explain Auschwitz without explaining it away.

So, why was Tajfel so keen to commend Bernstein's work? The answer does not lie in the nature of social identity theory or even in Tajfel's unique contribution to the social psychology of prejudice. It lies in Tajfel's knowledge about anti-Semitism and his deep fear that history in the late 1970s might be about to repeat itself. And if it did repeat itself, the result would not be, as Marx once famously commented, that tragedy would be repeated as comedy.

In his foreword, Tajfel quoted Bernstein, who in his own prologue had talked about his early difficulties in finding a publisher. Back in the 1920s, according to Bernstein, there had been an aversion to discussing anti-Semitism. Tajfel then commented: 'We have now come back to where Bernstein had started from.'[53] After the end of the Second World War, he claimed, there had been a great deal of writing about anti-Semitism, and there had been no way of avoiding the subject. However, now in the late 1970s and early 1980s 'the "aversion" is back with us'.[54] Some outward forms of anti-Semitism were changing, with old ideas about Jewish conspiracies now appearing as 'anti-Zionism' and the extreme right often employing codes to avoid directly mentioning Jews: 'Although it would be preposterous to claim that all anti-"Zionists" are anti-Semitic, there is very little doubt that the new terminology and the Middle East conflict have caused much old wine to be poured into new bottles.'[55] Tajfel feared that there was a parallel between the late 1970s and the 1920s, for people were being faced 'with a combination of circumstances very similar to that which Bernstein had to overcome when he tried to publish his book in the early twenties'.[56]

If it had proved inappropriate in the 1920s to adopt a dispassionate tone, then, in the light of recent history, it would be just as inappropriate to adopt one fifty years later. Anti-Semitism could never be just another outcome o group formation or an expression of the search for a positive social identity; certainly it never could be so for Jews of Tajfel's and Bernstein's backgrounds. The Tajfel archives, now housed in the Wellcome Trust Library, reveal the depth of Tajfel's concern to combat new forms of fascism and anti-Semitism. He was a signatory member of the left-wing Anti-Nazi League, which advocated directed action against the far-right groups of the time.

[53] Tajfel, 'Foreword', p. 2. [54] *Ibid.*, p. 2.
[55] *Ibid.*, p. 3. [56] *Ibid.*, p. 3.

Tajfel was aware that the writers of history can be important for reproducing old myths in new forms. The archive reveals his concern in 1980 about a booklet, entitled *Arab-Israeli Conflict*, which the Schools Council History Project had produced to be circulated in British schools.[57] Tajfel wrote to the publishers to complain that the booklet was biased in its representation of the past. Tajfel specifically objected that the booklet contained no statement of the scale of the Holocaust and its impact on Jews; he also objected that the booklet ignored the fact that many of the post-war immigrants to Israel had come from Arab countries. Tajfel copied his letter to a number of prominent academics and politicians. The philosopher Isaiah Berlin wrote back to offer his support, praising Tajfel for his fight against bigotry. Tajfel replied to Berlin saying that both the far left and far right were producing 'the kind of rumblings that scare me out of my wits'.[58]

The issue is not whether Tajfel was correct in seeing a parallel between the anti-Semitism of the 1920s and that of the late 1970s and early 1980s. There are clear differences as well as similarities. Nevertheless, we can see why Tajfel sought to understand the present in terms of the past and, to do that, he could not simply put his faith in a universal theory. He understood that no social psychological theory, however much laboratory support its supporters could muster in its favour, could replace the need to understand the particularities of the past.

The present chapter has sought to support this point, but not by producing general, and therefore essentially non-historical, arguments about relations between psychological and historical knowledge – and how social psychologists need to maintain a historical consciousness. To have expressed the argument in general terms would have meant expressing it non-historically. By contrast, the point has been pursued by telling the singular story of a book. This story has encompassed the history of its author and of Henri Tajfel, who knew that the enormity of their experiences, and those of their families, communities and that generation of European Jewry, could not be contained within even the best of theories. For those like Bernstein and Tajfel, the particularities of the past would ever haunt their view of the present.

It is often assumed that history belongs to the winners. But academic history cannot be left to the winners, as they will all too readily write the history of their disciplines in ways that celebrate current ways of thinking. Self-congratulatory histories will only tell half the story and maybe

[57] Schools Council History Project (1977). *Arab-Israeli Conflict*. Edinburgh: Holmes McDougall. See the Tajfel archives, the Wellcome Library, London box PSY/TAJ/6/50.

[58] Letter dated 31 March 1980, *ibid.*

not even the most important half. As Tajfel's tribute to Bernstein shows, we can learn much from the history of those who have been unjustly neglected. We can recover forgotten ideas, which in Bernstein's case were substantial ideas, and we can confront the unfairness of history. In retelling the story of someone whose intellectual achievement has been largely overlooked, and whose background was destroyed, we are able to make, by our act of remembrance, a small protest against that unfairness.

12 Historical stereotypes and histories of stereotypes

Mark Knights

History and social psychology share interests in the public sphere, the arts of persuasion and the formation of attitudes. As a result, both disciplines are interested in the construction, manipulation, dissemination and evolution of stereotypes and the prejudices on which they feed. The first section of this chapter outlines themes, conclusions and approaches drawn from psychology that might be particularly useful for historical analysis. Much of the social psychology literature about stereotyping should be of significant interest to historians, even though, it seems, it is seldom used by them. I shall then examine historical approaches to stereotyping and highlight some of the benefits of using historical data, which, in turn, is strikingly absent from most of the published social psychology work in the field. At one time the social sciences and history drew frequently on one another; now, that relationship, at least as far as psychology is concerned, seems more distant, though there are good reasons for thinking that some sort of rapprochement may be taking place, and this chapter seeks to foster that process.[1] The final section of the chapter will take a case study, the stereotypes of reform and reformers in eighteenth and early nineteenth-century Britain, in order to bring the two approaches together, and also to show how an even broader interdisciplinary approach, integrating visual and linguistic concerns, might be a productive way forward.

Social psychology and stereotypes

Social psychologists seem to be agreed that stereotyping is a by-product of normal cognitive processes that help us to order, simplify and hence understand better the complex world around us.[2] A stereotype is thus

1 V. Glăveanu and K. Yamamoto (eds.), 'Bridging history and social psychology', Special Issue of *Integrative Psychological and Behavioral Science*, 46 (2012). See also note 4.

2 A helpful overview can be found in C. Stangor and M. Schaller, 'Stereotypes as individual and collective representations', in C. N. Macrae, C. Stangor and M. Hewstone (eds.), *Stereotypes and Stereotyping* (New York: Guilford Press, 1996); chapter 8 in D. Schneider,

simply an association of attributes with a certain group of people.[3] The human mind has to think with the help of categorizations that form part of an orderly mental outlook. All this has the advantage, for the historian, of considering stereotypes to be a result of a normal and ubiquitous mental process rather than as necessarily the product of a corrupted or distorted mind, and hence helps to make stereotypes appear as 'rational' rather than 'irrational' phenomena, even when they are highly emotionally charged. Such an approach also makes it imperative to consider stereotypes historically: if they are part of the way in which the human mind works, they are as much a part of the past as the present. Yet this raises a further question, worth investigating in itself, about whether cognitive processes in the modern era are the same as those of the pre-modern era or whether cognition is culturally constructed or at least influenced by the contemporary world. My assumption in what follows is that modern and pre-modern minds share enough similarities for recent research to have a bearing on how we understand the pre-modern mind. Although the culture of the past certainly shaped and perhaps even determined what people thought and (as recent work on the history of emotions suggests) felt, as well as how they behaved, I make the assumption that certain behavioural responses and cognitive functions relating to how information is processed by the brain remain the same or similar, sufficiently so for modern findings to have some relevance for the past or at least to raise interesting questions for the historian. I freely admit, however, that this is an untested and possibly controversial position that would benefit from further exploration.[4]

The Psychology of Stereotyping (New York: Guilford Press, 2005) offers another good starting point.

[3] A stereotype can, but need not necessarily, become a prejudice (an emotive prejudgement) and lead to active discrimination. The relationship between stereotypes, prejudices and discrimination is explored in Schneider, *The Psychology of Stereotyping*, and C. Stangor (ed.), *Stereotypes and Prejudice: Essential Readings* (London: Psychology Press, 2000). The relationship between prejudice and categorical thinking was first systematically explored by G. Allport, *The Nature of Prejudice* (Cambridge, MA: Addison-Wesley, 1954).

[4] W. M. Reddy, *The Navigation of Feeling: a Framework for the History of Emotions* (Cambridge University Press, 2001); T. Dixon, *From Passions to Emotions: the Creation of a Secular Psychological Category* (Cambridge University Press, 2003), B. Rosenwein, 'Worrying about emotions in history', *American Historical Review*, 107 (2002), 921–45; Rosenwein, 'Problems and methods in the history of emotions', in *Passions in Context: International Journal for the History and Theory of Emotions*, 1 (2010), 1–11; J. Liliequist (ed.), *A History of Emotions, 1200–1800* (London: Pickering & Chatto, 2012). For a sceptical discussion about 'transhistorical laws in social psychology' urging the need to recognize change over time see K. Gergen, 'Social psychology as history', *Journal of Personality and Social Psychology*, 26 (1973), 309–20. Nevertheless Gergen concludes that although expressions of behaviour are primarily culturally determined, some behaviour may be fixed and that

Broadly speaking, there are two different, but not necessarily incompatible, approaches to understanding stereotype formation: one examines the individual cognitive processes occurring in the individual; the other stresses the cultural and contextual factors that make for collective or shared social representations. The former stresses the way in which the mind works, whereas the latter highlights the influential role played by parents, teachers, political and religious leaders and, above all, the media and advertisements. This second approach, with its stress on cultural factors, might seem the more likely fit with cultural history; but the cognitive reaction of individuals is also surely important and can have implications for the historian, particularly, as suggested in what follows, in helping to understand the process by which stereotypes are constructed and maintained.

Indeed, despite the different schools there seems to be some common ground among social psychologists in attempting to explain why stereotypes form. One common suggestion is that they strengthen the identity and esteem of 'in-groups', that is to say, groups with which an individual identifies.[5] In-groups have an internal cohesion that is in part derived from the identification of an 'out-group' with which they are in competition or conflict or tension. Indeed, another interesting characteristic noted by psychologists is that the more a group is seen as a unity or entity, the greater readiness there is to stereotype it, even in small, face-to-face groups where groups have a good deal of individualized information about each other (everyday interaction which other parts of the literature suggests might be expected to counteract the stereotype).[6] When we see a group of people as an entity, we will often attribute something essential to it. That process is also recognizable from historical stereotypes. Moreover, the social psychology literature suggests that stereotypes are, to a surprising extent, self-fulfilling: the expectation that an individual will act in a stereotypical fashion influences how that individual actually behaves. The formation of a stereotype is thus in some ways cyclical and self-reinforcing.[7] Again, such a process is historically observable. Confessions by witches, for example, show the degree to which the hostile stereotype was internalized and shaped behaviour.[8]

'we have yet to tap the vast quantities of information regarding interaction patterns in earlier periods' (p. 318).

5 For an overview see Schneider, *The Psychology of Stereotyping*, chapter 7.

6 R. Brown, *Prejudice: Its Social Psychology* (Oxford: Wiley-Blackwell, 2010), pp. 77–8.

7 For an overview of this literature see Schneider, *The Psychology of Stereotyping*, pp. 215–24.

8 For witchcraft see Malcolm Gaskill, 'Witchcraft in early modern Kent: stereotypes and the background to accusations', in J. Barry, M. Hester and G. Roberts (eds.), *Witchcraft in Early Modern Europe: Studies in Culture and Belief* (Cambridge University Press, 1998), 257–87; J. Sharpe, *Instruments of Darkness: Witchcraft in Early Modern England*

Stereotypes are particularly common in times of crisis and stress, when the mind needs to impose order on a complex and challenging 'information-rich environment'. 'Research amply demonstrates that the use of social stereotypes increases in cognitively demanding situations … Needs to simplify and structure understanding may be heightened within societies during times of crisis, such as wars, economic recessions and natural disasters.'[9] These conclusions are particularly suggestive to the historian, since it was very often such periods of crisis in which the authority and identity of groups was contested, challenged and often vulnerable, requiring more frequent assertion and greater reinforcement, producing literatures rich in stereotypical observations.

Although the terms are rather old-fashioned in the social psychology literature, the notions of schema and prototype might also be useful to historians.[10] Schemas 'are abstract knowledge structures that specify the defining features and relevant attributes of a given concept' and since the historian often investigates concepts in the past, a means of thinking about concepts is particularly useful. Akin to the schema is the prototype, an 'averaged idea of the concept', a typical representation of it – again, something very familiar to the historian, as will be shown in the third part of this chapter.

The psychology literature also offers interesting suggestions about how stereotypes are maintained. One approach that straddles both the individual and cultural schools of social psychology is rooted in language. It has been noted that some pairings of words are much stronger than others and hence better remembered. Such strong or 'hot' associations help to form stereotypical associations.[11] Examining which words are associated with others thus helps us to understand how stereotypes are constructed and the emotive power they wield. The 'hot' associations may also help to explain why stereotypes are so enduring, often persisting across several generations. It has also been suggested, by Abric and

(Philadelphia, PA: University of Pennsylvania Press, 1997); R. Briggs, *Witches and Neighbours: the Social and Cultural Context of European Witchcraft*, 2nd edn (Oxford: Wiley-Blackwell, 2002); S. Clark (ed.), *Languages of Witchcraft: Narrative, Ideology and Meaning in Early Modern Culture* (Basingstoke: Palgrave Macmillan, 2001).

9 Stangor and Schaller, 'Stereotypes as individual and collective representations', pp. 21–2.

10 For an overview see *ibid.*, pp. 7–9; Schneider, *The Psychology of Stereotyping*, chapter 4.

11 D. L. Hamilton, P. M. Dugan and T. K Trolier, 'The formation of stereotypic beliefs: further evidence for distinctive-based illusory correlations', *Journal of Personality and Social Psychology*, 58 (1985), 5–17; B. Mullen and C. Johnson, 'Distinctiveness-based illusory correlations and stereotyping: a meta-analytical integration', *British Journal of Social Psychology*, 29 (1990), 11–28; W. Wagner, J. Valencia and F. Elejabarrieta, 'Relevance, discourse and the "hot" stable core of social representations – a structural analysis of word associations', *British Journal of Social Psychology*, 35 (1996), 331–52.

others, that a collective or social representation has a 'central core' that is fundamental to its character, with peripheral elements that are less important and which might change over time and context.[12] The ideas expressed in the stable core also tend to be 'hot' words, closely related to emotional and bodily experience.

Another interesting approach, led by Semin, Fiedler and Maass, has been to examine the language used to describe in-groups and out-groups.[13] It was found that undesirable characteristics in the out-group tend to be described in abstract terms that describe states of being. Thus A hitting B might be summarized not as an observable one-off event but abstracted as a personality trait: 'A is violent.' But desirable characteristics displayed by the out-group tended to be described in much more specific ways that could be explained away as single incidents or aberrations from normal expectations. Conversely, undesirable behaviour in one's own group tends to be described in very specific and hence limiting ways, with the more enduring abstractions being reserved for their desirable behaviour. Thus undesirable behaviour in one's own group tends to be excused as idiosyncratic, while that in an out-group tends to be generalized as characteristic of the group as a whole. Indeed, Semin and Fiedler, building on work by Roger Brown, drew up four categories of verbs (the 'linguistic category model') to describe the different ways in which language was being used, ranging from the abstract to the particular. The first two categories, 'descriptive action verb' and 'interpretative action verb', refer to specific events. The last two are more abstract: the third category, 'state verb', describes an emotional, affective or mental state, such as 'love', 'admire', 'desire', 'envy'; and the fourth category, 'adjectives', describes highly abstract character dispositions, such as 'honest', 'impulsive', 'reliable'. Given that information at an abstract level is open ended and resistant to change, the prevalence of abstractions in stereotypes might help to explain their longevity as well as why behaviour that does not conform to a stereotype can be discounted as isolated and untypical.[14]

[12] J. C. Flament and P. Moliner, 'Contribution expérimentale à la théorie du noyeau central d'une répresentation' in J.-L. Beauvois, R.-V. Joule and J.-M. Monteil (eds.), *Perspectives cognitive et conduites sociales. Tome 2. Répresentations et processus cognitifs* (Cousset: Del Val, 1989), 139–41; Jean-Claude Abric, 'Central system, peripheral system: their functions and roles in the dynamics of social representations', *Papers on Social Representations*, 2 (1993), 75–8; Abric, 'Les Représentations sociales: aspects théoriques' in J. C. Abric (ed.), *Pratiques socials et représentations* (Paris: Presses Universitaires de France, 2001), pp. 11–36.

[13] For an overview see Schneider, *Psychology of Stereotyping*, pp. 553–9.

[14] R. Brown and D. Fish, 'The psychological causality implicit in language', *Cognition*, 14 (1983), 237–73; G. R. Semin and K. Fiedler, 'The linguistic category model, its bases, applications and range', *European Review of Social Psychology*, 2 (1991), 1–30;

Moving away from explanations rooted in cognitive psychology a group of social psychologists – Jonathan Potter, Margaret Wetherell and Michael Billig prominent among them – also study discourse in order to emphasize how the phenomenon of categorization and stereotyping is a social practice involving certain sorts of language use.[15] As Potter-and Wetherell put it, 'discourse analysis focuses, above all, on quintessentially psychological activities – activities of justification, rationalization, categorization, attribution, making sense, naming, blaming and identifying. Discourse studies links those activities with collective forms of social action' and uncovers 'a discursive history', a process that mixes 'representation and reality'.[16] This comes close to the 'linguistic turn' taken by historians that has resulted in a heightened awareness of the power of language itself to shape behaviour, to create modern identities and mindsets, and to subvert the distinction 'between representation and reality'.[17]

Further possibilities for a fruitful exchange between psychologists and historians around the issue of language are highlighted by Billig's research that straddles both the pre-modern past and social psychology. His work on the importance of rhetoric as a way of thinking and arguing shows on the one hand the benefit to social psychologists of understanding how people in the pre-modern era were taught to think and speak. He shows how rhetoric's stress on duality, dialogue and dialectic helps to explain how thought is governed and shaped by cultural factors. There are, he shows, always opposing ways of categorizing any situation, often involving the creation of sub-categories by splitting categories into parts ('particularization') and prejudices are thus necessarily fluid, variable

G. R. Semin and K. Fiedler, 'The inferential properties of interpersonal verbs', in G. R. Semin and K. Fiedler (eds.), *Language, Interaction and Social Cognition* (London: Sage, 1992); A. Maass, D. Salvi, L. Arcuri and G Semin, 'Language use in intergroup contexts: the linguistic intergroup bias', *Journal of Personality and Social Psychology*, 57 (1989), 981–93; A. Maass and L. Arcuri, 'The role of language in the persistence of stereotype', in Semin and Fiedler (eds.), *Language, Interaction and Social Cognition*; A. Maass, A. Milesi, S. Zabbini and D. Stahlberg, 'Linguistic inter-group bias: differential expectancies or in-group protection', *Journal of Personality and Social Psychology*, 68 (1995), 116–26.

[15] J. Potter and M. Wetherell, *Discourse and Social Psychology. Beyond Attitudes and Behaviour* (London: Sage, 1987); M. Wetherell and J. Potter, *Mapping the Language of Racism. Discourse and the Legitimation of Exploitation* (Hemel Hempstead: Harvester Wheatsheaf, 1992)

[16] Wetherell and Potter, *Mapping the Language*, pp. 2, 4 and 40.

[17] P. Joyce, *Democratic Subjects: the Self and the Social in Nineteenth-Century England* (Cambridge University Press, 1994), p. 2. For an overview see E. A. Clark, *History, Theory, Text: Historians and the Linguistic Turn* (Cambridge, MA: Harvard University Press, 2004); G. S. Jones, *Languages of Class: Studies in Working Class History 1832–1982* (Cambridge University Press, 1984).

and adaptable.[18] This work has implications for historians. Billig's assertion that 'all the major themes of modern social psychology can be found in classical rhetoric' should alert historians to finding ways of drawing on that literature about persuasion, categorization and ways of thinking.[19]

Indeed, this interest in language is where the historian (and literary historian) perhaps comes nearest to the psychologist. Rhetoric was learned by all educated people after the Renaissance.[20] Teaching the techniques of speaking well and persuasively, rhetoric had much in common with stereotyping. It stressed the need to arouse emotion, even to the extent of moving, exciting and agitating the audience, and some rhetorical manuals encouraged orators to whip up hatred by denigrating their opponents. The author of the *Rhetorica Ad Herennium* thus argued that it was justifiable to turn adversaries into objects of hatred 'if we can pin on them such attributes as violence, lust for power, factiousness, excessive wealth, and promiscuousness'.[21] Moreover, rhetoric encouraged exaggeration and re-description, which could convert virtues into vices or insinuate that vice was being disguised under a veil of virtue. The rhetorician thus 'uncovered' the vice of an antagonist – rather in the way that a stereotype claims to reveal the truth or reality about a group or an individual representing a group. And in trying to arouse emotion, rhetoricians also sought to conjure up what Walter Lippmann, when coining the term 'stereotype' in 1922, called 'speaking pictures', in the minds of their audience. These vivid mental pictures could use metaphor to make them even more striking, but it was also permissible to use ridicule and distortion. Rhetoric also encouraged thinking – or at least speaking – in terms of the binaries so familiar to students of stereotypes. Thomas Wilson's *Arte of Rhetorique* argued that 'by contraries set together, thynges oftentimes appere greater'.[22]

For the historian, then, the psychological literature contains a number of fruitful conclusions. There is an advantage in studying stereotypes as the following: products of everyday mental processes; interactions between individual cognition and cultural constructions; influenced by media representations; ways in which every individual and every society makes sense of the complexities around them; phenomena more likely

18 M. Billig, 'Prejudice, categorization and particularization: from a perceptual to a rhetorical approach', *European Journal of Social Psychology*, 15 (1985), 79–103.

19 M. Billig, *Arguing and Thinking: a Rhetorical Approach to Social Psychology*, 2nd edn (Cambridge University Press, 1996), p. 84.

20 For an overview see J. Richards, *Rhetoric* (London: Routledge, 2007).

21 Quoted by Q. Skinner, *Reason and Rhetoric in the Philosophy of Hobbes* (Cambridge University Press, 1997), p. 131.

22 Thomas Wilson, *The Arte of Rhetorique* (London, 1553), p. 69; cf. Skinner, *Reason and Rhetoric*, p. 413.

to occur at times of tension, crisis and conflict; means of bolstering an in-group over another; being remarkable persistent over time and yet, at the periphery, responding to change; based on entitative abstractions of group rather than individual behaviour and on shared schemas and prototypes; drawing a good deal of emotive power from the associations of particular words or labels, and using language in very particular ways that reinforce stereotypical concepts. Many of these approaches have inherently historical implications or might be tested using historical data. Language, at least in it written form, can at least be recovered from the past and analysed. Historians can thus study the part played by language in the construction and maintenance of stereotypes.

Nevertheless, the lack of a historical perspective in much of the social psychology literature is striking and Billig was self-consciously aware that his approach differed radically from that adopted by many of his colleagues, to the extent that he found himself 'cut off from the wider academic world' of social psychology.[23] Perhaps because of its methodological reliance on experimenting with live subjects, almost the entire literature focuses on the present and ignores the data available from the past. Despite the recognition that stereotyping is a normal cognitive function, and hence must be common to mankind across time, there is an implicit assumption, seldom examined or even fully stated, that modern mass society has in some way been transformative, ruling out historical data as of relevance to modern conceptions. Of course, it is true that modern visual and virtual media is in some ways different to earlier print and manuscript means of communication, but the differences can easily be exaggerated and a good deal might be learned from studies of earlier stereotypical representations.

The lack of a pre-modern historical perspective pervades not only the social psychology literature but also work done by sociologists and students of the media. For example, from a media studies perspective, Michael Pickering's rather illuminating work draws on twentieth-century history but goes no further back in time.[24] The focus on the present and the very recent past may have something to do with the foundation of stereotyping as a concept: Lippmann was a political journalist trying to analyse the effects of modern mass media. Yet the lack of a historical perspective curtails some aspects of social psychology's investigations. For example, one important element of stereotypes has to do with how far and fast they can change over time (and hence also how negative prejudices

[23] Billig, *Arguing and Thinking*, pp. 6–7.

[24] M. Pickering, *Stereotyping: the Politics of Representation* (Basingstoke: Palgrave Macmillan, 2001).

can be overcome or diminished). David Schneider, for example, says that culture is important in the development of stereotypes 'but its role is often indirect and hard to document', a problem to which the historian is nevertheless accustomed and equipped with certain tools to deal with.[25] Similarly if stereotypes are not fixed but can either evolve or even be modified, as is now generally recognized in the literature, then they are inherently historical things that demand to be tracked over time.[26]

Historical approaches to stereotyping

If much of the social psychology literature is curiously ahistorical, the historical literature on stereotypes also makes little use of social psychology. The term 'stereotype' is quite often used by historians; yet it is a concept that is seldom theorized; or, more generously, it has been theorized through engagement with other cognate disciplines such as literature, linguistics, sociology, political science and anthropology rather than psychology. What follows is an attempt to sketch some of the ways in which historians have thought about the process of stereotyping and the fields of study in which historical work on stereotypes has been conducted. My focus for the latter will be on my own area of expertise, premodern history, but I hope to raise methodological issues that extend beyond this period and hence have a wider application.

There is now a considerable body of historical work that explores stereotypes in what is known as the 'early modern' period, from about 1500 to about 1800.[27] Historians have charted their pervasive use in religious controversies that raged as a result of the Protestant Reformation and the Catholics' own Reformation and Counter-Reformation. Some of the most interesting material in the British context relates to polemical constructs of the 'hotter sort of Protestants' known as Puritans[28] and the construction of prejudices against Catholics – work to which we shall

[25] Schneider, *The Psychology of Stereotyping*, p. 23.

[26] For a discussion of how stereotypes change see *ibid.*, chapter 10.

[27] An extensive bibliography for the points made in this paragraph can be found in M. Knights, 'Taking a historical turn: possible points of connection between social psychology and history', *Integrative Psychological and Behavioral Science*, 46 (2012), 584–98.

[28] P. Collinson, 'The Puritan character: Polemics and polarities in early seventeenth century English culture', in Collinson, *From Cranmer to Sancroft* (London: Continuum International, 2006); Collinson, 'Ecclesiastical vitriol: religious satire in the 1590s and the invention of puritanism', in J. Guy (ed.), *The Reign of Elizabeth I: Court and Culture in the Last Decade* (Cambridge University Press, 1994), pp. 150–70; C. Haigh, 'The character of an anti-puritan', *The Sixteenth Century Journal*, 35 (2004), 671–88; P. Lake, 'Puritan identities', *Journal of Ecclesiastical History*, 35 (1984), 112–23; P. Lake, 'Anti-puritanism: the structure of a prejudice', in K. Fincham and P. Lake (eds.), *Religious Politics in Post-Reformation England: Essays in Honour of Nicholas Tyacke* (Woodbridge: Boydell Press, 2006), pp. 80–97.

return shortly.[29] At the same time, stereotypes of unorthodox belief, such as atheism and Judaism, have been studied, though most attention has focused on witchcraft, which has provided a very rich supply of stereotypical material. Perhaps closer to the social psychology literature has been the work on race and gender. Stereotypes of women, homosexuals and blacks have been explored quite extensively, together with analysis of the poor and outcast. Work on the role of the printing press – the new technology of the pre-modern period that was later to give the stereotype its name, after a process developed in the eighteenth century to fix type – also relates to the social sciences literature in exploring how the media helped to shape collective representations. Historical work on national identity, including the emergence and fostering of a sense of Britishness, and on partisan politics also offers insights into the construction of in and out groups. Finally, some of the literary and visual techniques associated with stereotyping have been explored through studies of rhetoric and satire, both verbal and visual.

This work has both generated and borrowed from some interesting approaches, some of which have run in parallel with those of social psychology but amplify it in important ways. One influential concept has been the 'imagined community' first introduced by a historically minded political scientist, Benedict Anderson.[30] Applying his idea to nationalism, Anderson suggests that the nation was itself an imagined construct made possible by historical conditions such as the growth of the press and the erosion of the ideology of divine right monarchy. An 'imagined community' was thus a cultural construct, historically determined in the late eighteenth and early nineteenth centuries, creating a prototype replicated elsewhere.

Identity also proved a fertile concept for the literary critic Edward Said who, in his exploration of the prejudices against oriental culture, stressed the process of 'Othering' by which false images of Asian and Middle Eastern culture had been created and against which Western identity was shaped. Western writings about the Orient depict it as an irrational, weak, feminized 'Other', contrasted with the rational, strong, masculine West. Thus, the stereotypes of the oriental helped to define both East

[29] P. Lake, 'Anti-popery: the structure of a prejudice', in R. Cust and A. Hughes (eds.), *Conflict in Early Stuart England* (London: Longman, 1989), pp. 72–106; A. Milton, 'A qualified intolerance: the limits and ambiguities of early Stuart anti-Catholicism', in A. Marotti (ed.), *Catholicism and Anti-Catholicism in Early Modern English Texts* (Basingstoke: Palgrave Macmillan, 1999), pp. 85–115; A. Walsham, *Church Papists: Catholicism, Conformity and Confessional Polemic in Early Modern England* (Woodbridge: Boydell Press, 1993).

[30] B. Anderson, *Imagined communities: reflections on the origin and spread of nationalism* (London: Verso, 1991).

and West, permeated all Western attitudes and literature, and also in turn justified Western imperialism.[31] Both the 'imagined community' and the process of 'Othering' have been widely taken up in historical works, particularly (but by no means exclusively) by those concerned with issues of national identity.

The binaries at work in Said's approach were also the subject of historian Stuart Clarke's approach to the study of witchcraft.[32] Clarke analysed an early modern mindset that he argued was culturally predetermined to think in terms of opposites or 'contrarieties' and hence which readily and rationally accepted notions of divergent orthodox and unorthodox religious beliefs that were expressed in a persecuting prejudice against witches. The language of inversion, antithesis and contrariety and the habit of binary thinking that permeated contemporary attitudes supplied, he argues, the essential discursive framework within which the concept of witchcraft made sense. Moreover, he shows how this framework pervaded a variety of subjects – language, science, history, religion and politics – that collectively shaped attitudes to witches. This stress on the need to examine a holistic 'system of thought' offers a rigorous and satisfying explanation for the construction of a prejudice, though whether the binary mentality that he identified ended with the Enlightenment and hence coincided with the end of witch-hunts seems unconvincing. Indeed, a binary mentality clearly endured well beyond the end of the witch craze, as will become apparent in the third section.

Binary oppositions in religious polemic have proved a particularly rich source for historians, because of the crisis created by the Protestant and Catholic reformations in the sixteenth and seventeenth centuries. Protestant demonization of the Catholic other, and Catholic or moderate Protestant hatred of Protestant zealotry produced in Britain the powerful and enduring prejudices of 'anti-popery' and 'anti-puritanism'. Peter Lake, in an influential article examining the 'construction of a prejudice', suggested that 'anti-popery' (i.e. hostility not just to the Catholic Church but also to the political and cultural authority it wielded) was a complex entity, made up of different strands of argument and narrative. The various elements could be combined by different individuals and groups into different versions of 'popery', thereby constructing different versions of the groups defining themselves against it. Thus 'anti-popery' and 'anti-puritanism', Lake argued, were enduring but not fixed stereotypes: aspects that were central to one polemical moment or group identity

[31] E. Said, *Orientalism* (New York: Pantheon Books, 1978).

[32] S. Clark, 'Inversion, misrule and the meaning of witchcraft', *Past and Present*, 87 (1980), 98–127; S. Clark, *Thinking with Demons: the Idea of Witchcraft in Early Modern Europe* (Oxford University Press, 1997).

might, in different circumstances, or in the hands of other polemicists, become peripheral. 'We are not dealing with coherent ideological positions, but rather with constellations of ideas, attributes and narratives, which could be arranged into a number of differently inflected syntheses, to meet a variety of polemical circumstances and forward a range of often very different, indeed sometimes mutually exclusive political purposes.'[33] Such a view makes a stereotype a highly fluid, contingent entity, constituted by many different parts, each of which might be stressed at any one time, depending on the context, with the result that the stereotype could and did change over time.[34] In short, Lake argues, the stereotype has a history, an argument entirely compatible with, and reinforcing of, the conclusions of social psychologists Billig, Potter and Wetherell.

The role of polemic in the construction of anti-popery and anti-puritanism highlights the importance of the new technology of the printing press in the construction, articulation and absorption of stereotypes but there is relatively little agreement amongst historians about how far the press fabricated stereotypes. For many historians of the pre-modern period oral and manuscript cultures were as important in shaping popular attitudes, and oral, print and scribal cultures worked symbiotically rather than in tension with one another.[35] Stereotypes were thus created through conversation as well as through the media that represented or replicated it. For other historians, however, the print revolution, with its capacity to reproduce the same text more extensively, penetrated all social levels and provided a shared set of cultural attitudes.[36]

Historians, when invoking the term 'stereotype', have thus made use of a variety of notions and approaches: an imagined community, 'Othering', binary mentalities, the manipulability and mutability of stereotypes for polemical purposes, the nature of print, the role of conversation and the power of words. These approaches in some way overlap with or touch on

[33] Lake, 'Anti-puritanism', pp. 82 and 96; Lake, 'Anti-popery', pp. 72–83 and 98–103.

[34] Lake does not, however, see the stereotype as full of agency, creating what it sought to attack, although another eminent historian of the Reformation, Patrick Collinson, clearly did: for Collinson anti-puritanism helped to create Puritanism. For Collinson, understanding the stereotype is essential to understanding the past, since stereotypes were not simply a reflection of antipathies but helped to constitute them.

[35] A. Fox, *Oral and Literate Culture in England 1500–1700* (Oxford University Press, 2000); A. Fox and D. Woolf (eds.), *The Spoken Word: Oral Culture in Britain, 1500–1850* (Manchester: Manchester University Press, 2002); H. Love, *Scribal Publication in seventeenth century England* (Oxford: Clarendon Press, 1993).

[36] E. L. Eisenstein, *The Printing Press as an Agent of Change* (2 vols.) (Cambridge University Press, 1979). For tensions over the role of the press see also D. Lemmings and C. Walker (eds.), *Moral Panics and the Law in Early Modern England* (Basingstoke: Palgrave Macmillan, 2009), which examines the 'moral panic' model advocated by Stanley Cohen.

those adopted by psychologists. 'Othering' and 'out-groups', or 'imagined communities' and 'social representations' are not too dissimilar and there is a common interest in binaries and the role of the media. Similarly, the capacity of words to shape cognition is recognized in both the social psychology literature and the historical-literary works that investigate rhetorical practices. To be sure, there are interesting differences. Abric's stable core and changeable periphery, for example, has something in common with Lake's notion of constellations of attributes that could be arranged and rearranged to stress different elements, but Lake's model has a far less stable, and more manipulable, core than Abric allows for. Yet it is clear that historians and social psychologists are often pursuing similar problems from slightly different perspectives and that historical work (both in terms of approach and data) might greatly enrich the perspective of the currently very present-centred psychologist.

Reform and reformers in eighteenth- and early nineteenth-century Britain

This final section will attempt to bring together some of the historical and psychological approaches in order to examine stereotypes that are part of a polemical battle. Building on the linguistic approach taken by both sets of secondary literature, I will show how rival groups sought to 'capture' key terms and attributes in order to win popular support. The analysis aims to offer a dynamic, contested and even dialectical explanation for how stereotypes evolve. In this version, alternative and competing visions of particular groups struggled for the control of the stereotype, in order to achieve positive rather than negative associations. They did this by trying to wrest from opponents the usage of a positively charged word or attribute to attach to their cause; or by trying to attach a negatively charged word to their opponents' identity. The two sides engaged *in a contest* with each other, so that there were different constructions of the same phenomenon, even at the same time. These different constructions were necessarily closely related to one another: the positive and negative stereotypes were two different representations of the same phenomenon that were fought over in a struggle that itself shaped how the two sides interacted. The stereotyping process was thus dialogic, as the two groups responded to each other's interventions.

The section also seeks to make methodological points about the importance of images in the process of stereotyping. Lippmann's 'pictures in the mind' can be taken more literally than he perhaps intended, for images can embody stereotypical attributes, not least because they could also contain or echo the linguistic construction of the stereotype. The pre-modern mind, like the modern one, was also conditioned to thinking visually. Even if Protestantism was distrustful of religious imagery, the Renaissance 'emblem' was a ubiquitous genre, combining an instructive image of a concept or keyword with a set of verse that explained the image's iconography. The 'emblem' was still in use at the beginning of the eighteenth century and continued to influence the representation of concepts. Increasingly, however, a new form, the graphic satire, was becoming a useful vehicle for the visual manipulation of stereotypes. Initially these graphic satires emulated the emblem, with titles, images and texts; but increasingly the explanatory text became minimized or embedded within the image itself. By the late eighteenth century, such images were a common part of polemical battles and provided a rich source for the study of stereotypes.[37] Fortunately, the superb British Museum website, which contains most of the extensive collection of prints and drawings, is searchable by keyword, so that such analyses are possible.[38] Even if visual material is not as well catalogued as the printed word, we still have enough to show the merits of using such material. In other words, a study of stereotypes offers a way not only of bringing history and social psychology together but also of uniting them with other disciplines, such as art history but also sociology, media studies and literary criticism.[39] Such a multi-disciplinary approach, it is hoped, will not only be of appeal to a wide audience but also show the large degree of common ground between the disciplines, as well as the gaps and differences between them.

I shall illustrate these points through an analysis of images of 'reform' and reformers in the late eighteenth and early nineteenth centuries. 'Reform' became an important term in the second half of the eighteenth century, though it continued to resonate with the legacy of 'reformation' that had been used to describe the religious changes of the sixteenth and seventeenth centuries.[40] The term 'reform' increasingly became associated with parliamentary reform, though it could also embrace other forms too (such as 'economical reform', which meant the state's, especially the Crown's, financial and patronage structures and influence). Reform was a wide-reaching but also a disturbing and divisive process

[37] V. Gatrell, *City of Laughter: Sex and Satire in Eighteenth-Century London* (London: Atlantic Books, 2006).

[38] See British Museum's database search page at www.britishmuseum.org/research/search_the_collection_database.aspx [accessed 15 February 2013].

[39] The role of visual culture in a history of concepts is explored in I. Hampsher-Monk, K. Tilmans and F. van Vree (eds.), *History of Concepts: Comparative Perspectives* (Amsterdam: Amsterdam University Press, 1998).

[40] For an excellent history of the term see J. Innes, '"Reform" in English Public Life: the fortunes of a word', in A. Burns and J. Innes (eds.), *Rethinking the Age of Reform: Britain 1780–1850* (Cambridge University Press, 2003), pp. 71–97.

because it raised so many questions about what line of reform to take and how best to pursue it. Reform was thus a polarizing process that encouraged binary representations to depict advocates as either good or bad. Reform and reformers were endowed by sympathizers and critics with very different characteristics: the stereotype of the reformer was contested. My concern here is less with the history of reform and more with how it can shed light on stereotyping processes.

Anti-reform graphic satire was common in the 1790s, when opponents of reform sought to associate it with what they saw as the horrors of the French Revolution. In other words, this was one of those 'moments of crisis' that so often produced and hardened stereotypes. Such images also often associate reform with the controversial politician and leader of the Whig Party, Charles James Fox, who often voiced critiques of the existing system and whose distinctive face and perceived vices became associated with the reformer. An individual was therefore used to epitomize the group and to make the threat posed by the group seem real – here the stereotype was less of a group than of a particular individual who was made to symbolize the group, thereby enabling the group to be tainted with his alleged vices. The negative depiction of reform also involved embedding the word in a network of associated terms, each of which had its own set of associations and histories. Very often, as the following section makes clear, these terms were the abstractions noted by proponents of the Linguistic Category Model discussed earlier. Thus although reform was tied closely to the Fox and his vices, the stereotype was universalized through the suggestion that the abstract traits depicted in the images, by means of keywords or labels, were shared ones among other reformers. We can also discern rhetorical ways of thinking and arguing being invoked, with the articulation of counter-arguments within these prints and a flexibility in how the stereotype came to be used.

These points can be illustrated by analysis of the images themselves.

Figure 12.1 depicts Fox as the devilish serpent tempting John Bull with a maggoty apple labelled 'reform'. Other diseased apples on the wizened tree (which is labelled 'Opposition', and shown as having roots of 'ambition', 'envy' and 'disappointment', suggesting that personal slights rather than principle were the principal drivers of the reformist cause) construct a network of abstract, associated pejorative terms: 'slavery', 'atheism', 'blasphemy', 'democracy', 'plunder', 'revolution', 'Whig club', 'deism', 'impiety' and 'conspiracy'. In the background, by contrast, is a flourishing tree, with a trunk of 'justice', with branches of 'law' and 'religion', with a crown in its leaves and healthy apples labelled with very positive abstractions: 'happiness', 'security' and 'freedom'. John Bull, in the foreground, collects the sound applies, indicating, should the viewer

Figure 12.1. James Gillray, *The Tree of Liberty* (1798). BM Satires 9214 © Trustees of the British Museum

Figure 12.2. Thomas Rowlandson, *The Contrast* (1792). BM Satires 8149 © Trustees of the British Museum

be in any doubt, which tree bore the best fruit, a message also driven home by the title, which reinforces the association between reform and the undermining of 'liberty'.

The image thus works with a binary divide: reform is associated with a list of negatively charged terms, whilst the healthy tree in the background suggests that the status quo, in terms of the law, Crown and church, led to a flourishing state.[41] The negatively charged, abstract terms occur frequently in other images, often in the same grouping, suggesting a shared set of associations. Thus many of the image's anti-reform 'hot words' relate to irreligion – 'atheism', 'blasphemy', 'impiety' and 'deism' (the belief in a non-Christian god) – and were contrasted with the flourishing 'religion' in the background. In late eighteenth-century Britain religious feelings were particularly emotive: the old hostility against Puritans and dissenters (those who challenged the established Church of England) had plenty of vigour, re-animated both by attempts to reform the church and by the French Revolution's attack on orthodox Christianity. A parallel

41 For the importance of binaries and inversions see Gustav Jahoda, 'Beyond Stereotypes', *Culture and Psychology*, 7 (2001), 309–20.

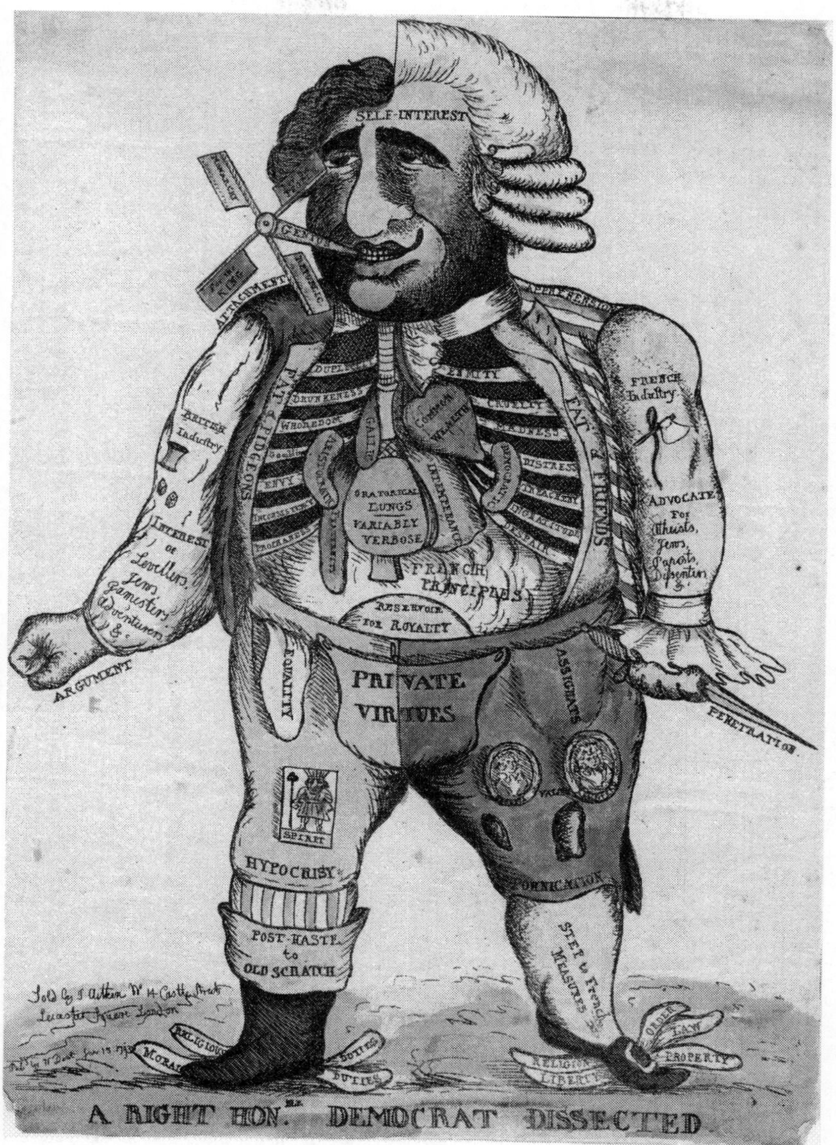

Figure 12.3. William Dent, *A Right Hon. Democrat Dissected* (1793). BM Satires 8291 © Trustees of the British Museum

Figure 12.4. George Cruikshank, *Death or Liberty! Or Britannia & the Virtues of the Constitution in danger of Violation from the gr[ea]t Political Libertine. Radical reform!* (1819). BM Satires 13279 © Trustees of the British Museum [cf. *A second sight view of the blessings of radical reform BM* Satires 11328]

image by a different artist, Thomas Rowlandson, strikingly echoes the network of terms used by Gillray and also widens it to include other associated terms (see Figure 12.2).

In Figure 12.2, 'French liberty' is thus, as in the Gillray print, associated with 'atheism', and contrasted, in binary fashion (indeed, as though these are almost literally two sides of the same coin), with the 'religion' and 'morality' associated with 'English liberty'. Similarly the 'plunder' associated with reform in the Gillray images is echoed by the 'national and private ruin' in the Rowlandson image; and the pejorative 'revolution' in the Gillray is the theme of the Rowlandson print. It is interesting to note that all the positively charged terms used by Gillray – religion, law, justice, happiness – were also deployed by Rowlandson, suggesting a tightly constructed network of positively charged, emotive abstractions. Here, then, was a 'core' of attributes. Liberty, it seems from these images, does not need reform.

The charged network of terms apparent in the Gillray satire is also reminiscent of a third image, by William Dent, showing Fox as a

Figure 12.5. *The Reformers' Attack on the Old Rotten Tree* (1831). BM Satires 16650 © Trustees of the British Museum

'democrat' and also further widening the cluster of associated terms (see Figure 12.3).

Figure 12.3 makes use of the terms 'envy' and 'ingratitude', which had formed the roots of Gillray's diseased tree, as labels for Fox's ribs (as do 'madness', 'treachery' and 'cruelty', which feature in the Rowlandson's depiction of revolutionary liberty), and his right arm carries the maxim 'Advocate for Atheists, Jews, Papists and Dissenters', reinforcing the association with those who were thought to attack the Church of England. 'Religion', 'liberty', 'property', 'law' and 'morality' are again being crushed under Fox's feet. The image also suggests (as rhetoric taught and as many other stereotypes did) that Fox's external persona hid a conspiratorial inner one. Asch and Zukier argue that people distinguish between an inner and outer person, in order to resolve inconsistencies – thus a person might exhibit a trait on the outside but the perceivers might conclude it did not reflect the true, inner person, and hence there was no need to change their mental stereotype.[42] Hence 'hypocrisy' is labelled clearly on Fox's knee.

[42] S. E. Asch and H. Zukier, 'Thinking about persons', *Journal of Personality and Social Psychology*, 46 (1984), 1230–40.

The Managers LAST KICK,

OR, THE DISTRUCTION OF THE

BOROUGHMONGERS.

Printed and Sold by J. QUICK, Bowling Green Lane, Clerkenwell, where Hawkers and Shopkeepers may be Supplied.—PRICE ONE PENNY

AIR.—Adam and Eve.

ALL you that dwell in Britains Isle now,
I pray one moment list awhile now,
We soon shall see some alteration,
In every quarter of the Nation,
Reform you know is England's watchword,
And William is a noble Landlord,
With the lies of his servants he'll not disemble,
And he will make the Boroughmongers tremble.

CHORUS.

Oppression shortly will be ended,
And we shall see the times soon mended.

We will no longer be in malencholy,
Behold John Bull so fat and jolly,
There's Will the Landlord now I say sir,
Swiftly carried by his noble Grey sir;
There's 8 in Bedlam peeping through the grating,
And Russell's Purge is operating,
The Tories who for gold will barter,
While England bawles out Magna Charta.

There's gallant Althorpe next you see sir,
With his friend Lord Melbourne does agree sir,
There's Lawyer Brougham seldom sleeping,
The rubbish out he's cleverly sweeping,
There's Hobhouse and his daddy Frank too,
Wood, Waithman, and Hume will play a prank too,
They'll with others play a tune sir,
Upon the 20th. day of June sir.

Poor Soldier Bob does now bewail sir,
With a Kettle fastened to his tail sir,
Another Tory has had a fall sir,
In Boro'bridge he'll Weather-all sir;
There's A——r for old Sarum,
If stuck in a field the crows would scare him,
Poor Sadler is gone among the flats sir,
In Tamworth P——l's confined in a den of rats sir.

There's poor old Bags alas, lamenting,
There's wicked A——r too repenting,
There's S———t got the typus fever,
There's V——t too that sad deceiver;

There's O'Connel for the Union bawling,
For the nation's rights aloud he's calling
There's Hunt at last that has long been clacking,
Now smothered in his Matchless Blacking.

King William and his men so clever,
Does nobly shout Reform for ever,
To them we look for our protection,
They nobly gain'd the last Election;
We are sure Reform will now be granted,
And that is the thing we long have wanted,
With joy the King will over whelm
The nation, while he guides the helm.

William is a Sailor bold sir,
And on the waves he has often roll'd sir,
He wants no Marquesses wives or Daughters,
To spend his time at Virginea waters;
He goes to neither Parks or Races,
A slobbering ladies' pretty faces,
He guides the helm and keeps his station,
And knows what is wanted through the nation.

We shall no longer be oppressed sir,
We shall see the times of Old Queen Bess sir,
Of tyranny we will soon be empty,
And we shall live in peace and plenty,
We have a monarch that's a man sir,
And one that well can rule the land sir,
All goodness ever does possess him,
So let us rejoice and sing god bless him.

CHORUS.

So now my simple song is ended,
I hope that you are not offended.

A DIALOGUE BETWEEN

JOHN BULL AND HIS FRIEND,

Concerning the Row at the King's Theatre with the Manager and the upstart over grown Performers.

Ah! friend John, how do you do—pray explain the meaning why you look so merry.

J. B. Why at the MANAGERS LAST KICK to be sure, which has made a fine Kick up, as well as being a Kick toes the Rogues who were always picking my pocket.

Fd. Why indeed John it must have been a pleasant FARCE which could have taken such an effect of You!

J. B. Farce! No no, it was no farce, but a first rate Comedy

Fd. Indeed! what was the Plot?—

J. B. REFORM! But it was so well managed, that it puzzled some of the wisest heads among the performers to tell what part to take; all the Characters were well drawn—

Fd. Why, when did it make its first appearance?

J. B. The first time that I had an opportunity to applaud it, was on the 1st. of March, when the performers had the impudence to dispute the Manager's having it announced, but he was determined, when some of the company who feared the loss of their engagement, kicked up such a row that I was afraid the piece would have been damned—but I supported it, and so did some of my friends, we therefore had it repeated.

Fd. Bravo! that was right, but who dared dispute when you and the Manager approved of the piece?

J. B. Who! a hoste of Rascals, and some of my servants who were put in trust by me, as well as others who had received good Salaries and Great Friendship from the Manager

Fd. Indeed! Who were they?

J. B. Why Nosey, Lemon Peel, Harriot Wilson's Luttrell, sweet smelling Rose, merry Andrew Allweather, the Old Rider and his Saddle—r, the Taylor, Smith, Blacking Maker, and last though not least, the favourite Will. old Bill's Son: but it would take too much time to tell all their names, for there were no less than 299 who conducted themselves worse towards their Master than a set of Colliers.

Fd. That the Blacking man should turn his Coat is no wonder, but I am certainly astonished at Will; what an ungrateful fellow after having his Salary raised by the Manager and promising so many times to behave himself well;—well, the old saying is a true one, "that ingratitude is worst than witchcraft." I hope they were all discharged?

J. B. Yes they were, but the Manager added a New Scene at the end of the piece—he got upon an Old Grey, with a Russell and Brougham on each side, and a hoste of staunch fellows behind; he then had a Scene of a high rock at the bottom of which was the SLOUGH OF DESPOND, he then began to prance on his good Old Grey and with his wip drove the refactory ones into the Muddy Slough which he had well filled to receive them.

Fd. Bravo! Well done John, and Manager William.

Figure 12.6. Charles Jameson Grant, *The Managers Last Kick*, or, the Distruction of the Boroughmongers (*c.*1830–5). BM Satires 17342 © Trustees of the British Museum

Figure 12.7. Anonymous print of 1832. *BM Satires 16924* © Trustees of the British Museum

One powerful means of creating a sense of a stereotypical in-group against reform was the use of Britannia (seen in Figure 12.2) and John Bull (in Figure 12.1). The representation of Britannia as a beautiful virgin seated on a rock with shield and spear first appeared on a coin in 1672, when Britain was threatened by Dutch power. The ravishing of Britannia in Figure 12.4 by a skeleton of death wearing only a cloak of 'radical reform' (the pejorative adjective further charging the word), despite her shield of 'religion' and a fiery sword of 'the laws', was clearly another means of invoking the props of 'British liberty' depicted in Figure 12.2. The French cap of liberty, given such prominence in Figure 12.1 as a sign of the excessive and foreign notion of liberty associated with reform, is again apparent on the figure of death in Figure 12.4. Similarly, Figure 12.1 used the figure of John Bull, much to the same effect. John Bull was the stereotype invented at the beginning of the eighteenth century in order to symbolize British national identity and common sense.[43] John Bull's resistance of French liberty/reform is clear.

In these images, then, we have a tight network of associated terms, both positively and negatively charged, that shape the way in which a bundle of concepts – reform, liberty, Britishness – were represented both linguistically and visually. Yet the core sets of values were not stable and could be appropriated, even by reformers. Reformers contested the notion that their cause meant revolution and a threat to property, law, justice and religion. Indeed, they suggested that without reform these good things were threatened. Thus the positively charged associations were appropriated by the reformers from their critics. This process can be demonstrated in more detail through another set of images.

In Figure 12.5 the image of the diseased tree (powerfully deployed *against* reform in Figure 12.1) is now used to represent the rotten parliamentary boroughs that created an unjust political system in which 'cormorants' nested – a bird associated for several centuries with greed and corruption. As with Figure 12.1, a binary 'good' is depicted in the background, showing 'Constitution Hill', the monarchy and John Bull bathed in sunlight. Bull's reconfiguration as a supporter of reform underlines how Figure 12.5 inverts Figure 12.1's message by recruiting the positively charged Bull to its cause. In the foreground the axe of 'reform' is wielded against the rotten tree.[44] Reform could thus be depicted as loyal and pro-monarchy, and hence as the means to secure law and peace.

Figure 12.6 shows King William IV riding 'the good old Grey' (an allusion to the reformist Earl Grey), with 'reform' exhaling from the horse's

[43] For an excellent history of John Bull see M. Taylor, 'John Bull and the iconography of public opinion in England c.1712–1929', *Past and Present*, 134 (1992), 93–128.

[44] A remarkably similar image, Henry Heath's *The Tree of Corruption* (1831), uses very much the same idea of the reform bill cutting down corruption. See also *The champions of reform destroying the monster of corruption* (1831), which shows the monster of corruption being attacked. Other images use the idea of the reform bill as a broom sweeping away the rotten boroughs (e.g. Henry Heath, *The Revolution of 1831* (1831, BM Satires 16690) and George Cruikshank, *Sweeping Measure* (1831, BM Satires 16612)).

mouth, and the ground on which they stand is 'Magna Charter', the embodiment of the legal tradition. Whereas in the 1790s reform was stereotyped as a threat to law and the monarchy, by the 1830s those who *opposed* reform were now stereotyped in the same way. What had previously been depicted as French and anti-patriotic could now be represented as British and patriotic. This is a point forcibly made by an image of Britannia with a banner of reform (see Figure 12.7).

Indeed the symbolism of Figure 12.7, with Britannia, the ship of state and the British lion, is almost the exact reverse of earlier anti-reform images such as Figure 12.2, with reform now associated with the positive attributes depicted there.

Conclusion

The first two sections of this chapter examined ways in which social psychology might be useful to history, and how history might in turn be useful to social psychology. The third section offered a case study that sought to bring these two perspectives together.

The evidence presented in the case study supports many of the findings made by social psychologists about the nature of in-groups and out-groups, about the persistence of binaries as a way of thinking, about the importance of the media in constructing and disseminating stereotypes, and about the importance of networks of abstract, highly charged and emotive terms. But it also modifies and challenges some conclusions. First, the role played in stereotypes by 'state' verbs – that describe states of being – might be extended to include charged abstract concepts or keywords such as 'liberty', 'happiness', 'prosperity' and 'religion'. Verbs were thus only part of a much wider linguistic framework that helped to construct, maintain and change stereotypes. Recovering how such keywords worked in relation to stereotypes is thus a fertile area for research, one which can (and perhaps can only) be explored in an interdisciplinary fashion. Second, the notion that stereotypes have a fixed, unchanging 'core' with a periphery that is more responsive to context may hold true for some stereotypes – and it may be that gender and race are less subject to change – but others are more fluid and malleable, manipulable by groups that sought to wrest control of key concepts, symbols and terms.[45]

Above all, the diverging representations of reform suggest that stereotypes could be, and were, contested in polemical battles in which both

[45] This is related to but also seems to go beyond the 'attitudinal ambivalence' discussed in K. Jonas, P. Broemer and M. Diehl, 'Attitudinal ambivalence', *European Review of Social Psychology*, 11 (2000), 35–74.

sides sought to appropriate key attributes and symbols for their own side. In other words, stereotypes were not so much fixed as part of a moving battle, in which very different constructions could be pitted against one another and in which groups could appropriate attributes from each other. The findings of the case study of 'reform' support Lake's suggestion, supported by Billig, that stereotypes were complex entities with histories that are worth charting, and that they are both historical (being clearly pervasive well before the advent of modern mass society) and have histories that change over time. It would, of course, be interesting to know more about the particular terms and symbols that helped to constitute them, since these also clearly had histories of their own. Some of the attributes associated with the reform controversy had short histories – 'radical', in its modern sense of seeking to overturn the established order, for example, was an eighteenth-century term – but others, such as 'corruption' or 'liberty', reached far back in time and even to different contexts. We might also chart histories of the vices and virtues that played such a prominent role in stereotype construction. In other words, there is a historical legacy of charged words, concepts and symbols that it would be useful to reconstruct.

It may, of course, be that polemical battles between two groups, both of which had access to print media, resulted in slightly unusual kinds of stereotype. More often, it might be said, stereotypes reflect a dominant majority demonizing and exercising power over a minority. There is something to be said for that view. On the other hand, the reformers who in the 1790s were very much in a minority managed over time to build a majority and reform was enacted in 1832. The changes in the stereotype of reformers might therefore have a wider resonance. Not only do they highlight the importance of a historical view of the evolution of a stereotype, they also indicate the degree to which stereotypes can be contested and challenged, even by out-groups, and that, when successful, this process involves the reconfiguration and appropriation of networks of attributes. Control of context-dependent key terms, traits and symbols is, history suggests, contestable.

This chapter has sought to highlight the importance of analysing stereotypes historically and the advantages that might exist were social psychologists to do so more systematically than they have done so far. Similarly, historians might do more to problematize how far cognitive processes changed over time, acknowledge stereotyping as a normal rather than aberrant or irrational process, and also be more sensitive to how different types of language shaped the mental pictures created by them (an issue that should also draw in expertise from linguists as well and offers an area of common concern across the disciplines). Given shared interests in the public sphere, the arts of persuasion and the formation of attitudes, historians might also explore the social psychology literature on these themes in order to distinguish between fixed or durable social phenomena and those subject to historical context, an enterprise that could harness the energies of both groups of scholars.

13 Psychology, the Viennese legacy and the construction of identity in the former Yugoslavia

Cathie Carmichael

With its proximity to Vienna and the intellectual world of the late Habsburg monarchy, a knowledge and consciousness about psychology was present at the inception of the first Yugoslavia in 1918.[1] A century later, the influence of the discipline still permeates the arts, popular culture and the discourses of everyday life in the successor states. Forms of self-deprecation and stereotypes about ethnic groups, especially about the people from the Dinaric region and Muslims, have had a profound impact on the countries of the former Yugoslavia. The continual interplay between intellectuals and the public has meant that life has at times imitated science.

In 1898 Sigmund Freud went to Hercegovina as part of a medical delegation. This visit and his excursion to Kotor were mentioned on several occasions in his later work. Freud, who had a deep interest and engagement with the Mediterranean world, was one of many Austrian visitors who travelled overland from Ragusa (Dubrovnik) to the hinterland after the administration of the region had been taken over by the Habsburg Monarchy in 1878.[2] It was in Trebinje, a town with a mixed Muslim and Christian population, that he began to think about his first essay on the mechanics of the unconscious.[3] Peter Swales has argued that this excursion saw the development of Freud's notion of Signorelli parapraxis

[1] I am grateful for discussions with the editors of this volume, Mat Savelli, Chris Jones, Maja Šimunjak, Mark Thompson, Richard Mills, Mike Bowker and Marko Živković, on this subject.

[2] G. Ricci, *Le città di Freud: Itinerari, emblemi, orizzonti di un viaggiatore* (Milan: Jaca Book, 1995), p. 69.

[3] D. I. Bjelić, *Normalizing the Balkans: Geopolitics of Psychoanalysis and Psychiatry* (Farnham: Ashgate, 2011), p. 38. See also D. Bjelić, 'Madness as a political factor', *Psychoanalysis, Culture & Society*, 15 (2010), 20–36. By 1879, the Muslim population of Hercegovina had declined to only 24 per cent, from a much higher percentage before the loss of Ottoman power. See J. McCarthy, 'Archival sources concerning Serb rebellions in Bosnia 1875–76', in M. Koller and K. H. Karpat (eds.), *Ottoman Bosnia. A History in Peril* (Madison: University of Wisconsin Press), pp. 204 and 145.

(often referred to as the 'Freudian slip').[4] It is also likely that Freud began to see sexual drive differently at this time and this change in attitude is reflected in his own sexual habits and practices. He made a personal decision that one should always seize the moment ('carpe diem') as life is short and death imminent.[5] According to Freud's notes, one local patient had told his doctor, 'when that no longer works, life has no worth'. He also observed that 'These Muslims [*Türken*] value the sexual drive above all else and if their drive fails, they fall into a despondency [*Verzweiflung*] which makes a striking contrast to their resignation in the face of death.'[6] Many years later, Alija Izetbegović used the Viennese psychoanalyst to defend his religious world-view: 'Freud proved that sexuality cannot be destroyed but only repressed: the repressed sexual urge brings about even more troubles. However sublime the Christian postulate for chastity and restraint is, the Islamic idea of a controlled and moderate sexual life suits man better as it recognises the issue.'[7]

By the time of his visit to Hercegovina, Freud was clearly working towards his celebrated theory concerning the drive for creativity or oblivion (*Eros* and *Mortido*, which was later referred to as *Thanatos*). He was fascinated by the fatalism of the Bosnian Muslims, recounting that the carers of a mortally sick person would answer 'Sir what is there to be said? I know that if he could have been saved [*retten*], then you would have done so.'[8] In Kotor, he encountered a man in the market who had told him that his name was 'Popović', which Freud somewhat absurdly equated with a rude German children's word, assessing that the man had blushed when he told him his name.[9] Given that Popov or variants of the name are ubiquitous in the Orthodox world, Freud's speculation reveals his *naivety* about local culture as well as his urge to extrapolate about areas well beyond his real expertise.

Freud's view of Muslim sexuality was one of professional curiosity, but was also dwelt upon in a less positive light by Yugoslav writers, many of whom trained in the Habsburg Monarchy. Vladimir Dvorniković completed a doctorate in psychology in Vienna as early as 1911 and subsequently published *Karakterologija Jugoslovena* (*The Study of Character of the Yugoslavs*) in Belgrade in 1939. His assessment of the legacy of

4 P. Swales, 'Freud, death and sexual pleasures. On the psychical mechanism of Dr. Sigm. Freud'. *Arc de Cercle*, 1 (2003), 4–74.

5 S. Freud, *Die Traumdeutung* (Leipzig/Vienna: Franz Deuticke, 1914), pp. 156–7.

6 S. Freud, *Zur Psychopathologie des Alltagslebens (Über Vergessen, Versprechen, Vergreifen, Aberglaube und Irrtum)* (Berlin: Verlag von S. Karger, 1904), pp. 5–6.

7 A. Izetbegović, *Islam between East and West* (Selangor: Islamic Book Trust, 1984), p. 234.

8 Freud, *Zur Psychopathologie*, p. 5.

9 'Er nannte mir seinen Namen und drückte mir errötend die Hand', Freud, *Die Traumdeutung*, p. 156.

the Ottoman period was that it was a 'black historical mire' of 'trouble, lament, tears and shame' which had left its mark on the Yugoslavs.[10] Similarly, Čedomil Mitrinović, who published *Naši muslimani* (*Our Muslims*) in Belgrade in 1926, attributed virtues to Orthodox Christianity, while viewing the impact of Islam as negative. The negative influences included 'vanity, wastefulness, lasciviousness, sensuality, rooted mysticism, and fatalism'.[11] Two year earlier in 1924, the young Ivo Andrić had completed a doctoral dissertation in Graz on the development of spiritual life in Bosnia under Turkish rule. This work is widely thought to have encouraged the negative views of the Islamic legacy.[12]

Dušan I. Bjelić has suggested that '[s]tories about Christian Muslim bloodshed still permeated the atmosphere in Trebinje when Freud arrived'.[13] The link between violence, sexuality and the Balkan Muslim–Christian border was forged in the rest of Europe, as the influence of the Ottoman Empire and Islam waned. '[W]orks of popular culture – including some that combined politics and pornography in the most astonishing ways – abounded', as Irvin Çemıl Schick has argued.[14] One of the best known of these texts was Gottfried Sieben's *Balkangreuel* (*Balkan Cruelty*) published in Vienna in 1909. Pirate editions followed in English and Czech and the book was reprinted as a series of postcards. The lithographs typically depict mass rapes of (naked) Christian women by Balkan Muslims in fezzes.[15] In many of the lithographs, the rapists are already assumed to have killed the local men, whose bodies (stabbed or hanged) are also in the pictures. In one, the mass rape takes place in an Orthodox Church while the bound priest looks on helplessly.

Although partially wrested from Viennese control in 1918, the new Yugoslav state continued to look towards Austria for cultural influence. Many Serbs who had never lived under the Habsburgs had studied in Central Europe both in the decades before the First World War and afterwards, and were quite 'Europeanized'.[16] The first use of the term 'psychology' (coined from the Greek words to mean 'study of the soul')

10 V. Dvorniković, *Karakterologija Jugoslovena* (Belgrade: Kosmos 1939), p. 117.

11 B. Aleksov, 'Adamant and treacherous. Serbian historians on religious conversions' in Pål Kolstø (ed.), *Myths and Boundaries in South-Eastern Europe* (London: Hurst, 2005), p. 175.

12 I. Andrić, *Die Entwicklung des geistigen Leben in Bosnien unter der Entwicklung der türkischen Herrschaft* (University of Graz, 1924).

13 Bjelić, *Normalizing the Balkans*, p. 37.

14 I. Schick, 'Christian maidens, Turkish ravishers: the sexualization of national conflict in the late Ottoman period', in Amila Buturović and I. Schick (eds.), *Women in the Ottoman Balkans: Gender, Culture, and History* (London: I. B. Tauris, 2007), p. 273.

15 Schick 'Christian maidens, Turkish ravishers', p. 292.

16 On Belgrade, see D. Stojanović, *Kaldrma i asfalt: Urbanizacija i evropeizacija Beograda 1890–1914* (Belgrade: Udruženje za društvenu istoriju, 2008).

is often attributed to the Dalmatian humanist Marko Marulić, whose *Psichiologia de ratione animae humanae* was published in Venice in the early sixteenth century.[17] However it was the discipline of psychology as it developed in Vienna during the late Habsburg Monarchy that was to have the greatest impact on Yugoslav ways of thinking about themselves. Many Central and Eastern Europeans were keen enthusiasts for this new language and science of human nature, which had developed in the German language universities in the late nineteenth century.[18] In *La Péninsule balkanique* (1918), Serbian academician Jovan Cvijić, who had received his doctorate from the University of Vienna in 1893, developed some of his ideas about the character of the South Slavs. He argued that men from the Dinaric mountain region were forceful, brave and had a long memory. By linking their own daily struggles to a kind of collective historical 'memory' of the medieval defeat by the Ottomans, they had an almost inbred sense of revenge on Muslims, an innate concept of freedom and bloody-minded independence.[19] Cvijić's construction essentially cut across the Orthodox–Catholic divide in the Dinaric region, which runs through Croatia, Hercegovina and Montenegro.

Discourses about the Dinaric region had a long vintage. In part they have their origins in the region's liminality, for centuries on the edges of the Habsburg, Adriatic and Ottoman worlds. When individuals fled from the firmer political authority of Venice, Vienna or Istanbul, they sometimes escaped to the mountains, creating what one anthropologist has called a 'refuge area'.[20] In this region, generally dominated by transhumance, pastoralism, banditry and smuggling, autonomous traditions prevailed. By the mid nineteenth century, a juxtaposition between the Turk and the Christian bandit or *hajduk* from the Dinaric region was already popular in Croatian literature.[21] As Marko Živković has argued, once the stereotypes about the Dinaric people were made a topic of scholarly writing, they 'percolated back to the popular level, if not directly through Cvijić's writings, then from his

[17] K. Marinković, 'The history of psychology in former Yugoslavia: an overview', *Journal of the History of the Behavioral Sciences*, 28 (1992), 240–51.

[18] J. Janoušek and I. Sirotkina, 'Psychology in Russia and Central and Eastern Europe', in *The Cambridge History of Science* (Cambridge University Press, 2003), vol. VII, p. 447.

[19] J. Cvijić, *La Péninsule Balkanique. Geographie Humaine* (Paris: A. Colin, 1918), pp. 281–379.

[20] C. Boehm, *Montenegrin Social Organization and Values: Political Ethnography of a Refuge Area Tribal Adaptation* (New York: AMS Press, 1983).

[21] M. Šolić, 'Women in Ottoman Bosnia as seen through the eyes of Luka Botić, a Christian poet', *in* A. Buturović and I. Ç. Schlick (eds.), *Women in the Ottoman Balkans: Gender, Culture, and History* (London: I. B. Tauris, 2007), p. 307. On the development of the cult of the *hajduk*, see I. Žanić, *Prevarena povijest. Guslarska estrada, kult Hajduka i rat u Hrvatskoj i Bosni i Hercegovini 1990–1995. Godine* (Zagreb: Durieux, 1998).

numerous popularizers and became firmly entrenched as a genre of folk ethnopsychology'.[22] Rudolf Bićanić, for example, travelled in the Dinarics or what he referred to as the 'passive regions'. His concern for the people and their ways of life was, like those of Cvijić, intended to be positive and was driven by a genuine humanism. He found the people trapped by such a harsh existence that they could barely afford to eat.[23] Intrigued by the choice of peasants to spend money on luxuries, alcohol and clothes before they spent it on food, he attributed this to their psychology.[24]

One of the most notorious texts written about the Balkans was the memorandum to the Yugoslavian cabinet penned by Vasa Čubrilović in 1937. Entitled simply 'The Emigration of the Albanians', it advised the Belgrade government that they needed to break up Muslim Albanian influence in the south of the country by force and thus provoke a wave of widespread emigration to Turkey and Albania. Like many of his contemporaries, Čubrilović saw the existence of Muslim groups within the new state as part of a largely undesirable Ottoman legacy. Čubrilović, who was Professor of History at Belgrade University for most of his career, was not just an armchair theorist of violence. In his youth he had been one of the assassins in Sarajevo in 1914. His older brother had been executed by the Habsburgs for his part in the murder of Franz Ferdinand. Interestingly, Čubrilović later advised the post-1945 government to expel the German and Italian populations.

The 1937 text was heavily influenced by a notion of national character and by contemporary ideas about the mind. Čubrilović suggested that 'to bring about the relocation of a whole population ... the first task is the creation of the suitable psychosis. This can be created in many ways. As is known the Muslim masses, in general, are very readily influenced, especially by religion and are superstitious and fanatical.' He advocated targeting religious personnel, who could be used to make migration to Turkey seem more attractive. He also believed that 'a tide of Montenegrins should be launched from the mountain pastures in order to create a large-scale conflict with the Albanians in Metohija [i.e. Kosovo]'. He continued by advising that '[t]he state ... must settle its own colonists there immediately after the departure of the Albanians ... The first to be settled in these villages should be the Montenegrins who are arrogant, spiteful and merciless and will drive the remaining Albanians away with

[22] M. Živković, *Serbian Dreambook: National Imaginary in the Time of Milošević* (Bloomington: Indiana University Press, 2011), p. 79.

[23] R. Bićanić, *Kako Živi Narod. Život u Pasivnim Krajevima* (Zagreb: Tisak Tipografija, 1936), p. 8.

[24] *Ibid.*, pp. 102–5.

their behaviour.[25] It was an extraordinarily frank document, which survives in the archives in Belgrade and has been published several times. For many readers, it would appear odd that Čubrilović argued that the Montenegrins, who he sincerely regarded as part of his own Serb people, were inclined to violence and could be used by the state to frighten off susceptible Muslims. Rather than depicting his own group as virtuous, a central tenet for most nationalists, he presented them as 'uncontrolled' and with a penchant for violence.

In 1948 the Croatian American émigré writer Dinko Tomašić wrote a popular text, *Personality and Culture in East European Politics*. Although it was published in English, the text was reasonably well-known in the former Yugoslavia. In many respects this was a Cold War era extension of the ideas of Cvijić and Dvorniković. Irrational and violent behaviour was imagined to be an integral part of the construction of a distinct personality type whose 'traditions and practices, supported by the fierceness of the Dinaric temper[,] made professional banditry flourish until present times ... a certain restlessness among the Orthodox in Herzegovina made men most eager to fight whenever the occasion arose'.[26] Dvorniković had also argued in *Karakterologija Jugoslovena* that Dinaric peoples had a strong tradition of violence, which he evidently admired.[27]

At the beginning of the 1920s, the illiteracy rate in Yugoslavia was approximately 50 per cent (and was especially high among women). The state of the nation's health was a grave concern to many, especially in the poorer regions. By the early 1980s after several decades of modernization, which included the provision of hospitals and schools by the both the Royalist and Communist regimes, the illiteracy figure was reduced to about 10 per cent and many of the scourges of rural and urban life such as tuberculosis were being tackled.[28] Modernization brought new problems, not least of which was the phenomenon of alcoholism amongst workers. Mat Savelli's research on the communist period has demonstrated the way in which the language of psychology and psychiatry had a prominent place in everyday life. Medical professionals were deeply influential and wrote for high-circulation newspapers, which gave ordinary people

25 V. Čubrilović, 'Iseljavanje Arnauta', in M. Brandt, B. Čović, R. Pavić, Z. Tomac, M. Valentić and S. Zuljić (eds.), *Izvori Velikosrpske Agresije: Rasprave, Dokumenti, Kartografski Prikazi*, (Zagreb: August Cesarec, Školska knjiga, 1991), pp. 106–24.

26 D. Tomašić, *Personality and Culture in East European Politics*, (New York: Stewart, 1948), p. 56.

27 R. *Yeomans*, 'Of "Yugoslav barbarians" and Croatian gentleman scholars: Nationalist ideology and racial anthropology in interwar Yugoslavia' in M. Turda and P. Weindling (eds.) *Blood And Homeland: Eugenics And Racial Nationalism in Central And Southeast Europe, 1900–1940* (Budapest: Central Eastern University Press, 2006), pp. 94–8.

28 J. B. Allcock, *Explaining Yugoslavia* (London: Hurst, 2000), p. 356.

a chance to indulge in self-reflection about their apparent collective failings especially with regard to perceived endemic drunkenness.[29]

Yugoslavia's rapid change was also reflected in a growth of the higher education system. Within Tito's Yugoslavia, psychology as a discipline and related clinical practice took off. Many psychologists adapted their ideas towards the prevailing Marxism-Leninism of the regime and the spirit of the times. Rudi Supek, already on the Left when he trained in Paris in the 1930s, generally rejected geographical and historical determinism in his work.[30] His distinguished predecessor Ramiro Bujas had trained in Graz and established the so-called Zagreb School of Psychology. In his capacity as one of the editors of the *Praxis* journal, Supek invited Herbert Marcuse to their Korčula summer school. Marcuse, whose 1955 book *Eros and Civilization: a Philosophical Inquiry into Freud* had attempted to merge Freudian ideas with Marxism, enjoyed his trips to Yugoslavia immensely. He was one of the growing number of people to take advantage of the boom in tourism to the Adriatic coast after 1960s.[31]

In Belgrade, psychology also took off as a discipline. Professor Branislav (Brana) Petronijević, a charismatic and progressive teacher, had studied medicine in Vienna and psychology in Leipzig with Wilhelm Wundt.[32] He encouraged his students to study abroad for higher degrees. His colleague Borislav Stevanović, who taught in Belgrade for many years, completed a doctoral dissertation in London under Charles Spearman, who had also been a pupil of Wundt. Baja Bajić, who like Supek had also studied in Paris and written a doctoral dissertation in 1927 on the 'Psychology of Dreaming'. This establishment with its dual pillars in Belgrade and Zagreb trained a generation of academics and practitioners. Through the work of Živorad (Žiža) Vasić, the reading public was introduced to many of the concepts of psychology, in much the same way that the American public developed an acquaintance with Freud via the work of Bruno Bettelheim.

The Yugoslavian public became familiar with the theories of the Viennese psychiatrist Wilhelm Reich after the controversial film *WR: Misterije organizma* (*WR: the Mysteries of the Organism*), directed by Dušan Makavejev, was released in 1971. It is a long exploration of Reich's idea about the mass psychology of fascism and sexual repression and includes some clips of Reich's period of exile in the United States. The film was duly criticized by the Yugoslav authorities as very much an attack on

29 M. Savelli 'Diseased, depraved or just drunk? The psychiatric panic over alcoholism in communist Yugoslavia', *Social History of Medicine*, 25 (2012), 462–80.

30 Marinković, 'The history of psychology', 251–340.

31 Personal communication from the late John Merrington.

32 M. Magazinović, *Moj Život* (ed. Jelena Šantić) (Belgrade: Clio, 2000), p. 176.

the authoritarian and controlling aspects of Soviet Communism as well as fascism. When Mark Thompson talked to Makavejev almost 20 years after its release, he sensed that the film 'operates at a level of psychological awareness far too demanding for the 1990s'.[33] In an interview with Ray Privett in 2000, the film-maker discussed his early education.

> I studied in a good Psychology department. Some of the early professors in the first years were old, German educated people ... We got Gestalt psychology, then later some Freudian stuff because we had a Professor who studied in Vienna with one of Freud's pupils. I discovered Wilhelm Reich in the early '50s, and tried to read him, but I could not find anything ... I tried to order his books from the States, but was told the publishing company does not exist anymore.[34]

Public debates about psychology emerged again after the death of Tito. In 1981, six adolescents in the town of Medjugorje in Herzegovina claimed to have seen apparitions of the Virgin Mary in the countryside while walking and tending sheep. The town in a particularly rocky area of the Hercegovina Karst was close to places where many of the local Serbs had been thrown to their deaths into a ravine by the Ustaša regime during the Second World War. Medjugorje itself had a predominantly Catholic population. The authorities were initially very hostile to the phenomenon, which mirrors Marian cults elsewhere in Europe (i.e. Knock, Lourdes, Marpingen and Fatima). One of the children's Franciscan tutors, padre Slavko Barbarić, had earned a Master's degree in child psychology in Rome. Suspicion was cast on the authenticity of the visions and the Bishop of Mostar, Pave Žanić, appointed a special commission of fifteen theologians, psychologists and psychiatrists to examine the case.[35] The children were wired up to brain monitors during their ecstasy, but the results were inconclusive. Although most of the commission decided that the apparitions were not genuine, a cult was created that saw the arrival of millions of tourists in the 1980s, a pilgrimage that continues to this day.

Yugoslav literature often engaged very consciously with psychology. Danilo Kiš later remarked about his 1965 novel *Bašta, pepeo* (Garden Ashes) that '[i]t's almost a Freudian subject: during a certain stage the father is, for the child, the *king* – the omnipotent'.[36] Elsewhere in his

[33] M. Thompson, *A Paper House. The Ending of Yugoslavia* (London: Hutchinson Radius 1992), p. 215.

[34] R. Privett, 'The country of movies: an interview with Dusan Makavejev', December 2000, online at http://sensesofcinema.com/2000/11/makavejev/ [accessed 20 February 2013].

[35] V. Perica, *Balkan Idols. Religion and Nationalism in Balkan States* (Oxford University Press, 2002), pp. 111–12.

[36] B. Lemon, 'A conversation with Danilo Kiš' *The Review of Contemporary Fiction*, 14 (1994), p. 109.

posthumously published short stories *Lauta i ožiljci* (*The Lute and the Scars*) (1994), Kiš compared his own father Eduard to Freud, drawing on their shared Jewish heritage and alluding to his father's death in Auschwitz (Freud's four sisters also perished in Nazi death camps). Both men had stood and looked out from the same 'magical' vantage point in Kotor.[37] When Freud had visited the Adriatic town in 1898, it was known as Cattaro and was part of the Habsburg Monarchy. It was there that he had his 'three Fates' dream.[38] By the time Eduard Kiš visited, some forty-one years later, it was part of the Kingdom of Yugoslavia. Elsewhere Kiš consciously drew upon Freud's interpretation of dreams.[39] In his 1983 collection of short stories *Enciklopedija mrtvih* (*The Encyclopedia of the Dead*), Kiš explicitly wanted to forge new areas of representation: 'My use of women narrators ... is also the result for a quest for change, for a new psychological register and a new voice.'[40] In some sense he was also engaged in a posthumous dialogue with Freud, believing that the latter had underestimated the role of reading before going to sleep upon the content of dreams.[41]

Discourses about the Dinaric personality and Muslim depravity were revived in the 1980s in different forms. As Wendy Bracewell has shown, debates about the sexual abuse of a Kosovo Serb farmer Djordje Martinović by Albanians were turned into a media circus. Apparently respectable publications discussed the Muslim penchant for 'deviant' behaviour after the farmer claimed he had been sodomized with a broken beer bottle by his Muslims neighbours.[42] It later emerged that the damage was self-inflicted and that Martinović was in all likelihood a fantasist who subsequently returned home safely after a spell recuperating in hospital. The damage that this incident did to ethnic relations was much more long lasting. Bracewell's article is arguably one of the most important contributions to our understanding of the wars of the 1990s. Although a causal link between discourse and violence cannot be proved (i.e. we cannot say absolutely that paranoia about putative rape in Kosovo in the 1980s led to widespread actual rape of Bosnian Muslims in the 1990s), we do know that particular views of Muslim sexuality were commonplace

37 'Taj je isti prizor posmatrao moj otac, godine 1939 (pet godina pre nego što će nestati u Aušvicu), a godine 1898. gospodin Sigmund Frojd, koji će posle toga usniti svoj čuveni san o trima Parkama', Danilo Kiš, *Lauta i ožiljci* (Belgrade: BIGZ, 2000), p. 45.

38 Freud, *Die Traumdeutung*, p.156.

39 J. Creet, 'The Archive and the uncanny: Danilo Kiš's "Encyclopedia of the Dead" and the fantasy of hypermnesia' *Lost in the Archives: Alphabet City*, 8 (2002), 265–76.

40 D. Kiš, *Homo poeticus*, (1983) cited in Creet, 'The archive and the uncanny', 9, fn. 12.

41 Lemon, 'Conversation with Danilo Kiš', p. 110.

42 W. Bracewell, 'Rape in Kosovo: Masculinity and Serbian nationalism', *Nations and Nationalism*, 6 (2000), 563–90.

in popular culture at that time. After the Martinović case, everyday life became a discursive battleground between ethnic groups that was – at the very least – reinforced by stereotypes about innate character.

At this juncture in the 1980s, it was not just the 'character' of Muslims that was important and in the public mind. Crucially, the notion of a special character among people of Dinaric stock, who were assumed to be carrying some kind of historical burden, was also revived. Sociologist Stjepan Meštrović (with co-authors, Slaven Letica and Miroslav Goreta) argued that there was a link between the type of fighting in the former Yugoslavia and the Dinaric personality in *Habits of the Balkan Heart*, published in 1993. 'The Yugoslav civil war exhibited barbaric acts of cruelty – massacres and the mutilation of the living as well as corpses that beg for an explanation. Our explanation is that when one examines the history of the Balkans, such savagery appears to be fairly typical.'[43] Croat historian Ivo Rendić-Miočević blamed national character for the war and violence. He saw Dinaric (or what he refers to as the 'tribe with no name') society as an example of barbarism within.[44]

In 1990, the Croatian Serb Jovan Rašković published a book called *Luda zemlja* (*Mad Country*), in which he argued that the Serbs as a people had been traumatized by the genocide of the 1940s.[45] He also argued that Croatians had not succumbed to a collective guilt about the genocide, which had created asymmetrical memories of recent history. Rašković was not a fringe figure, but a respected academic and psychiatrist. Perhaps more importantly he was an adolescent survivor of the Ustaša genocide and had seen at first-hand what impact the loss of an entire family could have after witnessing the behaviour of a bereaved man in Kistanje in 1941, who was clearly suffering from a deep trauma.[46] Worried by the impact of the rise of other nationalisms on the position of Serbs within Yugoslavia, he founded the Serbian Democratic Party in Croatia in 1990. He then contacted a professional colleague in Bosnia, Radovan Karadžić, and urged him to found a similar party in Bosnia. According to Dušan I. Bjelić, Rašković and Karadžić 'ushered in a kind of psychiatric politics of madness, escalating to the level of military action against Muslim and Croat minorities'.[47]

43 S. Meštrović, S. Letica and M. Goreta, *Habits of the Balkan Heart. Social Character and the Fall of Communism* (College Station: Texas A&M University Press, 1993), p.61.
44 I. Rendić-Miočević, *Zlo Velike Jetre: Povijest i Nepovijest Crnogoraca, Hrvata, Muslimana i Srba* (Split: Književni krug, 1996), pp. 51–131.
45 J. Rašković, *Luda Zemlja* (Belgrade: Akvarijus, 1990).
46 S. M. Weine, *When History Is a Nightmare: Lives and Memories of Ethnic Cleansing in Bosnia-Herzegovina* (New Brunswick, NJ: Rutgers University Press, 1999), p. 95.
47 Bjelić, *Normalizing the Balkans*, p.152.

Radovan Karadžić toured Bosnia with Rašković in 1990, working up their audience into a state of frenzy and paranoia. The rallies they held were generally made up of a mixture of patriotic songs, speeches and vows to protect Serbs everywhere, but at all times the idea of violence as a first resort was mooted. In *Luda Zemlja* and earlier in an article for *Intervju* magazine in September 1989, he discussed how the Serbs had an instinct for leadership, but with aggressive tendencies. They had overcome the Oedipus complex and dared to kill the father. Croats, according to Rašković, were suffering from a castration complex and afraid of being abused; whereas Muslims, who were fixated in the anal phase, valued people only by their property and had a tendency towards accumulating goods.[48] None of the national or ethnic characteristics suggested by Rašković were entirely positive and he broke up a crucial aspect of the Dinaric thesis by radically differentiating between Serbs and Croats. As a politician, Rašković seems to have favoured dialogue with Croat politicians, but his theories did serve to naturalize the role of violence in political discourse.

Rašković was very well aware of the problems of 'mass psychology'. Slobodan Milošević remembered in 2002 that 'Rašković said that anyone who uses his own head thinks a little differently from the next person'.[49] Beyond his contact with the Serb masses, he often expressed his fear about their 'madness'. He felt that 'Serb myths have entered the Serb spirit, but with a dose of poison, spite, vengeance, regression', which he felt had to be 'controlled' in order to make them less poisonous'.[50] It is plausible that both leaders actually used their scientific knowledge to deflect away from their own extreme political agenda. In The Hague, Milošević remembered that 'Rašković, who by occupation was a psychiatrist, often came across as a therapist even among his own people. When I went there, I always tried to calm things down rather than spur them on in this conflict.'[51] In Buković near Benkovac in 1990, Rašković responded to an angry crowd of predominantly young men who were shouting 'We will kill [Franjo] Tudjman. We will kill Ustaše' with words of calm, telling them not to seek weapons from him, but suggesting that

48 Rašković, *Luda Zemlja*, pp. 129–33.

49 Transcript of the trial of Slobodan Milošević, ICTY, The Hague, 26 November 2002, www.icty.org/x/cases/slobodan_milosevic/trans/en/021126ED.htm [accessed 20 February 2013].

50 Bjelić, *Normalizing the Balkans*, p. 151.

51 Transcript of the trial of Slobodan Milošević, ICTY, The Hague, 24 August 2005, www.icty.org/x/cases/slobodan_Milošević/trans/en/050824IT.htm [accessed 20 February 2013].

they could obtain them elsewhere.[52] This very indirect rhetorical style may have been a conscious use of autosuggestion.

In the Zagreb journal *Vjesnik* in January 1992, Rašković stated: 'I feel responsible because I made the preparations for this war, even if not the military preparations. If I hadn't created this emotional strain in the Serbian people, nothing would have happened.'[53] As Dušan I. Bjelić has so aptly commented, 'one may read Rašković's confession as one more example, perhaps the final one, of his professional delusion'.[54] In his working life, Rašković had written about aggression, narcissism and paranoia.[55] Karadžić was also aware of the potential of mass psychology and would use 'group hypnosis' methods when he coached football players in order to instil a 'winning attitude'.[56] He was described by poet Semezdin Mehmedinović in his *Sarajevo Blues*: 'in all of our meetings he seemed to present very reasonable suggestions … He seldom spoke when we hung out in a group at cafes, he just listened. When he did join a conversation, his words were calm and reassuring, perhaps because of his years as a psychiatrist.'[57]

The ritualized nature of the violence in the former Yugoslavia in the 1990s is very well known. The 'ludic' element within acts of violence has been noted by scholars of genocide. Many of those who carried out atrocities wore costumes, grew long beards and appeared to act out a part.[58] A 1986 hit song about unrequited love by Bosnian Muslim Sinan Sakić 'Pusti me da živim' ('Let me live!') was used to taunt inmates in the Omarska camp before they were tortured.[59] This juxtaposition between the 'everyday' and atrocities reoccurred throughout the war, a phenomenon that has been referred to as 'cognitive dissonance' by Ben Lieberman.[60] In addition, many of those who committed violence had no previous history of abusive behaviour and had often been on very good

[52] 'Hvala, hvala vam. Nemojte od mene tražiti oružje. Nemojte od mene tražiti oružje. Ali ako treba oružja, valjda će se naći neko ko će vam ga dati', see 'Jovan Rašković, Benkovac 1990' www.youtube.com/watch?v=LhkaQdzhm8s.

[53] Weine, *When History Is a Nightmare*, p. 91.

[54] D. I. Bjelić, 'Mad country, mad psychiatrists: psychoanalysis and the Balkan genocide', in S. Gourgouris (ed.), *Freud and Fundamentalism: the Psychical Politics of Knowledge* (New York: Fordham University Press, 2010), p. 226.

[55] Weine, *When History Is a Nightmare*, p. 92.

[56] J. M. Post, *Leaders and Their Followers in a Dangerous World. The Psychology of Political Behavior* (Ithaca, NY: Cornell University Press, 2004), p. 176.

[57] S. Mehmedinović, *Sarajevo Blues* (San Francisco: City Light Books 1998), p. 14.

[58] M. Sells, *The Bridge Betrayed: Religion and Genocide in Bosnia* (Berkeley: University of California Press, 1998), p. 77.

[59] E. Vulliamy, 'Bosnia – 20 years on', *Observer* (8 April 2012).

[60] B. Lieberman, 'Nationalist narratives, violence between neighbours and ethnic cleansing in Bosnia-Hercegovina: a case of cognitive dissonance?', *Journal of Genocide Research*, 8 (2006), 295–309.

terms with their neighbours. Many contemporary observers noted that Serbs would often say what seemed like very odd things, while referring more vaguely to the *longue durée* and historical injustices against them.[61]

Although there were atrocities in Croatia in 1991, sexual violence was not as widespread. It was in Bosnia and against Muslims that most of the rapes took place. During the 1990s (and since) the unofficial anthem of Serb nationalists was *Marš na Drinu* (March on the Drina), Stanislav Binički's 1915 song composed to celebrate the Austrian rout at the Battle of Cer the previous year. The first stanza is a call to heroism and sacrifice, '*U boj, krenite junaci svi, Kren'te i ne žal'te život svoj*'' ('Go into battle, all of you heroes and do not have regrets about your own life'). For several days before the main mosque in Zvornik was blown up in 1992, the sound of the Drina March was broadcast from the minaret.[62] Very often the violence in Bosnia had a specifically sexual content and seemed to be meted out as a kind of collective punishment. Women held in a Bosnian camp knew that whenever they heard the *Marš na Drinu*, in the loudspeaker system, they would be raped.[63] Even the clothes that Muslim women wore were sometimes targeted. Returning to her apartment in the Sarajevo suburb of Grbavica at the end of the war, Professor Lamija Hadžiosmanović remembered that her favourite red dress was full of bullet holes.[64]

In 1993, the Croatian writer Miro Gavran penned a play set in Vienna in 1919 called *Pacijent doktora Freuda* (*A Patient of Dr Freud*). In the play, Adolf Hitler and his girlfriend Christine, a widow, consult Freud about the problems they have experienced consummating their relationship. Gavran's Hitler personifies a destructive personality type that is ultimately beyond the help of the doctor. In one scene Freud asks Hitler to tell him what is on his mind. Hitler answers, 'a destroyed town, house, tree, pig, church; a burnt hen, woman, hand, eyes', at which point his doctor tells him quite urgently to stop.[65] Given that this play was written at the height of the Bosnian War, it is difficult to disassociate this passage

61 I. Čolović, 'Vreme i prostor u savremenoj političkoj mitologiji', in M. Prošić-Dvornić (ed.), *Kulture u tranziciji* (Belgrade: Plato, 1994), p. 125.

62 M. Thompson, *Forging War. The Media in Serbia, Croatia, Bosnia and Hercegovina* (Luton: University of Luton Press, 1999), p. 74.

63 *Seventh Report on War Crimes in the Former Yugoslavia*, part II: *Abuse of Civilians in Detention Centers*, 20, July–August, 92: at http://ess.uwe.ac.uk/documents/sdrpt7b.htm [accessed 20 February 2013].

64 BBC Storyville: 'The love of books. A Sarajevo story"', broadcast Wednesday 19 September 2012.

65 '... Srušeni grad. Srušena kuća. Srušeno stablo, Srušena svinja, Srušena crkva, Spaljena kokoš, Spaljena žena, Spaljena ruka, Spaljene oči', Miro Gavran, *Pacijent doktora Freuda*, (Zagreb: AGM, 1994), p. 34.

from those violent events. In an infamous interview with the Russian poet Edward Limonov in 1992, Radovan Karadžić gave a version of the history of the region and discussed his own poetry. He continued, 'there is a poem of mine about Sarajevo ... "I can hear disaster walking, city is burning out like a tamjan [i.e. incense in an Orthodox Church]" ... many other poems have something of prediction, which frightens me sometimes'.[66]

Since the 1990s, popular interpretations of psychological language were frequently employed in an attempt to delegitimize the nationalisms that had developed in the former Yugoslav republics.[67] In 1994, Tony Judt published a highly influential review article in which he described the recrudescence of nationalism as 'the narcissism of minor differences'.[68] Whether Judt was conscious of this or not, Rašković had used the same term in *Luda Zemlja*.[69] Sigmund Freud had used the term *'[der] Narzissmus der kleinen Differenzen'* in 1930 when comparing the 'relatively harmless appeasement of an inclination towards aggression' between neighbours such as Portugal and Spain who might 'feud' with or 'ridicule' each other.[70] In the Yugoslav context the term often had a connotation of self-deprecation or a studied form of detachment, which is much more value laden than Freud had intended.

After the break-up of the former Yugoslavia, many forms of popular culture have remained essentially 'Yugoslav' and have often operated as a form of imaginary dialogues between the new nationalities, which may or may not actually take place in everyday life. In Goran Marković's 2008 film *Turneja* (*The Tour*), a surgeon, who is compulsively and repeatedly washing blood from his hands, gives a short lecture to a group of actors about the 'irrational' nature of a war fought by people with the 'same mentality and same emotions' (*'isti mentalitet i ista osećanja'*). In the drama it is likely that the surgeon represents an ideal-type of rational and humane 'Yugoslav', a voice of sanity and a mood of conciliation in the middle of war. When he is killed later in the film, he is found to have been reading a dog-eared, open copy of Freud's 1905 book *Dosetka i njen odnos prema nesvesnom* (*The Joke and Its Relation to the Unconscious*). The writer Dubravka Ugrešić, who for many years was based in Zagreb, has also consciously engaged with psychology. Her short story 'Hrenovka u

[66] Paweł Pawlikowski (dir.), *Serbian Epics* (1992), available at www.pawelpawlikowski.co.uk/page3/ [accessed 20 February 2013].
[67] See, for example, S. Boym, 'Dubravka Ugrešić', *Bomb* 80 (Summer 2002), available at http://bombsite.com/issues/80/articles/2498 [accessed 20 February 2013].
[68] T. Judt, 'The new old nationalism', *New York Review of Books*, (4 May 1994).
[69] Rašković, *Luda Zemlja*, p. 132.
[70] S. Freud, *Das Unbehagen in der Kultur* (Vienna: Internationaler Psychoanalytischer Verlag, 1930), p. 85.

vrućem pecivu' ('*Frankfurter on a warm bun*') not only consciously echoes Nikolai Gogol's story *Nos* (*The Nose*), but is also a playful dialogue with both Freud and Lacan.[71]

Perhaps the most well-known interpreter of psychology in the former Yugoslavia has been the writer Slavoj Žižek, whose work enjoys both a popular and an academic audience.[72] He has been a particularly strident critic of (post)-Yugoslav nationalisms. In a deft discussion of the rivalry between the republics of Serbia and Slovenia, he made the following observation:

> At its most elementary, paranoia consists in this very externalization of the function of castration in a positive agency appearing as the 'thief of enjoyment'. By means of a somewhat risky generalization of the foreclosure of the Name-of-the-Father (the elementary structure of paranoia, according to Lacan), we could perhaps sustain the thesis that Eastern Europe's national paranoia stems precisely from the fact that Eastern Europe's nations are not yet fully constituted as 'authentic states'.[73]

The notion of insecurity about identity has been at the heart of many of the analyses of the crisis that tore the former Yugoslavia apart in the early 1990s.[74] By interpreting the ideas Lacan and Freud, Žižek anticipated the later work on the subject by some years.

Since the Yugoslav wars of dissolution, a kind of popular psychology has reappeared in cultural genres. *Kenjac* (*The Donkey/Ass*) directed by Antonio Nuić is a 2009 film about a small family in Drinovci in Hercegovina, very close to the border with Croatia. Set in the hot, dusty summer of 1995 and against the backdrop of Croatian military victory, the film explores the impact of the war and crisis on two brothers who have returned to their native village. Few of the locals are able to express their feelings directly and resort to violence and alcohol abuse. The drama centres on Lake Krenica and recurrent themes of suicide, drowning and despair. In the director's statement to the European Film Awards, Nuić, whose own father came from the region, explained that '[e]ach character in the film … swam in the lake on several occasions regardless of its actual danger. With this I want to render a deeply irrational, dark side of the people from Herzegovina, otherwise extremely religious and cautious

71 L. Lydic, '"Noseological" parody, gender discourse, and Yugoslav feminisms: following Gogol's "Nose" to Ugrešić's "Hot dog on a warm bun"', *Comparative Literature*, 62 (2010), 161–78.

72 His best-known book is probably S. Žižek, *The Sublime Object of Ideology* (London: Verso, 1989).

73 S. Žižek, 'Eastern Europe's Republics of Gilead', *New Left Review*, 183 (September–October 1990), 50–62.

74 M. Todorova, *Imagining the Balkans* (Oxford University Press, 1997), p. 183.

people'.[75] The film, which won widespread critical acclaim is also, implicitly, a discourse on the 'Dinaric personality' and would be understood by its target audience as such. Croats from Croatia proper continue to insist that people in Hercegovina are different from themselves.[76]

The engagement with psychology in the former Yugoslavia and its successor states is deeply paradoxical. On the one hand, this new discourse enriched everyday life and helped to shape the ideas of distinguished filmmakers, intellectuals, writers and playwrights. Before his early death in 1989, it was widely rumoured that Danilo Kiš was being considered for the Nobel Prize in literature, which cannot be awarded posthumously. The writers in the Ljubljana 'Lacanian Circle' are some of the best-known public intellectuals in the world. Film from the former Yugoslavia enjoys a wide audience and critical acclaim outside the region. The intellectual ambition of artists to carry out what Bosnian Director Pjer Žalica has described as 'mikrohirurgija ljudske duše' ('microsurgery on the soul') remains a constant.[77] On the other hand, the fusion of psychological concepts and *Karakterologija* into popular culture has led to the reification of negative forms of self-ascription, especially when referring to Dinaric people and Muslims. Stereotypes that depicted Muslims as both lascivious and fatalistic made an implicit link between sex and death, but also more crucially placed them as a group outside the circle of responsibility (or non-Muslims), leaving them both unprotected and unwanted. Stereotypes that depicted the Dinaric peoples as essentially violent and vengeful were embraced by individuals who had previously been exemplary citizens with no record of violence. Negative ideas may have reinforced patterns of behaviour *in extremis* especially during the 1990s wars, especially when trained professionals, such as Jovan Rašković and Radovan Karadžić, entered the political arena.

[75] A. Nuić, 'Director's statement', website of the European Film Awards, http://europeanfilmawards.eu/en_en/film/160 [accessed 20 February 2013].

[76] I. Žanić, 'The most Croat', *War Report*, 38 (November/December 1995), 41–2.

[77] A. Burić, 'Nije lako odlučiti da budeš sretan', *Dani*, 376 (27 August 2004), 46.

Conclusion: barriers to and promises of the interdisciplinary dialogue between psychology and history

Cristian Tileagă and Jovan Byford

Chapters published in this volume represent a collection of interdisciplinary explorations on topics of interest to both psychologists and historians. Our contributors represent an eclectic combination of established and emerging psychologists and historians, whose work represents only a small selection of the many schools of thought and methodological approaches within the two disciplines. Each has engaged with interdisciplinarity differently, in a way that transcends the established, conventional ways of thinking about interdisciplinary scholarship, namely appropriation, borrowing, translation and reduction.[1] Rather than offering a prescriptive guide about how to do interdisciplinarity, the present volume explores the possible forms that the dialogue between psychology and history can take.

We shall conclude the book by discussing briefly three interrelated themes and areas of concern which run through the volume and which we see as important foundations for interdisciplinary conversation: *epistemological critique*, *conceptual reflexivity* and *interdisciplinary communication*.

Epistemological critique

Transcending the boundaries between the two disciplines requires some degree of epistemological critique and the questioning of the fundamental assumptions of both psychology and history. In his essay, 'The Burden of History', Hayden White makes the point that historians 'claim occupancy of an epistemologically neutral middle ground that supposedly exists between art and science'. This makes it the 'special task' of the historian to join 'together two modes of comprehending the world that would normally be unalterably separated'.[2] Mainstream psychology, on the other hand, claims to occupy the high ground of science. One of the most common critiques of psychology is that it is present-centric,

[1] See our Introduction for a detailed discussion.
[2] H. White, 'The burden of history', *History & Theory*, 5 (1966), 111.

ahistorical, and only interested in drawing general and universal conclusions about human conduct that apply across time and contexts. Firm believers in the superiority and far-reaching implications of their findings, keen promoters of theories of human behaviour that transcend history, psychologists, in the words of Michael Billig, contend that 'history belongs on the side of the undisciplined. Historians have no rigorously repeatable methods that enable them time and again to produce "true facts"'.[3] History is 'methodologically undisciplined', having to 'rely on judgment, guesswork, and worst of all, imagination'.[4]

According to White, the epistemological 'middle ground' can 'block serious consideration of the more significant advances in literature, social science and philosophy in the twentieth century'.[5] In the same way, psychology's belief in the primacy of the empirical can erect impermeable and impenetrable boundaries between psychology and other disciplines, including history. As William James, the doyen of early American psychology put it in his lecture 'On a Certain Blindness in Human Beings', 'neither the whole truth nor the whole of good is revealed to any single observer, although each observer gains a partial superiority of insight from the peculiar position in which he [*sic*] stands'.[6] Psychologists and historians will both feel privileged by the supposed superiority of insight proffered by their specific epistemological position, yet they will often remain 'blind' to what they have to say to each other.

A related tension between the two modes of enquiry, which was mentioned in several chapters in this volume, is between the *universal* and the *particular*. Some historians will argue very convincingly that history is a discipline of the particular. It is the story of a specific historical context, an account or interpretation of a particular event, issue or biography played out by particular actors in a particular time and place. Many psychologists, on the other hand, will argue that psychology is a discipline of the general and the universal, one that aspires to uncover the universal laws of human behaviour, laws that transcend particular contexts and unique experiences of individuals. As Billig argued in this volume, psychologists tend to treat 'universal concepts as primary, using the particularities of the world to serve the categories of their theories, rather than vice versa. In their hands, general concepts become greedy concepts, devouring the individual, unique features of the social world' (see p. 236). Historians, on the contrary, treat the unique features of the social world as primary,

[3] M. Billig, *The Hidden Roots of Critical Psychology* (London: Sage, 2008), 10.
[4] *Ibid*, p. 11. [5] White, 'The burden of history', p. 111.
[6] W. James, *Talks to Teachers on Psychology: and to Students on Some of Life's Ideals* (New York: Henry Holt, 1910), p. 264.

and use them to develop a theory that would account for or explain those features.

Yet, it would be misleading to confine the general to psychology, and the particular to history. The most general psychological processes that psychologists study (attitudes, beliefs, memory, etc.) are also the most particular, in that they are integral to how people live their lives; they are intimately bound with sociocultural, political and historical contexts, which they make possible and within which they are constituted. Conversely, the study of history requires the consideration of phenomena that are general: the socio-psychological make-up of individuals, groups, communities, their representations, feelings, beliefs, values, dispositions and other characteristics by which they are defined. As Margaret Wetherell noted recently, non-psychologists are increasingly attempting 'to infuse their investigations with what could be called psychosocial "texture". They have a new interest in understanding how people are moved, and what they are attracted to – repetitions, pains and pleasures, feelings, and memories.'[7] Social and cultural historians have been at the forefront of this move. They are in the process of identifying certain themes, points of connections, areas of overlap, between psychological theory and history that might allow for the weaving of a psychosocial 'texture' into historians' narratives.

By contrast, psychologists, at least those working in the mainstream of the discipline have been less keen to add a historical 'texture' to their investigations. This is in spite of attempts to initiate a more widespread social and historical turn within psychology. For example Kenneth Gergen has argued that social psychology must be concerned with the 'systematic study of social history', while Serge Moscovici advocated a social psychology that takes on the form of 'anthropology of modern culture'.[8] What Gergen, Moscovici and others have pointed to is the need for social psychology to be a true discipline of the social, recognizing behaviour as socially and historically bounded. Also, the pretensions of universalism always harbour the danger of reducing wider social issues to a set of trivial research questions. As Billig argues in this volume, psychologists 'must get down to the particularities of the world; otherwise they will end up with bland generalities' (see p. 236).

These calls for an 'historical social psychology' and 'anthropological social psychology' have been largely ignored by mainstream psychological

[7] M. Wetherell, 'The winds of change: some challenges in reconfiguring social psychology for the future', *British Journal of Social Psychology*, 50 (2011), 402.

[8] K. Gergen, 'Social psychology as history', *Journal of Personality and Social Psychology*, 26 (1973), 319; S. Moscovici, 'Answers and questions', *Journal for the Theory of Social Behaviour*, 17 (1987), 513–28.

work in the experimental tradition. Psychology's intellectual and empirical priorities are still defined by a disregard for historical 'texture', and for contingency, variability and plurality of social life. Universalist models of human behaviour, values, belief systems, and so on, backed up by the quantification apparatus of inferential statistics, determine the kinds of questions that psychologists are asking, and the kinds of interpretations they offer. Instead of getting closer to studying actual behaviour in its cultural and historical context, mainstream social psychology is moving away from it, by insisting on staying in the laboratory, using hypothetical experimental scenarios, questionnaire ratings, reaction time measures, or self-reports of experience.[9] It is perhaps time for psychologists to enter the archive, to learn more from the history of their own discipline, more from the historian, anthropologist or ethnographer, learn more from popular culture. They ought to consider 'natural' rather than 'made up' settings and contexts, problem- rather than method-based approaches, actual instances of human behaviour rather than imagined scenarios and aggregation of statistical data.[10] As Marková argues in her chapter, approaches such as the Social Representations Theory have moved in this direction, in that they recognize that 'humans live in concrete conditions and their actions, passions, intentions and thinking is context-dependent' (see p. 126). The project of shifting mainstream psychology's centre of gravity is, or course, fraught with many difficulties; yet it is one worth pursuing.

Historians, as well as psychologists, may have a role to play in this undertaking. This is demonstrated by several historians among our contributors. In her chapter on psychoanalysis and history, Joan Scott identifies the tensions between the two modes of enquiry and reflects on the limits of 'instrumentalizing' psychological knowledge and using 'diagnostic categories' and 'labels' in historical explanation. She shows that there can be a productive relationship between psychoanalysis and history, especially when it comes to forcing historians to question their certainty about facts, narrative and cause and engage with issues of unconscious motivation. Paradoxically, however, according to Scott, the productive potential for interdisciplinary dialogue lies in the incommensurability of psychoanalysis and history. Scott's argument echoes and extends that of Elizabeth Wilson on neuroscience and psychoanalysis. Wilson argues that 'too concerned with producing a strong, polished alloy out of various elements of neuroscience and psychoanalysis' researchers tend to

[9] R. Baumeister, K. Vohs and D. Funder, 'Psychology as the science of self-reports and finger movements: whatever happened to actual behavior', *Perspectives on Psychological Science*, 2 (2007), 396–403.

[10] J. Potter, 'Re-reading *Discourse and Social Psychology*: transforming social psychology', *British Journal of Social Psychology*, 51 (2012), 436–55.

'overlook lines of fissure', the inconsistencies and 'fractures' generated by the bringing together of two seemingly disparate fields. Rather than treating these fractures as an obstacle, researchers need to recognize their creative potential.[11]

Rob Boddice on the other hand unpacks historians' method of historicizing emotions, a concept that is part of the vocabulary of psychologists, biologists, anthropologists or neuroscientists. Historians have appropriated emotions, which are usually portrayed by other disciplines as universal and hard-wired in the make-up of individuals, and turned them into cultural and historical products, useful for understanding social behaviour at different points in time and in different contexts. Thus emotion is not treated as strictly a psychological concept, but also a historical one: it helps shed light not only on 'collective feelings', but also 'collective practices' and 'causes of emotional and moral change over time'. Boddice also points out that there is more than one way of doing the 'history of emotions': this body of work is at present 'a cluster of different ways of doing history' (see pp. 163 and 165).

Similarly Carolyn Dean critically appraises some of psychology's central assumptions about human sexuality. She shows how historians are able to nuance psychology's focus on the universal, by identifying and locating particular psychological expressions and responses in specific local conditions and times. While psychology treats sexuality as an 'object' of analysis, history of sexuality goes beyond any particular psychological model of social behaviour. Dean is sceptical about the explanatory potential of psychological theory, mainly because of its tendency to impose universalist assumptions about gender and sex that have in many cases been damaging. For Dean, the history of sexuality (just like the history of emotions in the case of Rob Boddice) demonstrates how psychology's stance can be refined and improved, and exposes the role of psychology as not just a means of examining human behaviour, but also as a 'technology' for regulating it.

Finally, Jeremy Burman's chapter highlights some of the epistemological tensions underpinning history's turn to the 'brain', in the context of the project of 'neurohistory'. He warns against an uncritical importation of psychological and evolutionary assumptions into historical scholarship. Although 'neurohistory' can open the way for new questions and avenues of enquiry, it also reproduces problematic assumptions about evolution, neurological correlates of behaviour and social action.

Epistemological critique, of the kind encountered in this volume, challenges and problematizes the assumptions of both psychology and history,

[11] E. Wilson, 'Another neurological scene', *History of the Present*, 1 (2011), 149–50.

and in doing so clears different paths for interdisciplinary research. It leads to the realization that neither psychology nor history offer a path to objective truth, but are two among other possible ways of knowing and apprehending social and cultural life. This realization helps scholars to qualify, nuance and justify their arguments whilst still being rigorous in conducting systematic enquiries. It facilitates dialogue about which models of the mind and human behaviour are best suited to describe and explain how people behave in society; why, and how change happens, how memories or emotions are transmitted, or how groups or communities experience (or have experienced) the reality which they inhabit. This includes also critical explorations into the status of 'explanation' in history and psychology, and assumptions about the self, the brain, about individuals and collectives, causalities and temporalities.

Conceptual reflexivity

In addition to epistemological critique, one of the foundations of interdisciplinary dialogue is conceptual reflexivity: the continuous re-evaluation of a discipline's conceptual apparatus and its history.

In the case of psychology, conceptual reflexivity implies developing a consciousness of history and seeking to be historically self-reflexive.[12] Psychologists need to explore the roots of psychological ideas, and recognize their historical and cultural contingency. For historians, reflexivity involves developing a psychological consciousness, and recognizing that the study of phenomena such as stereotyping, gender, sexuality, the self, memory, and so on, requires engagement with psychological knowledge.

Conceptual reflexivity is especially necessary when dealing with topics that lie at the interface between psychological and historical enquiry. These include, among others, the study of mentalities, of the crowd and other collective psychological phenomena, which represent some of the earliest points of contact between psychology and history.[13] The importance attributed to a psychological understanding of history is reflected

[12] See, for instance, M. Billig's exploration of critical psychology's early foundations in *The Hidden Roots of Critical Psychology* (London: Sage, 2008); K. Danziger's excellent history of memory, *Marking the Mind* (Cambridge University Press, 2008), or R. Smith's *Between Mind and Nature: a History of Psychology* (London: Reaktion Books, 2013).

[13] The works of Le Roy Ladurie on mentalities, George Rudé on popular disturbances, and Pierre Sorlin on the history of anti-Semitism, are relevant examples; E. Le Roy Ladurie, *The Peasants of Languedoc* (Champaign: University of Illinois Press, 1976); G. Rudé. *The Crowd in History: a Study of Popular Disturbances in France and England, 1730–1848* (Oxford: Wiley, 1964); P. Sorlin, *'La Croix' et les Juifs (1880–1899). Contribution à l'histoire de l'antisémitisme contemporain* (Paris: Grasset, 1967).

in Arthur Marwick's suggestion that psychology, especially social psychology, 'may in some cases be a *sine qua non* of the intelligent analysis of certain historical problems'.[14] More recently Mark Knights, who shares Marwick's optimism, has identified several further points of connection, including the nature of modernity, the uses of the past, collective memory, ideology and political discourse, the public sphere, stereotypes, language and partisanship.[15]

As we have noted in the introduction, it is not uncommon for historians and psychologists to come together to solve problems, and address questions posed by the need to shed light on motivations, feelings and behaviour at a particular point in history. Yet, collaboration usually involves the historian bowing to the psychologist's expertise in the domain of human behaviour and disposition, while the psychologist recognizes the historian's superior knowledge about the details of the historical 'context'. A contemporary example is the book *Soldaten*, co-authored by the historian Sönke Neitzel and social psychologist Harald Welzer.[16] *Soldaten* represents an attempt to understand the 'mentality' of Nazi soldiers through the analysis of secret recordings of conversations among German prisoners of war. This is how Harald Welzer justifies the need for a cooperative enterprise:

> as a social psychologist without a profound knowledge of the Wehrmacht, I would never be able to interpret the material historically. Conversely, someone with a purely historical perspective would never be able to decode all the communicative and psychological aspects of the protocols.[17]

Underpinning this collaborative project is a division of expertise: the psychologist and the historian carefully avoid treading on each other's territory, maintaining disciplinary boundaries firmly in place. While this form of partnership is better than researchers politely ignoring each other, it demonstrates a lack of awareness of the aforementioned need to engage in conceptual reflexivity. In the case of Neitzel and Welzer's work, 'decoding' the psychological aspects of the recorded conversations treats the 'data' ahistorically. The authors do not seem to take sufficiently into account the fact that the recordings do not offer direct access to the soldier's experience and mentality, but are themselves an artefact with its own history, mediated by specific interactional context and the institutional, social, legal and political dynamic of surveillance work in Allied

14 A. Marwick, *The Nature of History* (Palgrave Macmillan, 1989), p. 166.

15 M. Knights, 'Taking a historical turn: possible points of connection between social psychology and history', *Integrative Psychological and Behavioral Science*, 46 (2012), 584–98.

16 S. Neitzel and H. Welzer, *Soldaten: On Fighting, Killing, and Dying* (London: Simon & Schuster, 2012).

17 Neitzel and Welzer, *Soldaten*, p. ix.

prisons during the Second World War. Similarly, in *Soldaten* interpreting the material 'historically' mainly involves borrowing psychological concepts and using them as 'decorative tools' to enhance and embellish historical interpretation.[18]

By contrast, chapters in this volume have shown that interdisciplinarity between psychology and history requires more than the selective and strategic borrowing of psychological concepts. Psychology must become an indispensable ingredient of historical scholarship, which helps illuminate empirical problems or puzzles identified by the historian. Mark Blum, for example, uses the notion of cognitive orientation to illustrate how historians might use psychologically informed approaches in the study of political decision making by historical figures. However, Blum warns that psychological concepts are only to be used in the context of a 'thorough understanding of the society' inhabited by the specific political figure. Mark Knights and Geoff Cubitt, on the other hand, offer a more nuanced view of the role of psychological concepts in historical scholarship. Knights demonstrates how the notion of 'stereotypes' is both a psychological and historical construction, and can act as the pivot on which the historian's analysis can turn, especially when what is at stake is meaning-making in what can broadly be called the 'public sphere'. Cubitt shows how the notion of 'social memory' is not just a joint topic of interest for both psychologists and historians, but a social, political and ideological phenomenon that needs to be understood and studied both psychologically and historically. What is important about this kind of interdisciplinary engagement is that it does not treat psychological concepts as tools at the historian's disposal, or mere 'labels' that point to (putative) mental states or processes. It recognizes them as historical constructs that reflect the contingency and dynamic nature of human behaviour. As such, psychological concepts are 'sensitizing' concepts, which guide, rather than prescribe, the form of enquiry, and which are scrutinized and challenged through historical analysis.[19]

Among contributions by psychologists there is a similar recognition that psychological concepts, such as prejudice or self-esteem, have deeper histories. To be fair, history is not entirely absent from mainstream psychological writing, but it tends to be limited to 'shallow' history, namely the historical background of a specific piece of research or

[18] M. de Certeau, *The Writing of History* (New York: Columbia University Press, 1988), p. 289.

[19] H. Blumer, 'What is wrong with social theory?', *American Sociological Review*, 18 (1954), 3–10.

area of study.[20] Contributions by Durrheim and by Turner, Condor and Collins show the importance of engagement with the 'deeper history' of psychological concepts such as prejudice and self-esteem. Similarly, Billig draws attention to the need to look beyond the conventional history of psychology, which is all too often written in ways that commend current ways of thinking. And yet, in all of these contributions the argument goes beyond the notion that psychologists need to know their own past. They must also overcome the assumption about the trans-historical nature of psychological knowledge. As Gergen argued in the Preface, 'whatever psychologists claim to be true about human nature is nothing more than their application of historically and culturally fashioned concepts to the ever-shifting conventions of the times' (see p. xii).

As we have seen, both psychology and history have their own forms of, and need for, conceptual reflexivity. And yet, interdisciplinarity is not just about being self-reflexive either as a psychologist or as a historian. It involves more than equipping historians with the tool of understanding history through the eyes of a psychologist, or enabling psychologists to analyse historical material. The conversation between psychology and history ought to be based on the increased recognition of the idea that people live in a historical context that is 'distributed' beyond one's mind, and that history is inescapably bound up with understanding the contingency of people's mentalities, social representations, stereotypes, inner conflicts, memories, habits, and so on. Thus, what is required is bringing together both kinds of reflexivity. It is about treating the human condition as being, at all times, both psychological *and* historical.

Interdisciplinary communication

Fostering conceptual reflexivity and epistemological critique is predicated upon psychology and history communicating with each other. It is often taken for granted that reflexivity in any field can be advanced through conversation with other fields and disciplines. And yet, what tends to be overlooked are the resources and interventions that are needed to keep the conversation open, to interrogate and continuously reassess the channels of communication. In the case of psychology and history, the lines of communication are often obstructed by an amalgam of institutional and intellectual barriers.

More often than not institutional arrangements within universities are not conducive to the interaction and dialogue between historians and psychologists. Disciplines guard their borders and are kept separate by

20 See K. Danziger, 'Does the history of psychology have a future', *Theory and Psychology*, 4 (1994), 467–84, for the distinction between 'deep' and 'shallow' histories.

firm theoretical and methodological delineations: those found trespassing beyond their specialism often risk being pushed to the periphery. Psychohistory, one of the earliest and most direct attempts to 'marry' psychology and history, is a relevant example: it ended up marginalized by both mainstream psychology and mainstream history. And yet, as Paul Elovitz has shown in his chapter, psychohistory survived in spite of this, and thrived on the periphery of both disciplines. What is more, as Elovitz points out, psychohistory's position in the landscape of historical and psychological scholarship was determined as much by internal divisions and strife as by the thwarted negotiations with the mainstream. Although united by the shared belief in the value of psychoanalysis in interpreting historical phenomena, those who align themselves with the psychohistory movement do not necessarily form a homogenous community.

A further barrier is the emergence of divisions not just between, but also *within* academic disciplines. The proliferation of sub-disciplines, schools of thought, methodological approaches and narrower and narrower specialist subjects and interests, leads to boundaries within disciplines becoming as relevant as those between them. For both historians and psychologists, navigating the expanses of specialist knowledge requires caution. Lawrence Stone warned historians to tread carefully when engaging with the growing specialism of human and social sciences. The historian should 'never forget the limitations imposed by his [*sic*] relative ignorance ... an ignorance inescapably dictated by the enormous growth of knowledge, and its fragmentation into specialized watertight disciplines'.[21]

The readiness of any particular specialism to engage with interdisciplinarity is closely tied up with its relative status within its own subject. Margaret Wetherell notes how 'just as social psychology seems to be entering a period of uncertain location, likely hardship, and a potential loss of institutional clout' it has 'reached perhaps a point of maximum possible dialogue with scholars in the humanities and social sciences'.[22] By contrast, other areas approach interdisciplinarity from a position of strength. The recent rise in popularity of neuroscience and neuropsychology has resulted in many other disciplines – including history – reaching out to it, seeking insights from it and exploring opportunities for collaboration. Thus, the emerging vocabulary and techniques of neurosciences exert a strong gravitational pull, with researchers from other disciplines carefully negotiating their orbiting trajectory. Some will be drawn inexorably towards the 'core' whereas others will try to push away from it,

[21] L. Stone, *The Past and the Present Revisited* (London: Routledge & Kegan Paul, 1987), p. 21.

[22] Wetherell, 'The winds of change', p. 402.

whilst submitting to the gravitational forces exerted by other disciplines and schools of thought.

When it comes to interdisciplinarity, however, the question is not just about how to overcome ignorance or reach the point of maximum possible dialogue. It is also about making small steps that move the dialogue forward, as well as maintaining an awareness of where the dialogue is and where it could go. Implicit in the very notion of 'discipline' is the fact that it *disciplines* those who are associated with it, and instils certain habits of thinking but also ways of writing that are not easily changed. Psychologists and historians need to learn to write for each other, but also read each other's work. In the Introduction we already mentioned psychology's penchant for technical jargon, at the expense of narrative coherence and clarity. This is not just an issue of style. In the words of Michael Billig, orthodox social science and psychology are 'depopulated': they are 'filled with abstract concepts, broad judgments and descriptions of general processes' but at the same time 'devoid of people'.[23] Reconstructing psychological but also inherently *historical* patterns of thinking and behaviour requires bringing real people into psychological writing. Psychology should always give a sense of how actual individuals, groups and communities live (or have lived), how they voice (or have voiced) their desires, fears and concerns. A 'repopulated' psychology would go some way towards clearing the path towards less reductionist, more insightful and comprehensive interpretations of individual and group behaviour. It would also make psychological concepts, ideas and theories more accessible and appealing to historians.

A related issue is that, at present, psychologists and historians, when engaging with each other, tend to rely on secondary literature. Psychologists will read synthetic works of history; historians will rely on general accounts of psychological theory and research. Interdisciplinarity can take the form of a much more intimate arrangement whereby primary historical sources and archival material would be made the topic of psychological research while the laboratory and other sources of psychological insight would be subjected to history's unique perspective and approach to interpretation. This would inevitably make history more 'psychological' and psychology more 'historical'.

Final remarks

Epistemological critique, conceptual reflexivity and interdisciplinary communication can take many different forms and the above discussion

[23] H.W. Simons and M. Billig, *After Postmodernism: Reconstructing Ideology Critique* (London: Sage, 1994), p. 151.

has focused only on a narrow selection of relevant issues and concerns. Interdisciplinarity, after all, is a dynamic process, not a fixed state that can be achieved through the application of a particular method or by following a prescribed recipe. What is important is that scholars continue to solve puzzles and answer questions about the human condition in a way that fosters reflexivity and close interdisciplinary engagement. On some occasions, this engagement will seek to create a unified programme or approach; on others it will be mainly a fortuitous enterprise. This is fine, as long as it does not stop being a conversation. Put differently, historians and psychologists will inevitably venture into each other's domains and what matters is not how far they choose to travel, but whether or not their digression leads to the realization that the seemingly distant domains of knowledge are in fact closer than initially imagined. Our contention, supported we hope by the arguments of our contributors, is that the dialogue between psychology and history can be driven forward by the idea that amid all the differences there is common ground, and that exchanges are both possible and desirable. Therefore, chapters in this volume should be seen as examples of how this common ground can be explored. None of them provides a definitive solution, but a starting point for reflection, and a convincing argument for why interdisciplinarity is a project worth pursuing.

As a final point, it might be useful to consider why interdisciplinarity actually matters. Psychology and history are essential to the make-up of the modern social imaginary, what Charles Taylor calls the 'modern moral order'.[24] In their development, both disciplines have instituted particular conceptions of the individual and society, inner and outer worlds, ways of seeing and conceiving selves, emotions and associated ideas about causality and 'being'. In that sense, both have encouraged human beings to reflect upon themselves, and as such have become an essential part of everyday social life. Psychology has contributed perhaps the most to our 'understanding of the conditions under which our present way of thinking about and acting upon human beings have taken shape'.[25] But the psychological and the historical imagination are not independent of each other. Their shared role is to create and reproduce the terms in which it is conceivable to talk about and describe human beings living their lives in past or present societies. As Kurt Danziger suggested, 'human subjectivity, the reality behind the objects of psychological investigation, is itself strongly implicated in the historical process,

[24] C. Taylor, *Modern Social Imaginaries* (Durham, NC: Duke University Press, 2004).
[25] N. Rose, *Inventing Our Selves: Psychology, Power and Personhood* (Cambridge University Press, 1998), p. 1.

both as agent and as product'.[26] The past and the present generate both psychological and historical subjects.

Furthermore, since their early inception as disciplines, both history and psychology were construed as serving a *social function*. In his essay *Clio, A Muse* (1913), the British historian George Macaulay Trevelyan claimed that history ought to help people 'remove prejudice', 'suggest ideals' and develop 'certain qualities of mind and heart'.[27] William James was expressing similar hopes when talking to teachers and students about the applications of psychology to practical life and 'some of life's ideals'.[28] Trevelyan and James believed that their disciplines are not just tools for the accumulation and interpretation of facts about the past and present, but also vehicles for the exposition of intellectual, emotional and social values.

Thus, psychology and history are brought together by a shared humanist message. Of course, psychological and historical knowledge have not always been forces for good. They have, on occasion, been placed in the service of inequality, the maintenance of the status quo, even the legitimization of violence and oppression. As the chapter by Cathie Carmichael has shown, in the 1990s psychological theories about collective mentalities and a psychologically informed understanding of history were instrumental in persuading the peoples of the former Yugoslavia that ethnic divisions are essential and violence is unavoidable. And yet, this should not distract from the fact that values of emancipation, collective mobilization, anti-discriminatory practice, and so on, permeate the argumentative fabric of many works of psychology and history. Throughout history, the two disciplines have helped make sense of individual and collective behaviours and practices and addressed challenging topics, such as nationalism, prejudice and inequality. They have challenged entrenched ways of thinking, demystified self-serving fictions and helped bring about valuable social change.

In order to continue to fulfil their common social role, psychology and history need to be acknowledged as relevant. Serge Moscovici has argued that psychology's 'gates' must be wide open not only to other sciences but also to the 'demands of society'.[29] Along the same lines, Roger Smith contends that 'the domain of psychology was never an empty land waiting for psychologists to march in to claim their kingdom. Psychologists

26 Danziger, 'Does the history of psychology have a future?', p. 475.

27 G. M. Trevelyan, *Clio, A Muse, and Other Essays Literary and Pedestrian* (Longmans, Green, 1913), pp. 4 and 22.

28 James, *Talks to Teachers on Psychology*.

29 S. Moscovici, 'Theory and society in social psychology' in J. Israel and H. Tajfel (eds.), *The Context of Social Psychology* (London: Academic Press, 1992), p. 62.

and ordinary people, who are psychologists too, created this land: it was a historical achievement.'[30] Both statements could be applied to history as well. This is, perhaps, why psychology and history hold enormous appeal for the general public: they tell stories that are at the same time both 'ordinary' and familiar, and original and new. With this in mind, it becomes clear that both disciplines will benefit if they abandon the notion that they constitute two separate intellectual 'cultures', with different priorities and audiences.

Only when brought together in a productive dialogue do psychological and historical insights become about real people and their past and present experiences, about the vagaries, dilemmas, contents and discontents of common lives, addressing recognizable and real concerns. In other words they become familiar and relevant. While discussions in this volume were limited to dialogues among western scholars, and mainly about their culturally specific concerns, we are aware that interdisciplinary engagement in different cultural and historical contexts inevitably generates different conversations around different topics and possibly with different outcomes. But our endeavour is envisaged only as the beginning, one that points the way to a profitable future cross-fertilization, wherever it takes us. After all, understanding how to advance the dialogue between psychology and history does not lie in past encounters between the two fields. Quite the contrary, it is all before us.

[30] Smith, *Between Mind and Nature*, p. 278.

Index

Printed in Great Britain
by Amazon